The Spirit, Giver of Life and Love

A Catechesis on The Creed

Pope John Paul II

With a Foreword by
Rev. George T. Montague, S.M.

Pauline
BOOKS & MEDIA
BOSTON

Library of Congress Cataloging in Publication Data

John Paul II, Pope, 1920-
    The Spirit, giver of life and love : a catechesis on the creed / Pope John Paul II.
       p. cm.
    Includes index.
    ISBN 0-8198-6987-2
    1. Holy Spirit—Papal documents. 2. Catholic Church—Doctrines—Papal documents. I. Title.
BT121.2.J64   1996
231'.044—dc20   95-39281
                                                      CIP

Reprinted with permission from *L'Osservatore Romano,* English Edition.

Cover: Titian (Tiziano Vecellio).
         Pentecost (Descent of the Holy Ghost).
         S. Maria della Salute, Venice, Italy.

Copyright © 1996, Daughters of St. Paul

Printed and published in the U.S.A. by Pauline Books & Media, 50 St. Paul's Avenue, Boston, MA 02130.

Pauline Books & Media is the publishing house of the Daughters of St. Paul, an international congregation of women religious serving the Church with the communications media.

1 2 3 4   99 98 97 96

The following abbreviations are used in the text to indicate certain documents:

AG	*Ad Gentes* (Decree on Mission Activity)
DViv	*Dominum et Vivificantem* (On the Holy Spirit)
LG	*Lumen Gentium* (Dogmatic Constitution on the Church)
MD	*Mulieris Dignitatem* (On the Dignity and Vocation of Women)
PO	*Presbyterorum Ordinis* (Decree on the Ministry and Life of Priests)
RM	*Redemptoris Mater* (Mother of the Redeemer)
DS	indicates citations from Denzinger-Schönmetzer

Contents

Foreword 11

The Coming of the Spirit of Truth

"I Believe in the Holy Spirit" 15

The Paraclete—the Spirit of Truth 20

The Holy Spirit as Advocate 26

The Coming of the Holy Spirit in the Light
of the Old Testament Promises 32

Preparation for the Coming of the Holy Spirit 37

Mary's Presence in the Upper Room at Jerusalem 41

Pentecost Was Originally a Celebration
of the First Fruits of the Harvest 46

Pentecost Is a Powerful Manifestation of God 52

Pentecost: An Outpouring of Divine Life 58

Pentecost: God's Gift of Divine Adoption 63

Pentecost Is the Fulfillment of the New Covenant 67

Pentecost: The Law of the Spirit 72

Pentecost: People of God, a Holy People 76

The Birth of the Church 80

Baptism in the Holy Spirit 84
The Intrinsic Link between the Eucharist
and the Gift of the Holy Spirit 90
Pentecost Marks the Beginning
of the Church's Mission 95
The Church's Universality and Diversity 100
Peter's Discourse after the Descent of the Holy Spirit 105
The Initial Apostolic Preaching 110
The Effect of Peter's Discourse at Pentecost 115
The Presence of Christ's Kingdom in Human History 120
The Holy Spirit in the Life of the Primitive Church 126
The Pentecost of the Gentiles 131
The Holy Spirit in the Mission to the Gentiles 137
The Fruitfulness of Pentecost 143
The Meaning of "Spirit" in the Old Testament 149
The Creative Action of the Divine Spirit 155
The Guiding Action of the Spirit of God 160
"Spirit Lifted Me..." 166
The Holy Spirit as Sanctifier 172
God's Spirit Purifies 177
The Spirit, the Word and Wisdom 182

The Holy Spirit in the Mission of Jesus

The Spirit's Greatest Wonder Is Christ 191
Virginal Conception 195
The Spirit's Special Presence in the Blessed Virgin Mary 201
A "New Anthropology" from the Spirit 206
Christ Is Totally Holy 210
The Spirit at Work in Mary's Visitation 214

The Presentation in the Temple 218
The Spirit and the Child Jesus 222
The Spirit Helps Mary Understand 226
The Spirit Working at Jesus' Baptism 230
The Spirit Led Jesus into the Desert 235
The Spirit of Prayer Fueled the Master's Active Life 240
The Spirit at Work on Calvary 245
The Resurrection of the Body 250

The Holy Spirit: A Divine Person

The Revelation of the Person of the Spirit 257
The New Testament Fully Reveals the Trinity 261
The Spirit: Active Agent in Jesus' Work 265
An Advocate Who Dwells in Us 270
The Spirit in St. Paul's Letters 274
The Spirit "Searches Everything" 278
Wind and Fire: Signs of the Spirit 283
Anointing: Biblical Sign of the Spirit 287
The Holy Spirit in the Creed 292
The Spirit and the *Filioque* Debate 298
The Spirit as "Love Proceeding" 304
The Spirit as Gift 310

The Spirit and the Church

The Soul of the Church 319
The Spirit of Unity 325
The Spirit Is the Source of Holiness 330
The Spirit: Source of Catholicity 336

The Spirit: Safeguard of the Apostolic Bond 341
The Spirit: Guardian of Sacred Tradition 346
The Spirit: Source of Sacramental Life 351
The Spirit: Source of All Ministry 356
The Spirit: Source of Spiritual Gifts 362
The Spirit: Another Comforter 368
The Spirit: Dwelling in Individuals 373
The Spirit: Source of New Life 378
The Spirit: Source of Interior Life 384
The Spirit: Source of Prayer Life.. 389
The Holy Spirit: Light of the Soul 395
The Holy Spirit Is the Vital Principle of Faith...................... 401
The Spirit: Life-Giving Source of New Love 407
The Spirit: Principle of Peace 412
Only the Holy Spirit Gives True Joy 417
The Spirit Gives Strength to Christians 422
The Spirit: Pledge of Eschatological Hope........................... 427

Index 433

Foreword

When the Holy Spirit fell upon the disciples in the upper room on Pentecost, St. Peter stood up to explain the extraordinary phenomenon to the nations represented by the pilgrims gathered for the feast. The nascent church had been so overcome with joy, praise and enthusiasm that the some of the spectators said they were drunk. But no, Peter said, this was exactly what Scripture had foretold through the prophet Joel —that the day would come when God would pour out his Spirit on the lowliest as well as the highest. Using more biblical texts, Peter went on to announce that God had sent his Spirit to proclaim the Messianic enthronement of his Son— Jesus, once crucified but now risen and glorified.

Two thousand years later the two hundred and sixty-third successor of Peter has done the same, in a series of addresses in which he unwraps the gift of the Holy Spirit for the church. Like Peter, Pope John Paul II draws heavily on Scripture to explain what we have received in our baptism and what we should be experiencing in our daily lives. So pervasive is the Pope's use of Scripture that he often sounds, if not like St. Peter in Acts, at least like the early Church fathers who fashioned their homilies as a tissue of biblical texts. Thus his catecheses (as the Pope himself calls these addresses) are pastorally oriented and easy to read. They lend themselves to contemplation and to prayer. Though less technical than his massive encyclical on the Holy Spirit, *Dominum et Vivificantem,* they nevertheless contain a profound and Scripturally sound theology of the Holy Spirit, from the simple explanation of the biblical symbols of the Spirit to the complex *Filioque* dispute which divided the Eastern and Western churches for centuries. The latter historical controversy, he says, is really no longer an obstacle to reunion with the Orthodox churches.

Perhaps the most neglected area of theology in the West is that of the Holy Spirit. Some years ago one of the best known Catholic biblical scholars in the United States complained about how little scholarly research had been done on the Holy Spirit. In recent years more scholars have taken an interest in filling the vacuum. Pope John Paul's addresses make a significant contribution to this literature. What is remarkable is the breadth, even the encyclopedic nature, of his reflections on the Spirit. He explores the relation of the Holy Spirit to the life of the Church as a whole, to that of the individual Christian, to the sacraments, to the church's eschatological hope, and to ministry—to name but a few.

I have one caution for the reader. You will enjoy this book most if you sip and savor it like good wine instead of trying to swallow it in one gulp. It will serve best if used as food for prayer.

> George T. Montague, S.M.
> St. Mary's University, San Antonio, Texas

THE COMING OF
THE SPIRIT OF TRUTH

"I Believe in the Holy Spirit"

In our reflections on the Apostles' Creed, we now pass from the articles which concern Jesus Christ, the Son of God made man for our salvation, to the article in which we profess our faith in the Holy Spirit. The Christological cycle is followed by that which is called pneumatological. The Apostles' Creed expresses this concisely in the words: "I believe in the Holy Spirit."

The Nicene-Constantinopolitan Creed develops this at greater length: "I believe in the Holy Spirit, the Lord and giver of life, who proceeds from the Father and the Son. With the Father and the Son he is worshipped and glorified. He has spoken through the prophets."

The creed, a profession of faith formulated by the Church, refers us back to the biblical sources where the truth about the Holy Spirit is presented in the context of the revelation of the Triune God. The Church's pneumatology is based on Sacred Scripture, especially on the New Testament, although to a certain extent the Old Testament foreshadows it.

The first source to which we can turn is a text from John's Gospel in Christ's farewell discourse to his disciples on the day before his passion and death on the cross. Jesus speaks of the coming of the Holy Spirit in connection with his own "departure," by announcing the coming (or descent) of the Spirit upon the apostles. "I tell you the truth; it is to your advantage that I go away, for if I do not go away, the Counselor will not come to you; but if I go, I will send him to you" (Jn 16:7).

The content of this text may appear paradoxical. Jesus, who makes a point of emphasizing "I tell you the truth," presents his own "departure" (and therefore his passion and death on the cross) as an advantage: "It is to your advantage...." However, he explains immediately what the value of his death consists in. Since it is a redemptive death, it is the condition for the fulfillment of God's salvific plan which will be crowned by the coming of the Holy Spirit. It is therefore the condition of all that this coming will bring about for the apostles and for the future Church, as people will receive new life through the reception of the Spirit. The coming of the Spirit and all that will result therefrom in the world will be the fruit of Christ's redemption.

If Jesus' departure takes place through his death on the cross, one can understand how the evangelist John can already see in this death the power and glory of the crucified. However, Jesus' words also imply the ascension to the Father as the definitive departure (cf. Jn 16:10), according to what we read in the Acts of the Apostles: "Being exalted at the right hand of God, and having received from the Father the promise of the Holy Spirit" (Acts 2:33).

The descent of the Holy Spirit occurred after the ascension into heaven. It is then that Christ's passion and redemptive death produce their full fruit. Jesus Christ, Son of Man, at the climax of his messianic mission, received the Holy Spirit from the Father, in the fullness in which this Spirit is to be given to the apostles and to the Church throughout all ages.

Jesus foretold: "I, when I am lifted up from the earth, will draw all men to myself" (Jn 12:32). This clearly indicates the universality of redemption both in the extensive sense of salvation for all humanity, and in the intensive sense of the totality of graces offered to the redeemed. This universal redemption, however, must be accomplished by means of the Holy Spirit.

The Holy Spirit is he who comes as a result and by virtue of Christ's departure. The words of John 16:7 express a causal relationship. The Spirit is sent by virtue of the redemption effected by Christ: "If I go, I will send him to you" (cf. *DV* 8). Indeed, "according to the divine plan, Christ's 'departure' is an indispensable condition for the 'sending' and the coming of the Holy Spirit, but these words also say that what begins now is the new salvific self-giving of God, in the Holy Spirit" *(DV* 11).

Through his being "lifted up" on the cross, Jesus Christ will "draw all people to himself" (cf. Jn 12:32). In the light of the words spoken at the Last Supper we understand that that "drawing" is effected by the glorified Christ through the sending of the Holy Spirit. It is for this reason that Christ must go away. The Incarnation achieves its redemptive efficacy through the Holy Spirit. By departing from this world, Christ not only leaves his salvific message, but gives the Holy Spirit, and to that is linked the efficacy of the message and of redemption itself in all its fullness.

A distinct Person

The Holy Spirit, as presented by Jesus especially in his farewell discourse in the upper room, is evidently a Person distinct from himself: "I will pray the Father, and he will give you another Counselor" (Jn 14:6). "But the Counselor, the Holy Spirit, whom the Father will send in my name will teach you all things, and bring to your remembrance all that I have said to you" (Jn 14:26). In speaking of the Holy Spirit, Jesus frequently uses the personal pronoun "he." "*He* will bear witness to me" (Jn 15:26). *"He* will convince the world of sin" (Jn 16:8). "When the Spirit of truth comes, *he* will guide you into all the truth" (Jn 16:13). *"He* will glorify me" (Jn 16:14). From these texts it is evident that the Holy Spirit is a Person, and not merely an impersonal power issuing from Christ (cf. e.g., Lk 6:19: "Power came forth from him..."). As a Person, he has his own proper activity of a personal character. When speaking of the Holy Spirit, Jesus said to the apostles: "You know him, for he dwells in you, and will be in you" (Jn 14:7). "He will teach you all things, and bring to your remembrance all that I have said to you" (Jn 14:26). "He will bear witness to me" (Jn 15:26). "He will guide you into all the truth." "Whatever he hears he will speak" (Jn 16:13). He "will glorify" Christ (cf. Jn 16:14), and "he will convince the world of sin" (Jn 16:8). The Apostle Paul, on his part, states that the Spirit "cries in our hearts" (Gal 4:6); "he apportions" his gifts "to each one individually as he wills" (1 Cor 12:11); "he intercedes for the saints" (Rom 8:27).

The Holy Spirit revealed by Jesus is therefore a personal being (the third Person of the Trinity) with his own personal activity. However, in the same farewell discourse, Jesus showed the bonds that unite the person of the Holy Spirit with the Father and the Son. He announced the descent of the Holy Spirit, and at the same time the definitive revelation of God as a Trinity of Persons.

Jesus told the apostles: "I will pray the Father, and he will give you another Counselor" (Jn 14:16), "the Spirit of truth who proceeds from the Father" (Jn 15:26), "whom the Father will send in my name" (Jn 14:26). The Holy Spirit is therefore a Person distinct from the Father and from the Son and, at the same time, intimately united with them. "He proceeds" from the Father, the Father "sends" him in the name of the Son and this is in consideration of the redemption effected by the Son through his self-offering on the cross. Therefore, Jesus Christ said: "If I go, I will send him to you" (Jn 16:7). "The Spirit of truth who proceeds from the Father" is announced by Christ as the Counselor, whom "I shall send to you from the Father" (Jn 15:26).

John's text which narrates Jesus' discourse in the upper room contains the revelation of the salvific action of God as Trinity. I wrote in the encyclical *Dominum et Vivificantem*: "The Holy Spirit, being consubstantial with the Father and the Son in divinity, is love and uncreated gift from which derives as from its source *(fons vivus)* all giving of gifts vis-à-vis creatures (created gifts): the gift of existence to all things, through creation; the gift of grace to human beings through the whole economy of salvation" (n. 10).

The Holy Spirit reveals the depths of the divinity: the mystery of the Trinity in which the divine Persons subsist, but open to human beings to grant them life and salvation. St. Paul refers to that when he writes in the First Letter to the Corinthians that "the Spirit searches everything, even the depths of God" (1 Cor 2:10).

General audience of April 26, 1989

The Paraclete—the Spirit of Truth

Several times we have quoted Jesus' words in his farewell discourse to the apostles in the upper room when he promised the coming of the Holy Spirit as a new and definitive defender and counselor: "I will pray the Father and he will give you another Counselor to be with you forever...the Spirit of truth, whom the world cannot receive, because it neither sees him nor knows him" (Jn 14:16-17). That farewell discourse, situated in the solemn account of the Last Supper (cf. Jn 13:2), is a source of primary importance for pneumatology, the theological discipline concerning the Holy Spirit. Jesus spoke of him as the Paraclete who "proceeds" from the Father, and whom the Father "will send" to the apostles and to the Church "in the name of the Son" when the Son himself "will go away," a departure which will be effected by the sacrifice of the cross.

We must consider the fact that Jesus called the Paraclete the "Spirit of truth." He also called him this at other times (cf. Jn 15:26; 16:13).

We recall that Jesus in that same farewell discourse, in reply to a question from the apostle Thomas about his identity, said of himself: "I am the way, and the truth, and the life" (Jn

14:6). From this twofold reference to the truth made by Jesus to define both himself and the Holy Spirit, one deduces that if he calls the Paraclete the "Spirit of truth," this means that the Holy Spirit is he who, after Christ's departure, will preserve among the disciples the truth which he had announced and revealed and, indeed, which he himself is. The Paraclete is the truth, as Christ is the truth. John said so in his First Letter: "The Spirit is the witness, because the Spirit is the truth" (1 Jn 5:7). In that same letter John also writes: "We are of God. Whoever knows God listens to us, and he who is not of God does not listen to us. By this we know the spirit of truth and the spirit of error" (1 Jn 4:6). The Son's mission and that of the Holy Spirit meet, are connected and are mutually completed in the affirmation of the truth and in victory over error. Their fields of action are the human spirit and the history of the world. The distinction between truth and error is the initial stage of that work.

To remain in the truth and to act in the truth is the essential task of Christ's apostles and disciples, both in the early times and in all succeeding generations of the Church down the centuries. From this point of view the announcement of the Spirit of truth has a key importance. Jesus said in the upper room: "I have yet many things to say to you, but you cannot bear them now" (Jn 16:12). Jesus' messianic mission lasted a short time, too short to disclose to the disciples all the contents of revelation. And not only was the available time short, but the preparation and intelligence of the hearers were limited. On several occasions it is stated that the apostles themselves "were utterly astounded" (cf. Mk 6:52), and "did not understand" (cf. e.g., Mk 8:21), or even misunderstood Christ's words and deeds (cf. e.g., Mt 16:6-11).

This explains the full significance of the Master's words: "When the Spirit of truth comes, he will guide you into all the truth" (Jn 16:13).

The first confirmation of this promise of Jesus will be had on the day of Pentecost and the subsequent days, as the Acts of the Apostles attests. The promise is not limited to the apostles and their immediate companions in evangelization. It extends to the future generations of disciples and confessors of Christ. The Gospel is destined for all nations and for all the successive generations which will arise in the context of diverse cultures and of the manifold progress of human civilization. Viewing the whole range of history Jesus said: "The Spirit of truth who proceeds from the Father will bear witness to me" (Jn 15:26). "He will bear witness," that is to say, he will show the true meaning of the Gospel within the Church, so that she may proclaim it authentically to the whole world. Always and everywhere, even in the ceaselessly changing events of the life of humanity, the "Spirit of truth" will guide the Church "into all the truth" (Jn 16:13).

The relationship between the revelation communicated by the Holy Spirit and that of Jesus is very close. It is not a question of a different disparate revelation. This can be deduced from the actual words of Christ's promise: "The Counselor, the Holy Spirit, whom the Father will send in my name will teach you all things, and bring to your remembrance all that I have said to you" (Jn 14:26). The "bringing to remembrance" is the function of memory. By recalling, one returns to what has been, to what has been said and done, thus renewing the awareness of things past, and as it were, making them live again. In regard to the Holy Spirit, the Spirit of a truth endowed with divine power, his mission is not limited to recalling the past as such. "By recalling" the words, deeds and the entire salvific mystery of Christ, the Spirit of truth makes him continually present in the Church. The Spirit ensures that he takes on an ever new "reality" in the community of salvation. Thanks to the action of the Holy Spirit, the Church not only recalls the truth, but remains and lives in the truth received from her Lord. The words of Christ are fulfilled also in this way: "He (the Holy Spirit) will bear witness to me" (Jn 15:26). This witness of the Spirit of truth is thus identified with the presence of the ever living Christ, with the active power of the Gospel, with the redemption increasingly put into effect and with a continual exposition of truth and virtue. In this way the Holy Spirit "guides" the Church "into all the truth." The Church goes out to meet the glorious Christ.

This truth is present in the Gospel, at least implicitly. What the Holy Spirit will reveal has already been said by Christ. He himself revealed it when, speaking of the Holy Spirit, he emphasized that the Spirit "will not speak on his own authority, but whatever he hears he will speak.... He will glorify me, for he will take what is mine and declare it to you" (Jn 16:13-14). The Christ, glorified by the Spirit of truth, is first of all the same Christ who was crucified, stripped of everything and as it were "emptied" in his humanity for the redemption of the world. Precisely by the work of the Holy Spirit the "word of the cross" was to be accepted by the disciples, to whom the Master himself had said: "...but you cannot bear them now" (Jn 16:12). The shadow of the cross was looming up before those poor men. A profound intervention was needed to make their minds and hearts capable of discerning "the glory of the redemption," which was accomplished precisely in the cross. A divine intervention was required to convince and transform interiorly each one of them, in preparation especially for the day of Pentecost, and then for the apostolic mission in the world. Jesus informed them that the Holy Spirit "will glorify me, for he will take what is mine and declare it to you." According to St. Paul only the Spirit, who "searches the depths of God" (1 Cor 2:10), knows the mystery of the Son-Word in his filial relationship with the Father and in his redemptive relationship with the people of every age. He alone, the Spirit of truth, can open human minds and hearts and make them capable of accepting the inscrutable mystery of God and of his incarnate Son, crucified and risen, Jesus Christ the Lord.

Again Jesus said: "The Spirit of truth...will declare to you the things that are to come" (Jn 16:13). What is the meaning of this prophetic and eschatological projection? In it, Jesus placed under the ray of the Holy Spirit the entire future of the Church, the entire historical journey it is called upon to carry out down the centuries. It means going to meet the glorious Christ, toward whom it reaches out as expressed in the invocation inspired by the Spirit: "Come, Lord Jesus!" (Rev 22:17, 20). The Holy Spirit leads the Church toward a constant progress in understanding of revealed truth. He watches over the teaching of that truth, over its preservation and over its application to changing historical situations. He stirs up and guides the development of all that serves the knowledge and spread of that truth, particularly in scriptural exegesis and theological research. These can never be separated from the guidance of the Spirit of truth nor from the Magisterium of the Church, in which the Spirit is always at work.

Everything happens in faith and through faith under the action of the Holy Spirit, as was stated in the encyclical *Dominum et Vivificantem:* "For the mystery of Christ taken as a whole demands faith, since it is faith that adequately introduces man into the reality of the revealed mystery. The 'guiding into all the truth' is therefore achieved in faith and through faith: and this is the work of the Spirit of truth and the result of his action in man. Here the Holy Spirit is to be man's supreme guide and the light of the human spirit. This holds true for the apostles, the eyewitnesses, who must now bring to all people the proclamation of what Christ did and taught, and especially the proclamation of his cross and resurrection. Taking a longer view, this also holds true for all the generations of disciples and confessors of the Master, since they will have to accept with faith and confess with candor the mystery of God at work in human history, the revealed mystery which explains the definitive meaning of that history" (n. 6).

In this way the Spirit of truth continually announces the things that are to come. He continually shows to humanity this divine future, which is above and beyond every temporal future, and thus fills with eternal value the future of the world. Thus the Spirit convinces man, making him understand that with all that he is and has and does, he is called by God in Christ to salvation.

Thus the Paraclete, the Spirit of truth, is man's true Counselor. Thus he is the true defender and advocate. He is the guarantor of the Gospel in history. Under his influence the good news is always the same and always near, and in an ever new way he illumines man's path in the perspective of heaven with "words of eternal life" (Jn 6:68).

General audience of May 17, 1989

The Holy Spirit as Advocate

In the previous reflection on the Holy Spirit we began with John's text of Jesus' farewell discourse. In a certain way this is the principal gospel source of pneumatology. Jesus announced the coming of the Holy Spirit, the Spirit of truth, who "proceeds from the Father" (Jn 15:26). He will be sent by the Father to the apostles and the Church in Christ's name, by virtue of the redemption effected in the sacrifice of the cross, according to the eternal plan of salvation. In the power of this sacrifice the Son also "sends" the Spirit, for he announced that the spirit will come as a consequence, and at the price of his own departure (cf. Jn 16:7). There is a connection stated by Jesus himself between his death-resurrection-ascension and the outpouring of the Holy Spirit, between the Pasch and Pentecost. Indeed, according to the fourth Gospel, the giving of the Holy Spirit took place on the very evening of Easter Sunday (cf. Jn 20:22-25). It may be said that the wound in Christ's side on the cross opened the way for the outpouring of the Spirit, which will be a sign and a fruit of the glory obtained though the passion and death.

We learn from Jesus' discourse in the upper room that he called the Holy Spirit the "Paraclete": "I will pray the Father, and he will send you another Paraclete, to be with you forever" (Jn 14:16). Similarly we read in other texts: "the Paraclete, the Holy Spirit" (cf. Jn 14:16; 15:26; 16:7). Instead of "Paraclete" many translations use the word "Counselor." That term is acceptable, though it is necessary to have recourse to the original Greek word *Parákletos* to grasp the full meaning of what Jesus says about the Holy Spirit.

Parákletos means literally, "one who is called or appealed to" (from *para-kaléin,* "to call to one's assistance"). He is therefore the defender," "the advocate," as well as the "mediator" who fulfills the function of intercessor. It is this meaning of "advocate-defender" that now interests us, while not forgetting that some Fathers of the Church use *parákletos* in the sense of "Counselor" particularly in reference to the Holy Spirit's action in regard to the Church. For the present we shall speak of the Holy Spirit as the Paraclete-Advocate-Defender. This term enables us to grasp the close relationship between Christ's action and that of the Holy Spirit, as can be seen from a further analysis of John's text.

Christ himself is the first Paraclete

When Jesus in the upper room, on the eve of his passion, announced the coming of the Holy Spirit, he did so in the following terms: "The Father will give you another Paraclete." These words indicate that Christ himself is the first Paraclete, and that the Holy Spirit's action will be like that of Christ and in a sense prolong it.

Jesus Christ, indeed, was the "defender" and remains such. John himself will say so in his First Letter: "If anyone does sin, we have an advocate *(parákletos)* with the Father, Jesus Christ the righteous" (1 Jn 2:1).

The advocate (defender) is he who, taking the part of those who are guilty because of sin committed, defends them from the penalty due to their sins, and saves them from the danger of losing eternal life and salvation. This is precisely what Jesus Christ did. The Holy Spirit is called the Paraclete because he continues Christ's redemptive work which freed us from sin and eternal death.

The Paraclete will be "another advocate-defender" also for a second reason. Remaining with Christ's disciples, he will watch over them with his omnipotent power. "I will pray the Father," Jesus said, "and he will give you another Paraclete to be with you forever" (Jn 14:16). "He dwells in you, and will be in you" (Jn 14:16). This promise must be taken together with the others made by Jesus when going to the Father: "I am with you always, to the close of the age" (Mt 28:20). We know that Christ is the Word who "became flesh and dwelt among us" (Jn 1:14). When going to the Father he said: "I am with you always, to the close of the age" (Mt 28:20). It follows that the apostles and the Church must continually find, by means of the Holy Spirit, that presence of the Word-Son which, during his earthly mission, was physical and visible in his incarnate humanity, but which, after his ascension to the Father, is completely immersed in mystery. The Holy Spirit's presence which, as Jesus said, is interior to souls and to the Church ("He dwells with you, and will be in you": Jn 14:17), will make the invisible Christ present in a lasting manner "until the end of the world." The transcendent unity of the Son and the Holy Spirit will ensure that Christ's humanity, assumed by the Word, will be present at work wherever the trinitarian plan of salvation is being put into effect through the power of the Father.

The Holy Spirit-Paraclete will be the advocate-defender of the apostles, and of all those down through the centuries in the Church who will be the heirs of their witness and apostolate. This is especially so in difficult moments when they are tested to the point of heroism. This was Jesus' prophecy and promise: "They will deliver you up to councils...you will be dragged before governors and kings.... When they deliver you up, do not be anxious how you are to speak or what you are to say...for it is not you who speak, but the Spirit of your Father speaking through you" (Mt 10:17-20; likewise Mk 13:11; Lk 12:12 says: "for the Holy Spirit will teach you in that hour what you ought to say").

Even in this very practical sense the Holy Spirit is the Paraclete-Advocate. He is close and even present to the apostles when they must profess the truth, justify it and defend it. He himself then inspires them. He himself speaks through their words, and together with them and through them he bears witness to Christ and his Gospel. Before their accusers he becomes the invisible advocate of the accused, by the fact that he acts as their counselor, defender and supporter.

Especially during persecutions in all ages, those words of Jesus in the upper room are verified: "When the Paraclete comes, whom I shall send to you from the Father...he will bear witness to me; and you also are witnesses, because you have been with me from the beginning" (Jn 15:26-27).

The action of the Holy Spirit is that of "bearing witness." It is an interior, "immanent" action in the hearts of the disciples, who then bear witness to Christ externally. Through that immanent presence and action, the transcendent power of the truth of Christ who is the Word-Truth and Wisdom, is manifested and advances in the world. From him, through the Spirit, the apostles obtained the power to bear witness according to his promise: "I will give you a mouth of wisdom, which none of your adversaries will be able to withstand or contradict" (Lk 21:15). This happened already in the case of the first martyr Stephen, of whom we read in the Acts of the Apostles that he was "full of the Holy Spirit" (6:5). His adversaries "could not withstand the wisdom and the spirit with which he spoke" (Acts 6:10). Also in the following centuries the opponents of the Christians continued to rage against the heralds of the Gospel. At times they stifled the Christians' voice in their blood, but without succeeding in suffocating the truth of which they were the messengers. That truth continued to flourish in the world through the power of the Spirit.

The Holy Spirit—the Spirit of truth, the Paraclete—is he who according to the words of Christ, "will convince the world of sin and of righteousness and of judgment" (Jn 16:8). Jesus' own explanation of these terms is significant: "Sin" signifies the lack of faith that Jesus met with among "his own," those of his own people who arrived at the point of condemning him to death on a cross. In speaking of "righteousness," Jesus seems to have in mind that definitive righteousness which the Father will confer upon him ("...because I go to the Father") in the resurrection and ascension into heaven. In this context "judgment" means that the Spirit of truth will demonstrate the guilt of the world in rejecting Christ, or more generally, in turning its back upon God. Because Christ did not come into the world to judge and condemn it but to save it, then in actual fact that "convincing the world of sin" on the part of the Spirit of truth must be understood as an intervention directed to the salvation of the world, to the ultimate good of humanity.

"Judgment" refers particularly to the "prince of this world," namely, Satan. From the very beginning he tried to turn the work of creation against the covenant and union of man with God: knowingly he opposes salvation. Therefore, he "is already judged" from the beginning, as I explained in the encyclical *Dominum et Vivificantem* (n. 27).

If the Holy Spirit, the Paraclete, is to convince the world precisely of this "judgment," undoubtedly he does so to continue Christ's work aimed at universal salvation.

We can therefore conclude that in bearing witness to Christ, the Paraclete is an assiduous (though invisible) advocate and defender of the work of salvation, and of all those engaged in this work. He is also the guarantor of the definitive triumph over sin and over the world subjected to sin, in order to free it from sin and introduce it into the way of salvation.

General audience of May 24, 1989

The Coming of the Holy Spirit in the Light of the Old Testament Promises

"Behold, I send the promise of my Father upon you" (Lk 24:49). After the announcements made by Jesus to the apostles on the day before his passion and death, we find recorded in Luke's Gospel the promise of their proximate fulfillment. Our previous reflections were based especially on the text of the farewell discourse in John's Gospel. We analyzed what Jesus said at the Last Supper about the Paraclete and his coming. This is a fundamental text inasmuch as it records the announcement and promise of Jesus who, on the eve of his death, linked the descent of the Holy Spirit to his own "departure." The former, he emphasizes, will take place "at the price" of his departure. Therefore, Jesus said: "It is to your advantage that I go away" (Jn 16:7).

The final part of Luke's Gospel also contains important statements of Jesus on this subject after the resurrection. He said: "Behold, I send the promise of my Father upon you; but stay in the city, until you are clothed with power from on high" (Lk 24:49). At the beginning of the Acts of the Apostles, Luke repeats this same admonition: "While staying with them he charged them not to depart from Jerusalem, but to wait for the promise of the Father" (Acts 1:4).

The Coming of the Holy Spirit...

In speaking of the promise of the Father, Jesus indicates the coming of the Holy Spirit, already foretold in the Old Testament. We read in the book of the prophet Joel: "And it shall come to pass afterward, that I will pour out my spirit on all flesh; your sons and your daughters shall prophesy; your old men shall dream dreams and your young men shall see visions. Even upon the menservants and maidservants in those days, I will pour out my spirit" (Joel 3:1-2). St. Peter will refer to this text in his first discourse of Pentecost, as we shall see later. In speaking of the "promise of the Father," Jesus also referred to the announcement of the prophets, significant even though generic. Jesus' announcements at the Last Supper are explicit and direct. If after the resurrection he refers to the Old Testament, it is a sign that he wishes to emphasize the continuity of pneumatological truth in the whole of revelation. It means that Christ brings to fulfillment the promises already made by God in the old covenant.

The prophet Ezekiel (36:22-28) gives particular expression to these promises. Through the prophet God announced the revelation of his own holiness, which had been profaned by the sins of the Chosen People, especially by the sin of idolatry. He also announced that he will again assemble Israel, purifying her from all stain. And then he promises: "A new heart I will give you, and a new spirit I will put within you. I will take out of your flesh the heart of stone and give you a heart of flesh. I will put my spirit with you, and cause you to walk in my statutes.... You shall be my people, and I will be your God" (Ez 36:26-28).

Ezekiel's prophecy, with the promise of the gift of the Spirit, makes more precise Jeremiah's famous prophecy on the new covenant: "Behold the days are coming, says the Lord, when I will make a new covenant with the house of Israel and the house of Judah.... I will put my law within them, and I will write it upon their hearts. I will be their God, and they shall be my people" (Jer 31:31, 33). In this text the prophet emphasizes that this new covenant will be different from the previous one—from that which was linked to the liberation of Israel from the bondage of Egypt.

Before going to the Father shortly before the day of Pentecost, Jesus recalled the promises of the prophets. He had particularly in mind the eloquent texts of Ezekiel and Jeremiah which explicitly refer to the new covenant. That prophetic announcement and promise of "putting a new spirit within them" is addressed to the heart, to man's interior, spiritual essence. The result of this insertion of a new spirit will be the placing of God's law within man ("within them") and therefore a profound bond of a spiritual and moral nature. This will be the essence of the new law infused into the human heart *(indita),* as St. Thomas says (cf. *Summa Theol.,* I-II, q. 106, a. 1), in reference to the prophet Jeremiah and to St. Paul, following in the steps of St. Augustine (cf. *De Spiritu et littera,* cc. 17, 21, 24: *PL* 44, 218, 224, 225).

According to Ezekiel's prophecy, it is not merely a case of the law of God infused into the human soul, but rather of the gift of the Spirit of God. Jesus announced the proximate fulfillment of this stupendous prophecy: the Holy Spirit, author of the new law, and himself the new law, will be present and active in human hearts. "You know him, for he dwells with you, and will be in you" (Jn 14:17). On the evening after his resurrection, in presenting himself to the apostles assembled in the upper room, Christ said to them, "Receive the Holy Spirit" (Jn 20:22).

The "outpouring of the Spirit," therefore, does not merely imply the "placing," the writing of the divine law in the depths of man's spiritual essence. By virtue of Christ's redemptive Pasch it also effects the gift of a divine Person: the Holy Spirit is "given" to the apostles (cf. Jn 14:16) that he may "dwell" in them (cf. Jn 14:17). It is a gift in which God communicates himself to man in the intimate mystery of divinity, so that the latter, sharing in the divine nature, in the trinitarian life, may bear spiritual fruit. This gift is therefore the basis of all the supernatural gifts, as St. Thomas explains (cf. *Summa Theol.,* I, q. 38, a. 2). It is the root of sanctifying grace which sanctifies precisely through "participation in the divine nature" (cf. 2 Pet 1:4). It is clear that this sanctification implies a moral transformation of the human spirit. Thus what was expressed by the prophets as "putting God's law in the heart" is confirmed, clarified and enriched in meaning in the new dimension of the "outpouring of the Spirit." On the lips of Jesus and in the gospel texts the promise acquires the fullness of meaning: the gift of the Person of the Paraclete.

This outpouring, this gift of the Spirit, also has as its purpose the consolidation of the apostles' mission when the Church makes her first appearance in history, and later throughout the whole development of the apostolic mission. Indeed, when taking leave of the apostles Jesus told them, "You will be 'clothed with power from on high'" (Lk 24:49). "You shall receive power when the Holy Spirit has come upon you; and you shall be my witnesses in Jerusalem and in all Judea and Samaria and to the ends of the earth" (Acts 1:8).

"You shall be witnesses": the apostles had already heard this during the farewell discourse (cf. Jn 15:27). In that same discourse Jesus had linked their human, firsthand and historical witness to him with the witness of the Holy Spirit: "He will bear witness to me" (Jn 15:26). Therefore, "in the witness of the Spirit of truth, the human testimony of the apostles will find its strongest support. And subsequently it will also find therein the hidden foundation of its continuation among the generations of Christ's disciples and believers who succeed one another down the ages" *(DV* 5).

Then and later, it was a question of bringing into being the kingdom of God as understood by Jesus. Indeed, in the same conversation prior to the ascension into heaven, he again insisted with the apostles that this kingdom (Acts 1:3) is to be understood in its universal and eschatological sense. It should not be understood as a merely temporal "kingdom of Israel" (Acts 1:6), which they still had in mind.

At the same time Jesus charged the apostles to remain in Jerusalem after the ascension. It is there that "they will receive power from on high"; and there the Holy Spirit will descend on them. Once again the bond and continuity between the old and new covenants is emphasized. Jerusalem, the point of arrival of the history of the People of God in the old covenant, must now become the departure point of the history of the People of God of the new covenant, that is, the Church.

Jerusalem was chosen by Christ himself (cf. Lk 9:51; 13:33) as the place of the fulfillment of his messianic mission. It was the place of his death and resurrection ("Destroy this temple, and in three days I will raise it up": Jn 2:19), and the place of the redemption. With the Pasch of Jerusalem the "time of Christ" is prolonged in the "time of the Church": the decisive moment will be the day of Pentecost. "Thus it is written that the Christ should suffer and on the third day rise from the dead, and that repentance and forgiveness of sins should be preached in his name to all nations, beginning from Jerusalem" (Lk 24:46-47). This beginning will take place under the action of the Holy Spirit who, at the beginning of the Church, as the Creator Spirit *(Veni, Creator Spiritus)* prolongs the work of the first creation when the Spirit of God "hovered over the waters" (Gen 1:2).

General audience of May 21, 1989

Preparation for the Coming of the Holy Spirit

We know Jesus' final promise and last order to the apostles before the ascension: "I send the promise of my Father upon you; but stay in the city until you are clothed with power from on high" (Lk 24:49; cf. Acts 1:4). We have spoken of this in a previous reflection, emphasizing the continuity and development of the pneumatological truth between the old covenant and the new. Today we learn from the Acts of the Apostles that that order was carried out by the apostles, who "when they had entered the city went up to the upper room, where they were staying.... All these with one accord devoted themselves to prayer" (Acts 1:13-14). Not only did they remain in the city, but they assembled in the upper room as a community. They remained there in prayer together with Mary, the mother of Jesus, as an immediate preparation for the descent of the Holy Spirit. They also waited and for the first external manifestation, through the work of the Holy Spirit, of the Church born from the death and resurrection of Christ. The whole community as such was preparing for that, and each one personally.

It was a prayerful preparation: "All these with one accord devoted themselves to prayer" (Acts 1:14). It was a repetition or a prolongation of the prayer through which Jesus of Nazareth prepared for the descent of the Holy Spirit at the moment of his baptism in the Jordan, when he was to begin his messianic mission: "When Jesus...was praying, the heaven was opened, and the Holy Spirit descended upon him" (Lk 3:21-22).

One might ask: why keep on praying for what has already been promised? Jesus' prayer at the Jordan shows that it is indispensable to pray for the timely reception of "the perfect gift from above" (cf. Jas 1:17). The community of the apostles and of the first disciples had to prepare for the reception of this very gift which comes from above: the Holy Spirit who was to initiate the mission of Christ's Church on earth.

In moments of particular importance the Church acts in like manner. She joins herself to that assembly of the apostles in prayer together with Christ's mother. In a certain sense she returns to the upper room. Thus it was, for example, at the beginning of the Second Vatican Council. Every year, moreover, the solemnity of Pentecost is preceded by a novena to the Holy Spirit, which reproduces the experience of the first Christian community awaiting in prayer the coming of the Holy Spirit.

The Acts of the Apostles emphasizes that the prayer was with "one accord." This detail indicates that an important transformation had already taken place in the hearts of the apostles. Previously there had been differences and even rivalry (cf. Mk 9:34; Lk 9:46; 22:24). It was a sign that Jesus' priestly prayer had begun to bear fruit. In that prayer Jesus had asked for the unity of his disciples: "that they may all be one; even as you, Father, are in me, and I in you, that they also may be in us" (Jn 17:21). "I in them and you in me, that they may become perfectly one, so that the world may know that you have sent me and have loved them even as you have loved me" (Jn 17:23).

Throughout all ages and in every Christian generation

this prayer of Christ for the unity of the Church is always relevant. How appropriate are those words to our own times, characterized by ecumenical efforts on behalf of Christian unity! Perhaps never more than today have they had a significance closer to that very special meaning with which they were uttered by Christ at the moment when the Church was about to be launched into the world! Today also one gets the impression on all sides of a start toward a new world, one more united and drawn together.

Moreover, the prayer of the community of the apostles and disciples before Pentecost was persevering: "they devoted themselves to prayer." It was not a prayer of momentary exaltation. The Greek word used by the author of the Acts of the Apostles suggests a patient assiduousness, in a certain sense even a "stubbornness," implying sacrifice and the overcoming of difficulty. It was therefore a prayer of the most complete dedication, not only of the heart but also of the will. The apostles were aware of the task that awaited them.

That prayer was itself a fruit of the interior action of the Holy Spirit, for it is he who urges to prayer and helps one to be devoted to prayer. Again there comes to mind the analogy with Jesus himself who, before beginning his messianic mission, went into the wilderness. The Gospels stress that "the Spirit drove him" (Mk 1:12; cf. Mt 4:1), that "he was led by the Spirit in the wilderness" (Lk 4:1).

If the gifts of the Spirit are manifold, it must be said that during the period in the upper room at Jerusalem, the Holy Spirit was already at work in the secrecy of prayer. This was so that on the day of Pentecost they might be ready to receive this great and "decisive" gift, by means of which the life of Christ's Church was to begin definitively on earth.

In the united community of prayer other persons were present besides the apostles, and some of them were women. Christ's recommendation, at the moment of his departure to return to the Father, concerned the apostles directly. We know that "he charged them not to depart from Jerusalem, but to wait for the promise of the Father" (Acts 1:4). To them he had entrusted a special mission in his Church.

If other persons, including women, now take part in the preparation for Pentecost, this is simply a continuation of Jesus' own way of acting, as is evident from different passages of the Gospels. Luke even tells us the names of some of these women who were followers, collaborators and benefactors of Jesus: Mary called Magdalene, Joanna the wife of Chuza, Herod's steward, Susanna, and many others (cf. Lk 8:1-3). The gospel proclamation of the kingdom of God took place not only in the presence of the Twelve and of the disciples in general, but also of these women in particular. The evangelist speaks of them when he said that they "provided for them (Jesus and the apostles) out of their means" (Lk 8:3).

From this it follows that "women on a parity with men are called to share in the kingdom of God which Jesus announced, to be part of it and also to contribute to its growth among people," as I explained at length in the Apostolic Letter *Mulieris Dignitatem.*

From this viewpoint, the presence of women in the upper room at Jerusalem, during the preparation for Pentecost and the birth of the Church, takes on particular importance. Men and women, the simple faithful, took part in the entire event alongside the apostles and together with them. From the very beginning the Church has been a community both of apostles and disciples, of men and women alike.

There is no doubt that the presence of the mother of Christ had a great importance in the preparation of the apostolic community for the coming of the Spirit at Pentecost. However, this is a subject for a separate reflection.

General audience of June 21, 1989

Mary's Presence in the Upper Room at Jerusalem

"All these with one accord devoted themselves to prayer, together with the women and the mother of Jesus, and with his brethren" (Acts 1:14). In these simple words the author of Acts records the presence of Christ's mother in the upper room during the days of preparation for Pentecost.

In the previous reflection we entered the upper room and saw that the apostles, in obedience to Jesus' command prior to his departure to the Father, were assembled and "with one accord devoted themselves" to prayer. They were not alone, for other disciples, both men and women, were present with them. Among these persons pertaining to the original Jerusalem community, St. Luke, the author of Acts, also names Mary, Christ's mother. He names her among those present without adding anything special in her regard. We know, however, that Luke in his Gospel wrote at length about Mary's divine and virginal motherhood, on the basis of the information obtained by him in the Christian communities for a precise methodological motive (cf. Lk 1:1 ff.: Acts 1:1 ff.). This information was traced back at least indirectly to the earliest source of all data about Mary, namely, the mother of Jesus herself. Consequently, in Luke's twofold narrative, just as the coming into the world of God's Son is set in close relationship with the person of Mary, so now the birth of the Church is likewise linked with her. The simple statement that she was present in the upper room at Pentecost is sufficient to indicate to us the great importance attributed by Luke to this detail.

The Acts of the Apostles reveals Mary as one of those taking part in the preparation for Pentecost as a member of the first community of the Church which was coming into being. On the basis of Luke's Gospel and of other New Testament texts a Christian tradition on Mary's presence in the Church was formed, which the Second Vatican Council summed up by hailing her as a preeminent and wholly unique member of the Church (cf. *LG* 53), inasmuch as she is the mother of Christ, the Man-God, and therefore the mother of God. The Council Fathers recalled in the introductory message the words of the Acts of the Apostles which we have reread. It was as though they wished to emphasize that just as Mary was present at the beginning of the Church, so likewise they desired her presence in the assembly of the apostles' successors gathered together in the second half of the twentieth century in continuity with the community of the upper room. In coming together for the work of the Council, the Fathers also wished "to devote themselves with one accord to prayer with Mary the mother of Jesus" (cf. Acts 1:14).

At the annunciation Mary had experienced the descent of the Holy Spirit. The angel Gabriel had said to her: "The Holy Spirit will come upon you, and the power of the Most High will overshadow you; therefore the child to be born will be called the Son of God" (Lk 1:35). Through the Spirit's coming down upon her, Mary was associated in a unique way with the mystery of Christ. In the encyclical *Redemptoris Mater* I wrote: "In the mystery of Christ she is present even 'before the creation of the world' (cf. Eph 1:4), as the one whom the Father 'has chosen' from eternity as mother of his Son in the

Incarnation. And what is more, together with the Father, the Son has chosen her, entrusting her eternally to the Spirit of holiness" *(RM* 8).

In the upper room in Jerusalem, as the Paschal Mystery of Christ on earth reached its fulfillment, Mary together with the other disciples prepared for a new coming of the Holy Spirit which would mark the birth of the Church. It is true that she was already a "temple of the Holy Spirit" *(LG* 53) by her fullness of grace and by her divine motherhood. But she took part in the prayers for the Spirit's coming so that through his power there should burst out in the apostolic community the impulse toward the mission which Jesus Christ, on coming into the world, had received from the Father (cf. Jn 5:36), and on returning to the Father, had transmitted to the Church (cf. Jn 17:18). From the very beginning Mary was united to the Church as a disciple of her Son and as the most outstanding image of the Church in her faith and charity (cf. *LG* 53).

The Second Vatican Council emphasized this in the *Constitution on the Church* where we read: "By reason of the gift and role of divine maternity, by which she is united with her Son, the Redeemer, and with his singular graces and functions, the Blessed Virgin is also intimately united with the Church. As St. Ambrose taught, the mother of God is a type of the Church in the order of faith, charity and perfect union with Christ. For in the mystery of the Church...the Blessed Virgin stands out in eminent and singular fashion.... By her belief and obedience, not knowing man but overshadowed by the Holy Spirit she brought forth on earth the very Son of the Father" *(LG* 63).

Mary's prayer in the upper room in preparation for Pentecost has a special significance, precisely because of the bond with the Holy Spirit established at the moment of the mystery of the Incarnation. Now this bond comes up again, enhanced with a new reference point.

In saying that Mary "stands out" in the order of faith, the Council seems to hark back to Elizabeth's greeting to her cousin, the Virgin of Nazareth after the annunciation: "Blessed is she who believed" (Lk 1:45). The evangelist writes that "Elizabeth was filled with the Holy Spirit" (Lk 1:41) in replying to Mary's greeting and uttering those words. Moreover, according to the same Luke, "they were all filled with the Holy Spirit" in the upper room in Jerusalem on the day of Pentecost (Acts 2:4). Therefore she also who "was found to be with child of the Holy Spirit" (cf. Mt 1:18) received at Pentecost a new fullness of the Holy Spirit. From that day onward her pilgrimage of faith, charity and perfect union with Christ was linked with the Church's own pilgrim journey.

The apostolic community needed her presence and that devotedness to prayer together with her, the mother of the Lord. It may be said that in that prayer with Mary, one perceives her special mediation deriving from the fullness of the gifts of the Holy Spirit. As his mystical spouse, Mary implores his coming upon the Church born from the pierced side of Christ on the cross, and now about to be revealed to the world.

As can be seen, Luke's brief mention in Acts of the presence of Mary among the apostles and all those who "devoted themselves to prayer" in preparation for Pentecost and the outpouring of the Holy Spirit, has a very rich content.

In the Constitution *Lumen Gentium* the Second Vatican Council expressed this richness of content. According to this important conciliar text, she who in the midst of the disciples in the upper room devoted herself to prayer, is the mother of the Son, predestined by God to be "the first-born among many brethren" (cf. Rom 8:29). The Council however adds that she herself cooperated "in the regeneration and formation" of these "brethren" of Christ, with her motherly love. The Church in her turn—from the day of Pentecost—"by her preaching brings forth to a new and immortal life the sons who are born to her in baptism, who are conceived of the Holy Spirit and born of God" *(LG* 64). The Church, therefore, by becoming herself a mother in this way, looks to the mother of Christ as her model. The Church's looking to Mary began in the upper room.

General audience of June 28, 1989

Pentecost Was Originally a Celebration of the First Fruits of the Harvest

From the foregoing reflections on the article of the creeds on the Holy Spirit, one observes the rich biblical foundation of the pneumatological truth. At the same time, however, we must also note the difference of delineation, in divine revelation, of this truth in relation to the Christological truth. It is evident indeed from the sacred texts that the eternal Son, one in being with the Father, is the fullness of God's self-revelation in human history. In becoming "son of man," "born of woman" (cf. Gal 4:4), he was manifested and acted as true man. As such he also definitively revealed the Holy Spirit, announcing his coming and making known his relationship with the Father and the Son in the mission of salvation and therefore in the mystery of the Trinity. According to the announcement and promise of Jesus, the Church, the body of Christ (cf. 1 Cor 12:27) and sacrament of his presence "with us until the end of the world" (cf. Mt 28:20), has her beginning with the coming of the Paraclete.

However, the Holy Spirit, one in being with the Father and Son, remains the "hidden God." While operating in the Church and in the world, he is not manifested visibly, unlike the Son. The Son assumed human nature and became like us, so that the disciples, during his mortal life, could see him and "touch him with (their) hands," he, the Word of life (cf. 1 Jn 1:1).

On the other hand, the knowledge of the Holy Spirit, based on faith in Christ's revelation, is not supported by the vision of a divine Person living among us in human form, but only by the observation of the effects of his presence and operation in us and in the world. The key point of this knowledge is the Pentecost event.

In the religious tradition of Israel, Pentecost was originally the feast of the first fruits of the harvest. "Three times in the year shall all your males appear before the Lord God, the God of Israel" (Ex 34:23). The first time was for the feast of the Pasch; the second for the harvest festival; the third for the so-called Feast of Tabernacles.

The "feast of harvest, of the first fruits of your labor, of what you sow in the field" (Ex 23:16), was called "Pentecost" in Greek, because it was celebrated fifty days after the feast of the Pasch. It was also called the feast of weeks, because it fell seven weeks after the Pasch. The feast of ingathering was celebrated separately, toward the end of the year (cf. Ex 23:16; 34:22). The books of the law contained detailed instructions for the celebration of Pentecost (cf. Lev 23:15ff.; Num 28:26-31), which later also became the feast of the renewal of the covenant (cf. 2 Chr 15:10-13), as we shall see in due course.

The descent of the Holy Spirit on the apostles and on the first community of Christ's disciples who, in the upper room of Jerusalem, "devoted themselves with one accord to prayer," together with Mary the mother of Jesus (cf. Acts 1:14), is linked with the Old Testament meaning of Pentecost. The feast of harvest becomes the feast of the new "harvest" for which the Holy Spirit is responsible: the harvest in the Spirit.

This harvest is the fruit of the seed sown by Christ. We

recall Jesus' words in John's Gospel: "I tell you, lift up your eyes, and see how the fields are already white for harvest" (Jn 4:35). Jesus gave the apostles to understand that only after his death would they reap the harvest of the seed he had sown: "'one sows and another reaps.' I sent you to reap that which you did not labor; others have labored, and you have entered into their gain" (Jn 4:37-38).

From the day of Pentecost, through the work of the Holy Spirit, the apostles will become the reapers of the seed sown by Christ. "He who reaps receives wages, and gathers fruit for eternal life, so that sower and reaper may rejoice together" (Jn 4:36). And indeed on the day of Pentecost, after Peter's first discourse, there was an abundant harvest. "Some three thousand" were converted (Acts 2:41): a cause of great joy both for the apostles and their Master, the divine Sower.

The harvest is the fruit of Christ's sacrifice. Jesus spoke of the sower's "toil," and this consists especially in his passion and death on the cross. Christ is that "other one" who has labored for this harvest. He is "another" who has opened the way for the Spirit of truth, who, from the day of Pentecost, begins to work effectively by means of the apostolic kerygma.

The way was opened through Christ's self-offering on the cross: through his redemptive death, confirmed by the pierced side of the crucified. From his heart "there issued at once blood and water" (Jn 19:34), a sign of physical death. However, one can see in this fact the fulfillment of the mysterious words spoken by Jesus on one occasion on the last day of the Feast of Tabernacles, concerning the coming of the Holy Spirit: "If any one thirsts, let him come to me and drink. He who believes in me, as the scripture has said, 'Out of his heart shall flow rivers of living water.'" The evangelist comments: "He said this about the Spirit, which those who believed in him were to receive" (Jn 7:37-39). This was as if to say that the believers would have received much more than the rain prayed for on the Feast of Tabernacles, drawing on a fountain from which would truly have come the living water of Sion, announced by the prophets (cf. Zech 14:8; Ez 47:1 f.).

Concerning the Holy Spirit Jesus had promised: "When I go away I will send him to you" (Jn 16:7). Truly, the water that issues from the pierced side of Christ (cf. Jn 19:34) is the sign of this sending. It will be an abundant outpouring: actually a "river of living water," a metaphor expressing a special generosity and kindness in God's self-giving to man. That Pentecost at Jerusalem confirmed this divine abundance, promised and granted by Christ through the Spirit.

In Luke's narrative the same circumstances of the feast seem to have a symbolic meaning. The descent of the Spirit occurs at the conclusion of the feast. The expression used by the evangelist suggests a fullness. He said, "When the day of Pentecost had come..." (Acts 2:1). On the other hand, St. Luke again recounts that "they were all together": not only the apostles, but the entire original group of the nascent Church, men and women, together with the mother of Jesus. It is the first detail to be borne in mind. However, in the description of that event there are also other details which are no less important from the point of view of the "fullness."

Luke writes: "Suddenly a sound came from heaven like the rush of a mighty wind, and it filled all the house where they were sitting.... And they were all filled with the Holy Spirit" (Acts 2:2, 4). One should note that emphasis on fullness ("filled the house," "they were all filled"). This observation can be taken in conjunction with what Jesus said when going to the Father: "Before many days you shall be baptized with the Holy Spirit" (Acts 1:5). "Baptized" means "immersed" in the Holy Spirit: this is expressed by the rite of immersion in water during Baptism. The "immersion" and the "being full" signify the same spiritual reality, caused in the apostles and in all present in the upper room by the descent of the Holy Spirit.

That "fullness" experienced by the small original community on the day of Pentecost can be considered a spiritual continuation of the fullness of the Holy Spirit that "dwells" in Christ, in whom there is "all fullness" (cf. Col 1:19). As we read in the Encyclical *Dominum et Vivificantem*, all that Jesus "says of the Father and of himself—the Son, flows from the fullness of the Spirit which is in him, which fills his heart, pervades his own 'I,' inspires and enlivens his action from the depths" (n. 21). For this reason the Gospel can say that Jesus "rejoiced in the Holy Spirit" (Lk 10:21). Thus "the fullness" of the Holy Spirit which is in Christ was manifested on the day of Pentecost by the "filling with the Holy Spirit" of all those assembled in the upper room. Thus there was instituted that Christ-Church reality to which the apostle Paul alludes: "You have come to fullness of life in him, who is the head of all rule and authority" (Col 2:10).

It may be added that the Holy Spirit on Pentecost "becomes the master" of the apostles by demonstrating his power over their humanity. The manifestation of this power has the character of a fullness of the spiritual gift which is manifested as a power of the spirit, a power of mind, will and heart. St. John writes that "to him whom God has sent...he gives the Spirit without measure" (Jn 3:34). This applies in the first place to Christ; but it can also be applied to the apostles to whom Christ has given the Spirit, so that they in turn may transmit him to others.

Finally, we note that on Pentecost the prophecy of Ezekiel was fulfilled: "I will give you a new heart and a new spirit I will put within you" (36:26). Truly this "breath" has brought joy to the reapers, so that it can be said with Isaiah: "They rejoice before you as with joy at the harvest" (9:3).

Pentecost—the ancient feast of the harvest—is now presented in the center of Jerusalem with a new meaning, as a special "harvest" of the divine Paraclete. Thus is fulfilled the prophecy of Joel: "In those days I will pour out my spirit on all flesh" (Joel 2:28).

General audience of July 5, 1989

Pentecost Is a Powerful Manifestation of God

Our knowledge of the Holy Spirit is based on what Jesus tells us about him, especially when Jesus speaks about his own departure and his return to the Father. "When I shall have gone away...the Holy Spirit will come to you" (cf. Jn 16:7). Christ's paschal "departure" through the cross, resurrection and ascension finds its culmination in Pentecost, that is, in the descent of the Holy Spirit upon the apostles. They were "of one accord devoted to prayer" in the upper room "together with the mother of Jesus" (cf. Acts 1:14) and the group of persons who formed the nucleus of the original Church.

In that event the Holy Spirit remains the mysterious God (cf. Is 45:15), and such he will remain throughout the entire history of the Church and of the world. It could be said that he is hidden in the shadow of Christ, the Son-Word, one in being with the Father, who in visible form "became flesh and dwelt among us" (Jn 1:14).

In the Incarnation the Holy Spirit was not visibly manifested—he remained the hidden God—and he enveloped Mary in the mystery. The angel said to the Virgin, the woman chosen for God's definitive approach to man: "The Holy Spirit will come upon you, and the power of the Most High will overshadow you" (Lk 1:35).

Similarly at Pentecost the Holy Spirit "overshadows" the nascent Church, so that under his influence she may be empowered to "announce the mighty works of God" (cf. Acts 2:11). What took place in Mary's womb in the Incarnation now finds a further fulfillment. The Spirit operates as the "hidden God," invisible in his person.

However, Pentecost is a theophany, that is to say, a powerful divine manifestation. It completes the manifestation on Mount Sinai, after Israel had gone forth from the bondage of Egypt under the guidance of Moses. According to rabbinical tradition, the manifestation on Mount Sinai occurred fifty days after the Pasch of the Exodus, the day of Pentecost.

"Mount Sinai was wrapped in smoke, because the Lord descended upon it in fire; and its smoke went up like the smoke of a kiln, and the whole mountain quaked greatly" (Ex 19:18). The absolute transcendence of "he who is" (cf. Ex 3:14) then manifested it. Already at the foot of Mount Horeb, Moses had heard from the midst of the burning bush the words: "Do not come near; put off your shoes from your feet, for the place on which you are standing is holy ground" (Ex 3:5). Now at the foot of Mount Sinai the Lord said to him: "Go down and warn the people, lest they break through to the Lord to gaze and many of them perish" (Ex 19:21).

The theophany of Pentecost is the last of the series of manifestations in which God progressively made himself known to man. With it God's self-revelation reaches its culmination; through it he wished to infuse into his people faith in his majesty and transcendence and, at the same time, in his immanent presence of "Emmanuel," of "God with us."

At Pentecost there is a theophany which, together with Mary, directly touches the whole Church in its initial nucleus, thus completing the long process begun under the old covenant. If we analyze the details of the event in the upper room recorded in Acts (2:1-13), we find there different elements which recall previous theophanies, especially that of Sinai, which Luke seems to have in mind when describing the descent of the Holy Spirit. According to Luke's description, the theophany in the upper room takes place by means of phenomena resembling those of Sinai: "When the day of Pentecost had come, they were all together in one place. And suddenly a sound came from heaven like the rush of a mighty wind, and it filled all the house where they were sitting. And there appeared to them tongues as of fire, distributed and resting on each one of them. And they were all filled with the Holy Spirit and began to speak in other tongues, as the Spirit gave them utterance" (Acts 2:1-4).

Three basic elements mark the event—the sound of a mighty wind, tongues as of fire, and the charism of speaking in other languages. All these are rich in a symbolic value which must be borne in mind. In the light of these facts one understands better what the author of Acts had in mind when he said that those present in the upper room "were filled with the Holy Spirit."

"A sound like the rush of a mighty wind." From the linguistic point of view there is an affinity here between the wind (the breath of wind) and "the spirit." In Hebrew, as in Greek, "wind" is a homonym of "spirit": *"ruah—pneuma."* We read in the Book of Genesis (1:2): "The spirit *(ruah)* of God was moving over the face of the waters," and in John's Gospel: "The wind *(pneuma)* blows where it wills" (Jn 3:8).

In the Bible a strong wind "announces" the presence of God. It is the sign of a theophany. "He was seen upon the wings of the wind," we read in the Second Book of Samuel (22:11). "Behold, a stormy wind came out of the north, and a great cloud, with brightness round about it, and fire flashing forth continually," is the theophany described at the beginning of the Book of the Prophet Ezekiel (1:4). In particular, the breath of wind is the expression of the divine power which draws forth from chaos the order of creation (cf. Gen 1:2). It is also the expression of the freedom of the Spirit: "The wind blows where it wills, and you hear the sound of it, but you do not know whence it comes or whither it goes" (Jn 3:8). "A sound like the rush of a mighty wind" is the first element of the theophany of Pentecost, a manifestation of the divine power at work in the Holy Spirit.

The second element of the Pentecost event is fire: "There appeared to them tongues as of fire" (Acts 2:3). Fire is always present in the manifestations of God in the Old Testament. We see this in the covenant between God and Abraham (cf. Gen 15:17); likewise when God revealed himself to Moses in the burning bush which was not consumed (cf. Ex 3:2); again, in the columns of fire which guided the people of Israel by night through the desert (cf. Ex 13:21-22). Fire is present particularly in the manifestation of God on Mount Sinai (cf. Ex 19:18), and also in the eschatological theophanies described by the prophets (cf. Is 4:5; 64:1; Dan 7:9 etc.). Fire, therefore, symbolizes the presence of God. On several occasions Sacred Scripture states that "our God is a consuming fire" (Heb 12:29; Dt 4:24; 9:3). In the rites of holocaust the destruction of the thing offered was of less importance than the sweet perfume which symbolized the raising up of the offering to God, while fire, also called the "minister of God" (cf. Ps 104:4) symbolized man's purification from sin, just as silver is refined and gold is tested in the fire (cf. Zech 13:8-9).

In the theophany of Pentecost there is the symbol of the tongues as of fire which rested on each of those present in the upper room. If fire symbolizes God's presence, the tongues of fire distributed and resting on their heads seem to indicate the "descent" of God the Holy Spirit on those present, the gift of himself to each of them to prepare them for their mission.

The symbolism of the multiplication of languages

The gift of the Spirit, the fire of God, assumes a particular form, that of "tongues." Its meaning is immediately explained when the author adds: "They began to speak in other tongues, as the Spirit gave them utterance" (Acts 2:4). The words that come from the Holy Spirit are "like fire" (cf. Jer 5:14; 23:29). They have an efficacy that mere human words do not possess. In this third element of the manifestation of God at Pentecost, God the Holy Spirit, in giving himself to men, produced in them an effect which was both real and symbolic. It was real in that it concerned the faculty of speech which is a natural property of man. However, it was also symbolic since these men "from Galilee," while using their own language or dialect, spoke "in other languages," so that in the multitude that speedily gathered each one heard "his own language," although representatives of many different people were present (cf. Acts 2:6).

The symbolism of the "multiplication of languages" is very significant. According to the Bible the diversity of languages was the sign of the multiplication of peoples and of nations, and indeed of their dispersal following the construction of the tower of Babel (cf. Gen 11:5-9). Then the one common language understood by everyone was divided into many languages, thus causing a confusion of mutual incomprehension. Now the symbolism of the tower of Babel is succeeded by that of the languages of Pentecost, which indicates the opposite of that confusion of languages. One might say that the many incomprehensible languages have lost their specific character, or at least have ceased to be a symbol of division. They have given way to the new work of the Holy Spirit, who through the apostles and the Church brings to spiritual unity peoples of different origins, languages and cultures in view of the perfect communion in God announced and implored by Jesus (cf. Jn 17:11, 21-22).

We conclude with the words of Vatican Council II in the *Constitution on Divine Revelation:* "Christ established the kingdom of God on earth, manifested his Father and himself by deeds and words, and completed his work by his death, resurrection and glorious ascension and by the sending of the Holy Spirit. Having been lifted up from the earth, he draws all men to himself (cf. Jn 12:32), he who alone has the words of eternal life (cf. Jn 6:68). This mystery had not been manifested to other generations as it was now revealed to his holy apostles and prophets in the Holy Spirit (cf. Eph 3:4-6), so that they might preach the Gospel, stir up faith in Jesus, Christ and Lord, and gather together the Church" *(DV* 17). This is the great work of the Holy Spirit and of the Church in human hearts and in history.

General audience of July 12, 1989

Pentecost:
An Outpouring of Divine Life

The Pentecost event in the upper room of Jerusalem was a special divine manifestation. We have already considered its principal external elements: "the sound of a mighty wind," the "tongues of fire" above those assembled in the upper room, and finally the "speaking in other languages." All these elements indicate not only the presence of the Holy Spirit, but also his special descent on those present, his "self-giving," which produced in them a visible transformation, as is evident from the text of the Acts of the Apostles (2:1-12). Pentecost closes the long cycle of divine manifestations in the Old Testament, among which the most important was that to Moses on Mount Sinai.

From the beginning of this series of pneumatological reflections, we have also mentioned the link between the Pentecost event and Christ's Pasch, especially under the aspect of his departure to the Father through his death on the cross, his resurrection and ascension. Pentecost is the fulfillment of Jesus' announcement to the apostles on the day before his passion, during his "farewell discourse" in the upper room of Jerusalem. On that occasion Jesus had spoken of the "new Paraclete": "I will pray the Father, and he will give you another Paraclete, to be with you forever, even the spirit of truth" (Jn 14:16). Jesus emphasized: "When I go, I will send him to you" (Jn 16:7). Speaking of his departure through his redemptive death on the cross, Jesus had said: "Yet a little while and the world will see me no more, but you will see me; because I live also" (Jn 14:19).

Here we have a new aspect of the link between the Pasch and Pentecost: "I live." Jesus was speaking of the resurrection. "You will live": the life, which will be manifested and confirmed in my resurrection, will become your life. The transmission of this life, manifested in the mystery of Christ's Pasch, is effected definitively at Pentecost. Indeed, Christ's words echo the concluding part of Ezekiel's prophecy in which God promised: "I shall put my Spirit within you, and you shall live" (37:14). Therefore Pentecost is linked organically to the Pasch. It pertains to Christ's paschal mystery: "I live and you will live."

By virtue of the coming of the Holy Spirit, Christ's prayer in the upper room is also fulfilled: "Father, the hour has come; glorify your Son that the Son may glorify you, since you have given him power over all flesh, to give eternal life to all whom you have given him" (Jn 17:1-2).

In the paschal mystery, Jesus Christ is the principle of this life. The Holy Spirit gives this life, drawing on the redemption effected by Christ: "He will take what is mine" (Jn 16:14). Jesus himself had said: "It is the Spirit that gives life" (Jn 6:63). Similarly St. Paul proclaims that "the written code kills, but the Spirit gives life" (2 Cor 3:6). Pentecost radiates the truth professed by the Church in the words of the creed: "I believe in the Holy Spirit, the Lord, the giver of life." Together with the Pasch, Pentecost is the climax of the divine Trinity's economy of salvation in human history.

The apostles were assembled on the day of Pentecost in the upper room of Jerusalem together with Mary, the mother of

Jesus, and other "disciples" of the Lord, men and women. They were the first to experience the fruits of Christ's resurrection.

For them Pentecost was the day of resurrection, of new life in the Holy Spirit. It was a spiritual resurrection which we can discern in the transformation of the apostles in the course of all those days; from the Friday of Christ's passion, through Easter day, until the day of Pentecost. The capture of the Master and his death on the cross were a terrible blow for them, from which they found it difficult to recover. This explains their mistrust and doubts on receiving news of the resurrection, even when they met the risen one. The Gospels refer to it several times: "They would not believe" (Mk 16:11); "some doubted" (Mt 28:17). Jesus himself rebuked them gently: "Why are you troubled and why do questionings arise in your hearts?" (Lk 24:38). He tried to convince them about his identity, by showing them that he was not "a spirit" but had "flesh and bones." It was for this reason that he even ate a piece of broiled fish before them (cf. Lk 24:37-43).

The Pentecost event definitively leads the disciples to overcome this attitude of mistrust: the truth of the resurrection fully pervades their minds and wins over their wills. Truly then "out of their hearts flow rivers of living water" (cf. Jn 7:38), as Jesus himself had foretold in a metaphorical sense when speaking of the Holy Spirit.

Through the work of the Holy Spirit the apostles and the other disciples became an "Easter people," believers in and witnesses to Christ's resurrection. Without reserve, they made the truth of that decisive event their own. From the day of Pentecost they were the heralds of "the mighty works of God" *(magnalia Dei)* (Acts 2:11). They were made capable of it from within. The Holy Spirit effected their interior transformation by virtue of the new life that derived from Christ in his resurrection and now infused by the new Paraclete into his followers. We can apply to this transformation what Isaiah prophesied metaphorically: "until the Spirit is poured upon us from on high, and the wilderness becomes a fruitful field, and the fruitful field is deemed a forest" (Is 32:15). Truly on Pentecost the gospel truth is radiant with light: God "is not the God of the dead, but of the living" (Mt 22:32), "for all live to him" (Lk 20:38).

The Pentecost theophany opens to all the prospect of newness of life. That event is the beginning of God's new "self-giving" to humanity. The apostles are the sign and pledge not only of the "new Israel," but also of the "new creation" effected by the paschal mystery. As St. Paul writes: "One man's act of righteousness leads to acquittal and life for all men.... Where sin increased, grace abounded all the more" (Rom 5:18-20). This victory of life over death, of grace over sin, achieved by Christ, works in humanity by means of the Holy Spirit. Through him it brings to fruition in our hearts the mystery of redemption (cf. Rom 5:5; Gal 5:22).

Pentecost is the beginning of the process of spiritual renewal, which realizes the economy of salvation in its historical and eschatological dimension, casting itself over all creation.

In the Encyclical on the Holy Spirit, *Dominum et Vivificantem,* I wrote: "It is a new beginning in relation to the first original beginning of God's salvific self-giving, which is identified with the mystery of creation itself. Here is what we read in the very first words of the Book of Genesis: 'In the beginning God created the heavens and the earth...and the Spirit of God *(ruah Elohim)* was moving over the face of the waters' (1:1f.). This biblical concept of creation includes not only the call to existence of the very being of the cosmos, that is to say, the giving of existence, but also the presence of the Spirit of God in creation, that is to say, the beginning of God's salvific self-communication to the things he creates. This is true first of all concerning man, who has been created in the image and likeness of God" (n. 12). At Pentecost the "new beginning" of God's salvific self-giving is united to the paschal mystery, source of new life.

General audience of July 22, 1989

Pentecost:
God's Gift of Divine Adoption

We have analyzed the external elements recorded in the Acts of the Apostles of the divine manifestation in the theophany of Pentecost in Jerusalem, namely, "the sound of a mighty wind," "the tongues of fire" above those assembled in the upper room, and finally that psychological-vocal phenomenon whereby the apostles are understood even by those who speak "other languages." We have also seen that among all those external manifestations the important and essential element is the interior transformation of the apostles. It is precisely this transformation that expresses the presence and action of the Spirit-Paraclete, whose coming had been promised to the apostles by Christ at the time of his return to the Father.

The descent of the Holy Spirit is closely connected with the paschal mystery, which is effected in the redemptive sacrifice of the cross and in Christ's resurrection which generates new life. On the day of Pentecost the apostles—by the work of the Holy Spirit—fully partake in this life, and thus there matures within them the power of the witness which they will bear to the risen Lord.

At Pentecost the Holy Spirit is manifested as the giver of

life. This is what we profess in the creed when we proclaim him "the Lord, the giver of life." This completes the economy of God's self-communication which began when he gave himself to man, created in his image and likeness. This divine gift of self—which originally constituted the mystery of the creation of man and of his elevation to supernatural dignity—after sin is projected in history as a promise of salvation. It is fulfilled in the mystery of the redemption effected by Christ, the God-Man, through his sacrifice. Linked to Christ's paschal mystery, "God's self-giving" is fulfilled in Pentecost. The theophany of Jerusalem signifies the new beginning of God's self-giving in the Holy Spirit. The apostles and all those present on that day with Mary, the mother of Christ, in the upper room, were the first to experience this new outpouring of divine life which—in them and through them, and therefore in the Church and through the Church—has been made available to everyone. It is universal, just as redemption is universal.

The beginning of the new life is acquired through the gift of divine adoption. This is obtained for all by Christ through the redemption and extended to all by the Holy Spirit. By grace, the Spirit remakes and as it were recreates man in the likeness of the only-begotten Son of the Father. In this way the incarnate Word renews and reinforces God's "gift of self," by offering man through the redemption that "participation in the divine nature" mentioned in the Second Letter of Peter (cf. 2 Pet 1:4). St. Paul also, in the Letter to the Romans, speaks of Jesus Christ as "designated Son of God in power according to the Spirit of holiness by his resurrection from the dead" (1:4).

The fruit of the resurrection, which realizes the fullness of the power of Christ, Son of God, is therefore shared with those who are open to the action of the Spirit as a new gift of divine adoption. After having spoken of the Word made flesh, St. John says in the prologue of his Gospel that "to all who received him, who believed in his name, he gave power to become children of God" (1:12). The two apostles John and Paul understood the concept of divine adoption as a gift to man of this new life, effected by Christ through the Holy Spirit.

The adoption is a gift coming from the Father, as we read in the First Letter of John: "See what love the Father has given us, that we should be called children of God; and so we are" (1 Jn 3:1). In the Letter to the Romans Paul expounds the same truth in the light of God's eternal design: "For those whom he foreknew he also predestined to be conformed to the image of his Son, in order that he might be the first-born among many brethren" (8:29). The same apostle in the Letter to the Ephesians speaks of a sonship due to divine adoption, since God has predestined us "to be his adopted sons through Jesus Christ" (1:5).

Moreover, in the Letter to the Galatians Paul speaks of the eternal design conceived by God in the depth of his trinitarian life. It was accomplished in the "fullness of time" with the coming of the Son in the Incarnation to make us his adopted sons: "God sent forth his Son, born of a woman...so that we might receive adoption as sons" (Gal 4:4-5). According to the Apostle, the mission of the Holy Spirit is closely connected with the Son's "mission" *(missio)* in the trinitarian economy. He adds: "And because we are sons, God has sent the Spirit of his Son into our hearts, crying, 'Abba! Father!'" (Gal 4:6).

Here we touch the goal of the mystery expressed in Pentecost: the Holy Spirit descends "into our hearts" as the Spirit of the Son. Precisely because he is the Spirit of the Son, he enables us to cry out to God together with Christ: "Abba, Father."

This cry expresses the fact that not only are we called to be sons of God, "but we are so indeed," as the Apostle John emphasizes in his First Letter (3:1). Because of this gift, we truly share in the sonship proper to the Son of God, Jesus

Christ. This is the supernatural truth of our relationship with Christ, a truth that can be known only by those who "have known the Father" (cf. 1 Jn 2:13).

This knowledge is possible only by virtue of the Holy Spirit, through the witness which he gives from within to the human spirit. There, he is present as the principle of truth and life. The Apostle Paul tells us: "The Spirit himself bears witness with our spirit that we are children of God, and if children, then heirs, heirs of God and fellow heirs with Christ" (Rom 8:16-17). "You did not receive the spirit of slavery to fall back into fear, but you have received the spirit of sonship whereby we cry, 'Abba! Father!'" (Rom 8:15).

The Spirit reproduces in man the image of the Son, thus establishing the intimate fraternal bond with Christ which leads us to "cry out with him, 'Abba! Father!'" Hence the Apostle writes that "all who are led by the Spirit of God are sons of God" (Rom 8:14). The Holy Spirit "breathes" in the hearts of believers as the Spirit of the Son, establishing in man the divine sonship in the likeness of Christ and in union with Christ. The Holy Spirit forms the human spirit from within according to the divine exemplar which is Christ. Thus, through the Spirit, the Christ known in the pages of the Gospel becomes the "life of the soul." In thinking, loving, judging, acting and even in feeling, man is conformed to Christ, and becomes "Christlike."

This work of the Holy Spirit has its new beginning at Pentecost in Jerusalem, at the apex of the paschal mystery. From then onward Christ is with us and works in us through the Holy Spirit, putting into effect the eternal design of the Father, who has predestined us "to be his adopted sons through Jesus Christ" (Eph 1:5). Let us never tire of repeating and meditating on this marvelous truth of our faith.

General audience of July 26, 1989

Pentecost Is the Fulfillment of the New Covenant

The Pasch of Christ's cross and resurrection reached its climax in the Pentecost of Jerusalem. The descent of the Holy Spirit on the apostles, assembled in the upper room with Mary and the first community of Christ's disciples, was the fulfillment of the promises and announcements made by Jesus to his disciples. Pentecost is the solemn public manifestation of the new covenant made between God and man "in the blood" of Christ: "this is the new covenant in my blood," Jesus had said at the Last Supper (cf. 1 Cor 11:25). This is a new, definitive and eternal covenant, prepared by previous covenants spoken of in the Old Testament. Those already contained the announcement of the definitive pact which God would make with man in Christ and in the Holy Spirit. The revealed word in Ezekiel's prophecy was an invitation to view the Pentecost event in this light: "And I will put my spirit within you" (Ez 36:27).

God's covenants with Noah and Abraham

We have previously noted that whereas Pentecost had at one time been the feast of the harvest (cf. Ex 23:14), it was later celebrated also as a memorial and a renewal of the covenant made by God with Israel after the liberation from the Egyptian bondage (cf. 2 Cor 15:10-13). In any event we read in the Book of Exodus that Moses "took the book of the covenant, and read it in the hearing of the people; and they said 'All that the Lord has spoken we will do, and we will be obedient.' And Moses took the blood and threw it upon the people and said, 'Behold the blood of the covenant which the Lord has made with you in accordance with all these words'" (Ex 24:7-8).

The covenant of Sinai had already been made between the Lord God and Israel. Before that there had been, according to the Bible, God's covenants with the patriarch Noah and with Abraham.

In the covenant with Noah after the flood, God showed his intention to establish a covenant not only with humanity but also with the whole of creation in the visible world: "Behold, I establish my covenant with you and your descendants after you, and with every living creature that is with you...with all animals that come from the ark" (Gen 9:9-10).

The covenant with Abraham had also another meaning. God chose a man and made a covenant with him because of his descendants: "I will establish my covenant between me and you and your descendants after you throughout their generations for an everlasting covenant, to be God to you and to your descendants after you" (Gen 17:7). The covenant with Abraham revealed God's plan to choose a specific people, Israel, from which the promised Messiah would be born.

The divine law was given in the covenant of Sinai

The covenant with Abraham did not contain a law in the true and proper sense. The divine law was given later, in the covenant of Sinai. God promised it to Moses who had gone up the mountain in answer to God's call: "Now therefore, if you will obey my voice and keep my covenant, you shall be my own possession among all peoples; for all the earth is mine.... These are the words which you shall speak to the children of Israel" (Ex 19:5). Moses informed the elders of Israel of the divine promise, "and all the people answered together and said, 'All that the Lord has spoken we will do.' And Moses reported the words of the people to the Lord" (Ex 19:8).

This biblical description of the preparation of the covenant and of the mediating action of Moses sets out in relief the figure of this great leader and lawgiver of Israel, showing the divine origin of the code which he gave to the people. But it also wishes to make it understood that the covenant of Sinai involved commitments on both sides: the Lord chose Israel as his special possession, "a kingdom of priests and a holy nation" (Ex 19:6). But it was on the condition that they would remain faithful to his law in the Ten Commandments, and to the other prescriptions and norms. The people of Israel on their part pledged themselves to this fidelity.

The history of the old covenant shows many instances of Israel's infidelity to God. The prophets especially rebuked Israel for their infidelities, and they interpreted the mournful events of their history as divine punishment. They threatened further punishment, but at the same time they announced another covenant. For example, we read in Jeremiah: "Behold, the days are coming says the Lord, when I will make a new covenant with the house of Israel and the house of Judah, not like the covenant which I made with their fathers when I took them by the hand to bring them out of the land of Egypt, my covenant which they broke" (31:31-32).

The new and future covenant will involve man more intimately. Again we read: "This is the covenant which I will make with the house of Israel after those days, says the Lord: I will put my law within them, and I will write it upon their hearts; and I will be their God, and they shall be my people" (Jer 31:33).

This new initiative of God concerns especially the "interior" person. God's law will be put in the depths of the human "being" (of the human "I"). This character of interiority is confirmed by the words, "I will write it upon their hearts." It is therefore a law with which man is identified interiorly. Only then is God truly "their" God.

According to the prophet Isaiah the law constituting the new covenant will be established in the human spirit by means of the spirit of God. The Spirit of the Lord "shall rest upon a shoot from the stump of Jesse" (Is 11:2), that is, on the Messiah. The words of the prophet shall be fulfilled in him: "The Spirit of the Lord God is upon me, because the Lord has anointed me" (Is 61:1). Guided by the Spirit of God, the Messiah will fulfill the covenant and will make it new and eternal. This is what Isaiah foretold in prophetic words floating above the obscurity of history: "And as for me, this is my covenant with them, says the Lord: my spirit which is upon you, and my words which I have put in your mouth, shall not depart out of your mouth, or out of the mouth of your children, or out of the mouth of your children's children, says the Lord, from this time forth and for evermore" (Is 59:21).

Whatever may be the historical and prophetic periods within which Isaiah's vision is set, we can well say that his words are fully fulfilled in Christ, in the Word who is his own but also "of the Father who sent him" (cf. Jn 5:37); in his Gospel which renews, completes and vivifies the law; and in the Holy Spirit who is sent by virtue of Christ's redemption through his cross and resurrection, thus fully confirming what God had already announced through the prophets in the old covenant. With Christ and in the Holy Spirit there is the new covenant, of which the prophet Ezekiel had prophesied as the mouthpiece of God: "I will give you a new heart and a new spirit: I will take out of your flesh the heart of stone and give you a heart of flesh. And I will put my spirit within you, and cause you to walk in my statutes and be careful to observe my ordinances...and you shall be my people, and I will be your God" (Ez 36:26-28).

In the Pentecost event of Jerusalem the descent of the Holy Spirit definitively fulfilled God's new and eternal covenant with humanity sealed in the blood of the only-begotten Son, as the crowning moment of the "Gift from on high" (cf. Jas 1:17). In that covenant the Triune God "gives himself," no longer merely to the Chosen People, but to all humanity. Ezekiel's prophecy, "you shall be my people and I will be your God" (Ez 36:28), acquires a new and definitive dimension: universality. It realizes to the full the dimension of interiority, because the fullness of the gift—the Holy Spirit—must fill all hearts, giving to all the necessary power to overcome all weakness and sin. It acquires the dimension of eternity: it is a "new and eternal" covenant (cf. Heb 13:20). In that fullness of the gift the Church has its beginning as the People of God of the new and eternal covenant. This fulfilled Christ's promise concerning the Holy Spirit sent as "another Counselor" *(Parákletos)*, "to be with you forever" (Jn 14:16).

General audience of August 2, 1989

Pentecost: The Law of the Spirit

The descent of the Holy Spirit on Pentecost was the definitive completion of the paschal mystery of Jesus Christ. It was the full realization of the announcements of the Old Testament, especially those of the prophets Jeremiah and Ezekiel, concerning a new, future covenant which God would establish with man in Christ and an "outpouring" of God's Spirit "on all mankind" (Joel 3:1). However, this also means a new inscription of God's law in the depths of man's being, or, as the prophet says in the "heart" (cf. Jer 31:33). Thus we have a new law, or a law of the spirit, which we must now consider for a more complete understanding of the mystery of the Paraclete.

We have already emphasized the fact that the old covenant between God and the people of Israel, established by means of the theophany of Sinai, was based on the law. At its center we find the Decalogue. The Lord exhorted his people to observe the commandments: "If you will obey my voice and keep my covenant, you shall be my own possession among all peoples; for all the earth is mine, and you shall be to me a kingdom of priests and a holy nation" (Ex 9:5-6).

Since that covenant had not been faithfully kept, God

announced through the prophets that he would establish a new covenant: "This is the covenant which I will make with the house of Israel after those days, says the Lord: I will put my law within them, and I will write it upon their hearts." These words of Jeremiah, already quoted in the previous catechesis, are joined to the promise: "and I will be their God, and they shall be my people" (Jer 31:33).

The law of love for God and neighbor

Therefore the new (future) covenant announced by the prophets was to be established by means of a radical change in man's relationship with God's law. Instead of being an external rule, written on tablets of stone, the law was to become, thanks to the action of the Holy Spirit on the human heart, an interior guideline established "in the depths of man's being."

According to the Gospel, this law is summarized in the commandment of love for God and neighbor. When Jesus stated that "on these two commandments depend all the law and the prophets" (Mt 22:40), he made it clear that they were already contained in the Old Testament (cf. Dt 6:5; Lev 19:18). Love for God is "the great and first commandment"; love for our neighbor is "the second (which) is like the first" (Mt 22:37-39). It is also a condition for observing the first: "for he who loves his neighbor has fulfilled the law" (Rom 13:8).

The commandment of love for God and neighbor is the essence of the new law established by Christ by word and example (even to giving "his life for his friends": cf. Jn 15:13). It is written in our hearts by the Holy Spirit. For this reason it becomes the "law of the Spirit."

As the Apostle writes to the Corinthians: "You show that you are a letter from Christ delivered by us, written not with ink but with the Spirit of the living God, not on tablets of stone but on tablets of human hearts" (2 Cor 3:3). Therefore the law of the Spirit is man's interior imperative. Rather, it is the same Holy Spirit who thus becomes man's teacher and guide in the depths of his heart.

A law thus understood is far removed from every form of external constraint to which man may be subjected in his actions. The law of the Gospel, contained in the word and confirmed by the life and death of Christ, consists in a divine revelation which includes the fullness of the truth about the good of human actions. At the same time it heals and perfects man's inner freedom, as St. Paul writes: "The law of the Spirit of life in Christ Jesus has set me free from the law of sin and death" (Rom 8:2). According to the Apostle, the Holy Spirit who gives life, because through him the human spirit shares in God's life, becomes at the same time the new principle and source of human activity: "in order that the just requirement of the law might be fulfilled in us, who walk not according to the flesh but according to the Spirit" (Rom 8:4).

In this teaching St. Paul would have been able to appeal to Jesus himself, who in the Sermon on the Mount had pointed out: "Do not think that I have come to abolish the law and the prophets; I have come not to abolish them but to fulfill them" (Mt 5:17). This fulfillment of God's law by Jesus Christ through word and example constitutes the model of walking according to the Spirit. In this sense, the law of the spirit, written by him on tablets of human hearts, exists and operates in those who believe in Christ and share in his Spirit.

As we see from the Acts of the Apostles, the whole life of the primitive Church was a demonstration of the truth expressed by St. Paul. According to him, "God's love has been poured into our hearts through the Spirit who has been given to us" (Rom 5:5). In spite of the limitations and defects of its members, the community of Jerusalem shared in the new life which "is given by the Spirit"; it lived out of God's love. We also have received this life as a gift from the Holy Spirit, who fills us with love—love for God and neighbor—the essential content of the greatest commandment. Thus the new law, stamped in human hearts by love as a gift of the Holy Spirit, is the law of the Spirit within them. It is the law which gives freedom, as St. Paul writes: "The law of the spirit of life in Christ Jesus has set me free from the law of sin and death" (Rom 8:2).

The beginning of a new morality

For this reason, insofar as it is "the pouring into our hearts" of God's love (cf. Rom 5:5), Pentecost marks the beginning of a new human morality based on the law of the Spirit. This morality is more than mere observance of the law dictated by reason or by revelation itself. It derives from and at the same time reaches something more profound. It derives from the Holy Spirit and makes it possible to live in a love which comes from God. It becomes a reality in our lives by means of the Holy Spirit who "has been poured into our hearts."

The Apostle Paul was the greatest proclaimer of this higher morality, rooted in the law of the spirit. He who had been a zealous Pharisee, an expert, a meticulous observer and a fanatical defender of the letter of the old law, and who later became an apostle of Christ, could write about himself: "God...has qualified us to be ministers of a new covenant, not in a written code but in the Spirit: for the written code kills, but the Spirit gives life" (2 Cor 3:6).

General audience of August 9, 1989

Pentecost:
People of God, a Holy People

On the day of Pentecost at Jerusalem, the apostles received the Holy Spirit, together with the first community of Christ's disciples, assembled in the upper room with Mary, the mother of the Lord. Thus the promise which Christ made to them when he left this world to return to the Father was fulfilled for them. On that day the Church, which had her origins in the Redeemer's death, was revealed to the world. I shall speak about this in the next catechesis.

Now I would like to show that the coming of the Holy Spirit, as the fulfillment of the new covenant in Christ's blood, gives rise to the new People of God. This is the community of those who have been "sanctified in Christ Jesus" (1 Cor 1:2); those from whom Christ has made "a kingdom of priests to his God and Father" (Rev 1:6; cf. 5:10; 1 Pet 2:9). All this happened by virtue of the Holy Spirit.

In order to grasp fully the significance of this truth, announced by the Apostles Peter and Paul and by the Book of Revelation, we must return for a moment to the establishing of the old covenant between the Lord God and Israel. It was represented by its leader, Moses, after the liberation from the slavery of Egypt. The texts which speak of it indicate clearly that the strict covenant was not reduced to a mere pact founded on bilateral duties. It was the Lord God who chose Israel as his people, so that the people became his property, while he himself would be their God from then onward.

Thus we read: "Now therefore, if you will obey my voice and keep my covenant, you shall be my own possession among all peoples; for all the earth is mine, and you shall be to me a kingdom of priests and a holy nation" (Ex 19:5-6). The Book of Deuteronomy repeats and confirms what God proclaims in Exodus. "For you (Israel) are a people holy to the Lord your God; the Lord your God has chosen you to be a people for his own possession, out of all the peoples that are on the face of the earth" (Dt 7:6; cf. 26:18). (Incidentally, we may note that the expression *sequllah* means "the king's personal treasure.")

Such a choice on God's part derives totally and exclusively from his love, a completely gratuitous love. We read: "It was not because you were more numerous than any other people that the Lord set his love upon you and chose you, for you were the fewest of all peoples; but it is because the Lord loves you and is keeping the oath which he swore to your fathers, that the Lord has brought you out with a mighty hand, and redeemed you from the house of bondage" (Dt 7:7-8). The Book of Exodus expresses the same thing in picturesque language: "You have seen what I did to the Egyptians, and how I bore you on eagles' wings and brought you to myself" (Ex 19:4).

God acts out of gratuitous love. This love binds Israel to the Lord God in a particular and exceptional way. Through it Israel became God's property. Yet such love requires a return, and therefore a response of love on Israel's part: "You shall love the Lord your God with all your heart" (Dt 6:5).

Thus in the covenant a new people, the People of God, came into being. Being the "property" of the Lord God means being consecrated to him, being a holy people. It is what the

Lord God makes known to the entire community of the Israelites through Moses: "You shall be holy, for I, the Lord your God, am holy" (Lev 19:2). By that very choice God gave himself to his people in that which is most characteristic of him, holiness, and he asked it from Israel as a quality of life.

As a people consecrated to God, Israel is called to be a priestly people: "You shall be called the priests of the Lord; men shall speak of you as ministers of our God" (Is 61:6).

The new covenant, new and eternal, comes strictly "in Christ's blood" (cf. 1 Cor 11:25). By virtue of this sacrifice, the "new Counselor" *(Parákletos)* (cf. Jn 14:16)—the Holy Spirit—is given to those who are "sanctified in Christ Jesus, called to be saints" (1 Cor 1:2). "To all God's beloved in Rome, who are called to be saints" (Rom 1:7), St. Paul addressed his letter to the Christians of Rome. He expressed himself similarly to the Corinthians: "To the Church of God which is at Corinth, with all the saints who are in the whole of Achaia" (2 Cor 1:1); to the Philippians: "To all the saints in Christ Jesus who are at Philippi" (Phil 1:1); to the Colossians: "To the saints and faithful brethren in Christ at Colossae" (Col 1:2); and to those of Ephesus: "To the saints who are at Ephesus" (Eph 1:1).

We find the same mode of expression in the Acts of the Apostles: "Peter...came down also to the saints that lived at Lydda" (Acts 9:32; cf. 9:41; also 9:13 "to your saints at Jerusalem").

All these cases refer to Christians, or to the faithful, that is, to the brethren who have received the Holy Spirit. The Holy Spirit is the direct builder of that holiness upon which, through participation in the holiness of God himself, the whole Christian life is built: "You were sanctified...in the Spirit of our God" (1 Cor 6:11; cf. 2 Thess 2:13; 1 Pet 1:2).

The same must be said of the consecration which, in virtue of the Holy Spirit, causes the baptized to become "a kingdom of priests to his God and Father" (cf. Rev 1:6; 5:10; 20:6). The First Letter of Peter fully develops this truth: "Like living stones be yourselves built into a spiritual house, to be a holy priesthood, to offer spiritual sacrifices acceptable to God through Jesus Christ" (1 Pet 2:5). "You are a chosen race, a royal priesthood, a holy nation, God's own people, that you may declare the wonderful deeds of him who called you out of darkness into his marvelous light" (1 Pet 2:9). We know that "it was revealed to them" with the voice of the Gospel "through the Holy Spirit sent from heaven" (1 Pet 1:12).

The Constitution *Lumen Gentium* of the Second Vatican Council expressed this truth in the following words: "Christ the Lord, high priest taken from among men (cf. Heb 5:1-5), made the new people 'a kingdom of priests to God, his Father' (Rev 1:6; cf. 5:9-10). The baptized, by regeneration and the anointing of the Holy Spirit, are consecrated to be a spiritual house and a holy priesthood, that through all those works which are those of the Christian they may offer spiritual sacrifices and proclaim the power of him who has called them out of darkness into his marvelous light (cf. 1 Pet 2:4-10)" (n. 10).

Here we arrive at the very essence of the Church as People of God and community of saints, to which we shall return in the next catechesis. However, the texts quoted clarify already that the unction, that is, the power and action of the Holy Spirit, is expressed in the condition of holiness and consecration of the new people.

General audience of August 16, 1989

The Birth of the Church

The Church, which originated in Christ's redemptive death, was manifested to the world on Pentecost Day by the work of the Holy Spirit. This is the theme of today's catechesis, introduced by the previous one on the descent of the Holy Spirit, which gave rise to the new People of God. We have seen how, in reference to the old covenant between the Lord God and Israel as his "chosen" people, the people of the new covenant made "in Christ's blood" (cf. 1 Cor 11:25) are called in the Holy Spirit to holiness. It is the people consecrated through "the anointing of the Holy Spirit" in the sacrament of Baptism. It is the "royal priesthood" called to offer "spiritual gifts" (cf. 1 Pet 2:9). By forming the people of the new covenant in this way, the Holy Spirit manifests the Church which flowed from the Redeemer's heart wounded on the cross.

In the Christological cycle of catecheses, we have already shown that Jesus Christ, by "transmitting to the apostles the kingdom received from the Father" (cf. Lk 22:2; Mk 4:11), laid the foundations for building his Church. He did not limit himself to attracting listeners and disciples by means of the words of the Gospel and the signs worked by him. He clearly stated that he wished "to build the Church" on the apostles, and in particular on Peter (cf. Mt 16:18). When the hour of his passion, the evening of the previous day, arrived, he prayed for their "consecration in the truth" (cf. Jn 17:17); he prayed for their unity: "That they may all be one; even as you, Father, are in me, and I in you...so that the world may believe that you have sent me" (cf. Jn 17:21-23). Finally, he gave his life "as a ransom for many" (Mk 10:45), "to gather into one the children of God who are scattered abroad" (Jn 11:52).

The conciliar Constitution *Lumen Gentium* emphasizes the connection between the Paschal mystery and Pentecost: "When Jesus, who had suffered the death of the cross for mankind, had risen, he appeared as the one constituted as Lord, Christ and eternal Priest, and he poured out on his disciples the Spirit promised by the Father" (n. 5). This happened in accordance with what Jesus announced during the supper before his passion, and repeated before his final departure from this earth to return to the Father: "You shall receive power when the Holy Spirit has come upon you; and you shall be my witnesses in Jerusalem...and to the end of the earth" (Acts 1:8).

This fact is culminating and decisive for the Church's existence. Christ announced and instituted her, and then finally "generated" her on the cross through his redemptive death. However, the Church's existence became evident on the day of Pentecost when the Holy Spirit descended and the apostles began to "bear witness" to Christ's paschal mystery. We can speak of this event as a birth of the Church, as we speak of a person's birth at the moment when he comes forth from his mother's womb and "is manifested" to the world.

In the Encyclical *Dominum et Vivificantem* I wrote: "The era of the Church began with the 'coming,' that is to say, with the descent of the Holy Spirit on the apostles gathered in the upper room in Jerusalem, together with Mary, the Lord's mother. The time of the Church began at the moment when the promises and predictions that so explicitly referred to the Counselor, the Spirit of truth, began to be fulfilled in complete power and clarity upon the apostles, thus determining the birth of the Church.... The Holy Spirit assumed the invisible—but in a certain way 'perceptible'—guidance of those who after the departure of the Lord Jesus felt deeply that they had been left orphans. With the coming of the Spirit they felt capable of fulfilling the mission entrusted to them. They felt full of strength. It is precisely this that the Spirit worked in them, and this is certainly at work in the Church, through their successors" (n. 25).

The Church's birth is like a "new creation" (cf. Eph 2:15). We can make an analogy with the first creation, when "the Lord formed man of dust from the ground, and breathed into his nostrils the breath of life" (Gen 2:7). To this breath of life man owes the spirit which makes him a human person. We must refer back to this creative breath when we read that the risen Christ, appearing to the apostles assembled in the upper room, "breathed on them, and said to them: 'Receive the Holy Spirit. If you forgive the sins of any, they are forgiven; if you retain the sins of any, they are retained'" (Jn 20:22-23). This event, which took place the very evening of the Pasch, can be considered as a Pentecost in anticipation, not yet public. Then followed the day of Pentecost, the public manifestation of the gift of the Spirit. Jesus Christ, "exalted at the right hand of God, and having received from the Father the gift of the Holy Spirit, poured out this Spirit" (Acts 2:33). Therefore through the work of the Holy Spirit there has been "the new creation" (cf. Ps 104:30).

Besides the analogy with the Book of Genesis, we can find another in a passage from the Book of Ezekiel where we read: "Thus says the Lord God: Come from the four winds, O breath, and breathe upon these slain, that they may live" (Ez 37:9). "Behold, I will open your graves, and raise you from your grave, O my people; and I will bring you home into the land of Israel" (Ez 37:12). "And I will put my Spirit within you, and you shall live...you shall know that I, the Lord, have spoken" (Ez 37:14). "...and the breath came into them, and they lived, and stood upon their feet" (Ez 37:10).

This magnificent and penetrating prophetic vision concerns the messianic restoration of Israel after the exile, announced by God after the long period of suffering (cf. Ez 37:11-14). The same announcement of revival and new life was given by Hosea (cf. 6:2; 13; 14) and by Isaiah (26:19). Yet the symbolism used by the prophet gave Israel the desire for an individual resurrection, perhaps already foreseen by Job (cf. 19:25). As other passages show, this idea would develop gradually in the Old Testament (cf. Dan 12:2; 2 Macc 7:9-14; 23-36; 12:43-46) and in the New (Mt 22:29-32; 1 Cor 15). However, that idea prepared for the concept of the new life which would be revealed in Christ's resurrection and would come down on those who would believe, through the work of the Holy Spirit. We believers in Christ can also read a certain paschal analogy in the text of Ezekiel.

Here is a final aspect of the mystery of the Church's birth at Pentecost through the Spirit's action. In it Christ's priestly prayer in the upper room is realized: "that they may all be one; even as you, Father, are in me, and I in you, that they also may be in us, so that the world may believe that you have sent me" (Jn 17:21). Descending upon the apostles assembled with Mary, Christ's mother, the Holy Spirit transforms and unites them, "filling them" with the fullness of the divine life. They become "one," an apostolic community, ready to bear witness to the crucified and risen Christ. This is the new creation which flowed from the cross and was given life by the Holy Spirit, who gave it its historical beginning at Pentecost.

General audience of August 30, 1989

Baptism in the Holy Spirit

When the Church, originating in the sacrifice of the cross, began her early journey by means of the descent of the Holy Spirit in the upper room at Pentecost, "her time" began. "It was the time of the Church" as collaborator of the Spirit in the mission of making the redemption by Christ fruitful among humanity from generation to generation. In this mission and in collaboration with the Spirit, the Church realizes the sacramentality which the Second Vatican Council attributes to her when it teaches: "The Church is in Christ like a sacrament or as a sign and instrument both of a very closely knit union with God and of the unity of the whole human race" *(LG* 1). This sacramentality has a deep significance in relation to the mystery of Pentecost, which gives the Church the strength and the charisms to work visibly among the whole human family.

In this catechesis we wish to consider principally the relationship between Pentecost and the sacrament of Baptism. We know that the coming of the Holy Spirit had been announced at the Jordan together with the coming of Christ. John the Baptist was to link the two comings, and indeed to show their intimate connection when speaking of baptism: "He will baptize you with the Holy Spirit" (Mk 1:8). "He will baptize you with the Holy Spirit and with fire" (Mt 3:11). This link between the Holy Spirit and fire is found in the context of biblical language, which already in the Old Testament showed fire as the means adopted by God to purify consciences (cf. Is 1:25; 6:5-7; Zech 13:9; Mal 3:2-3; Sir 2:5 etc.). In its turn, the baptism practiced in Judaism and in other ancient religious was a ritual immersion, which signified a regenerating purification. John the Baptist had adopted this practice of baptizing with water, while emphasizing that its value was not merely ritual but oral, because it was "for conversion" (cf. Mt 3:2, 6, 8, 11; Lk 3:10-14). Besides, it was a kind of initiation through which those who received it became the Baptist's disciples and formed around him a community characterized by its eschatological expectation of the Messiah (cf. Mt 3:2, 11; Jn 1:13-14). Nevertheless, it was a baptism with water. It therefore did not have the power of sacramental purification. Such power would have been characteristic of the baptism of fire— in itself an element much more powerful than water—brought by the Messiah. John proclaimed the preparatory and symbolic function of his baptism in relation to the Messiah, who was to baptize "with the Holy Spirit and with fire" (Mt 3:11; cf. 3, 7, 10, 12: Jn 1:33). He added that the Messiah would thoroughly purify with the fire of the Spirit those who were well disposed, gathered like "wheat in the granary." Yet he would burn "the chaff...with unquenchable fire" (Mt 3:12), like the "hell of fire" (cf. Mt 18:8-9), a symbol of the end destined for all who did not let themselves be purified (cf. Is 66:24; Jdt 16:17; Sir 7:17; Zeph 1:18; Ps 21:10, etc.).

While developing his role as prophet and precursor along the lines of Old Testament symbolism, the Baptist one day met Jesus by the Jordan. He recognized him as the Messiah, proclaimed that he is "the Lamb of God, who takes away the sin of the world" (Jn 1:29), and baptized him at his request (cf. Mt

3:14-15). Yet at the same time he testified to the messiahship of Jesus, whose mere announcer and precursor he claimed to be. This testimony of John was supplemented by his own statement to his disciples and hearers concerning the experience which he had on that occasion, and which perhaps had reminded him of the Genesis narrative about the end of the flood (cf. Gen 8:10): "I saw the Spirit descend as a dove from heaven, and it remained on him. I myself did not know him, but he who sent me to baptize with water said to me: 'He on whom you see the Spirit descend and remain, this is he who baptizes with the Holy Spirit...'" (Jn 1:32-33; cf. Mt 3:16; Mk 1:8; Lk 3:22).

"Baptizing in the Holy Spirit" means regenerating humanity with the power of God's Spirit. That is what the Messiah does. As Isaiah had foretold (11:2; 42:1), the Spirit rests on him, filling his humanity with divine strength, from his Incarnation to the fullness of the resurrection after his death on the cross (cf. Jn 7:29; 14:26; 16:7, 8; 20:22; Lk 24:49). Having acquired this fullness, Jesus the Messiah can give the new baptism in the Spirit of whom he is full (cf. Jn 1:33; Acts 1:5). From his glorified humanity, as from a fountain of living water, the Spirit will flow over the world (cf. Jn 7:37-39; 19:34; cf. Rom 5:5). This is the announcement which the Baptist made when bearing witness to Christ on the occasion of his baptism, in which are found the symbols of water and fire, expressing the mystery of the new life-giving energy which the Messiah and the Spirit have poured out on the world.

During his ministry, Jesus also spoke of his passion and death as a baptism which he himself must receive: a baptism, because he must be totally immersed in the suffering symbolized by the cup which he must drink (cf. Mk 10:38; 14:36). But it was a baptism which Jesus connected to the other symbol of fire. In this it is easy enough to glimpse the Spirit who "pours out" his humanity, and who one day, after the fire of the cross, would flow over the world. He would spread the baptism of fire which Jesus so longed to receive that he was in anguish until it was accomplished in him (cf. Lk 12:50).

In the Encyclical *Dominum et Vivificantem* I wrote: "The Old Testament on several occasions speaks of fire from heaven which burnt the oblations presented by men. By analogy one can say that the Holy Spirit is the fire from heaven which works in the depths of the mystery of the cross. The Holy Spirit as Love and Gift comes down, in a certain sense, into the very heart of the sacrifice which is offered on the cross. Referring here to the biblical tradition we can say: he consumes this sacrifice with the fire of the love which united the Son with the Father in the trinitarian communion. And since the sacrifice of the cross is an act proper to Christ, also in this sacrifice he receives the Holy Spirit. He receives the Holy Spirit in such a way that afterward—and he alone with God the Father—can give him to the apostles, to the Church, to humanity. He alone sends the Spirit from the Father. He alone appears to the apostles in the upper room, breathes on them and says: 'Receive the Holy Spirit; if you forgive the sons of any, they are forgiven' (cf. Jn 20:23)" (n. 41).

Thus John's messianic announcement at the Jordan is fulfilled: "He will baptize you with the Holy Spirit and with fire" (Mt 3:11; cf. Lk 3:16). Here also is found the realization of the symbolism by which God himself is shown as a column of fire which guides the people through the desert (cf. Ex 13:21-22); as the word of fire through which "the mountain (Sinai) burned with fire to the heart of heaven" (Dt 4:11); as a fire of ardent glory with love for Israel (cf. Dt 4:24). What Christ himself promised when he said that he had come to cast fire on the earth (cf. Lk 12:49) is fulfilled, while the Book of Revelation would say of him that his eyes are blazing like a fire (cf. Rev 1:14; 2:18; 19-12). Thus it is clear that the Holy

Spirit is represented by the fire (cf. Acts 2:3). All this happens in the paschal mystery, when Christ "received the baptism with which he himself was to be baptized" (cf. Mk 10:38) in the sacrifice on the cross, and in the mystery of Pentecost, when the risen and glorified Christ pours his Spirit on the apostles and on the Church.

According to St. Paul, by that "baptism of fire" received in his sacrifice, Christ in his resurrection became the "last Adam," "a life-giving spirit" (cf. 1 Cor 15:45). For this reason the risen Christ announced to the apostles: "John baptized with water but before many days you shall be baptized with the Holy Spirit" (Acts 1:5). By the work of the "last Adam," Christ, "the life-giving Spirit" (cf. Jn 6:83) would be given to the apostles and to the Church.

On Pentecost Day this baptism is revealed. It is the new and final baptism which purifies and sanctifies through a new life. It is the baptism in virtue of which the Church is born in the eschatological perspective which extends "to the close of the age" (cf. Mt 28:20); not merely the Church of Jerusalem of the apostles and the Lord's immediate disciples, but the entire Church, taken in her universality, realized through the times and in the places where she is established on earth.

The tongues of fire which accompanied the Pentecost event in the upper room at Jerusalem are the sign of that fire which Jesus Christ brought and enkindled on earth (cf. Lk 12:43): the fire of the Holy Spirit.

In the light of Pentecost we can also understand better the significance of Baptism as a first sacrament, insofar as it is a work of the Holy Spirit. Jesus himself had referred to it in his conversation with Nicodemus: "Truly, truly, I say to you, unless one is born of water and the Spirit, he cannot enter the kingdom of God" (Jn 3:5). In this same conversation Jesus referred also to his future death on the cross (cf. Jn 3:14-15) and to his heavenly glory (cf. Jn 3:13). It is the baptism of the sacrifice, from which the baptism by water, the first sacrament of the Church, received power to effect her birth from the Holy Spirit and to open to humanity the "entrance to God's kingdom." Indeed, as St. Paul writes to the Romans, "Do you not know that all of us who have been baptized into Christ were baptized into his death? We are buried therefore with him by baptism into death, so that as Christ was raised from the dead by the glory of the Father, we too might walk in newness of life" (Rom 6:3-4). This baptismal walk in newness of life began on Pentecost day at Jerusalem.

Several times in his letters the Apostle points out the significance of Baptism (cf. 1 Cor 6:11; Tit 3:5; 2 Cor 1:22; Eph 1:13). He sees it as a "washing of regeneration and renewal in the Holy Spirit" (Tit 3:5); a portent of justification "in the name of the Lord Jesus Christ" (1 Cor 6:11; cf. 2 Cor 1:22); as a "seal of the promised Holy Spirit" (cf. Eph 1:13); as "a guarantee of the Spirit in our hearts" (cf. 2 Cor 1:22). Given this presence of the Holy Spirit in the baptized, the Apostle recommends to the Christians of that time and also repeats to us today: "Do not grieve the Holy Spirit of God, in whom you were sealed for the day of redemption" (Eph 4:30).

General audience of September 6, 1989

The Intrinsic Link between the Eucharist and the Gift of the Holy Spirit

Jesus' promise "...before many days you shall be baptized with the Holy Spirit" (Acts 1:5), indicates the special link between the Holy Spirit and baptism. We saw in the previous reflection that beginning with John's baptism of penance at the Jordan when he announced the coming of Christ, we are brought close to him who will baptize "with the Holy Spirit and with fire." We are also brought close to that unique baptism with which he himself was to be baptized (cf. Mk 10:38): the sacrifice of the cross offered by Christ "through the eternal Spirit" (Heb 9:14). He became "the last Adam who became a life-giving spirit," according to the statement of St. Paul (cf. 1 Cor 15:45). We know that on the day of the resurrection Christ granted to the apostles the Spirit, the giver of life (cf. Jn 20:22), and also later at Pentecost when all were "baptized with the Holy Spirit" (cf. Acts 2:4).

There is therefore an objective relationship between Christ's paschal sacrifice and the gift of the Spirit. Since the Eucharist mystically renews Christ's redemptive sacrifice, one can easily see the intrinsic link between this sacrament and the gift of the Spirit. In founding the Church through his coming on the day of Pentecost, the Holy Spirit established it in objective relationship to the Eucharist, and ordered it toward the Eucharist.

Jesus had said in one of his parables: "The kingdom of heaven may be compared to a king who gave a marriage feast for his son" (Mt 22:2). The Eucharist is the sacramental anticipation and, in a certain sense, a "foretaste" of that royal feast which the Book of Revelation calls "the marriage supper of the Lamb" (cf. Rev 19:9). The bridegroom who is at the center of that marriage feast and of its Eucharistic foreshadowing and anticipation is the Lamb who "took away the sins of the world," the Redeemer.

In the Church born of the baptism of Pentecost, when the apostles and with them the other disciples and followers of Christ, were "baptized with the Spirit," the Eucharist is and remains until the end of time the sacrament of the Body and Blood of Christ.

In it is present "the blood of Christ, who through the eternal Spirit offered himself without blemish to God" (Heb 9:14); the blood "poured out for many" (Mk 14:24) "for the forgiveness of sins" (Mt 26:28); the blood "which purifies your conscience from dead works" (cf. Heb 9:14); the "blood of the covenant" (Mt 26:28). When instituting the Eucharist, Jesus himself said: "This cup...is the new covenant in my blood" (Lk 22:20; cf. 1 Cor 11:25), and he told the apostles: "Do this in remembrance of me" (Lk 22:19).

In the Eucharist—on each occasion—there is re-presented the sacrifice of the Body and Blood offered by Christ once for all on the cross to the Father for the redemption of the world. The Encyclical *Dominum et Vivificantem* states: "In the sacrifice of the Son of Man the Holy Spirit is present and active.... The same Christ Jesus in his own humanity opened himself totally to this action...[which] from suffering enables salvific love to spring forth" (n. 40).

The Eucharist is the sacrament of this redemptive love, closely connected with the Holy Spirit's presence and action. At this point how can we fail to recall Jesus' words in the synagogue of Capernaum, after the multiplication of the bread (cf. Jn 6:27), when he proclaimed the necessity of being nourished on his body and blood? Many of his hearers thought his discourse "on eating his body and drinking his blood" (cf. Jn 6:53) "a hard saying" (Jn 6:60). Realizing their difficulty, Jesus said to them: "Do you take offense at this? Then what if you were to see the Son of Man ascending where he was before?" (Jn 6:61-62). That was an explicit allusion to his future ascension into heaven. At that very point he added a reference to the Holy Spirit which would be fully understood only after the ascension. He said: "It is the Spirit that gives life, the flesh is of no avail; the words that I have spoken to you are spirit and life" (Jn 6:63).

Jesus' hearers understood that first announcement of the Eucharist in a "material" sense. The Master immediately explained that his words would be clarified and understood only through the "Spirit, the giver of life." In the Eucharist Christ gives us his body and blood as food and drink, under the appearance of bread and wine, just as during the paschal meal at the Last Supper. Only through the Spirit, the giver of life, can the Eucharistic food and drink produce in us "communion," that is to say, the salvific union with Christ crucified and glorified.

A significant fact is linked to the Pentecost event: from the earliest times after the descent of the Holy Spirit the apostles and their followers, converted and baptized, "devoted themselves to the breaking of bread and the prayers" (Acts 2:42). It was as if the Holy Spirit himself had directed them toward the Eucharist. In the Encyclical *Dominum et Vivificantem* I stated: "Guided by the Holy Spirit, the Church from the beginning expressed and confirmed her identity through the Eucharist" (n. 62).

The primitive Church was a community founded on the teaching of the apostles (Acts 2:42). It was completely animated by the Holy Spirit who enlightened the believers to understand the Word, and gathered them together in charity around the Eucharist. Thus the Church grew into a multitude of believers who "were of one heart and soul" (Acts 4:32).

In the same encyclical already quoted we read: "Through the Eucharist, individuals and communities, by the action of the Paraclete-Counselor, learn to discover the divine sense of human life" (n. 62). They discover the value of the interior life, realizing in themselves the image of the Triune God. This is always presented to us in the books of the New Testament and especially in St. Paul's letters, as the alpha and omega of our lives. That is to say, it is the principle according to which man is created and modeled, and the last end to which he is directed and led by the will and plan of the Father, reflected in the Son-Word and in the Spirit-Love. It is a beautiful and profound interpretation which patristic tradition has given of the key principle of Christian spirituality and anthropology. It was summarized and formulated in theological terms by St. Thomas (cf. *Summa Theol.,* I, q. 93, a. 8). This is how it is expressed in the Letter to the Ephesians: "For this reason I bow my knees before the Father, from whom every family in heaven and on earth is named, that according to the riches of his glory he may grant you to be strengthened with might through his Spirit in the inner man, and that Christ may dwell in your hearts through faith; that you, being rooted and grounded in love, may have power to comprehend with all the saints what is the breadth and length and height and depth, and to know the love of Christ which surpasses knowledge, that you may be filled with all the fullness of God" (3:14-19).

It is Christ who gives us this divine fullness (cf. Col 2:9 f.) through the action of the Holy Spirit. Thus, filled with divine life, Christians enter and live in the fullness of the whole Christ, which is the Church, and through the Church, in the new universe which is gradually being constructed (cf. Eph 1:23; 4:12-13; Col 2:10). At the center of the Church is the Eucharist, where Christ is present and active in humanity and in the whole world by means of the Holy Spirit.

General audience of September 13, 1989

Pentecost Marks the Beginning of the Church's Mission

In the Council's Decree *Ad Gentes*, on the Church's missionary activity, the Pentecost event and the historical beginning of the Church are closely connected: "On the day of Pentecost (the Holy Spirit) came down upon the disciples.... For it was from Pentecost that the 'acts of the apostles' took origin" *(AG* 4). If, therefore, from the moment of her birth, by going out into the world on the day of Pentecost, the Church is manifested as "missionary," this was through the work of the Holy Spirit. We can also add that the Church always remains such: she remains "in a state of mission" *(in statu missionis).* The missionary character belongs to her very essence. It is a constitutive property of the Church of Christ, because the Holy Spirit has made her missionary from her origin.

An analysis of the text of the Acts of the Apostles which records the event of Pentecost (Acts 2:1-13), indicates the truth of this conciliar assertion which pertains to the common patrimony of the Church.

We know that the apostles and the other disciples, assembled with Mary in the upper room, heard "a sound like the rush of a mighty wind," and there appeared to them "tongues as of fire, distributed and resting on each one of them" (cf. Acts 2:2-3). In the Jewish tradition fire was a sign of a special manifestation of God who spoke for the instruction, guidance and salvation of his people. The memory of the marvelous experience of Sinai was alive in the soul of Israel and disposed her to understand the meaning of the new communications contained under that symbolism, as is evident also from the Jerusalem Talmud (cf. Hag 2, 77b, 32; cf. also the Midrash Rabbah 5, 9 on Exodus 4:27). The same Jewish tradition had prepared the apostles to understand that the "tongues" signified the mission of proclamation, witness and preaching which Jesus himself had enjoined on them. The "fire" was in relation not only to the law of God, which Jesus had confirmed and brought to completion, but also to himself, to his person, and to his life, death and resurrection, since he was the new Torah to be proclaimed in the world. Under the action of the Holy Spirit, the "tongues of fire" became the word on the lips of the apostles: "They were all filled with the Holy Spirit and began to speak in other tongues, as the Spirit gave them utterance" (Acts 2:4).

Already in the history of the Old Testament there had been similar manifestations in which the spirit of the Lord was given for prophetic utterance (cf. Mic 3:8; Is 61:1; Zech 7:12; Neh 9:30). Isaiah tells us that one of the seraphim flew to him, "having in his hand a burning coal which he had taken with tongs from the altar." With it he touched his lips to cleanse him from all guilt, before the Lord entrusted him with the mission of speaking to his people (cf. Is 6:6-9 ff.). The apostles were aware of this traditional symbolism and were therefore able to grasp the meaning of what was happening to them on that Pentecost, as Peter testified in his first discourse, by linking the gift of tongues to Joel's prophecy about the future outpouring of the divine Spirit which was to enable the disciples to prophesy (Acts 2:17 ff.; Joel 3:1-5).

With the "tongues of fire" (Acts 2:3) each apostle received the multiform gift of the Spirit, just as the servants in the gospel parable had all received a certain number of talents to make fruitful (cf. Mt 25:14 ff.). That "tongue" was a sign of the awareness which the apostles had and kept alive concerning the missionary task to which they were called and dedicated. As soon as they were "filled with the Holy Spirit, they began to speak in other tongues, as the Spirit gave them utterance." Their power came from the Spirit, and they carried out the task consigned to them under an interior impulse from on high.

This happened in the upper room, but very soon the missionary proclamation and glossolalia or gift of tongues went beyond the place where they dwelt. Two extraordinary events took place, and they are described in the Acts of the Apostles. First of all, it describes the gift of tongues by which they spoke words pertaining to a multiplicity of languages and used to sing the praises of God (cf. Acts 2:11). The multitude summoned by the sound and amazed by that fact was made up of "devout Jews" who were in Jerusalem for the paschal feast. They belonged to "every nation under heaven" (Acts 2:5) and they spoke the languages of the peoples into whom they were civilly and administratively integrated, even though ethnically they were still Jews. Now that multitude assembled around the apostles "was bewildered, because each one heard them speaking in his own language. They were amazed and wondered, saying, 'Are not all these who are speaking Galileans? And how is it that each of us hears in his own native language?'" (Acts 2:6-8). At this point Luke does not hesitate to trace a kind of map of the Mediterranean world from which those devout Jews came. It was as though he placed that world of converts to Christ in opposition to the babel of languages and peoples described in Genesis (11:1-9), without failing to mention among the others, "visitors from Rome," "Parthians and

Medes and Elamites and residents of Mesopotamia, Judea and Cappadocia, Pontius and Asia, Phrygia and Pamphylia, Egypt and the parts of Libya belonging to Cyrene, and visitors from Rome, both Jews and proselytes, Cretans and Arabians" (Acts 2:11-19). In the mouths of them all Luke, as though reliving the event that had happened at Jerusalem and had been handed down in the early Christian tradition, places the words: "We hear from [the apostles, Galileans by origin] telling in our own tongues the mighty works of God" (Acts 2:11).

The event of that day was certainly mysterious, and also very significant. We can discover in it a sign of the universality of Christendom and of the Church's missionary character. The sacred writer presents it to us, knowing well that the message is destined for the people of every nation. It is the Holy Spirit who intervenes to ensure that each one understands at least something in his own language: "Each of us hears in his own native language" (Acts 2:8). Today we would speak of an adaptation to the linguistic and cultural conditions of each one. One can therefore see in all this a primary form of inculturation, effected by the work of the Holy Spirit.

The other extraordinary fact is the courage with which Peter and the eleven "stood up" and began to explain the messianic and pneumatological meaning of what was happening before the eyes of that bewildered multitude (Acts 2:14 ff.). We shall return to this matter in due course. Here we may make a final reflection on the contrast (a kind of analogy from contraries) between what happens at Pentecost and what we read in the Book of Genesis on the subject of the Tower of Babel (cf. Gen 11:1-9). There we are witnesses of the dispersion of the languages, and therefore of the people who, in speaking different languages, cannot understand one another. At Pentecost, on the contrary, under the action of the Spirit who is the "Spirit of truth" (cf. Jn 15:26), the diversity of languages no longer impedes the understanding of what is proclaimed in the name and to the praise of God. Thus there is a relationship of interhuman union which goes beyond the boundaries of languages and cultures, and this union is brought about in the world by the Holy Spirit.

It is an initial fulfillment of the words addressed by Christ to the apostles before ascending to the Father: "You shall receive power when the Holy Spirit has come upon you; and you shall be my witnesses in Jerusalem and in all Judea and Samaria and to the ends of the earth" (Acts 1:8).

The Second Vatican Council comments: "The Church, which the Spirit guides in the way of all truth and which he unified in communion and in works of ministry, he both equips and directs with hierarchical and charismatic gifts" *(LG* 4), "giving life, soul-like, to ecclesiastical institutions and instilling into the hearts of the faithful the same mission spirit which impelled Christ himself" *(AG* 4). From Christ, to the apostles, to the Church, to the whole world: under the action of the Holy Spirit the process of the universal unification in truth and love can and must unfold.

General audience of September 20, 1989

The Church's Universality and Diversity

We read in the Constitution *Lumen Gentium* of Vatican Council II: "When the work which the Father gave the Son to do on earth (cf. Jn 17:4) was accomplished, the Holy Spirit was sent on the day of Pentecost in order that he might continually sanctify the Church, and thus, all those who believe would have access through Christ in one Spirit to the Father (cf. Eph 2:18). He is the Spirit of life, a fountain of water springing up to life eternal (cf. Jn 4:47; 7:38-39).... The Spirit dwells in the Church and in the hearts of the faithful, as in a temple (cf. 1 Cor 3:16; 6:19).... In them he prays on their behalf and bears witness to their adoptive sonship (cf. Gal 4:6; Rom 8:15-16 and 26)" *(LG* 4).

Therefore, the Church's birth on the day of Pentecost coincides with the manifestation of the Holy Spirit. For this reason also our reflections on the mystery of the Church in relationship to the Holy Spirit are concentrated around Pentecost.

Through an analysis of this event we noted and explained in the previous reflection that the Church, through the work of the Holy Spirit, has been missionary from the very beginning.

Ever since, she has remained *in statu missionis* in all times and places.

The missionary character of the Church is intimately connected with her universality. At the same time, the Church's universality implies, on the one hand, a solid unity and on the other, a plurality and a multiformity, that is to say, a diversity. This is not an obstacle to unity, but rather give it the character of communion. The Constitution *Lumen Gentium* emphasizes that in a special way when it speaks of the "gift of union in the Holy Spirit" (cf. *LG* 13), a gift possessed by the Church from the day of her origin in Jerusalem.

An analysis of the passage of the Acts of the Apostles concerning the day of Pentecost entitles us to state that the Church came into being as a universal Church, and not merely as a particular church, that of Jerusalem, to which were later added other particular churches in other places. Certainly, the Church began at Jerusalem as a small original community of the apostles and of the first disciples; but the circumstances of her birth indicated from the very first moment the perspective of universality. One such circumstance was the apostles' "speaking in other tongues, as the Spirit gave them utterance" (cf. Acts 2:4), so that people of different nations, present in Jerusalem, heard "the mighty works of God" (cf. Acts 2:11). They heard them in their own languages, even though the speakers "were Galileans" (cf. Acts 2:7). We have already mentioned this in the previous reflection.

Moreover, the fact that the apostles were of Galilean origin is significant. Indeed, Galilee was a region of heterogeneous population (cf. 1 Macc 5:14-23), where the Jews had much contact with people of other nations. Hence, Galilee was known as "Galilee of the nations" (Is 9:1, quoted in Mt 4:15; 1 Macc 5:15). For this reason it was considered inferior, from the religious point of view, to Judea, the region of the authentic Jews.

The Church, therefore, was born at Jerusalem, but the message of faith was not proclaimed there by citizens of Jerusalem, but by a group of Galileans. Moreover, their preaching was not addressed exclusively to the inhabitants of Jerusalem, but to Jews and proselytes of whatever origin.

Following upon the witness of the apostles, shortly after Pentecost, communities (that is, local churches) arose in different places, and naturally also and first of all at Jerusalem. However, the Church which began with the descent of the Holy Spirit was not merely a Jerusalem church. From the moment of her birth the Church was universal with an aspect of universality, which would be manifested later by means of all the particular churches.

The Church's universal opening was confirmed in the so-called "council of Jerusalem" (cf. Acts 15:13-14) of which we read: "After they (Paul and Barnabas) finished speaking, James replied, 'Brethren, listen to me. Symeon has related how God first visited the Gentiles, to take out of them a people for his name'" (Acts 15:13-14). In that "council" it is to be noted that Paul and Barnabas were witnesses of the spread of the Gospel among the Gentiles. James, who then spoke, authoritatively represented the Judaeo-Christian position typical of the Church of Jerusalem (cf. Gal 2:12), of which he became the leader upon Peter's departure (cf. Acts 15:13; 21:18). Peter was the herald of the universality of the Church which extended a welcome both to the Chosen People and to the pagans.

From the beginning the Holy Spirit wills the universality, the catholicity of the Church in the context of all the local and particular communities (that is, churches). This fulfills Jesus' significant words in his conversation with the Samaritan woman beside the well at Sychar: "Woman, believe me, the hour is coming when neither on this mountain (that is, Mount Garizim, in Samaria) nor in Jerusalem will you worship the

Father.... But the hour is coming, and now is, when true worshippers will worship the Father in spirit and truth, for such the Father seeks to worship him" (cf. Jn 4:21, 23).

That "worship of the Father in Spirit and in truth" began with the coming of the Holy Spirit on the day of Pentecost. It cannot be limited to one place because it is inscribed in man's vocation to recognize and honor the one God who is also Spirit, and is therefore open to universality.

Under the action of the Holy Spirit Christian universalism was therefore inaugurated. It was expressed from the beginning in the multitude and diversity of persons who shared in the first radiation of Pentecost, and in a certain way in the plurality of the languages, cultures, peoples and nations represented by the people at Jerusalem on that occasion. It is also expressed in the human groups and social strata from which the followers of Christ down the centuries would be drawn. Universality does not mean uniformity either for those of the earliest times or for successive generations.

The demands of universality and variety are expressed also in the essential, internal unity of the Church by means of the multiplicity and diversity of the gifts or charisms, and also of ministries and initiatives. In this regard we observe that, on the day of Pentecost, Mary also, the mother of Christ, received the confirmation of her maternal mission. This was not only in regard to the Apostle John, but to all the disciples of her Son, and to all Christians (cf. *RM* 24; *LG* 59). And of all those assembled on that day in the upper room of Jerusalem—both men and women—who were "baptized with the Holy Spirit" (cf. Acts 2:4), it can be said that, following upon this fundamental event, they were endowed with different gifts, of which St. Paul would speak later: "Now there are varieties of gifts, but the same Spirit; and there are varieties of service, but the same Lord: and there are varieties of working, but it is the same God who inspires them all in everyone. To each is given the manifestation of the Spirit for the common good" (1 Cor 12:4-7). "God has appointed in the Church first apostles, second prophets, third teachers, then workers of miracles, then healers, helpers, administrators and speakers in various kinds of tongues" (1 Cor 12:28). Through this range of charisms and ministries, from the very earliest times, the Spirit gathered together, governed and vivified Christ's Church.

St. Paul recognized and emphasized the fact that due to such a distribution of gifts to believers on the part of the Holy Spirit, the Church has a diversity of charisms and ministries for the unity of the entire body. As we read in the Letter to the Ephesians: "And his gifts were that some should be apostles, some prophets, some evangelists, some pastors and teachers, for the equipment of the saints, for the work of ministry, for building up the body of Christ, until we all attain to the unity of faith and of the knowledge of the Son of God, to mature manhood, to the measure of the stature of the fullness of Christ" (4:11-13).

Bringing together the witness of the apostles and of Christian tradition, the Constitution *Lumen Gentium* synthesizes as follows their teaching on the action of the Holy Spirit in the Church: "The Church, which the Spirit guides in the way of all truth and which he unified in communion and in works of ministry, he both equips and directs with hierarchical and charismatic gifts and adorns with his fruits. By the power of the Gospel he makes the Church keep the freshness of youth. Uninterruptedly he renews it and leads it to perfect union with its spouse. The Spirit and the bride both say to Jesus, the Lord, 'Come!'" (n. 4).

General audience of September 27, 1989

Peter's Discourse after the Descent of the Holy Spirit

We read in the Acts of the Apostles that, after the descent of the Holy Spirit, when the apostles began to speak in various languages, "all were amazed and perplexed, saying to one another, 'What does this mean?'" (Acts 2:12). The Acts en ables us to discern the meaning of that extraordinary fact, because the book has already described what took place in the upper room, when Christ's apostles and disciples—men and women—assembled together with Mary, his mother, and were "filled with the Holy Spirit" (Acts 2:4). In this event the Spirit-Paraclete himself remains invisible. However, the activity of those in whom and through whom the Spirit acts is visible. From the moment the apostles left the upper room, their unusual behavior was noted by the crowd that came running and gathered around them. They all asked themselves: "What does this mean?" The author of Acts does not fail to add that among the witnesses of the event there were also some who scoffed at the apostles' behavior, suggesting that they were probably "filled with new wine" (Acts 2:13).

Such a situation required a word of explanation to clarify the true meaning of what had happened. It was also necessary to make known to those who had gathered outside the upper room the Holy Spirit's action experienced by those assembled within when the Holy Spirit descended upon them.

It was a fitting occasion for Peter's first discourse. Under the inspiration of the Holy Spirit, he spoke also in the name of, and in communion with, the other apostles. Peter exercised for the first time his function of herald of the Gospel, preacher of divine truth and witness to the Word. It may be said that he initiated the mission of the Popes and bishops who were to succeed him and the other apostles down the centuries. "Then Peter, standing with the eleven, lifted up his voice" (Acts 2:14).

In this discourse of Peter one observes the Church's apostolic structure such as it was from the beginning. The eleven shared with Peter the same mission, the vocation to bear the same authoritative witness. Peter spoke as the first among them by virtue of the mandate received directly from Christ. No one called into question his duty and right to speak first and in the name of the others. This manifested the action of the Holy Spirit who, according to the Second Vatican Council, guides the Church in the way of truth and bestows upon her varied hierarchical and charismatic gifts, and in this way directs her (cf. *LG* 4).

Peter's words at Jerusalem, in communion with the eleven, remind us that the Church's primary pastoral task is proclaiming the Gospel: evangelization. This is what Vatican II teaches us: "For bishops are preachers of the faith, who lead new disciples to Christ, and they are authentic teachers, that is, teachers endowed with the authority of Christ, who preach to the people committed to them the faith they must believe and put into practice, and by the light of the Holy Spirit illustrate that faith. They bring forth from the treasury of Revelation new things and old, making it bear fruit and vigilantly warding off any errors that threaten their flock" *(LG* 25). Also "priests, as co-workers with their bishops, have the primary duty of proclaiming the Gospel of God to all. In this way they fulfill the command of the Lord: 'Going therefore into the whole world preach the Gospel to every creature' (Mk 16:15) and they establish and build up the People of God" *(PO* 4).

It may also be noted, according to that passage from Acts, that the spontaneous charismatic witnessing of individuals to Christ does not suffice for evangelization. These charismatic transports proceed from the Holy Spirit and under some aspects they provide the first witness to his work. This was seen in the "glossolalia" on the day of Pentecost. However, an authoritative, motivated and systematic evangelization is also essential. This took place in apostolic times and in the first community of Jerusalem with the kerygma and catechesis, which, under the action of the Holy Spirit, enabled the mind to discover in its unity and to comprehend in its meaning the divine plan of salvation. This is precisely what happened on the day of Pentecost. It was necessary that the event which had just taken place should be made known and explained to the people of different nations who had gathered outside the upper room. It was necessary to instruct them about God's salvific plan, expressed in what had happened.

Peter's discourse is also important from this point of view. For this very reason, before proceeding to examine its content, we should dwell for a moment on the person of the speaker. On two occasions before the passion, Peter had already professed his faith in Christ.

On one occasion, after the announcement of the Eucharist in the neighborhood of Capernaum, Jesus, on seeing many of his disciples turn their backs on him, asked the apostles: "Will you also go away?" (Jn 6:67). Peter replied with those words inspired from on high: "Lord, to whom shall we go? You have the words of eternal life; and we have believed and have come to know that you are the Holy One of God" (Jn 6:68-69).

On another occasion Peter's profession of faith took place near Caesarea Philippi, when Jesus asked the apostles: "Who do you say that I am?" According to Matthew, "Simon Peter replied: 'You are the Christ, the Son of the living God'" (Mt 16:15-16).

Now, on the day of Pentecost, Peter, by this time freed from the crisis of fear that had led him to deny Jesus on the eve of the passion, professed that same faith in Christ. Strengthened by the paschal event, he proclaimed openly before all those people that Christ was risen! (cf. Acts 2:24 ff.)

Moreover, in being the first to speak out, Peter revealed his own awareness and that of the other eleven that he bore the chief responsibility for preaching and teaching the faith in Christ, even though the eleven shared with him in the task and responsibility. Peter was aware of what he was doing when, in his first discourse, he exercised the mission of teacher deriving from his apostolic office.

On the other hand, Peter's discourse was in a certain way an extension of Jesus' own teaching. Just as Christ exhorted his hearers to believe, so likewise did Peter. Jesus carried out his ministry in the pre-paschal period—one might say, in the perspective of his resurrection, while Peter spoke and acted in the light of the Pasch which was already a fact. That confirmed the truth of the mission and Gospel of Christ. He spoke and acted under the influence of the Holy Spirit, the Spirit of truth, recalling Christ's words and deeds which shed light on the Pentecost event itself.

Finally, we read in the Acts of the Apostles that "Peter...lifted up his voice" (2:14). Here the author seems to want to refer not only to the strength of Peter's voice, but also and especially to the force of conviction and authority with which he spoke. Something happened similar to what the Gospels tell us about Jesus, namely, that when he taught, those who heard him "were astonished at his teaching, for he taught them as one who had authority" (Mt 1:22; cf. also Mt 7:29), "because he spoke with authority" (Lk 4:32).

On the day of Pentecost Peter and the other apostles, having received the Spirit of truth, could by his power speak after the manner of Christ. From his very first discourse Peter expressed in his words the authority of revealed truth itself.

General audience of October 25, 1989

The Initial Apostolic Preaching

Before his return to the Father, Jesus had promised the apostles: "You shall receive power when the Holy Spirit has come upon you; and you shall be my witnesses in Jerusalem and in all Judea and Samaria and to the end of the earth" (Acts 1:8). As I wrote in the Encyclical *Dominum et Vivificantem*, "On the day of Pentecost this prediction was fulfilled with total accuracy. Acting under the influence of the Holy Spirit, who had been received by the apostles while they were praying in the upper room, Peter comes forward and speaks before a multitude of people of different languages, gathered for the feast. He proclaims what he certainly would not have had the courage to say before" (n. 30). It is the first witness given publicly and one might say solemnly to the risen Christ, to Christ victorious. It is also the beginning of the apostolic preaching.

We already spoke about it in the previous reflection, examining it from the point of view of the teacher: "Peter with the eleven" (cf. Acts 2:14). Today we wish to analyze the content of that first sermon, as a model or schema of the many other proclamations which will follow in the Acts of the Apostles, and later in the history of the Church.

Peter addressed those who had assembled near the upper room: "Men of Judea and all who dwell in Jerusalem" (Acts 2:14). They were the same people who had witnessed the phenomenon of the glossolalia, and heard in their own languages the apostles speaking of "the mighty works of God" (cf. Acts 2:11). In his discourse Peter began by defending or at least explaining the condition of those who, "filled with the Holy Spirit" (Acts 2:4), were suspected of being drunk because of their unusual behavior. From the opening words he gave the answer: "These men are not drunk, as you suppose, since it is only the third hour of the day: but this is what was spoken by the prophet Joel" (Acts 2:15-16).

The passage from Joel is extensively quoted in Acts: "And in the last days it shall be, God declares, that I will pour out my Spirit upon all flesh, and your sons and your daughters shall prophesy" (Acts 2:17). This "outpouring of the Spirit" on both young and old, on menservants and maidservants, will have therefore a universal character. And it will be confirmed by signs: "I will show wonders in the heavens above and signs on the earth below" (Acts 2:19). These will be the signs of the "day of the Lord" which is approaching (cf. Acts 2:20). "And it shall be that whoever calls on the name of the Lord shall be saved" (Acts 2:21).

In the mind of the speaker the text from Joel aptly explains the meaning of the event of which those present saw the signs: "the outpouring of the Holy Spirit." It was a supernatural act of God joined to signs typical of the coming of God, foretold by the prophets and identified by the New Testament with the coming of Christ. This is the context in which Peter concentrated the essential content of his discourse, which is the very nucleus of the apostolic "kerygma": "Men of Israel, hear these words: Jesus of Nazareth, a man attested to you by God with mighty works and wonders and signs which God did through him in your midst, as you yourselves know—this

Jesus, delivered up according to the definite plan and foreknowledge of God, you crucified and killed by the hands of lawless men. But God raised him up, having loosed the pangs of death, because it was not possible for him to be held by it" (Acts 2:22-24).

Perhaps not all those present at Peter's discourse, having come from many regions for the Pasch and Pentecost, had taken part in the events in Jerusalem which ended with Christ's crucifixion. But Peter addressed them also as "men of Israel," belonging to an ancient world in which, by that time, the signs of the Lord's new coming were clear for everyone.

The signs and wonders to which Peter referred were certainly still within the recollection of the people of Jerusalem, but also of many others of his hearers. They must have at least heard Jesus of Nazareth spoken about. In any case, having recalled all that Jesus had done, Peter passed to the fact of Jesus' death on the cross, and spoke directly of the responsibility of those who had consigned him to death. However, he added that Christ "was delivered up according to the definite plan and foreknowledge of God" (cf. Acts 2:23). Peter therefore introduced his hearers into the vision of God's salvific plan which was fulfilled precisely by means of Christ's death. And he hastened to give the decisive confirmation of God's action through and beyond what had been done by men. This confirmation is Christ's resurrection: "God raised him up, having loosed the pangs of death, because it was not possible for him to be held by it" (Acts 2:24).

It is the culminating point of the apostolic kerygma concerning Christ the Savior who had vanquished death.

At this point Peter again had recourse to the Old Testament. He cited the messianic psalm 16 verses 8-11:

"I saw the Lord always before me,
for he is at my right hand that I may not be shaken;
therefore my heart was glad, and my tongue rejoiced;

moreover my flesh will dwell in hope.
For you will not abandon my soul to Hades
not let your Holy One see corruption.
You have made known to me the ways of life;
You will make me full of gladness with your presence"
(Acts 2:25-28).

It is a legitimate adaptation of the Davidic Psalm which the author of Acts quotes according to the Greek text of the Septuagint. It emphasizes the aspiration of the Jewish soul to escape death, in the sense of a hope of liberation from death even after it has taken place.

Doubtlessly Peter was at pains to stress that the words of the Psalm do not refer to David, whose tomb, he remarked, was with them to that day. They refer, rather, to his descendant, Jesus Christ: David "foresaw and spoke of the resurrection of Christ" (Acts 2:31). The prophetic words are therefore fulfilled: "This Jesus Christ God raised up, and of that we all are witnesses. Being therefore exalted at the right hand of God, and having received from the Father the promise of the Holy Spirit, he has poured out this which you see and hear.... Let all the house of Israel therefore know assuredly that God has made him both Lord and Christ, this Jesus whom you crucified" (Acts 2:32-33, 36).

On the day before his passion Jesus had told the apostles in the upper room, in reference to the Holy Spirit: "He will bear witness to me...and you also are witnesses" (Jn 15:26-27). As I wrote in the Encyclical *Dominum et Vivificantem*, "In the first discourse of Peter in Jerusalem this 'witness' finds its clear beginning: it is the witness to Christ crucified and risen, the witness of the Spirit-Paraclete and of the apostles" (n. 30).

In this testimony Peter wished to remind his hearers of the mystery of the risen Christ. But he also wished to explain the facts of Pentecost at which they were present, by showing that they were signs of the coming of the Holy Spirit. The

Paraclete really came by virtue of Christ's Pasch. He came and transformed those men of Galilee, to whom was entrusted the witness concerning Christ, "exalted at the right hand of the Father" (cf. Acts 2:33), that is to say, exalted by his victory over death. His coming was therefore a confirmation of the divine power of the risen Christ. "Let all the house of Israel know assuredly that God has made him both Lord and Christ, this Jesus whom you crucified" (Acts 2:36). In writing to the Romans Paul also proclaimed: "Jesus is Lord" (Rom 10:9).

General audience of November 8, 1989

The Effect of
Peter's Discourse at Pentecost

After recording Peter's first discourse on the day of Pentecost, the author of Acts informs us that those present "were cut to the heart" (Acts 2:37). These eloquent words indicate the action of the Holy Spirit in the souls of those who heard from Peter the first apostolic preaching, his witness concerning Christ crucified and risen, and his explanation of the extraordinary events which had taken place that day. In particular, that first public presentation of the paschal mystery reached the core of the expectations of the people of the old covenant, when Peter said: "God has made both Lord and Christ this Jesus whom you crucified" (Acts 2:36).

The same Holy Spirit who had descended upon the apostles was now at work in the hearts of those who heard the apostolic preaching. Peter's words touched their hearts, awakening in them "a conviction of their sinfulness," the beginning of conversion.

Filled with remorse, "...they said to Peter and the rest of the apostles: 'Brethren, what shall we do?'" (Acts 2:37). The question, "what shall we do?" shows their readiness of will. It was the interior good predisposition of Peter's listeners that made them aware that it was necessary to change their lives when they heard his words. They addressed Peter and the other apostles. They knew that Peter spoke for the eleven also, and that the eleven therefore (that is to say, all the apostles) were witnesses of the same truth and were charged with the same mission. It is also significant that they called them "brethren," echoing Peter who had spoken in a fraternal spirit in his discourse, in the latter part of which he addressed those present as "brethren."

Peter himself then replied to the question of those present. It was a simple reply which could well be described as lapidary: "Repent" (Acts 2:38). Jesus had begun his messianic mission with this exhortation (cf. Mk 1:15). Peter repeated it on the day of Pentecost, in the power of the Spirit of Christ who descended on him and on the other apostles.

Repentance, as I emphasized in the Encyclical *Dominum et Vivificantem*, is the crucial step in the process of conversion which the Holy Spirit works within us: "By becoming 'the light of hearts,' that is, the light of consciences, the Holy Spirit 'convinces concerning sin,' which is to say, he makes man realize his own evil [i.e. the evil committed by himself], and at the same time directs him toward what is good.... Thus the conversion of the human heart, which is an indispensable condition for the forgiveness of sins, is brought about by the influence of the Counselor" (n. 42).

On the lips of Peter "repent," means: change from the rejection of Christ to faith in the Risen One.

The crucifixion had been the definitive expression of the rejection of Christ, sealed by an ignominious death on Golgotha. Peter exhorted those who crucified Jesus to have faith in the risen one: "God raised him up, having loosed the pangs of death" (Acts 2:24). Pentecost, then, was the confirmation of Christ's resurrection.

The exhortation to conversion implies above all faith in Christ the Redeemer. Indeed, the resurrection is the revelation of that divine power which, by means of Christ's crucifixion and death, effects man's redemption and his liberation from sin.

If through Peter's preaching the Holy Spirit "convinces concerning sin," he does so "by virtue of the redemption accomplished by the blood of the Son of Man...." The Letter to the Hebrews says that this "blood purifies the conscience" (cf. 9:14). It therefore, so to speak, opens to the Holy Spirit the door into man's inmost being, namely, into "the sanctuary of human consciences" (*DViv* 42).

In his Pentecost discourse, Peter proclaimed and testified that this profound and inmost level is reached by the action of the Holy Spirit in virtue of Christ's redemption.

Peter went on to complete his message as follows: "Repent and be baptized every one of you in the name of Jesus Christ for the forgiveness of your sins; and you shall receive the gift of the Holy Spirit" (Acts 2:38). Here we have the echo of what Peter and the other apostles heard from Jesus after his resurrection, when "he opened their minds to understand the Scriptures, and said to them, 'Thus it is written that the Christ should suffer and rise from the dead... and that repentance and forgiveness of sins should be preached in his name to all nations, beginning from Jerusalem'" (Lk 24:45-47).

Following faithfully what Christ had laid down (cf. Mk 16:16; Mt 28:19), Peter called not only for repentance but also for baptism in Christ's name "for the forgiveness of...sins" (Acts 2:38). On the day of Pentecost the apostles were "baptized in the Holy Spirit" (cf. Acts 2:4). Therefore, in passing on the faith in Christ the Redeemer, they urged people to be baptized, for baptism is the first sacrament of this faith. Since it effects the forgiveness of sins, the faith should find in baptism its own sacramental expression so that man may share in the gift of the Holy Spirit.

This is the ordinary way of conversion and grace. Other ways are not excluded, for "the Spirit blows where it wills" (cf.

Jn 3:8). The Spirit can accomplish the work of salvation by sanctifying man apart from the sacrament, when its reception is not possible. It is the mystery of the meeting between divine grace and the human soul. Let this reference suffice for the moment, for we shall speak about it again, God willing, in the reflections on Baptism.

In the Encyclical *Dominum et Vivificantem* I analyzed the victory over sin won by the Holy Spirit in reference to the action of Christ the Redeemer. There I wrote: "The convincing concerning sin, through the ministry of the apostolic kerygma in the early Church, is referred—under the impulse of the Spirit poured out at Pentecost—to the redemptive power of Christ crucified and risen. Thus the promise concerning the Holy Spirit made before Easter is fulfilled: 'He will take what is mine and declare it to you.' When therefore, during the Pentecost event, Peter speaks of the sin of those who 'have not believed' and have sent Jesus of Nazareth to an ignominious death, he bears witness to victory over sin: a victory achieved, in a certain sense, through the greatest sin that man could commit: the killing of Jesus, the Son of God, consubstantial with the Father! Similarly, the death of the Son of God conquers human death: 'I will be your death, O death,' as the sin of having crucified the Son of God 'conquers' human sin: that sin which was committed in Jerusalem on Good Friday—and also every human sin. For the greatest sin on man's part is matched, in the heart of the Redeemer, by the oblation of supreme love that conquers the evil of all the sins of man" (n. 31).

It is therefore a victory of love! This is the truth contained in Peter's exhortation to conversion through Baptism.

By virtue of Christ's victorious love the Church also is born in sacramental Baptism through the work of the Holy Spirit on the day of Pentecost, when the first conversions to Christ took place.

We read that "those who received his word (that is, the

truth contained in Peter's words) were baptized, and there were added that day about three thousand souls" (Acts 2:41), that is, "they were added" to those who had been previously "baptized in the Holy Spirit," the apostles. Having been baptized "with water and the Holy Spirit," they become the community "of the adopted sons of God" (cf. Rom 8:15). As "sons in the Son" (cf. Eph 1:5) they become "one" in the bond of a new brotherhood. Through the action of the Holy Spirit they become the Church of Christ.

In this regard one must recall the event concerning Simon Peter which took place on the lake of Gennesaret. The evangelist Luke tells us that Jesus "said to Simon, 'Put out into the deep and let down your nets for a catch.' And Simon answered, 'Master, we toiled all night and took nothing. But at your word I will let down the nets.' And when they had done this, they enclosed a great catch of fish, and their nets were breaking...and they filled both the boats, so that they began to sink. But when Simon Peter saw it, he fell down at Jesus' knees, saying, 'Depart from me, for I am a sinful man, O Lord....' And Jesus said to Simon, 'Do not be afraid; henceforth you will be catching men.' And when they had brought their boats to land, they left everything and followed him" (Lk 5:4-8; 10-11).

That event-sign contained the announcement of the future victory over sin through faith, repentance and baptism, preached by Peter in Christ's name. That announcement became reality on the day of Pentecost, when it was confirmed by the work of the Holy Spirit. Peter the fisherman and his companions on the lake of Gennesaret found in this reality the paschal expression of Christ's power, and at the same time the meaning of their apostolic mission. They found the fulfillment of the announcement: "From now on you will be a fisher of men."

General audience of November 15, 1989

The Presence of Christ's Kingdom in Human History

As we have seen in the progressive unfolding of the pneumatological reflections, the Holy Spirit revealed himself in his salvific power on the day of Pentecost. He was revealed as "another Counselor" (cf. Jn 14:16), who "proceeds from the Father" (Jn 15:26), whom "the Father sends in the Son's name" (cf. Jn 14:26). He was revealed as "Someone" distinct from the Father and the Son, and at the same time consubstantial with them. He is revealed through the Son, even though he remained invisible. He was revealed through the power and action attributed to him, distinct from that of the Son, and at the same time intimately united to him. Such is the Holy Spirit according to Christ's statement on the day before his passion: "He will glorify me for he will take what is mine and declare it to you" (Jn 16:14). "He will not speak on his own authority, but whatever he hears he will speak, and he will declare to you the things that are to come" (Jn 16:13).

The Paraclete-Counselor does not replace Christ. He comes after him in virtue of Christ's redemptive sacrifice. He comes so that Christ can remain in the Church and work in her as Redeemer and Lord.

I wrote in the Encyclical *Dominum et Vivificantem*: "Between the Holy Spirit and Christ there thus subsists, in the economy of salvation, an intimate bond whereby the Spirit works in human history as 'another Counselor,' permanently ensuring the transmission and spreading of the Good News revealed by Jesus of Nazareth. Thus in the Holy Spirit Paraclete, who in the mystery and action of the Church unceasingly continues the historical presence on earth of the Redeemer and his saving work, the glory of Christ shines forth, as the following words attest: 'He (the Spirit of truth) will glorify me, for he will take what is mine and declare it to you'" (n. 7).

The truth contained in this promise of Jesus became evident at Pentecost: The Holy Spirit fully "reveals" the mystery of Christ, his messianic and redemptive mission. The primitive Church was aware of this fact, as is clear from Peter's first preaching and from many later episodes recorded in the Acts of the Apostles.

It is significant that in replying on Pentecost to his hearers' question, "What shall we do?" Peter exhorted them: "Repent and be baptized every one of you in the name of Jesus Christ" (Acts 2:38). In sending his apostles into the whole world, Jesus had ordered them to administer baptism "in the name of the Father and of the Son and of the Holy Spirit" (Mt 28:19). Peter echoed faithfully the Master's word and the result was that, on that occasion, "about three thousand persons" (Acts 2:41) were baptized "in the name of Jesus Christ" (Acts 2:38). This expression, "in the name of Jesus Christ," represents the key for entering with faith into the fullness of the Trinitarian mystery and thus becoming Christ's possession as persons consecrated to him. In this sense, the Acts speaks of the invocation of the name of Jesus in order to be saved (cf. 2:21; 3:16; 4:10-12; 8:16; 10:48; 19:5; 22:16). In his letters St. Paul insists on the same requirement in the order of salvation (cf. Rom 6:3; 1 Cor 6:11; Gal 3:27; cf. also James 2:7). During the Last Supper Jesus promised the trinitarian gift when he said to the apostles: "The Spirit of truth...will glorify me, for he will take what is mine and declare it to you. All that the Father has is mine; therefore I said he will take what is mine and declare it to you" (Jn 16:13-15). This trinitarian gift becomes a reality through baptism "in the Holy Spirit," conferred "in the name of Christ."

In all their activities carried out after Pentecost under the influence of the Holy Spirit, the apostles referred to Christ as the reason, the principle and the operative power. Thus in the cure of the lame man "near the gate of the temple which is called Beautiful" (Acts 3:2), Peter said to him: "I have no silver and gold, but I give you what I have; in the name of Jesus Christ of Nazareth, walk!" (Acts 3:6). This miracle drew many people to Solomon's portico, and Peter spoke to them, as on Pentecost day, of Christ crucified "whom God raised from the dead, and to this we are witnesses" (Acts 3:15). It was faith in Christ that cured the lame man: "Faith in his name has made this man strong whom you see and know; and the faith which is through Jesus has given the man this perfect health in the presence of all of you" (Acts 3:16).

When the apostles were summoned for the first time before the Sanhedrin, "Peter, filled with the Holy Spirit," in the presence of the "rulers of the people and elders" (Acts 4:8) bore witness yet again to Christ crucified and risen. He concluded his reply to the Sanhedrin as follows: "There is salvation in no one else, for there is no other name under heaven given to men by which we must be saved" (Acts 4:12). When they were released, the author of Acts tells us, "they went to their friends" and with them praised the Lord (Acts 4:23-24). Then there was a kind of minor Pentecost: "When they had prayed, the place in which they were gathered together was shaken; and they were all filled with the Holy Spirit and spoke the word of God with boldness" (Acts 4:31). Later, in the first Christian community and before the people, "with great power the apostles gave their testimony to the resurrection of the Lord Jesus, and great grace was upon them all" (Acts 4:33).

The deacon Stephen was a special example of this fearless witness to Christ. He was the first martyr, and we read in the account of his death: "Stephen, full of the Holy Spirit, gazed into heaven and saw the glory of God, and Jesus standing at the right hand of God; and he said, 'Behold, I see the heavens opened, and the Son of Man standing at the right hand of God.' But they cried out with a loud voice and stopped their ears and rushed together upon him" (Acts 7:55-59).

From these and other accounts in Acts it is clear that the apostles' teaching under the influence of the Holy Spirit has its reference point and keystone in Christ. The Holy Spirit enabled the apostles and their disciples to penetrate the truth of the Gospel proclaimed by Christ, and particularly his paschal mystery. He enkindled in them love for Christ to the point of sacrificing their lives. He ensured that the Church brought into being, from the very beginning, the kingdom brought by Christ. Under the action of the Holy Spirit and with the collaboration of the apostles, of their successors and of the entire Church, this kingdom will develop in history until the end of time. There is no trace in the Gospels, in the Acts or in the letters of the apostles of any kind of pneumatological utopianism whereby the kingdom of the Father (Old Testament) and of Christ (New Testament) should be succeeded by the kingdom of the Holy Spirit, represented by the claims of the "spirituals," exempt from all law, even from the evangelic law preached by Jesus. As St. Thomas Aquinas writes, "the old law was not only of the Father, but also of the Son, since the old law prefigures Christ.... So likewise the new law is not only of Christ, but also of the Holy Spirit, according to the words of St. Paul: 'The law of the spirit of life in Christ Jesus...' (Rom 8:2). Therefore we are not to expect another law which would be that of the Holy Spirit" *(Summa Theol.,* I, II, q. 106, a. 4, ad 3). During the Middle Ages there were some who, under the influence of the apocalyptic speculations of the pious Calabrian monk Joachim of Fiore (d. 1202), dreamed and predicted the coming of a "third kingdom" in which the universal renewal in preparation for the end of the world, foretold by Jesus, would be verified (cf. Mt 14:4). But St. Thomas further notes that "from the very beginning of the Gospel preaching Christ had stated: 'The kingdom of heaven is at hand' (Mt 4:17). Hence it is very stupid to say that Christ's Gospel is not the Gospel of the kingdom" *(Summa Theol.,* I, II, q. 106, a. 4, ad 4). It is one of the very few cases in which the holy Doctor used harsh words in judging an erroneous opinion, because in the thirteenth century the controversy engendered by the ravings of the "spirituals" was very much alive. They distorted Joachim's teaching, and St. Thomas saw the danger of the claims of independence and innovation founded on the presumption of charisms. They were to the detriment of the cause of the Gospel and of the true kingdom of God. Therefore he harked back to the necessity of the "fully successful preaching of the Gospel in the whole world, that is to say, with the foundation of the Church in every nation. And in this sense...the Gospel has not been preached in the whole world; the end of the world will come after this preaching" *(Summa Theol.,* I, II, q. 106, a. 4 ad 4).

This has been the Church's line of thought from the very beginning, on the basis of the preaching of Peter and the other apostles. There one finds not even the shadow of a dichotomy between Christ and the Holy Spirit. Rather, their preaching confirms what Jesus had said of the Paraclete during the Last Supper: "He will not speak on his own authority, but whatever he hears he will speak, and he will declare to you the things that are to come. He will glorify me, for he will take what is mine and declare it to you" (Jn 16:13-14).

At this point we cannot but rejoice at the amount of space devoted by the theology of our Eastern brothers to reflection on the relation between Christ and the Holy Spirit. This relation finds its most intimate expression in the Christ-Pneuma after the resurrection and Pentecost, in line with the words of St. Paul, "the last Adam became a life-giving spirit" (1 Cor 15:45). It is an open field for the study and contemplation of the mystery which is both Christological and Trinitarian. The Encyclical *Dominum et Vivificantem* states: "The supreme and complete self-revelation of God, accomplished in Christ and witnessed to by the preaching of the apostles, continues to be manifested in the Church through the mission of the invisible Counselor, the Spirit of truth. How intimately this mission is linked with the mission of Christ, how fully it draws from this mission of Christ, consolidating and enveloping in history its salvific results, is expressed by the verb 'take': 'he will take what is mine and declare it to you.' As if to explain the words 'he will take' by clearly expressing the divine and trinitarian unity of the source, Jesus adds: 'All that the Father has is mine; therefore I said that he will take what is mine and declare it to you.' By the very fact of taking what is 'mine' he will draw from 'what is the Father's'" (n. 7).

Let us recognize it frankly: this mystery of the trinitarian presence in humanity through the kingdom of Christ and of the Holy Spirit is the most beautiful and joyous truth that the Church could give to the world.

General audience of November 22, 1989

The Holy Spirit in the Life of the Primitive Church

The coming of the Holy Spirit on the day of Pentecost was a unique event, but it did not end there. Rather, it was the beginning of a lasting process, whose first phases are recorded in the Acts of the Apostles. They concern first of all the life of the Church at Jerusalem. After having borne witness to Christ and to the Holy Spirit and having obtained the first conversions, the apostles had to defend themselves before the Sanhedrin. They defended the right to existence of the first community of Christ's disciples and followers. The Acts of the Apostles tells us that even before the elders, the apostles were assisted by the same power they received at Pentecost: they were "filled with the Holy Spirit" (cf. e.g., Acts 4:8).

This power of the Spirit was manifested in some moments and aspects of the life of the Jerusalem community, which are particularly mentioned in Acts.

Let us summarize them briefly, beginning with the common prayer of the community. On returning from the Sanhedrin, the apostles reported to the brethren what had been said by the chief priests and elders. "Then they lifted their voices together to God..." (Acts 4:24). In their beautiful prayer recorded by Luke they recognized the divine plan in the persecution, recalling that God had spoken "through the Holy Spirit" (4:25). They quoted the words of Psalm 2 (vv. 1-2) on the rage unleashed by the kings and peoples of the earth "against the Lord and against his Anointed." They applied these words to Jesus' death: "Truly in this city there were gathered together against your holy servant Jesus, whom you anointed, both Herod and Pontius Pilate, with the Gentiles and the peoples of Israel, to do whatever your hand and your plan had predestined to take place. And now, Lord, look upon their threats, and grant to your servants to speak your word with all boldness" (Acts 4:25-29). It was a prayer full of faith and abandonment to God, at the end of which there was a new manifestation of the Spirit and a new Pentecost event, as it were.

"When they had prayed, the place in which they were gathered together was shaken" (Acts 4:31). There was then a new manifestation of the Holy Spirit's power, perceptible to the senses, as had happened on the first Pentecost. Moreover, the reference to the place in which the community was gathered together confirms the analogy to the upper room. It indicates that the Holy Spirit wished to involve the whole community with his transforming action. Then "all were filled with the Holy Spirit": not only the apostles who had confronted the leaders of the people, but all the "brethren" (4:23) gathered with them, who constituted the central and most representative nucleus of the first community. With the enthusiasm aroused by the new fullness of the Holy Spirit, we are told by Acts, "they spoke the word of God with boldness" (Acts 4:31). It was the answer to their prayer to the Lord: "Grant to your servants to speak your word with all boldness" (Acts 4:29).

The little Pentecost therefore made a new beginning of the evangelizing mission after the Sanhedrin had judged and imprisoned the apostles. The power of the Holy Spirit was manifested especially in the boldness which the members of the Sanhedrin had already noticed to their amazement in Peter and John, "for they perceived that they were uneducated, common men" (Acts 4:13). Now Acts again emphasizes that "they were filled with the Holy Spirit and spoke the word of God with boldness."

Moreover, the whole life of the primitive community at Jerusalem bore the signs of the Holy Spirit who was its invisible guide and inspirer. The overall view of it given by Luke enables us to see in that community the model of the Christian communities formed throughout the centuries. This includes parishes and religious congregations, in which the fruit of the "fullness of the Holy Spirit" is given tangible form in some basic forms of organization, codified in part in the law of the Church.

They are principally the following: "communion" *(koinonia)* in fraternity and love (cf. Acts 2:42), so that it could be said of the Christians that they were "of one heart and soul" (Acts 2:32); the community spirit in handing over their goods to the apostles for distribution to each according to his need (Acts 4:34-37), or in their use, while retaining their ownership, so that "no one said that any of the things he possessed was his own" (4:32; cf. 2:44-45; 4:34-37); communion in "devoting themselves to the apostles' teaching" (Acts 2:42) and their "testimony to the resurrection of the Lord Jesus" (Acts 4:33); communion in the "breaking of the bread" (Acts 2:42), that is, in the common meal according to the Jewish custom, into which the Christians, however, inserted the Eucharistic rite (cf. 1 Cor 11:16; 11:24; Lk 22:19; 24:35); communion in the prayers (Acts 2:42; 46-47). The word of God, the Eucharist, prayer and fraternal charity constituted the quadrilateral within which the community lived, grew and became strong.

On their part the apostles "with great power gave testimony to the resurrection of the Lord Jesus" (4:33). They worked "many signs and wonders" (5:12), as they had asked in the prayer in the upper room: "Stretch out your hand to heal, and signs and wonders are performed through the name of your holy servant Jesus" (Acts 4:30). They were signs of the presence and action of the Holy Spirit, to whom the entire life of the community was referred. Even the guilt of Ananias and Sapphira, who pretended to bring to the apostles and the community the whole price of the property they had sold while holding back part of the proceeds, was regarded by Peter as a fault against the Holy Spirit: "You have lied to the Holy Spirit" (5:3); "How is it that you have agreed together to tempt the Spirit of the Lord?" (Acts 5:9). It was not a case of a "sin against the Holy Spirit" in the sense in which the Gospel speaks (cf. Lk 12:10) and which would be handed down in the Church's moral and catechetical texts. Rather, it was a failure to maintain the unity of the Spirit in the bond of peace, as St. Paul would say (Eph 4:3). It was therefore a pretense in professing that Christian community in charity, whose soul is the Holy Spirit.

The awareness of the Holy Spirit's presence and action is found in the choice of the seven deacons, men "full of the Spirit and of wisdom" (Acts 6:3), and in particular of Stephen "a man full of faith and of the Holy Spirit" (Acts 6:5). Very soon he began to preach Jesus Christ with zeal, enthusiasm and boldness, working "great wonders and signs among the people" (Acts 6:8). Having aroused the anger and jealousy of some of the Jews who rose up against him, Stephen did not cease to preach and he did not hesitate to accuse his opponents of being heirs to their fathers in "resisting the Holy Spirit" (Acts 7:51). He thus went serenely to his martyrdom, as we read in Acts: "Stephen, full of the Holy Spirit, gazed into heaven and saw the glory of God, and Jesus standing at the right hand of God..." (Acts 7:55). In that attitude he was put to death by stoning. Thus the primitive Church, under the action of the Holy Spirit, added martyrdom to the experience of communion.

The Jerusalem community was composed of men and women of Jewish origin, like the apostles themselves and Mary. We cannot forget this fact, even though later those Jewish Christians, gathered around James when Peter set out for Rome, were dispersed and gradually disappeared. However, what we learn from Acts should inspire us with respect and gratitude for those distant "elder brothers and sisters," inasmuch as they belonged to those people of Jerusalem who showed their favor to the apostles (cf. Acts 2:47) who gave "their testimony to the resurrection of the Lord Jesus" (Acts 4:33). No less can we forget that after Stephen's stoning and Paul's conversion, the Church which had developed from that first community "had peace and was built up throughout all Judea and Galilee and Samaria; and walking in the fear of the Lord and in the comfort of the Holy Spirit it was multiplied" (Acts 9:31).

So the first chapters of the Acts of the Apostles attest to the fulfillment of the promise made by Jesus to the apostles in the upper room before his passion: "I will pray the Father, and he will give you another Counselor, to be with you for ever, the Spirit of truth" (Jn 14:16-17). As we have seen before, "Counselor" (in Greek *Parákletos)* also means Advocate or Defender. Both as Advocate or Defender and as Counselor the Holy Spirit is revealed as present and at work in the Church from her beginnings in the heart of Judaism. Soon we shall see that the same Spirit will lead the apostles and their collaborators to extend the experience of Pentecost to all nations.

General audience of November 29, 1989

The Pentecost of the Gentiles

The descent of the Holy Spirit on the day of Pentecost brought Christ's paschal mystery to its fulfillment with his "departure" through the sacrifice of the cross. It completed God's revelation of himself through his Incarnate Son. In this way "there is accomplished in its entirety the mission of the Messiah, that is to say of the one who has received the fullness of the Holy Spirit for the Chosen People of God and for the whole of humanity. 'Messiah' literally means 'Christ," that is, 'Anointed One,' and in the history of salvation it means 'the one anointed with the Holy Spirit.' This was the prophetic tradition of the Old Testament. Following this tradition, Simon Peter will say in the house of Cornelius: 'You must have heard about the recent happenings in Judaea...after the baptism which John preached: how God anointed Jesus of Nazareth with the Holy Spirit and with power" (Acts 10:37 f.) *(DViv* 15). Peter continued with a brief summary of the Gospel story, which is also a rudimentary creed, bearing witness to Christ crucified and risen, Redeemer and Savior of mankind, in the way of "all the prophets" (Acts 10:43).

On the one hand, Peter connected the descent of the Holy Spirit with the Old Testament tradition. On the other, he knew and proclaimed that on the day of Pentecost a new process began which would last down the centuries, bringing to complete fulfillment the history of salvation. The first stages of this process are described in the Acts of the Apostles. Peter himself was involved in a decisive moment of that process: the entrance of the first pagan into the Church, under the evident influence of the Holy Spirit who guided the action of the apostles. It was the case of the Roman centurion stationed at Caesarea. Peter had introduced him into the community of the baptized. He was aware of the decisive importance of that act which was undoubtedly not in conformity with existing religious practices. But at the same time he knew with certainty that God had willed it. On entering the centurion's house he "found many persons gathered; and he said to them, 'You yourselves know how unlawful it is for a Jew to associate with or to visit any one of another nation; but God has shown me that I should not call any man common or unclean" (Acts 10:28).

It was a great moment in the history of salvation. By that decision Peter made the primitive Church leave the ethnic-religious confines of Jerusalem and Judaism. He became the instrument of the Holy Spirit in launching it toward all peoples, according to Christ's command (cf. Mt 28:19). The prophetic tradition on the universality of God's kingdom in the world was thus fulfilled in a complete and higher way, far beyond the view of the Israelites attached to the old law. Peter had opened the way of the new law, in which the Gospel of salvation should reach all people without any distinction of nation, culture or religion, so that all might enjoy the fruits of redemption.

The Acts of the Apostles contains a detailed account of this event. In the first part we are informed about the interior process which made Peter aware of the step to be taken. We read that Peter, who was lodging for some days at the house of

The Pentecost of the Gentiles

"Simon, a tanner" (Acts 10:6) at Joppa, "went up on the housetop to pray, about the sixth hour. And he became hungry and desired something to eat; but while they were preparing it, he fell into a trance and saw the heaven opened, and something descending, like a great sheet, let down by four corners upon the earth. In it were all kinds of animals and reptiles and birds of the air. And then came a voice to him, 'Rise, Peter; kill and eat.' But Peter said, 'No, Lord; for I have never eaten anything that is common or unclean.' And the voice came to him again a second time, 'What God has cleansed, you must not call common.' This happened three times, and the thing was taken up at once to heaven" (Acts 10:9-16).

It was a vision which perhaps brought to the surface questions and uncertainties which had been fermenting in Peter's mind under the influence of the Holy Spirit in light of the experience gained during his early preaching. It was linked to the recollection of Christ's teaching and command about universal evangelization. It was a pause for reflection on that roof terrace at Joppa, opening on to the Mediterranean, which prepared Peter for the decisive step he had to take!

Indeed, "Peter was inwardly perplexed as to what the vision he had seen might mean" (Acts 10:17). Then while he "was pondering the vision, the Spirit said to him, 'Behold, three men are looking for you. Rise and go down, and accompany them without hesitation: for I have sent them'" (Acts 10:19-20). It is the Holy Spirit, therefore, who prepared Peter for the new task. He worked especially through the vision whereby he urged Peter to reflection, arranged the meeting with the three men—two servants and a devout solider (cf. Acts 10:7)—sent from Caesarea to seek and invite him. When the interior process was accomplished the Spirit gave Peter an explicit order. Obeying it, Peter decided to go to Caesarea to the house of Cornelius. He was received by the centurion and the members of his household with the respect due to a divine messenger. Peter recalled his vision and asked those present: "Why have you sent for me?" (Acts 10:29).

Cornelius, "an upright and God-fearing man" (Acts 10:22), explained how he got the idea of inviting him, an invitation also due to divine inspiration. And he concluded, saying: "Now therefore we are all here present in the sight of God, to hear all that you have been commanded by the Lord" (Acts 10:33).

Peter's reply, recorded in Acts, is full of theological and missionary significance. We read: "Peter opened his mouth and said: 'Truly I perceive that God shows no partiality, but in every nation anyone who fears him and does what is right is acceptable to him. You know the word which he sent to Israel, preaching good news of peace by Jesus Christ (he is Lord of all), the word which was proclaimed throughout all Judea, beginning from Galilee after the baptism which John had preached: how God anointed Jesus of Nazareth with the Holy Spirit and with power; how he went about doing good and healing all who were oppressed by the devil, for God was with him. And we are witnesses to all that he did both in the country of the Jews and in Jerusalem. They put him to death by hanging him on a tree; but God raised him on the third day and made him manifest; not to all the people but to us who were chosen by God as witnesses, who ate and drank with him after he rose from the dead. And he commanded us to preach to the people and to testify that he is the one ordained by God to be judge of the living and the dead. To him all the prophets bear witness that every one who believes in him receives forgiveness of sins through his name'" (Acts 10:34-43).

It was well to quote this text in full, for it is a further condensation of the apostolic preaching and a first synthesis of catechesis which would later receive definitive form in the creed. It is the preaching and catechesis of Jerusalem on the day of Pentecost, repeated at Caesarea in the house of the pagan Cornelius. The event of the upper room was renewed in what may be called the Pentecost of the pagans, similar to that of Jerusalem, as Peter himself observed (cf. Acts 10:47; 11:15; 15:8). We read that "while Peter was still saying this, the Holy Spirit fell on all who heard the word. And the believers from among the circumcised who came with Peter were amazed, because the gift of the Holy Spirit had been poured out even on the Gentiles" (Acts 10:44-45).

"Then Peter declared, 'Can any one forbid water for baptizing these people who have received the Holy Spirit just as we have?'" (Acts 10:47). He said this before "the believers from among the circumcised," that is to say, the converts from Judaism, who were amazed because they heard Cornelius' relatives and friends "speaking in tongues and extolling God" (cf. Acts 10:46), just as had happened at Jerusalem on the day of the first Pentecost. It was an analogy of events full of significance: indeed, it was as if it were the same event, a single Pentecost verified in different circumstances.

The conclusion is the same: Peter "commanded them to be baptized in the name of Jesus Christ" (Acts 10:48). We have, then, the baptism of the first pagans. By his apostolic authority and guided by the light of the Holy Spirit, Peter thus began the spreading of the Gospel and the extension of the Church beyond the frontiers of Israel.

The Holy Spirit, who descended on the apostles by virtue of Christ's redemptive sacrifice, had confirmed that the salvific value of this sacrifice extends to all humanity. Peter had heard the interior voice saying: "What God has cleansed, you must not call common" (Acts 10:15). He knew very well that the cleansing had taken place by means of the blood of Christ, the Son of God, who, as we read in the Letter to the Hebrews (9:14), "through the eternal Spirit offered himself without blemish to God." We are assured that that blood "will purify our consciences from dead works to serve the living

God." Peter had come to understand better that the new times had arrived when, as the prophets had foretold, even the sacrifices of the pagans would be pleasing to Yahweh (cf. Is 56:7; Mal 1:11; and also Rom 15:16; Phil 4:18; 1 Pet 2:5). Therefore he said with full awareness to the centurion Cornelius: "Truly I perceive that God shows no partiality," as Israel had already learned from Deuteronomy, echoed in Peter's words: "The Lord your God is God of gods and Lord of lords, the great, the mighty, and the terrible God who is not partial..." (Dt 10:17). The Acts testifies that Peter was the first to grasp the new sense of that old idea which was incorporated into the apostles' teaching (cf. 1 Pet 1:17; Gal 2:6; Rom 2:11).

Such is the interior genesis of those beautiful words spoken to Cornelius on the human relationship with God: "...in every nation any one who fears him and does what is right is acceptable to him" (Acts 10:35).

General audience of December 6, 1989

The Holy Spirit in the Mission to the Gentiles

After the baptism of the first pagans, carried out at Peter's command in the house of the centurion Cornelius at Caesarea, Peter remained for some days with the new Christians in response to their invitation (cf. Acts 10:48). This did not please the brethren at Jerusalem, and they criticized him for this on his return (cf. Acts 11:3). Rather than defend himself from the accusation, Peter preferred "to explain to them what had happened" (Acts 11:4), so that the converts from Judaism could appreciate the full importance of the fact that the "Gentiles also had received the word of God" (Acts 11:1).

He then told them of the vision he had at Joppa, of Cornelius' invitation, of the interior prompting of the Spirit that dispelled his hesitation (cf. Acts 11:12), and finally of the descent of the Holy Spirit on those in the centurion's house (cf. Acts 11:16). He concluded his account as follows: "I remembered the word of the Lord, how he said, 'John baptized with water, but you shall be baptized with the Holy Spirit.' If then God gave the same gift to them as he gave to us when we believed in the Lord Jesus Christ, who was I that I could withstand God?" (Acts 11:16-17).

This, according to Peter, was the real question, not the fact of his having accepted hospitality from a pagan converted from paganism, an unusual case and regarded as unlawful by the Christians of Jewish origin at Jerusalem. It is interesting to note the effect of Peter's words, for we read in Acts that "when they heard this, they were silenced. And they glorified God, saying, 'Then to the Gentiles also God has granted repentance until life'" (Acts 11:18).

It was the first victory over the temptation to socio-religious particularism which threatened the primitive Church inasmuch as it had its origin in the Jewish community at Jerusalem. The Apostle Paul, with Peter's help, would achieve another victory, in a still more striking manner. We shall speak of this later.

Let us pause now to consider how Peter continued on the way begun with Cornelius' baptism. Once again it will be seen that it was the Holy Spirit who guided the apostles in this direction.

The Acts tell us that the converts at Jerusalem, "scattered because of the persecution that arose over Stephen," continued the work of evangelization wherever they happened to be. But "they spoke the word to none except Jews" (Acts 11:19). Some of them, however, citizens of Cyprus and Cyrene, on coming to Antioch, the capital of Syria, began to speak also to the Greeks (that is, to the non-Jews), preaching the Good News of the Lord Jesus. "And the hand of the Lord was with them, and a great number that believed turned to the Lord. News of this came to the ears of the church in Jerusalem, and they sent Barnabas to Antioch" (Acts 11:21-22). It was a kind of inspection decided upon by the community which, as the original one, claimed the right of vigilance over the other churches (cf. Acts 8:14; 11:1; Gal 2:2).

Barnabas went to Antioch. When he arrived there and "saw the grace of God, he was glad; and he exhorted them all to remain faithful to the Lord with steadfast purpose; for he was a good man, full of the Holy Spirit and of faith. And a large company was added to the Lord. So Barnabas went to Tarsus to look for Saul; and when he had found him, he brought him to Antioch. For a whole year they met with the Church and taught a large company of people; and in Antioch the disciples were called Christians for the first time" (Acts 11:23-26).

It was another decisive moment for the new faith based on the covenant in Christ, crucified and risen. Moreover, the new name "Christians" manifested the strength of the bond that united the members of the community among themselves. The "Pentecost of the pagans" illumined by Peter's preaching and behavior brought progressively to fulfillment Christ's prediction about the Holy Spirit: "He will glorify me, for he will take what is mine and declare it to you" (Jn 16:14). Christianity's assertion of itself under the influence of the Holy Spirit realizes with increasing evidence the glorification of the "Lord Jesus."

In the context of the relations between the Church of Antioch and that of Jerusalem, Saul of Tarsus appeared upon the scene; he was brought to Antioch by Barnabas. The Acts tells us that "for a whole year they remained in that community and taught a large company of people" (Acts 11:26). A little later we are told that one day "while they were worshipping the Lord and fasting, the Holy Spirit said, 'Set apart for me Barnabas and Saul for the work to which I have called them.' Then after fasting and praying they laid their hands on them and sent them off. So, being sent out by the Holy Spirit, they went down to Seleucia; and from there they sailed to Cyprus" (Acts 13:2-4), the homeland of Barnabas (cf. Acts 4:36). Saul's vocation and mission in the company of Barnabas was indicated as willed by the Holy Spirit who thus initiated a new phase of development in the life of the primitive Church.

We all know the story of the conversion of Saul of Tarsus and its importance for the evangelization of the ancient world, which he undertook with all the drive and enthusiasm of his Herculean soul, when Saul became Paul, the Apostle of the nations (cf. Acts 13:9).

Here we shall recall only the words addressed to him by the disciple Ananias of Damascus, when by the Lord's command he went to find "in the house of Judas, in the street called Straight" (Acts 9:10), the persecutor of the Christians, who was spiritually transformed after his meeting with Christ.

According to Acts, "Ananias departed and entered the house. After laying his hands on him he said, 'Brother, Saul, the Lord Jesus who appeared to you on the road by which you came, has sent me that you may regain your sight and be filled with the Holy Spirit'" (Acts 9:17). Saul regained his sight and immediately began to bear witness in the synagogues first at Damascus "by proving that Jesus was the Christ" (Acts 9:22), and then at Jerusalem where, presented by Barnabas, he went in and out, "preaching boldly in the name of the Lord" and "disputing against the Hellenists" (Acts 9:29). These Greek-speaking Jews, violently opposed to all the Christian preachers (cf. Acts 6:9 f.; 7:58; 9:1; 21:27; 24:19), were particularly ferocious against Saul, even to the point of trying to kill him (cf. Acts 9:29). "And when the brethren knew it, they brought him down to Caesarea and sent him off to Tarsus" (Acts 9:30). It was there that Barnabas went to look for him to bring him to Antioch (cf. Acts 11:25-26).

We already know that the development of the Church of Antioch was due in large part to the influx of the Greeks who were converted to the Gospel (cf. Acts 11:20). This had aroused the interest of the Church at Jerusalem. However, even after Barnabas' inspection, there remained some perplexity about the procedure followed in admitting pagans into the Church without following the Mosaic observance. Indeed, on a certain occasion "some men came down from Judea [to Antioch] and were teaching the brethren, 'Unless you are circumcised according to the custom of Moses, you cannot be saved.' And when Paul and Barnabas had no small dissension and debate with them, Paul and Barnabas and some of the others were appointed to go up to Jerusalem to the apostles and the elders about this question" (Acts 15:1-2).

It was a fundamental problem which touched the very essence of Christianity as a doctrine and as a life based on faith in Christ, and its originality and independence from Judaism.

The problem was resolved in the "council of Jerusalem" (as it is usually called), by the apostles and elders, but under the action of the Holy Spirit. The Acts tells us that "after there had been much debate, Peter rose and said to them, 'Brethren, you know that in the early days God made a choice among you, that by my mouth the Gentiles should hear the word of the Gospel and believe. And God, who knows the heart, bore witness to them, giving them the Holy Spirit just as he did to us; and he made no distinction between us and them, but cleansed their hearts by faith'" (Acts 15:7-9).

It was the outstanding moment of the awareness of the "Pentecost of the pagans" on the part of the mother community in Jerusalem, where the highest representatives of the Church were gathered together. The whole community felt that it was living and acting "filled with the comfort of the Holy Spirit" (Acts 9:31). It knew that not only the apostles but also other brethren had taken this decision and acted under the movement of the Spirit, as for example, Stephen (Acts 6:5; 7:55), Barnabas and Saul (Acts 13:2, 4, 9).

It would soon have learned of a fact that happened at Ephesus, where Saul, who had now become Paul, had arrived. It is narrated by Acts as follows: "While Apollos [another preacher of the Gospel] was at Corinth, Paul passed through the upper country and came to Ephesus. There he found some disciples. And he said to them 'Did you receive the Holy Spirit when you believed?' And they said, 'No, we have never even heard that there is a Holy Spirit....' On hearing this, they were baptized in the name of the Lord Jesus. And when Paul had laid his hands upon them, the Holy Spirit came on them; and they spoke with tongues and prophesied" (Acts 19:1-2, 5-6). The Jerusalem community knew therefore that that kind of epic of the Holy Spirit was unfolding by means of many endowed with charisms and apostolic ministries. That first council, however, presented an ecclesiastical-institutional fact recognized as decisive for the evangelization of the whole world, in intimate connection between the assembly presided over by Peter and the Holy Spirit.

The apostles communicated in a significant formula the conclusions arrived at and the decisions taken: "It has seemed good to the Holy Spirit and to us" (Acts 15:28). This expressed their complete awareness of acting under the guidance of this Spirit of truth which Christ had promised them (cf. Jn 14:16-17). They knew that they derived from him the authority to make that decision, and the certainty of the decision taken. It was the Paraclete, the Spirit of truth, who at that moment ensured that the Pentecost of Jerusalem should become to an ever greater extent the "Pentecost of the pagans." Thus God's new covenant with humanity "in the blood of Christ" (cf. Lk 22:20) was opened to all peoples and nations, to the very ends of the earth.

General audience of December 13, 1989

The Fruitfulness of Pentecost

The previous reflections on the Holy Spirit were linked especially to the Pentecost event. We saw that from the day on which the apostles assembled in the upper room of Jerusalem were "baptized with the Holy Spirit" (cf. Acts 2:4), a process began. By various stages described in the Acts of the Apostles, it revealed the action of the Holy Spirit as that of the "other Paraclete" promised by Jesus (cf. Jn 14:16), who came to complete his saving work. He always remains the invisible "hidden God," and yet the apostles were fully aware that it was precisely he who was at work in them and in the Church. It was he who guided them and strengthened them to bear witness to Christ crucified and risen, even to the point of martyrdom, as in the case of the deacon Stephen. It was he who indicated to them how to approach the people, and it was he who by means of them converted all those who opened their hearts to his action. Many of them came also from outside Israel. The first was the Roman soldier Cornelius at Caesarea. Many others would follow at Antioch and in other places, and the Jerusalem Pentecost was spread far and wide and gradually reached people everywhere.

It may be said that in this whole process described by the Acts of the Apostles, one sees the fulfillment of Christ's prediction to Peter on the occasion of the miraculous catch of fish: "Do not be afraid; henceforth you will be catching men" (Lk 5:10; cf. also Jn 21:11, 15-17).

Moreover, in the trance at Joppa (cf. Acts 11:5), Peter had the idea of abundance impressed on him when he saw the great sheet coming down toward him and being drawn up to heaven. In it he saw "animals and beasts of prey and reptiles and birds of the air" while a voice said to him: "Rise, kill and eat" (Acts 11:6-7). That abundance could well represent the abundant fruits of the apostolic ministry which the Holy Spirit would produce through the action of Peter and the other apostles, as Jesus had foretold on the day before his passion: "Truly, truly, I say to you, he who believes in me will also do the works that I do; and greater works than these will he do, because I go to the Father" (Jn 14:12). Certainly the source of that abundance was not merely the human words of the apostles, but the Holy Spirit's direct action in the hearts and consciences of the people. The whole spiritual fruitfulness of the apostolic mission came from the Holy Spirit.

The Acts of the Apostles notes the progressive widening of the circle of those who believed and joined the Church, sometimes specifying their number, and at other times speaking of them more generically.

Thus regarding what happened on Pentecost day at Jerusalem, we read that "there were added that day about three thousand souls" (Acts 2:41). After Peter's second discourse we are informed that "many of those who heard the word believed; and the number of the men came to about five thousand" (Acts 4:4).

Luke makes a point of emphasizing this numerical increase of believers, on which he also insists later, though without specifying numbers: "And the word of God increased;

and the number of disciples multiplied greatly in Jerusalem, and a great many of the priests were obedient to the faith" (Acts 6:7).

Naturally what was most important was not the number, which might suggest mass conversions. Luke stresses the converts' relationship with God: "And the Lord added to their number day by day those who were being saved" (Acts 2:47). "And more than ever believers were added to the Lord, multitudes both of men and women" (Acts 5:14). However, the number has an importance of its own, as a proof or sign of the fruitfulness coming from God. Therefore Luke again informs us that "the increase in the number of the disciples" (cf. Acts 6:1) was the reason for the institution of the seven deacons. He tells us further that "the Church...was multiplied" (Acts 9:31). In another passage he informs us that "a large company was added to the Lord" (Acts 11:24), and "The churches were strengthened in the faith and they increased in numbers daily" (Acts 16:5).

In this numerical and spiritual increase the Holy Spirit showed himself as the Paraclete announced by Christ. Luke tells us that "the Church...was full of the comfort of the Holy Spirit" (Acts 9:31). This comfort did not abandon Christ's witnesses and confessors in the midst of persecutions and the difficulties of evangelization. We think of the persecutions of Paul and Barnabas when they were driven out of Antioch of Pisidia. This did not deprive them of their apostolic zeal and enthusiasm; rather, "they shook off the dust from their feet, and went to Iconium. And the disciples were filled with joy and with the Holy Spirit" (Acts 13:51-52).

This joy from the Holy Spirit strengthened the apostles in their trials, so that without giving way to discouragement they continued to bear Christ's saving message from place to place.

Thus, from the very day of Pentecost the Holy Spirit was revealed as the source of interior strength (gift of fortitude). At the same time he helps in the making of opportune choices (gift of counsel), especially in matters of decisive importance, as in the question of the baptism of the centurion Cornelius, the first pagan admitted to the Church by Peter, or in the council of Jerusalem, when the conditions were established for the admission of pagan converts among the Christians.

The signs or miracles spoken of in previous reflections also derive from the fruitfulness of Pentecost. They accompanied the apostles' activity, as repeatedly reported in Acts: "Many signs and wonders were done among the people by the hands of the apostles" (Acts 5:12). As in the case of Christ's teaching, these signs were intended to confirm the truth of the saving message. This is stated expressly in the case of the activity of the deacon Philip: "The multitudes with one accord gave heed to what was said by Philip, when they heard him and saw the signs which he did" (Acts 8:6). The author specifies that it was a question of freeing those possessed by unclean spirits and of healing the paralyzed and the lame. Then he concludes: "So there was much joy in that city" (Acts 8:6-8).

He thinks it worth noting that it was a city of Samaria (cf. Acts 8:9), a region inhabited by a population which, though of the same race and religion as Israel, was separated from it because of historical and doctrinal reasons (cf. Mt 10:5-6; Jn 4:9). However, the Samaritans also expected the Messiah (cf. Jn 4:25). The deacon Philip, led by the Spirit, was brought there to proclaim that the Messiah had come. He confirmed the Good News with miracles. This therefore explains the joy of the people.

The Acts adds an episode to which we should at least refer, because it demonstrates the high regard in which the Gospel preachers held the Holy Spirit.

In that city of Samaria, before the coming of Philip, there was "a man named Simon who had previously practiced magic and amazed the people, saying that he himself was somebody great. They all gave heed to him from the least to the greatest..." (Acts 8:9-10). Always the same story! "But when they believed Philip as he preached the Good News about the kingdom of God and the name of Jesus Christ, both men and women were baptized. Even Simon himself believed, and after being baptized he continued with Philip. And seeing signs and great miracles performed, he was amazed" (Acts 8:12-13).

When it became known at Jerusalem that "Samaria had received the word of God" preached by Philip, the apostles "sent to them Peter and John, who came down and prayed for them that they might receive the Holy Spirit: for it had not yet fallen on any of them, but they had only been baptized in the name of the Lord Jesus. Then they laid their hands on them and they received the Holy Spirit" (Acts 8:14-17).

It was then that Simon, desiring to acquire the power to "confer the Spirit," like the apostles through the laying on of hands, offered them money to obtain that supernatural power. (Hence the origin of the word "simony" signifying commerce in sacred things). But Peter responded with indignation for that attempt to acquire with money "the gift of God," which is precisely the Holy Spirit (Acts 8:20; cf. 2:38; 10:45; 11:17; Lk 11:9, 13), and then threatened Simon with divine retribution.

The two apostles then returned to Jerusalem, evangelizing the villages through which they passed. Philip, however, went to Gaza, and prompted by the Holy Spirit, he joined a minister of the queen of Ethiopia who was passing along the road seated in his chariot, and "he told him the Good News of Jesus" (Acts 8:25-26, 27, 35). This was followed by his Baptism. "And when they came up out of the water, the spirit of the Lord caught up Philip..." (Acts 8:39).

As can be seen, Pentecost spread and bore abundant fruit, stirring up many to accept the Gospel and to be converted in the name of Jesus Christ. The Acts of the Apostles is the history of the fulfillment of Christ's promise, namely, that the

Holy Spirit sent by him would descend upon his disciples and complete his work when he, having ended his "day of work" (cf. Jn 5:17) with the night of his death (cf. Lk 13:33; Jn 9:4), would have returned to the Father (cf. Jn 13:1; 16:28). This second phase of Christ's redemptive work began with Pentecost.

General audience of December 20, 1989

The Meaning of "Spirit" in the Old Testament

In our catecheses on the person and mission of the Holy Spirit, we have sought first of all to listen to the announcement and promise concerning him made by Jesus, especially at the Last Supper. We have sought to take up again the account of his coming that is given in the Acts of the Apostles. We have re-examined the texts of the New Testament that tell of the early Church's preaching concerning him and faith in him. Yet in our analysis we have often come upon the Old Testament. It is the apostles themselves who in their early preaching just after Pentecost expressly presented the coming of the Holy Spirit as the fulfillment of the ancient promises and prophecies. They considered the old covenant and the history of Israel as a time of preparation for receiving the fullness of truth and grace that was to come with the Messiah.

It is true that Pentecost was an event thrusting into the future. This is because it marked the beginning of the time of the Holy Spirit, whom Jesus himself had indicated as a protagonist, together with the Father and the Son, in the work of salvation—a work destined to be diffused from the cross into the whole world. Nevertheless, to understand all the more fully the revelation of the Holy Spirit, it is necessary to go back in time, that is, to the Old Testament, in order to find there the signs of the long preparation for the mystery of Easter and Pentecost.

We must reflect again, therefore, on the biblical facts concerning the Holy Spirit and on the process of revelation which rises gradually from the shadows of the Old Testament to the clear affirmations of the New. This is first expressed within creation and then in the work of redemption, first in the history and prophecy of Israel and then in the life and mission of Jesus the Messiah, from the moment of the Incarnation up to that of the resurrection.

In the first place, among the facts to be examined is the name that first suggests the Holy Spirit in the Old Testament and the different meanings that this name conveys.

We know that in the Hebrew mentality a name has the powerful significance of representing a person. We may recall on this point the importance that is given to the way of naming God in Exodus and in the whole tradition of Israel. Moses had asked the Lord God what his name was. The revelation of a name was considered a manifestation of the person himself: the sacred name established a relationship between the people and the transcendent yet present being of God himself (cf. Ex 3:13-14).

The name that serves to suggest the Holy Spirit in the Old Testament will help us to understand his properties, even though we only learn of his reality as a divine person, of one substance with the Father and the Son, through the revelation of the New Testament. It is legitimate to think that the term was chosen with accuracy by the sacred authors, and, what is more, that the Holy Spirit himself, who inspired them, guided the conceptual and literary process which led to the elaboration of an apt expression for signifying his person even in the Old Testament.

The Meaning of "Spirit" in the Old Testament

In the Bible, the Hebrew term for the Spirit is *ruah*. The first meaning of this term, and that of its Latin translation *spiritus,* is "breath." (In English the relationship between spirit and respiration is still apparent.) A breath is the most immaterial reality we perceive. It cannot be seen; it is intangible; it cannot be grasped by the hand; it seems to be nothing, and yet it is vitally important. The person who does not breathe cannot live. The difference between a living person and a dead one is that the former has breath and the latter no longer does. Life comes from God. Hence breath, too, comes from him, and he can take it away (cf. Ps 104:29-30). Seeing breath in this way, they came to understand that life depends on a spiritual principle, which was called by the same Hebrew word, *ruah*. Man's breath bears a relationship to a much more powerful external breath, the wind.

The Hebrew *ruah*, just as the Latin *spiritus,* also designates the blowing of the wind. No one sees the wind, yet its effects are impressive. It drives the clouds and shakes the trees. When it is violent, it can whip up the sea and sink ships (Ps 107:25-27). To the men of old the wind appeared to be a mysterious power that God had at his disposal (Ps 104:3-4). It could be called "God's breath."

In the Book of Exodus, a prose narrative says: "Yahweh drove back the sea with a strong easterly wind all night, and he made dry land of the sea. The waters parted and the sons of Israel went on dry ground right into the sea..." (Ex 14:21-22). In the next chapter the same events are described in a poetic manner and the blowing of the easterly wind is called "a blast from the nostrils" of God. Addressing God, the poet says: "A blast from your nostrils and the waters piled high.... One breath of yours you blew, and the sea closed over them" (Ex 15:8-10). This expresses in a very suggestive way the conviction that the wind was God's instrument in these circumstances.

From observations on the invisible and powerful wind

one came to conceive the existence of the "spirit of God." In the texts of the Old Testament one passes easily from one meaning to the other, and even in the New Testament we see that the two meanings are present. To help Nicodemus understand the way the Holy Spirit acts, Jesus used the comparison of the wind, and he employed the same term in both cases: "The wind blows wherever it pleases.... That is how it is with all who are born of the Wind [i.e. of the Holy Spirit]" (Jn 3:8).

The fundamental idea expressed in the biblical name of the Spirit is, therefore, not that of an intellectual power, but that of a dynamic impulse, similar to the force of the wind. In the Bible, the primary function of the spirit is not to give understanding, but to give movement; not to shed light, but to impart dynamism.

This aspect is not exclusive, however. Other aspects are expressed and they pave the way for the revelation to follow. First and foremost, there is the aspect of interiority. Indeed, breath enters into man. In biblical terms, this could be expressed by saying that God puts the spirit into people's hearts (cf. Ez 36:26; Rom 5:5). Since air is so tenuous, it penetrates not only into our body, but all of its spaces and clefts. This helps to understand that "the spirit of the Lord fills the whole world" (Wis 1:7) and that it penetrates especially "all intelligent, pure and most subtle spirits" (7:23), as the Book of Wisdom says.

Related to the aspect of interiority is the aspect of knowledge. "Who can know the depths of man," asks St. Paul, "if not his own spirit?" (1 Cor 2:11). Only our spirit knows our intimate reactions and thoughts not yet communicated to others. Similarly, and with stronger reason, the Spirit of the Lord present within all the beings of the universe knows all from within (Wis 1:7). Indeed, "the Spirit reaches the depths of everything, even the depths of God.... The depths of God can only be known by the Spirit of God" (1 Cor 2:10-11).

The Meaning of "Spirit" in the Old Testament

When it is a matter of knowledge and communication between persons, breath has a natural connection with the word. To speak we use our breath. The vocal chords make our breath vibrate, and it thus transmits the sounds of the words. Inspired by this fact, the Bible draws a comparison between the word and the breath (cf. Is 11:4), or the word and the spirit. Thanks to our breath, the word is propagated; from our breath it derives strength and dynamism. Psalm 33 uses this comparison with regard to the primordial event of creation and says: "By the word of Yahweh the heavens were made, their whole array by the breath of his mouth..." (v. 6).

In texts of this kind we can perceive a distant preparation of the Christian revelation of the mystery of the Blessed Trinity. God the Father is the origin of creation. He has brought it about by his Word, that is, by the Son, and by his Breath, the Holy Spirit.

The many meanings of the Hebrew term *ruah*, used in the Bible to designate the Spirit, seem to give rise to some confusion. Indeed, in a given text, it is often not possible to determine the exact meaning of the word. One might waver between wind and breath, between breath and spirit, or between created spirit and the divine Spirit.

This multiplicity, however, has a certain wealth, for it establishes a fruitful communication between so many realities. In this regard it is better to give up in part the pretenses of neat reasoning in order to embrace broader perspectives. When we think of the Holy Spirit, it is useful to remember that his biblical name means "breath," and that it is related to the powerful blowing of the wind and to our own intimate breathing. Rather than clinging to an over-intellectual and arid concept, we will find it helpful to take in this wealth of images and facts. Unfortunately, translations are unable to convey them to us completely, for they are often obliged to choose other terms. To render the Hebrew word *ruah*, the Greek translation of the Septuagint uses twenty-four different terms, and so does not permit one to see all the connections between the texts of the Hebrew Bible.

To end this terminological analysis of the Old Testament texts concerning *ruah*, we can say that the breath of God appears in them as the power that gives life to creatures. It appears as a profound reality of God which works deep within man. It appears as a manifestation of God's dynamism which is communicated to creatures.

Though not yet understood as a distinct Person in the context of the divine being, the "breath" or "Spirit" of God is distinguishable in some way from the God who sends it to operate in creatures. Thus, even from the literary point of view, the human mind is gradually prepared to receive the revelation of the Person of the Holy Spirit, who will appear as the expression of God's intimate life and omnipotence.

General audience of January 3, 1990

The Creative Action of the Divine Spirit

In biblical language, the emphasis given to *ruah* as "the breath of God" seems to demonstrate that the analogy between the invisible, spiritual, penetrating, omnipotent divine action, and the wind, was rooted in the psychology and tradition on which the sacred authors drew. At the same time it provided new food for thought. Despite the variety of derived meanings, the term always served to express a vital force at work from outside or within man and the world. Even when it did not denote directly a divine person, the term in reference to God—"Spirit (or breath) of God"—implanted and caused to grow in the mind of Israel the idea of a spiritual God who intervenes in history and human life. It prepared the ground for the future revelation of the Holy Spirit.

Thus we can say that already in the creation narrative of the Book of Genesis, the presence of the "spirit (or wind) of God," which was moving over the face of the waters while the earth was formless and void, and darkness was upon the face of the deep (cf. Gen 1:2), is a remarkably striking reference to that vital force. It suggests that the breath or spirit of God had a role in creation: a life-giving power, together with the "word" which imparts being and order to things.

The connection between the spirit of God and the waters, which we observe at the beginning of the creation account, is found in another form in different passages of the Bible and becomes still closer, because the Spirit himself is presented as a fruitful water, a source of new life. In the book of consolation, Deutero-Isaiah expresses this promise of God: "For I will pour water on the thirsty land, and streams on the dry ground; I will pour my Spirit upon your descendants, and my blessings on your offspring. They shall spring up like grass amid waters, like willows by flowing streams" (Is 44:3-4). The water which God promises to pour is his Spirit, which he will "pour out" on his people. Likewise the prophet Ezekiel announces that God "will pour out" his Spirit upon the house of Israel (Ez 39:29), and the prophet Joel takes up again the same expression which compares the spirit to water poured out: "I will pour out my spirit on all flesh" (Joel 3:1 in the Hebrew text).

The symbolism of water, with reference to the Spirit, will be taken up again in the New Testament and enriched with new shades of meaning. We shall have occasion to speak of them later.

In the creation account, after the initial mention of the spirit or breath of God that hovered over the waters (Gen 1:2), we do not again find the word *ruah*, the Hebrew word for spirit. However, the way in which the creation of man is described suggests a relationship with the spirit or breath of God. We read that, after having formed man from the dust of the ground, the Lord God "breathed into his nostrils the breath of life; and man became a living being" (Gen 2:7). The word "breath" (in Hebrew *neshama)* is a synonym of "wind" or "spirit" *(ruah),* as is evident from the parallelism with other texts. On the other hand, the action of "breathing" attributed to God in the creation account is ascribed to the Spirit in the prophetic vision of the resurrection (Ez 37:9).

Sacred Scripture therefore gives us to understand that

God has intervened by means of his breath or spirit to make man a living being. In man there is a "breath of life," which comes from the "breathing" of God himself. In man there is a breath or spirit similar to the breath or spirit of God.

When the Book of Genesis speaks in chapter two of the creation of the animals (v. 19), it does not hint at such a close relationship with the breath of God. From the previous chapter we know that man was created "in the image and likeness of God" (1:26-27).

Other texts, however, admit that the animals also have a vital breath or wind and that they received it from God. Under this aspect man, coming forth from the hands of God, appears in solidarity with all living beings. Thus Psalm 104 makes no distinction between men and animals when it says, addressing God the Creator: "These all look to you, to give them their food in due season. When you give to them, they gather it up" (vv. 27-28). The Psalmist then adds: "When you take away their breath, they die and return to their dust. When you send forth your Spirit, they are created; and you renew the face of the earth" (vv. 29-30). The creatures' existence therefore depends on the action of the breath-spirit of God, who not only creates but also conserves and continually renews the face of the earth.

The first creation was devastated by sin. But God did not abandon it to destruction, but prepared for its salvation, which was to constitute a "new creation" (cf. Is 65:17; Gal 6:15; Rev 21:5). The action of God's Spirit for this new creation is suggested by Ezekiel's famous prophecy on the resurrection. In a striking vision the prophet has before his eyes a vast valley "full of bones," and is ordered to prophesy to these bones and say to them: "O dry bones, hear the word of the Lord. Thus says the Lord God to these bones: 'Behold, I will cause breath to enter you, and you shall live...'" (Ez 37:1-5). The prophet carries out the divine command and "there was a noise, a rattling, and the bones came together, bone to its bone" (37:7). Then there were sinews on them, and flesh had come upon them, and skin had covered them; and finally, at the command of the prophet, breath came into them, and they lived, and stood upon their feet (cf. 37:8-10).

The primary meaning of this vision was to announce the restoration of the people of Israel after the devastation and exile: "These bones are the whole house of Israel," says the Lord. The Israelites were regarded as lost, without hope. God promises them: "I will put my Spirit within you, and you shall live" (37:14). However, in the light of Jesus' paschal mystery, the prophet's words acquire a higher meaning, that of announcing a real resurrection of our mortal bodies thanks to the action of God's Spirit.

The Apostle Paul expresses this certainty of faith in the words: "If the spirit of him who raised Jesus from the dead dwells in you, he who raised Christ Jesus from the dead will give life to your mortal bodies also through his Spirit who dwells in you" (Rom 8:11).

The new creation had its beginning through the Holy Spirit's action in Christ's death and resurrection. In his passion Jesus fully received the action of the Holy Spirit in his human nature (cf. Heb 9:14). He thus passed from death to a new life (cf. Rom 6:10), which he can now communicate to all believers by transmitting to them this same Spirit, initially in baptism, and then fully in the final resurrection.

On the evening of Easter, appearing to the disciples in the upper room, the risen Christ repeated over them the action of God the Creator over Adam. God had "breathed" on the body of the man to give him life. Jesus "breathed" on his disciples and said to them: "Receive the Holy Spirit" (Jn 20:22).

Jesus' human breath thus serves to produce a divine work still more marvelous than the initial one. It is not merely the creation of a living man, as in the first creation, but the introduction of human beings into the divine life.

Rightly, therefore, does St. Paul establish a parallelism and an antithesis between Adam and Christ, between the first and second creation, when he writes: "If there is a physical body there is also a spiritual body. Thus it is written, 'The first man Adam became a living being' (Gen 2:7), the last Adam became a life-giving spirit" (1 Cor 15:44-45). The risen Christ, the new Adam, is so permeated in his humanity by the Holy Spirit, that he himself can be called "spirit." His humanity not only possesses of itself the fullness of the Holy Spirit, but it also has the capacity to communicate the life of the Spirit to all humanity. "If anyone is in Christ," St. Paul also writes, "he is a new creation" (2 Cor 5:17).

The creative and renewing action of God's Spirit is thus fully manifested in the mystery of Christ's death and resurrection. The Church invokes the Spirit when she prays: *"Veni Creator Spiritus,"* "Come, Creator Spirit."

General audience of January 10, 1990

The Guiding Action of the Spirit of God

The Old Testament gives us valuable examples of the acknowledged role of the Spirit of God—as "breeze," "breath," "life force," symbolized by wind. These examples are found not only in the books collecting the religious and the literary output of the sacred writers, which mirror both the psychology and the vocabulary of Israel, but also in the very lives of the personages who led the people in their historic journey toward the messianic future.

According to the sacred writers, it is God's Spirit who acts upon the leaders. The Spirit sees to it that they not only work in God's name, but also that their actions truly serve to carry out God's plan. They should look not so much toward building up and increasing their own personal or dynastic power, seen from a monarchical or aristocratic point of view, but rather toward giving valuable service to others, and especially to the people. It can be said that, through the mediation of these leaders, God's Spirit enters into and guides Israel's history.

Already in the story of the patriarchs one can note that they are being guided and led in their journey, in their travels and in their experiences by a divine hand which is fashioning a plan regarding their descendants. One of them is Joseph in whom the Spirit of God lives as a spirit of wisdom. He is discovered by pharaoh who asks his officials: "Could we find another like him, a man so endowed with the spirit of God?" (Gen 41:38). God's spirit makes Joseph capable of administering the country and accomplishing extraordinary tasks not only for his family and its various genealogical branches, but also on the plane of the whole future history of Israel.

God's spirit acts on Moses as well, the mediator between Yahweh and the people. The spirit sustains him and leads him during the exodus which will bring Israel to a homeland and make it an independent people, capable of accomplishing its messianic role. When the families encamped in the desert experienced a tense moment and Moses lamented before God that he did not feel up to carrying "the weight of all this people" (Num 11:14), God ordered him to choose seventy men. With them he was to set up an initial governing structure for those wandering tribes, and God announced to him: "I will also take some of the spirit that is on you and will bestow it on them, that they may share the burden of the people with you, and you will then not have to bear it by yourself" (Num 11:17). And thus, with the seventy elders gathered around the meeting tent, "the Lord took some of the spirit that was on Moses and bestowed it on the seventy elders" (Num 11:25).

When at the end of his life Moses had to be concerned about leaving the community a leader so that "it might not become a flock without a shepherd," the Lord pointed out Joshua to him; he was a "man in whom the spirit was present" (Num 27:17-18). Moses laid "hands on him," with the result that he, too, was "full of the spirit of wisdom" (Dt 34:9). These are typical cases of the Spirit's presence and action in the lives of the shepherds of the people.

Anointing is a sign of divine investiture

At times the gift of the Spirit is conferred on a person who, while not a leader, is called by God to give a service of some importance in special times and circumstances. For example, when it was time to construct the meeting tent and the ark of the covenant, God told Moses: "See, I have called Bezalel by name...I have filled him with a divine spirit of skill and understanding and knowledge in every craft" (Ex 31:3; cf. 35:31). And furthermore, God adds even in regard to the workmates of this artisan: "I have also endowed all the experts with the necessary skill to make all the things I have ordered you to make: the meeting tent, the ark of the commandments" (Ex 31:6-7).

The Book of Judges celebrates the lives of persons who were called at first "hero liberators," but later were also governors of cities and districts during the time of settlement between the tribal and monarchical periods. According to the usage of the verb *shâfat*, "to judge," in Semitic languages related to Hebrew, these people were considered to be not only administrators of justice, but also leaders of their people. They were raised up by God who communicated to them his spirit (breath—*ruah*) in answer to pleas made to him during moments of crisis. Several times in the Book of Judges their appearance and their victorious deeds are attributed to a gift of the spirit. Thus in the case of Othniel, the first of the great judges whose history is summarized, it is said that "when the Israelites cried out to the Lord, he raised up for them a savior, Othniel...and he rescued them. The spirit of the Lord came upon him and he judged Israel" (Jgs 3:9-10).

In Gideon's case, emphasis is placed on the power of divine action: "The spirit of the Lord enveloped Gideon" (Jgs 6:34). It is also said of Jephthah that "the spirit of the Lord came upon Jephthah" (Jgs 11:29). And regarding Samson: "The spirit of the Lord began to stir him" (Jgs 13:25). In these cases the spirit of God is the giver of extraordinary strength, of courage in decision-making, and at times of strategic prowess, by which a person was made capable of carrying out a mission entrusted to him for the liberation and leadership of the people.

When the historical leap is made from judges to kings, when the Israelites ask to have "a king to govern us, as other nations have" (1 Sam 8:5), the elderly judge and liberator Samuel acts so as not to mar Israel's sense of belonging to God as the chosen people and to assure the essential element of theocracy, that is, recognition of God's rights over the people. The anointing of kings as an inaugural rite is a sign of divine investiture which places political power at the service of a religious and messianic purpose. In this sense Samuel tells Saul, after having anointed him and having foretold the meeting at Gibeath with a group of psalm-singing prophets: "The spirit of the Lord will rush upon you and you will join them in their prophetic state and you will be changed into another man" (1 Sam 10:6). Also when the first initiatives of war became evident, "The spirit of God rushed upon Saul" (1 Sam 11:16). The promise of protection and of God's covenant which Samuel had made to Saul was realized in him: "God will be with you" (1 Sam 10:7). When the spirit of God abandoned Saul, he was terrified by an evil spirit (cf. 1 Sam 16:14). David had already appeared on the scene, consecrated by the aged Samuel with oil by which "the spirit of the Lord, from that day on, rushed upon David" (1 Sam 16:13).

In David even more than in Saul the ideal of the king anointed by the Lord, a type of the future Messiah-King, who would be the real liberator and savior of his people, took hold. Although David's successors did not reach his stature in realizing messianic kingship, and not a few of them abused Yahweh's covenant with Israel, the ideal of the King-Messiah did not die. It was projected into the future in terms of expectation, rekindled by prophetic announcements.

164   THE SPIRIT, GIVER OF LIFE AND LOVE

Isaiah especially emphasizes the relationship between God's spirit and the Messiah: "The spirit of the Lord shall rest upon him" (Is 11:2). Again it will be a spirit of strength, but, above all, a spirit of wisdom: "a spirit of wisdom and understanding, a spirit of counsel and of strength, a spirit of knowledge and of fear of the Lord," that spirit which will drive the Messiah to act with justice on behalf of the afflicted, the poor and the oppressed (Is 11:2-4).

The Holy Spirit of the Lord (cf. Is 42:1; 61:1 f.; 63:10-13; Ps 50; 51:13; Wis 1:5; 9:17), his "life breath" *(ruah)* which runs throughout Bible history will thus be given to the Messiah in full. That very spirit which breathed upon the chaos prior to creation (cf. Gen 1:2), the spirit which gives life to all that is (cf. Ps 104:29-30; 33:6; Gen 2:7; Ez 37:5-6, 9-10), which raises up judges (cf. Jgs 3:10; 6:34; 11:29) and kings (cf. 1 Sam 11:6), which makes artisans capable of doing their work in the sanctuary (cf. Ex 31:3; 35:31), which gives Joseph wisdom (cf. Gen 41:38), and Moses and the prophets inspiration (cf. Num 11:17, 25-26; 24:2; 1 Sam 23:2), will fall upon the Messiah with the abundance of its gifts (cf. Is 11:2). It will enable him to accomplish his mission of justice and peace. He upon whom God will have "placed his Spirit" "shall bring forth justice to the nations" (Is 42:1). "He will not retreat or be disheartened until he establishes justice on the earth" (42:4).

In what way will he "establish justice" and free the oppressed? Will it be perhaps by strength of arms as the judges did, under the impetus of the spirit, and as the Maccabees did many centuries later? The Old Testament did not allow for a clear response to this question. Certain passages told of violent interventions, as, for example, the Isaian text which says: "I trampled down the peoples in my anger, I crushed them in my wrath, and I let their blood run out upon the ground" (Is 63:6). Others, however, insisted on abolishing all struggle: "One nation shall not raise the sword against another nor shall they train for war again" (Is 2:4).

The answer had to be revealed by the way in which the Holy Spirit led Jesus into his mission: from the Gospel we know that the Spirit prompted Jesus to reject the use of arms and any human ambition and carry out a divine victory by means of unlimited generosity, shedding his own blood to free us from our sins. Thus the directing action of the Holy Spirit was manifested in a decisive way.

General audience of January 17, 1990

"Spirit Lifted Me..."

By referring to the last catechesis, we can draw from the Biblical data already cited the prophetic aspect of the activity exercised by God's Spirit over the leaders of the people, the kings and the Messiah. This aspect requires further reflection, because prophecy is the course along which the history of Israel runs, dominated by the prominent figure of Moses, the prophet par excellence, "with whom the Lord spoke face to face" (Dt 34:10). Through the centuries the Israelites became more and more familiar with the dual concept of "the law and the prophets," as an expressive synthesis of the spiritual patrimony which God entrusted to his people. And it is through his spirit that God spoke and acted in the fathers, and from generation to generation prepared a new day.

Without doubt the prophetic phenomenon which is seen in history is linked to the word. The prophet is a person who speaks in the name of God and delivers to his or her hearers and readers what God wants to make known concerning the present and future. God's spirit animates the word and gives it life. It gives to the prophet and the prophet's word a certain divine pathos, by which the prophet becomes vibrant and at times passionate, sometimes laden with suffering, and always dynamic.

Often the Bible describes significant episodes where it becomes evident that God's spirit rests on someone, and this person immediately pronounces a prophetic utterance. That is what happened with Balaam: "God's spirit came upon him" (Num 24:2). Then "he gave voice to his oracle and said: 'The utterance of one who hears what God has to say, and knows what the Most High knows, of one who sees what the Almighty sees, enraptured and with eyes unveiled...'" (Num 24:3-4). It is the famous prophecy, which although referring immediately to Saul (cf. 1 Sam 15:8) and to David (cf. 1 Sam 30:1 ff.) in the war against the Amalekites, evokes the Messiah as well: "I see him, though not now; I behold him, though not near; a star shall advance from Jacob, a staff shall arise from Israel..." (Num 24:17).

Another aspect of the prophetic spirit in service to the word is that it is able to be communicated and almost divided as the needs of the people dictated. This happened in the case of Moses who worried that the number of Israelites to lead and govern totaled at that time "600,000 adult men" (Num 11:12). The Lord commanded him to choose and gather together "seventy men among the elders of Israel, known by him to be elders of the people and their authorities" (Num 11:16). That done, the Lord "took some of the spirit that was on Moses and bestowed it on the seventy elders; and as the spirit came to rest on them they prophesied..." (Num 11:25).

In the succession of Elisha to Elijah, the former wished to be given no less than "two thirds of the spirit" of the great prophet, a kind of double portion of the inheritance due to the eldest son (cf. Dt 21:17). This was so that he might be recognized as the principal spiritual heir among the multitude of prophets and "sons of the prophets" grouped into guilds (2 Kgs 2:3). But the spirit is not passed on from prophet to prophet like an earthly inheritance: it is God who grants it. However, it did happen so, and the "sons of the prophets" admitted it: "The spirit of Elijah rests on Elisha" (2 Kgs 2:15; cf 6:17).

In Israel's contact with neighboring peoples there was no lack of false prophecy, which led to the formation of ecstatic groups who substituted music and movements for the spirit which came from God. They belonged to the Baal cult. Elijah waged a decisive battle against such prophets (1 Kgs 18:25-29), and emerged from it alone in his greatness. For his part, Elisha had further contact with some of these groups who seemed to have come to their senses (cf. 2 Kgs 2:3).

In genuine Biblical tradition the true concept of the prophet is defended and insisted on as being a man of God's word, appointed by God, on a par with and in a line from Moses (cf. Dt 18:15 f.). God promised Moses: "I will raise up for them a prophet like you in the midst of their brethren and I will put my words in his mouth. He will speak what I command him" (Dt 18:18). This promise is accompanied with a warning against the abuses of prophecy: "If a prophet presumes to speak in my name an oracle that I have not commanded him to speak, or speaks in the name of other gods he shall die. If you say to yourselves, 'How can we recognize an oracle which the Lord has spoken?' know that even though a prophet speaks in the name of the Lord, if his oracle is not fulfilled or verified, it is an oracle which the Lord did not speak" (Dt 18:20-21).

Another aspect of this criterion for judging is fidelity to the doctrine of God given to Israel through resistance to the seduction of idolatry (cf. Dt 13:2 f.). This explains the hostility shown toward the false prophets (cf. 1 Kgs 22:6 ff.; 2 Kgs 3:13; Jer 2:26; 5:13; 23:9-40; Mi 3:11; Zech 13:2). The duty of the prophet, as a man of God's word, is to fight the "spirit of lies" which is found on the lips of the false prophets (cf. 1 Kgs 22:23), in order to protect the people from their influence. It is a mission received from God, as Ezekiel proclaimed: "Thus the word of the Lord came to me: 'son of man, prophesy against the prophets of Israel, prophesy! Say to those who prophesy their own thought: Hear the word of the Lord: Woe to those prophets who are fools, who follow their own spirit and have seen no vision'" (Ez 13:2-3).

A man of the word, the prophet must also be "a man of the spirit," as Hosea once called him (9:7). He must have the spirit of God, and not only his own spirit, if he is to speak in the name of God.

This concept was developed by Ezekiel above all, who allowed the awareness which already took place about the deep meaning of prophecy to be seen. To speak in God's name requires the presence of God's spirit in the prophet. This presence is manifested in a contact which Ezekiel calls "vision." In those who are granted it, the activity of God's spirit guarantees the truth of the words pronounced. We find here a new indication of the link between word and spirit, which linguistically and conceptually prepares the way for the link which in the New Testament is placed between the Word and the Holy Spirit.

Ezekiel was aware of being personally led by the spirit: "Spirit entered into me" (he writes), "it set me on my feet and I heard the one who spoke to me" (Ez 2:2). The spirit enters into the person of the prophet. It makes him stand up: therefore it makes of him a witness to God's word. It lifts him up and puts him into motion: "Spirit lifted me up...and carried me away" (Ez 3:12-14). Thus does the dynamism of the spirit manifest itself (cf. Ez 8:3; 11:1, 5, 24; 43:5). Furthermore, Ezekiel specifies that he is speaking of "the Lord's Spirit" (11:5).

The dynamic aspect of the prophetic action of the divine Spirit comes through strongly in the prophecies of Haggai and Zechariah who, after the return from the Exile, vigorously pushed the repatriated Hebrews to get to work rebuilding the

Temple of Jerusalem. The result of the first prophecy of Haggai was that "the Lord stirred up the spirit of the governor of Judah, Zerubbabel...and the spirit of the high priest Joshua...and the spirit of all the remnant of the people, so that they came and set to work on the house of the Lord of hosts" (Hg 1:14). In a second prophecy the prophet Haggai intervened once again and promised the powerful help of the Lord's spirit: "Courage Zerubbabel.... Courage, Joshua.... Courage, all people of the land, says the Lord...my spirit will be with you, do not fear" (Hg 2:4-5). Likewise the prophet Zechariah proclaimed: "This is the word of the Lord to Zerubbabel: neither by an army nor with might, but with my spirit, says the Lord of hosts" (Zech 4:6).

In the days immediately preceding the birth of Jesus, there were no longer prophets in Israel and no one knew how long that situation would last (cf. Ps 74:9; 1 Macc 9:27). Yet one of the last prophets, Joel, had announced a universal outpouring of God's spirit which was to take place "before the coming of the day of the Lord, the great and terrible day" (Joel 3:4). It was to be manifested with an extraordinary spreading of the gift of prophecy. The Lord had proclaimed through his agent: "I will pour out my spirit upon all mankind; your sons and daughters will prophesy; your old men shall dream dreams and your young men shall see visions" (3:1). Thus finally the wish expressed many centuries previously by Moses would be fulfilled: "Would that all were prophets among the Lord's people and would that the Lord might bestow his spirit on them all" (Num 11:29). Prophetic inspiration would thus reach even "the slaves, both men and women" (Joel 3:2), overcoming all distinctions of cultural level or social condition. Then salvation would be offered to all: "Whoever will call upon the name of the Lord will be saved" (Joel 3:5).

As we saw in a previous catechesis, this prophecy of Joel found its fulfillment on the day of Pentecost. Turning to the amazed crowd, the Apostle Peter was able to declare: "What the prophet Joel prophesied has come to pass"; and he repeated the oracle of the prophet (cf. Acts 2:16-21), explaining that Jesus, "exalted at the right hand of God, had received from the Father the promised Holy Spirit and had poured it out" abundantly (cf. Acts 2:33). From that day on, the prophetic activity of the Holy Spirit has been continually manifested in the Church to give her light and comfort.

General audience of January 14, 1990

The Holy Spirit as Sanctifier

According to the Bible, the divine spirit is not only a light which illumines by giving knowledge and prompting prophecy, but also a force which sanctifies. God's spirit communicates holiness, because he himself is "a spirit of holiness," "holy spirit." This title is attributed to the divine spirit in chapter 63 of the Book of Isaiah when, in the long poem or psalm devoted to praising the benefits of Yahweh and deploring the people's strayings during Israel's history, the sacred author says that "they rebelled and grieved his holy spirit" (Is 63:10). But he adds that, after God's punishment, "they remembered the days of old and Moses his servant," and they wondered: "Where is he who put his holy spirit in their midst?" (Is 63:11).

This title is echoed also in Psalm 51 where, in asking pardon and mercy of the Lord *(Miserere mei Deus, secundum, misericordiam tuam)*, the author pleads: "Do not cast me out from your presence nor take your holy spirit from me" (Ps 51:13). This is a reference to the intimate principle of good which operates within, leading one to holiness ("spirit of holiness").

The Book of Wisdom affirms the incompatibility of the Holy Spirit with all lack of sincerity and justice: "The holy spirit of discipline flees deceit and withdraws from senseless counsel; and when injustice occurs, it is rebuked" (Wis 1:5). This expresses a very close relationship between wisdom and the spirit. In wisdom, the inspired author says, "there is an intelligent and holy spirit" (7:22), which is therefore "unstained" and "loving the good." This spirit is the very spirit of God, because he is "all-powerful and all-seeing" (7:23). Without this "holy spirit of God" (cf. 9:17), which God "sends from on high," human beings cannot discern the holy will of God (9:13-17) and much less carry it out faithfully.

The necessity of holiness is strongly linked in the Old Testament to the cultural and priestly dimension of Israel's life. Worship must be carried out in a "holy" place, a place of the dwelling of God thrice holy (cf. Is 6:1-4). The cloud is the sign of the Lord's presence (cf. Ex 40:34-35; 1 Kgs 8:10-11). Everything, within the tent, in the Temple, on the altar and on the priests, starting with Aaron, the first to be consecrated (cf. Ex 29:1 ff.), must respond to the demands of the "holy." The holy is like a halo of respect and veneration created around persons, rites and places privileged by a special relationship with God.

Some Biblical texts affirm God's presence in the tent in the desert and in the Jerusalem Temple (Ex 25:8; 40:34-35; 1 Kgs 8:10-13; Ez 43:4-5). Still, in the account of the dedication of the Temple of Solomon, a prayer is recounted in which the king places this claim in doubt, saying: "Can it indeed be that God dwells among men on earth? If the heavens and the highest heavens cannot contain you, how much less this Temple which I have built" (1 Kgs 8:27). In the Acts of the Apostles, St. Stephen expresses the same conviction regarding the Temple: "Yet the Most High does not dwell in houses made by human hands" (Acts 7:48). The reason for that is explained by Jesus himself in his conversation with the Samaritan woman: "God is spirit, and those who worship him must worship in spirit and in truth" (Jn 4:24). A house made of materials cannot fully receive the sanctifying action of the Holy Spirit and therefore cannot be truly "the dwelling of God." The true house of God must be a "spiritual house," as St. Peter will say, formed of "living stones," that is, of men and women sanctified interiorly by God's Spirit (cf. 1 Pet 2:4-10; Eph 2:21-22).

For that reason God promised the gift of the Spirit in hearts, in Ezekiel's famous prophecy which says: "I will prove the holiness of my great name, profaned among the nations, in whose midst you have profaned it.... I will cleanse you from all your impurities and from all your idols; I will give you new heart and place a new spirit within you.... I will put my spirit within you..." (Ez 36:23-27). The result of this wonderful gift is holiness in the concrete, lived with sincere attachment to God's holy will. Thanks to the intimate presence of the Holy Spirit, hearts will be finally docile to God and the life of the faithful will conform to the Lord's law.

God says: "I will put my spirit within you and I will make you live according to my statutes and will make you observe my laws and put them into practice" (Ez 36:27). Thus the Spirit sanctifies the entire existence of the human person.

The "spirit of lies" fights against God's spirit (cf. 1 Kgs 22:21-23); the "unclean spirit" overpowers persons and peoples, making them bow to idolatry. In the oracle on Jerusalem's liberation found in the Book of Zechariah, within the messianic perspective the Lord himself promises to effect the conversion of the people, making the unclean spirit vanish: "On that day...I will destroy the names of the idols from the land.... I will also take away the prophets and the spirit of uncleanliness from the land..." (Zech 13:1-2; cf. Jer 23:9 f.; Ex 13:2 ff.).

Jesus fought the "unclean spirit" (cf. Lk 9:42; 11:24). In this regard, Jesus spoke of the intervention of the spirit of God and said: "If I cast out devils by the Spirit of God, then the kingdom of God has come upon you" (Mt 12:28). To his disciples Jesus promised the help of the "Counselor," who "will convict the world...in regard to condemnation, because the ruler of this world has been condemned" (Jn 16:8-11). In his turn, Paul will speak of the spirit which justifies by faith and love (cf. Gal 5:5-6), and will put in the place of the "works of the flesh" the "fruits of the spirit" (cf. Gal 5:19 ff.), teaching the new life "according to the Spirit": the new Spirit of which the prophets spoke.

All those individuals or peoples who follow the spirit that is in conflict with God, "grieve" God's spirit. That is an expression used by Isaiah which we have already cited and which is timely to repeat in this context. It is found in the meditation of the so-called Trito-Isaiah on the history of Israel: "It was not a messenger nor an angel, but he himself [God] saved them. Because of his love and pity he redeemed them himself, lifting them and carrying them all the days of old. But they rebelled and grieved his holy spirit" (Is 63:9-10). The prophet contrasts the generosity of the saving love of God for his people with their ingratitude. In his anthropomorphic description, the attribution to God's spirit of the sadness caused by the abandonment of the people conforms to human psychology. But in the language of the prophet one can say that the sin of the people saddens the spirit of God especially because this spirit is holy: the sin offends the divine holiness. The offense is more serious because the holy spirit of God has been not only placed by God within Moses his servant (cf. Is 63:11), but also given as a guide to his people during their Exodus from Egypt (cf. Is 63:14) as a sign and pledge of future salvation: "and they rebelled..." (Is 63:10).

Paul, also, as an heir of this concept and this vocabulary,

will recommend to the Christians of Ephesus: "Do not grieve the Holy Spirit of God with which you were sealed for the day of redemption" (Eph 4:30; 1:13-14).

The expression "sadden the Holy Spirit" shows well how the people of the Old Testament had passed gradually from a concept of sacral holiness, a rather external one, to the desire for interiorized holiness under the influence of God's Spirit.

The more frequent use of the title "Holy Spirit" indicates this evolution. Nonexistent in the most ancient books of the Bible, this title takes over little by little, precisely because it suggested the Spirit's role in sanctifying the faithful. The hymns of Qumran in various sections thank God for the interior purification which he has wrought by means of his Holy Spirit (e.g. *Hymns from the First Cave of Qumran*, 16:12; 17:26).

The intense desire of the faithful was no longer only to be freed from oppressors, as in the time of the judges, but above all to be able to serve the Lord "in holiness and justice, before him all our days" (Lk 1:75). For this to happen the sanctifying grace of the Holy Spirit was needed.

The Gospel message answers this expectation. It is significant that, in all four Gospels, the word "holy" appears for the first time in relation to the Spirit, both in speaking of the birth of John the Baptist and that of Jesus (Mt 1:18-20; Lk 1:15, 35), and in announcing the baptism in the Holy Spirit (Mk 1:8; Jn 1:33). In the account of the annunciation, the Virgin Mary hears the words of the angel Gabriel: "The Holy Spirit will come upon you...because he who will be born will be holy and called the Son of God" (Lk 1:35). Thus the crucial sanctifying activity of the Holy Spirit, destined to spread among all people, had its beginning.

General audience of February 21, 1990

God's Spirit Purifies

In the preceding catechesis, we quoted a verse of Psalm 51 in which the Psalmist, repentant after his serious sin, implores God's mercy and asks the Lord: "Do not deprive me of your holy spirit" (v. 13). The Psalm is the Miserere, a very well-known Psalm which is often repeated in the liturgy, as well as in the devotion and penitential practices of Christian people. It expresses feelings of repentance, trust and humility which easily arise in a "heart contrite and humbled" (Ps 51:19) after sinning. The Psalm merits study and meditation, in the tradition of the Fathers and writers of Christian spirituality; it offers us new dimensions of the concept "divine spirit" in the Old Testament. It helps us to translate doctrine into spiritual and ascetical practice.

Those who followed the references to the prophets made in the preceding catechesis will find it easy to discover the strong kinship of the Miserere with those texts, especially those of Isaiah and Ezekiel. The sense of standing in the sight of God in a sinful condition itself, found in the penitential passage of Isaiah (59:12; cf. Ez 6:9), and the sense of personal responsibility instilled by Ezekiel (18:1-32) are already present in this Psalm. Within the context of the experience of sin and the strongly felt need for conversion, the Psalm asks God for a purification of the heart together with a renewed spirit. The action of God's spirit thus takes on more concrete aspects and a more precise commitment on the level of a person's existential condition.

"Have pity on me, O God!" The Psalmist implores divine mercy to win purification from sin: "Wipe out my offense, thoroughly wash me of my guilt, and of my sin cleanse me!" (Ps 51:3-4). "Cleanse me of my sin with hyssop that I may be purified; wash me and I shall be whiter than snow" (v. 9). But he knows that God's pardon cannot be reduced to a simply external withholding of accusation, without there being an interior renewal: the human being, all alone, is incapable of that. Therefore he asks: "Create in me, O God, a clean heart, and a steadfast spirit renew within me. Cast me not out from your presence, and your holy spirit take not from me. Give me back the joy of your salvation and a willing spirit sustain in me" (vv. 12-14).

The Psalmist's choice of words is extremely expressive: he asks for a creation, that is, the exercise of God's almighty power with the intention of creating a new being. Only God can create *(barà)*, that is, bring something new into existence (cf. Gen 1:1; Ex 34:10; Is 48:7; 65:17; Jer 31:21-22). Only God can give a pure heart, a heart which is completely transparent in its total desire to conform to God's will. Only God can renew the intimate part of the human being, change the person from within, set aright the basic direction of his conscious life and his religious and moral life. Only God can justify the sinner, according to the vocabulary of theology and dogma itself (cf. *DS* 1521-1522; 1560), which translates in just that way the prophet's phrase: "to give a new heart" (Ps 51:12).

"A steadfast spirit" (Ps 51:12) is asked for next, or the injection of God's strength into the human spirit, freed from the moral weakness felt in and shown by sin. This strength, this steadfastness, can come only from the active presence of God's spirit, and therefore the Psalmist implores: "Do not deprive me of your holy spirit." It is the only time in the psalms that this expression is found: "God's holy spirit." In the Hebrew Bible it is used only in the Isaian text which, in meditating on Israel's history, laments to God about the rebellion by which "they grieved his holy spirit" (Is 63:10), and recalls Moses for whom God "put his holy spirit within him" (Is 63:11). The Psalmist is already aware of the intimate presence of God's spirit as a continuing source of holiness, and therefore prays: "Do not deprive me of it!" Thus the juxtaposition of this request with the other one: "Cast me not out from your presence," lets us understand the Psalmist's conviction that the possession of God's Holy Spirit is linked to the divine presence in a person's inner being. To be deprived of that presence would be the real misfortune. If the Holy Spirit remains in him, man stands in a relationship with God that is no longer just "face to face," as before a face to contemplate: no, he possesses in himself a divine strength which inspires his behavior.

After having asked not to be deprived of God's Holy Spirit, the Psalmist asks for the restitution of joy. Earlier he had already prayed for the same thing, when he asked God for his purification, hoping to become "whiter than snow": "Make me feel joy and gladness; the bones you have crushed will exalt for joy" (Ps 51:10). But in the psychological-reflective process in which prayer is born, the Psalmist feels that in order to enjoy this joy fully, it is not enough for all guilt to be wiped away. The creation of a new heart is needed, with a steadfast spirit linked to the presence of God's holy spirit. Only then can he ask: "Give me the joy of your salvation!"

Joy is part of the renewal included in the phrase "creation of a clean heart." It is the result of birth into a new life, as Jesus will explain in the parable of the prodigal son. The father who pardons is the first to rejoice and wants to communicate the joy of his heart to all (cf. Lk 15:20-32).

Along with joy, the Psalmist asks for a "willing spirit," that is, a spirit of courageous commitment. He asks it of him who, according to the Book of Isaiah, had promised salvation for the weak: "On high I dwell in holiness and with the crushed and dejected in spirit, to revive the spirits of the dejected, to revive the hearts of the crushed" (Is 57:15).

Once this request is made, the Psalmist immediately adds a declaration of his commitment to work with God on behalf of sinners, for their conversion: "I will teach transgressors your ways, and sinners shall return to you" (Ps 51:15). This is another characteristic element of the interior process of a sincere heart, which has won pardon for its own sins. Such a heart wishes to win the same gift for others, prompting their conversion. It has the intention of working and promises to work toward this goal. This "spirit of commitment" in such a person flows out of the presence of the "holy spirit of God" and is the sign of that presence. In the enthusiasm of conversion and in the fervor of commitment, the Psalmist expresses to God his conviction concerning the effectiveness of his own actions. For him it seems certain that "sinners will return to you." But here as well the awareness of the active presence of an inner power, that of the "holy spirit," is in play.

The deduction enunciated by the Psalmist has a universal value: "My sacrifice, O God, is a contrite spirit; a heart contrite and humbled, O God, you will not spurn" (Ps 51:19). Prophetically he foresees that the day will come when, in a restored Jerusalem, the sacrifices celebrated on the temple altar according to the law's prescriptions will be acceptable (cf. vv. 20-21). The rebuilding of the walls of Jerusalem will be the sign of divine pardon, as the prophets Isaiah (cf. 60:1 ff.; 62:1 ff.), Jeremiah (cf. 30:15-18) and Ezekiel (cf. 36:33) will also say. But it remains sure that what is of greater worth is that "sacrifice of the spirit" of the person who asks pardon humbly, moved by the divine spirit which, thanks to repentance and prayer, was not taken away from him (cf. Ps 51:13).

As is clear from this succinct presentation of its basic themes, the psalm Miserere is for us not only a beautiful prayer text and a guide in the asceticism of repentance. It is also a witness to the level of development achieved in the Old Testament regarding the concept of the "divine spirit," as it gradually comes closer to what will be the revelation of the Holy Spirit in the New Testament.

The Psalm is, therefore, a great page in the history of the spirituality of the Old Testament, in pilgrimage, although in shadow, toward the new Jerusalem which will be the Holy Spirit's dwelling place.

General audience of February 28, 1990

The Spirit, the Word and Wisdom

The experience of the Old Testament prophets accents especially the link between the word and the spirit. The prophet speaks in the name of God and through the spirit. Scripture itself is a word which comes from the Spirit, the recording of the spirit lasting through the ages. It is holy because of the spirit who brings about its effectiveness through the spoken and written word.

Even in some who are not prophets, the intervention of the spirit prompts the word. The First Book of Chronicles recounts that the "brave ones" who acknowledged his royalty joined David. It says that "the spirit enveloped Amasai, leader of the thirty [brave ones]" and made him say these words to David: "We are yours.... Peace, peace to you, and peace to him who helps you; your God it is who helps you." And "David received them and placed them among the leaders of his troops" (1 Chr 12:19). Even more dramatic is another example told in the Second Book of Chronicles, which Jesus will recall (cf. Mt 23:35; Lk 11:51). This took place at a time when temple worship was declining and Israel was yielding to the temptation to idolatry. When the prophets who were sent to the

Israelites by God so that they might return to him were left unheeded, "Then the Spirit of God possessed Zechariah, son of Jehoiada the priest. He took his stand above the people and said to them: 'God says, "Why are you transgressing the Lord's commands, so that you cannot prosper? Because you have abandoned the Lord, he has abandoned you."' But they conspired against him, and at the king's order they stoned him to death in the court of the Lord's temple" (2 Chr 24:20-21). These are meaningful examples of the connection between spirit and word, present in the mind and the vocabulary of Israel.

Another similar link is the one between spirit and wisdom. It is seen in the Book of Daniel, on the lips of King Nebuchadnezzar. In recounting his dream and Daniel's explanation of it, he recognized the prophet as "a man who has the spirit of the holy God" (Dan 4:5; cf. 4:6, 15; 5:11, 14), that is, divine inspiration, which the pharaoh in his day also recognized in Joseph through the wisdom of his counsel (cf. Gen 41:38-39). In pagan vocabulary the king of Babylon spoke repeatedly of "the spirit of the holy gods," while at the end of his account he spoke of "the king of heaven" (Dan 4:34), in the singular. In any case, he recognized that a divine spirit was manifest in Daniel, as King Belshazzar will also acknowledge: "I have heard that the spirit of the holy gods is in you, and that you possess brilliant knowledge and extraordinary wisdom" (Dan 5:14). And the author of the book stresses that "Daniel outshone all his supervisors and satraps, because an exceptional spirit was in him, and the king thought of giving him authority over the entire kingdom" (Dan 6:3).

The "extraordinary wisdom" and the "exceptional spirit" are rightly attributed to Daniel. These bear witness to the link between these qualities in Judaism of the second century BC. (when the book was written) to sustain the faith and hope of the Jews persecuted by Antiochus Epiphanes.

In the Book of Wisdom, a text edited almost at the threshold of the New Testament—that is, according to certain modern authors, in the second half of the first century BC, and in Hellenistic circles—the link between wisdom and the spirit is so stressed that the two are almost identical. From the beginning we find there that "wisdom is a kindly spirit" (Wis 1:6). It is manifested and communicated by the strength of a basic love for humanity. But this kindly spirit is not blind nor does it tolerate evil in people, even hidden evil. "Wisdom does not enter into a soul that plots evil, nor does she dwell in a body under debt of sin. For the holy spirit of discipline flees deceit and withdraws from senseless counsels.... She acquits not the blasphemer of his guilty lips because God is the witness of his innermost self and the sure observer of his heart and the listener to his tongue" (Wis 1:4, 6).

The spirit of the Lord, therefore, is a holy spirit, who wants to communicate his holiness and carry out an educational function: "The holy spirit who teaches" (Wis 1:5). The spirit opposes injustice. That is not a limit upon the spirit's love, but rather a demand of that love. In the fight against evil, the spirit opposes all iniquity, but without ever allowing himself to be tricked, because nothing escapes the spirit, "not even words spoken in secret" (Wis 1:11). The spirit "fills the world"; it is omnipresent. "And, all-embracing, the spirit knows what man says" (Wis 1:7). The effect of his omnipresence is knowledge of all things, even secret ones.

Being a "kindly spirit," the spirit does not intend only to watch over people, but to fill them with his voice and his holiness. "God did not make death, nor does he rejoice in the destruction of the living. For he fashioned all things that they might have being..." (Wis 1:13-14). The affirmation of this positive quality of creation reflects the biblical concept of God as "he who is" and as creator of the whole universe (cf. Gen 1:1 ff.). It gives a religious basis to the philosophical concept and to the ethics of relations with things; above all it launches a discussion of the final goal of the human being, which no philosophy would have been able to put forth without the aid of divine revelation. St. Paul will then say later that, if death had been introduced through man's sin, Christ came as the new Adam to redeem humanity from sin and free humanity from death (cf. Rom 5:12-21). The Apostle will add that Christ brought a new life in the Holy Spirit (cf. Rom 8:1 ff.), giving the name and, even more, revealing the mission of the divine Person sheathed in mystery in the pages of the Book of Wisdom.

King Solomon, who is presented as the author of this book by literary contrivance, says at a certain moment to his colleagues: "Listen, oh kings..." (Wis 6:1), inviting them to receive the wisdom which is the secret and norm for royalty, and explaining "what wisdom is..." (Wis 6:22). He praises wisdom with a long list of the divine spirit's traits, which he attributes to wisdom, almost personifying it: "In her is a spirit, intelligent, holy, unique, manifold..." (Wis 7:22-23). There are twenty-one descriptive attributes (three times seven), consisting of words taken in part from Greek philosophy and in part from the Bible. Here are the most important ones:

The spirit is "intelligent," that is, not a blind impulse, but a force led by the awareness of truth. It is a "holy" spirit, because it wants not only to enlighten people, but to make them holy. It is "unique and manifold," thus able to penetrate into everything. It is "subtle," and pervades all spirits. Its activity is thus essentially interior, as is the spirit's presence. The spirit is "omnipotent and all-seeing," but does not constitute a tyrannical or destructive power, because the spirit is "kind and a friend to mankind," desires their good and tends to "make friends for God." Love supports and directs the exercise of the spirit's power.

Wisdom, therefore, has the qualities of and carries out the roles traditionally attributed to the divine spirit: "spirit of wisdom and intelligence...etc." (Is 11:2 f.), because wisdom is identified with the spirit in the mysterious depths of the divine reality.

Among the functions of the Spirit-Wisdom there is that of making known the divine will: "Who ever knew your will, except you had given Wisdom and sent your holy spirit from on high?" (Wis 9:17). Unaided, the human person is not able to know God's will: "What man knows God's counsel?" (Wis 9:13). By means of his holy spirit, God makes known his own will, his plan for human life, much more deeply and surely than with a mere promulgation of a law in formulae of human language. Acting from within by the gift of the Holy Spirit, God permits "the paths of those on earth to be made straight; and men learned what was your pleasure, and were saved by wisdom" (Wis 9:18). At this point the author describes in ten chapters the work of the Spirit-Wisdom in history, from Adam to Moses, to the covenant with Israel, to the liberation, through the continuing care given God's people. And he concludes: "In all ways, O Lord, you have magnified and glorified your people; unfailing, you stood by them in every time and circumstance..." (Wis 19:22).

In this historical wisdom-literature remembrance, a passage emerges where in speaking to the Lord, the author recalls God's omnipresent spirit which loves and protects human life. That goes also for the enemies of God's people and, generally, for the godless, for sinners. In them, too, there is a divine spirit of love and life: "You spare all things because they are yours, O Lord, lover of souls, for your imperishable spirit is in all things" (Wis 11:26; 12:1).

"You spare...." Israel's enemies could have been punished in a way much more terrible than did happen. They could have been "winnowed out by your mighty spirit, but you have disposed all things by measure, number and weight" (Wis 11:20). The Book of Wisdom praises God's "moderation" and offers this reason for it: God's spirit does not act only as a strong wind, able to destroy the guilty, but as a spirit of wisdom which desires life and thereby shows its love. "But you have mercy on all, because you can do all things; and you overlook people's sins that they may repent. For you love all things that are and loathe nothing that you have made; for what you hated, you would not have fashioned. And how could a thing remain, unless you willed it; or be preserved had it not been called forth by you?" (Wis 11:23-25).

We are at the summit of religious philosophy, not only of Israel, but of all ancient peoples. Here the biblical tradition, already expressed in Genesis, answers the great questions unresolved even by Hellenistic culture. Here God's mercy united with the truth of his creation of all things. The universality of creation carries with it the universality of mercy. And all is under the power of the eternal love with which God loves all his creatures: love in which we now recognize the person of the Holy Spirit.

The Book of Wisdom already lets us perceive this Spirit-Love which, like Wisdom, takes on the qualities of a person, with the following characteristics: spirit which knows all and makes known to people the divine plans; spirit which cannot accept evil; spirit which, through the mediation of wisdom, wants to lead all to salvation; spirit of love which desires life; spirit which fills the universe with its beneficial presence.

General audience of March 14, 1990

THE HOLY SPIRIT IN THE MISSION OF JESUS

The Spirit's Greatest Wonder Is Christ

In earlier catecheses we showed how references and allusions to the existence of the divine Spirit appear throughout the Old Testament tradition. They appear almost as a prelude to the revelation given in the New Testament of the Holy Spirit as a person.

We know that God inspired and led Israel's sacred writers, preparing the definitive revelation which was to be accomplished by Christ and given by him to the Apostles, so that they might preach and spread it throughout the world.

The Old Testament contains an initial and gradual revelation of not only the Holy Spirit, but also the Messiah-Son of God, his redeeming action and his kingdom. This revelation makes a distinction between God the Father, the eternal Wisdom proceeding from him, and the powerful and kindly spirit with which God works in the world from the creation and directs history according to his plan of salvation.

Doubtlessly this was not yet a clear manifestation of the divine mystery. But it was at the same time a kind of preparatory course for future revelation. God himself was carrying it out during the period of the old covenant through "the law and the prophets" (cf. Mt 22:40; Jn 1:45) and the history of Israel itself, since *"omnia in figura contingebant illis."* Everything in that history had a figurative and preparatory value for the future (1 Cor 10:11; 1 Pet 3:21; Heb 9:24).

On the threshold of the New Testament we find some people—Joseph, Zechariah, Elizabeth, Anna, Simeon, and above all Mary—who, thanks to the inner enlightenment of the Spirit, knew how to discover the true meaning of Christ's coming into the world.

The reference which the evangelists Luke and Matthew make to the Holy Spirit in regard to these very devout representatives of the old covenant (cf. Mt 1:18, 20; Lk 1:15, 35, 41, 67; 2:26-27), documents a link between and, we can also say, a passage from the Old to the New Testaments. This was later fully recognized in the light of Christ's revelation and after the Pentecost experience. The fact remains significant that the apostles and evangelists used the term "Holy Spirit" to speak of God's intervention both in the Incarnation of the Word and in the birth of the Church on Pentecost day. It is worth pointing out that in both events Mary the virgin mother is at the center of the portrait described by Luke—Mary who conceived Jesus by the action of the Holy Spirit (cf. Lk 1:35; Mt 1:18). With the apostles and the other first members of the Church, she remained in prayer expecting the very same Spirit (cf. Acts 1:14).

Jesus himself illustrated the role of the Spirit when he explained to the disciples that they would be able to penetrate the depths of the mystery of his person and mission only with the Spirit's help: "When the Spirit of truth comes, he will guide you to all truth" (Jn 16:13-14). Therefore, it is the Holy Spirit who lets people grasp the greatness of Christ and thus glorifies the Savior. But it is also the same Spirit who reveals his role in Jesus' life and mission. This is a point of great interest, to which I wish to direct your attention with this new series of catecheses.

The Spirit's Greatest Wonder Is Christ

If previously we have shown the wonders of the Holy Spirit announced by Jesus and experienced at Pentecost and during the initial journey of the Church in history, the time has come to accent the fact that the first and greatest wonder accomplished by the Holy Spirit is Christ himself. It is toward this wonder that we want to direct our attention.

We have already reflected on the person, life and mission of Christ in the Christological series. But now we can return briefly to that topic under the heading of pneumatology, that is, in the light of the action accomplished by the Holy Spirit within the Son of God made man.

Treating the topic of the Son of God in catechetical instruction, one speaks about him after having considered God the Father, and before speaking of the Holy Spirit, who "proceeds from the Father and the Son." For this reason, Christology precedes pneumatology. And it is right that it is so, because even seen from a chronological standpoint, Christ's revelation in our world happened before the outpouring of the Holy Spirit who formed the Church on Pentecost day. Furthermore, that outpouring was the fruit of Christ's redemptive offering and the manifestation of the power acquired by the Son now seated at the Father's right hand.

Still a pneumatological integration with Christology seems to be inevitable—as the Orientals observe—by the fact that the Holy Spirit is found at the very origin of Christ as the Word Incarnate come into the world "by the power of the Holy Spirit," as the creed says.

In accomplishing the mystery of the Incarnation, there was a decisive presence of the Spirit, to the degree that, if we want to grasp and enunciate this mystery more fully, it is not enough for us to say that the Word was made flesh. We must also underline—as happens in the Creed—the Spirit's role in forming the humanity of the Son of God in the virginal womb of Mary. We will speak about this later. And we will attempt to follow the action of the Holy Spirit in the life and mission of Christ: in his childhood, in the inauguration of his public life through his baptism, in his sojourn in the desert, in prayer, in preaching, in sacrifice and finally in resurrection.

A basic truth emerges from examination of the Gospel texts: what Christ was, and what he is for us, cannot be understood apart from the Holy Spirit. That means that not only is the Holy Spirit's light necessary for penetrating Christ's mystery, but the influence of the Holy Spirit in the Incarnation of the Word and in the entire life of Christ must be taken into account to explain the Jesus of the Gospel. The Holy Spirit left the mark of his own divine personality on the face of Christ.

Therefore, arriving at a deeper awareness of Christ demands also a deeper awareness of the Holy Spirit. To know who Christ is and to know who the Spirit is are two indissolubly linked requirements, the one implying the other.

We can add that even the Christian's relationship with Christ is integrally joined to his or her relationship with the Spirit. The Letter to the Ephesians helps us understand this when it expressed the hope that believers may be "strengthened with power" by the Spirit of the Father in the inner man, in order to be able to "know Christ's love which surpasses all knowledge" (cf. Eph 3:16-19). That means that in order to reach Christ with our knowledge and love as happens in true Christian wisdom, we need the inspiration and the guidance of the Holy Spirit, the interior master of truth and life.

General audience of March 28, 1990

Virginal Conception

The entire "Christ event" is explained by the action of the Holy Spirit, as we said in the previous instruction. For this reason, a correct and complete reading of the "Christ event"—and of its various stages—is for us the privileged path for reaching full knowledge of the Holy Spirit. We read the truth regarding the Third Person of the Blessed Trinity especially in the life of the Messiah: of him who was "consecrated with the Spirit" (cf. Acts 10:38). This truth is particularly clear in certain moments of Christ's life, upon which we will reflect in coming instructions. The first of these moments is the Incarnation itself, that is, the coming into the world of God's Word. He took on human nature in his conception and was born of Mary by the power of the Holy Spirit: *"Conceptus de Spiritu Sancto, natus ex Maria Virgine,"* as we say in the creed.

It is the mystery hidden in the event which we hear about in the Gospel in the two versions of Matthew and Luke. We refer to them as substantially identical and also complementary sources. Working in the chronological order of the narrated events we ought to begin with Luke. But for purposes of our instruction it is opportune to use Matthew's text as a starting point. It gives the formal explanation of Jesus' conception and birth (perhaps in relationship to the first rumors which circulated in hostile Jewish circles). The evangelist writes: "This is how the birth of Jesus came about. When his mother Mary was betrothed to Joseph but before they lived together, she was found with child through the Holy Spirit" (Mt 1:18). The evangelist adds that Joseph was told of this fact by a divine messenger: "Behold, the angel of the Lord appeared to him in a dream and said, 'Joseph, son of David, do not be afraid to take Mary your wife into your home because it is through the Holy Spirit that this child has been conceived in her'" (Mt 1:20).

Matthew's intention, therefore, was to assert unequivocally the divine origin of this event, which he attributed to the Holy Spirit's intervention. And this explanation became a text of the Christian communities of the first centuries out of which came the Gospels, the creeds and conciliar definitions, and the tradition of the Fathers.

Luke's text, in its turn, specifies for us the moment and the mode in which Mary's virginal motherhood originated from the Holy Spirit (cf. Lk 1:26-38). These are the messenger's words as reported by Luke: "The Holy Spirit will come upon you and the power of the Most High will overshadow you. Therefore he who is to be born will be called holy, the Son of God" (Lk 1:35).

We note in the meantime the simplicity, the precision and the conciseness with which Matthew and Luke report the concrete circumstances of the Incarnation of the Word. The prologue of the Fourth Gospel will later offer a more complete theology. This makes us see how far removed our faith in Christ is from the mythological sphere to which certain religious interpreters, even contemporary ones, reduce the concept of a God made man. The Gospel texts, in their essence, bear the fragrance of historical truth through their direct or indirect dependence on eyewitnesses and above all on Mary as the principal source of the narration. But at the same time, they allow the conviction of the evangelists and of the first Christian communities to shine through concerning the presence of a mystery, or rather of a revealed truth, in that event which happened "by the power of the Holy Spirit." The mystery of divine intervention in the Incarnation, as a real event, literally true, although not verifiable by human experience, except in the "sign" (cf. Lk 2:12) of humanity, of "flesh," as John says (1:14), is a sign offered to humble human beings open to God's attraction. The Incarnation is presented to us as a historical event, and not as a myth or a symbolic narration by the evangelists, in apostolic and post-apostolic literature and by Christian tradition. It is a real event, which "in the fullness of time" (cf. Gal 4:4) brought about what even in certain myths of antiquity could have been hinted at as a dream, or as a nostalgic echo or perhaps also as a prediction of perfect communion between humanity and God. We say with no hesitation that the Incarnation of the Word and the intervention of the Holy Spirit, which the Gospel writers present to us as a historical fact of their times, are at the same time mystery, revealed truth and object of faith.

Please note the new elements and the originality of the event even in relation to the writings of the Old Testament, which spoke only of the descent of the (Holy) Spirit upon the future messiah: "A shoot shall sprout from the stump of Jesse, and from his roots a bud shall blossom. The Spirit of the Lord will rest upon him" (Is 11:1-2). "The Spirit of the Lord is upon me because he has anointed me" (Is 61:1). Luke's Gospel speaks instead of the descent of the Holy Spirit upon Mary, when she became mother of the Messiah. Part of this new element is also the fact that this time the descent of the Holy Spirit involves a woman, whose special participation in the messianic work of salvation is highlighted. Thus the role of the woman in the Incarnation and the link between the woman and the Holy Spirit in Christ's coming stand out at the same time. It sheds light also on the mystery of the woman. It will have to be investigated and illustrated further throughout history in regard to Mary, but also in its repercussions upon the status and mission of all women.

Another new element in the Gospel narrative is found in comparing it with the narrations of miraculous births handed down by the Old Testament (cf. e.g. 1 Sam 1:4-20; Jgs 13:2-24). These births occurred in the usual manner of human procreation, even though in an unusual fashion, and in their announcement the Holy Spirit was not mentioned. Instead, during the annunciation to Mary in Nazareth, it is said for the first time that the conception and birth of God's Son as her Son would come about by the working of the Holy Spirit. This is a matter of a virginal conception and birth, as the Lucan text already indicates with Mary's question to the angel: "How can this be? I do not know man" (Lk 1:34). With these words Mary affirmed her own virginity, and not only as a fact, but also, implicitly as her intent.

This intention is better understood as a total self-gift to God through her virginity when one sees her virginity as a result of the Holy Spirit's action within Mary. That can be picked up in the very greeting directed to her by the angel: "Hail! Favored one, the Lord is with you" (Lk 1:28). The evangelist will also say of the elderly Simeon that "the Holy Spirit was upon him, a man righteous and devout and awaiting the consolation of Israel" (Lk 2:25). But the words addressed to Mary say much more: they affirm that she has been "transformed by grace," "established in grace." This singular abundance of grace cannot be anything but the fruit of a preliminary action of the Holy Spirit in preparation for the mystery of the Incarnation. The Holy Spirit sees to it that Mary is perfectly prepared to become the mother of God's Son and that, in view of this divine motherhood, she is and remains a virgin. It is another element in the mystery of the Incarnation which shines through from the narrated event of the Gospels.

As for Mary's decision in favor of virginity, we can better realize that it is due to the working of the Holy Spirit if we consider the tradition of the old covenant in which she lived and was educated. In that tradition, the aspirations of the "daughters of Israel," also in reference to worship and God's law, went rather in the direction of motherhood since virginity was not an ideal which was embraced or even appreciated. Israel was completely caught up in the feeling of awaiting the Messiah. Women were psychologically oriented toward motherhood also in regard to the Messiah's coming. That personal and ethnic tendency rose to the level of prophecy which permeated the history of Israel, a people in whom the messianic expectation and woman's generative function were strictly connected. Marriage, therefore, took on a religious aspect for the "daughters of Israel."

But the Lord's ways were different. The Holy Spirit led Mary precisely in the direction of virginity, in which she stands at the origin of a new ideal of complete consecration—soul and body, emotions and will, mind and heart—in the heart of God's People of the new covenant, according to the invitation made by Jesus: "For the sake of the kingdom of God" (Mt 19:12). I spoke about this new evangelical ideal in the Apostolic Letter *Mulieris Dignitatem* (n. 20).

Mary, mother of Jesus Christ, the Son of God made man, as a virgin remains the irreplaceable point of reference for God's saving action. Even our day, which seems to be heading in the opposite direction, cannot cloud over the light of virginity (celibacy for the sake of God's kingdom) which is inscribed by the Holy Spirit in such a clear way within the mystery of the Incarnation of the Word. He who was "conceived of the Holy Spirit and born of the Virgin Mary" owes his birth and human existence to that virginal motherhood which made Mary the living symbol of woman's dignity, the synthesis of two humanly irreconcilable greatnesses—motherhood and virginity—and almost the identity card for the truth of the Incarnation. Mary is the true mother of Jesus, but God alone is his Father, by the power of the Holy Spirit.

General audience of April 4, 1990

The Spirit's Special Presence in the Blessed Virgin Mary

We have already seen that a correct and careful reading of the "Incarnation event" reveals truths about the Holy Spirit as well as truths about Christ the God-Man. The truths about Christ and the truths about the Holy Spirit make up the single mystery of the Incarnation. It is revealed to us in the New Testament and especially—as a biographical and historical fact, full of mysterious truths—in Matthew's and Luke's narratives of Jesus' conception and birth. We acknowledge it in our profession of faith in Christ, the eternal Son of God, when we say that he was made man by being conceived and born of Mary "by the power of the Holy Spirit."

That mystery shines through the account which the evangelist Luke devotes to Mary's annunciation, as an event occurring within the context of a deep, sublime personal relationship between God and Mary. The narrative casts light also on the personal relationship which God wants to have with every person.

God is present in all beings as the principle and the one who sustains their existence according to the nature of each. He makes himself present in a new way in each person who opens himself up to him and becomes his follower, welcoming the gift of grace by which he is able to know and love him supernaturally, as guest of the soul transformed into a holy temple (cf. St. Thomas, *Summa Theol.*, I, q. 8, a. 3, ad 4; q. 38, a. 1; q. 43, a. 3). But in Christ's humanity God brings about a still higher and more perfect indwelling—and a unique one, uniting it to himself in the person of the eternal Word-Son (cf. *Summa Theol.*, I, q. 8, a. 3, ad 4; III, q. 2, a. 2). One can say that he brought about a union and a special and privileged indwelling in Mary during the Incarnation of the Word, in the conception and birth of Jesus Christ, whose Father he alone is. It is a mystery which stands out when the Incarnation is considered in its fullness.

Let us reflect once more on the passage from Luke. It describes and documents God's very personal relationship with the Virgin, to whom his messenger communicated the call to be the mother of the Messiah, the Son of God, by the power of the Holy Spirit. On the one hand God communicated himself to Mary in the Trinity of Persons, which Christ one day would make more clearly known in their unity and distinction. The angel Gabriel announced to Mary that by God's will and grace she will conceive and bear him who will be acknowledged to be the Son of God; and that will happen by the power, that is by virtue, of the Holy Spirit, who, by overshadowing her, will cause her to be the human mother of this child. The term "Holy Spirit" resounds in Mary's soul as a Person's name; that is a new element compared to the tradition of Israel and the writings of the Old Testament. It is an anticipated revelation for her, who is allowed to share in what is at least a dim perception of the mystery of the Trinity.

In particular the Holy Spirit, who is made known in Luke's words reflected in the discovery which Mary made, appears as the one who, in a certain sense, "overcomes the distance" between God and man. It is the Person through whom God draws near to man in his humanity to "give himself as a gift" in his very divinity to man, and to bring about in every human being a new form of union and presence (cf. St. Thomas, *Summa Theol.*, q. 43, a. 3). Mary is privileged in this discovery by reason of the divine indwelling and her union with God in her motherhood. In view of this very high vocation, she was given a special grace which the angel recognized in his greeting (cf. Lk 1:28). And all this is the work of the Holy Spirit, the principle of grace in every person.

In Mary the Holy Spirit descended and acted, chronologically speaking, even before the Incarnation, that is, from the moment of her Immaculate Conception. But that happens in view of Christ, her Son, in the extra-temporal sphere of the mystery of the Incarnation. For her the Immaculate Conception constituted, in advance, a participation in the benefits of the Incarnation and redemption, as the highpoint and fullness of the "self-gift" which God makes to man. And that is accomplished by the power of the Holy Spirit. The angel said to Mary: "The Holy Spirit will come upon you and the power of the Most High will overshadow you. Therefore the child to be born will be call holy, the Son of God" (Lk 1:35).

In the Lucan passage, among other truths, there is also the fact that God waited for an act of consent on the part of the Virgin of Nazareth. In the books of the Old Testament which refer to births under extraordinary circumstances, there are cases where parents because of their age are no longer capable of generating the desired offspring. From the case of Isaac, born to Abraham and Sarah in their already advanced old age, we arrive at the threshold of the New Testament with John the Baptist, born of Zechariah and Elizabeth, these, too, of advanced age.

In Mary's annunciation something very different occurs. Mary gave herself completely to God in her virginity. To become the mother of God's Son, she did not have to do more than what was asked of her: give her consent to what the Holy Spirit will accomplish in her with his divine power.

Thus the Incarnation, the Holy Spirit's work, includes an act of free will on the part of Mary, a human being. A human being (Mary) responded consciously and freely to God's action; she welcomed the Holy Spirit's power.

In asking for a conscious and free response, God respected in her and brought to its highest expression the "dignity of causality" which he himself gives to all beings and especially to human beings. On the other hand, that beautiful answer by Mary: "Behold, I am the servant of the Lord. May it be done to me according to your word" (Lk 1:38) is already itself a fruit of the power of the Holy Spirit within her in her will and heart. It is an answer given by grace and in grace, which comes from the Holy Spirit. But this did not make it cease being an authentic expression of her freedom as a human creature, a conscious act of free will. The inner action of the Holy Spirit aimed to ensure that Mary's response—and that of every human being whom God calls—is precisely what it ought to be. It expressed in the most compete fashion possible the personal maturity of an enlightened and pious conscience, which knew how to give itself without reservation. This is mature love. The Holy Spirit, giving himself to the human will as (uncreated) Love, ensures that created love is born and grows in the subject; at the same time this action, as an expression of human will, constitutes the person's spiritual fullness. Mary gave her answer of love in a perfect way, and thus became the shining type for every person's personal relationship with God.

The "Nazareth event," described by Luke in the Gospel of the annunciation, is therefore a perfect image—and we can call it the model—of the God-man relationship. God wills that this relationship be founded in every person on the gift of the Holy Spirit, but also on personal maturity. At the threshold of the new covenant the Holy Spirit gave Mary a gift of immense spiritual greatness. He obtained from her an action of dedication and loving obedience, which is an example for all those who are called to faith and to the following of Christ, now that "the Word was made flesh and dwelt among us" (Jn 1:14). After the earthly mission of Jesus and Pentecost, the call, God's "self-gift," the action of the Holy Spirit which continues the Nazareth event will be repeated throughout the whole future of the Church. And it will always have to be that man's answer to the call and to God's gift be given with the same personal maturity which radiated throughout the fiat of the Virgin of Nazareth during the annunciation.

General audience of April 18, 1990

A "New Anthropology" from the Spirit

In the creed we profess that the Son, one in being with the Father, became man by the power of the Holy Spirit. In the Encyclical *Dominum et Vivificantem* I wrote that "the conception and birth of Jesus Christ are in fact the greatest work accomplished by the Holy Spirit in the history of creation and salvation: the supreme grace—'the grace of union,' source of every other grace, as St. Thomas explains (cf. *Summa Theol.*, III, q. 7, a. 13).... For the 'fullness of time' is matched by a particular fullness of the self-communication of the Triune God in the Holy Spirit. 'By the power of the Holy Spirit' the mystery of the 'hypostatic union' is brought about—that is, the union of the divine nature and the human nature, of the divinity and the humanity in the one Person of the Word-Son" (n. 50).

This refers to the mystery of the Incarnation. At the start of the new covenant, the mystery of the Holy Spirit is linked to the revelation of the Incarnation. We have seen this in the preceding catecheses which permitted us to illustrate this truth in its various aspects, beginning with the virginal conception of Jesus Christ, as we read in the Lucan passage on the annunciation (cf. Lk 1:26-38). It is difficult to explain the origin of this text without thinking of the narrative about Mary, who alone could have made known what had taken place within her at the moment of the conception of Jesus. The analogies which have been proposed between this passage and other accounts from the ancient world and especially Old Testament writings never refer to the most important and decisive point, that is, the virginal conception. That constitutes an absolutely new element.

It is true that in the parallel passage from Matthew we read: "All of this took place to fulfill what the Lord said through the prophet: 'Behold, the virgin shall be with child and bear a son, and they shall name him Emmanuel'" (Mt. 1:22-23). The result, however, always surpasses the expectations. That is, the event includes new elements which were not expressed in the prophecy. Thus, in the case that we are referring to, the Isaian oracle about the virgin who will conceive (cf. Is 7:14) remained incomplete and therefore lent itself to various interpretations.

The Incarnation event fulfilled it with unforseeable perfection. A truly virginal conception was brought about through the power of the Holy Spirit. The Son who was born is truly "God with us." We are no longer referring strictly to a covenant with God, but to God's real presence in the people's midst by virtue of the Incarnation of the eternal Son of God. This is an absolutely new element.

The virginal conception, therefore, is an integral part of the mystery of the Incarnation. The body of Jesus, conceived in virginal fashion by Mary, belongs to the person of the eternal Word of God. The Holy Spirit does precisely this as he comes upon the virgin of Nazareth. He brings it about that the man (the Son of Man) whom she conceived is the true Son of God, eternally begotten of the Father, one in substance with the Father, for whom the eternal Father is the only Father. While being born of Mary as a man, he continues to be the Son of the same Father of whom he is eternally begotten. See how in a special way the virginity of Mary stresses the fact that the Son she conceived by the power of the Holy Spirit is the Son of God. God alone is his Father.

The traditional iconography, which shows Mary with the child Jesus in her arms and does not picture Joseph beside her, constitutes a silent but firm statement of her virginal motherhood, and for that very reason, of the Son's divinity. This image, therefore, could be called the icon of Christ's divinity. We find it already at the end of the second century in a fresco in the Roman catacombs and afterward, in innumerable reproductions. It is especially depicted with very effective artistic touches and marks of faith in the Byzantine and Russian icons which have links with the most genuine sources of faith: the Gospels and the early tradition of the Church.

Luke reports the words of the angel who announced the birth of Jesus by the power of the Holy Spirit: "The Holy Spirit will come upon you, and the power of the Most High will overshadow you" (Lk 1:35). The Spirit of which the evangelist speaks is the Spirit "which gives life." Reference is not made solely to that "breath of life" which is the mark of living beings, but to the very life of God himself: the divine life. The Holy Spirit who is in God as a breath of love, the absolute (uncreated) Gift of the divine Persons, acts in the Incarnation of the Word as the breath of this love for humanity: for Jesus himself, for human nature and for all of humanity. This breath expresses the Father's love. He so loved the world that he gave his only begotten Son (cf. Jn 3:16). In the Son is the fullness of the gift of divine life for humanity.

This is what I called in the Encyclical *Dominum et Vivificantem* "the particular fullness of the self-communication of the triune God in the Holy Spirit" (n. 50). This is the deepest meaning of the "hypostatic union." This is a formula which reflects the thought of the Councils and of the Fathers on the mystery of the Incarnation, and therefore on the concepts of nature and person, elaborated and made use of on the basis of the experience of the distinction between nature and subject which every man perceives within himself. The idea of the person had never before been so clearly individuated and defined as it was in the work of the Councils, once the apostles and the evangelists had made known the event and the mystery of the Incarnation of the Word "by the power of the Holy Spirit."

We can say, therefore, that in the Incarnation the Holy Spirit laid the foundations for a new anthropology which sheds light on the greatness of human nature as reflected in Christ. In him, human nature reaches its highest point of union with God, "having been conceived by the power of the Holy Spirit in such a way that one and the same subject can be Son of God and Son of man" (St. Thomas, *Summa Theol.,* III, q. 2, a. 12, ad 3). It was not possible for man to rise up higher than this highpoint, nor is it possible for human thought to conceive of a closer union with the divinity.

General audience of May 23, 1990

Christ Is Totally Holy

"The Holy Spirit will come upon you and the power of the Most High will overshadow you. Therefore the child to be born will be called holy, the Son of God" (Lk 1:35). As we know, these words which the angel spoke to Mary at the annunciation in Nazareth refer to the mystery of the Incarnation of the Son-Word by the power of the Holy Spirit. They refer to a key truth of our faith which was the object of previous catecheses. By the power of the Holy Spirit—as we said—the hypostatic union is brought about: the Son consubstantial with the Father assumed a human nature from the Virgin Mary by which he became true man without ceasing to be true God. The union of divinity and humanity in the one Person of the Word-Son, that is the hypostatic union *(hypostasis*: "person") is the Holy Spirit's greatest accomplishment in the history of creation and in salvation history. Even though the entire Trinity is its cause, it is still attributed by the Gospel and by the Fathers to the Holy Spirit, because it is the highest work wrought by divine Love. It was wrought with the absolute gratuitousness of grace, in order to communicate to humanity the fullness of holiness in Christ. All these effects are attributed to the Holy Spirit (cf. St. Thomas, *Summa Theol.,* III, q. 32, a. 1).

Christ Is Totally Holy

The words addressed to Mary during the annunciation indicate that the Holy Spirit is the source of holiness for the Son who is to be born of her. At the instant in which the Eternal Word becomes man, a unique fullness of human holiness is accomplished in the assumed nature, a fullness which goes beyond that of any other saint, not only of the old but also of the new covenant. This holiness of the Son of God as man, as Son of Mary—a holiness from the source rooted in the hypostatic union—is the work of the Holy Spirit. He will continue to act in Christ to the point of crowning his masterpiece in the Easter mystery.

This type of holiness is a result of the unique consecration about which Christ himself will speak explicitly during a discussion with his hearers: "Can you say that the one whom the Father has consecrated and sent into the world blasphemes because I said: 'I am the Son of God'?" (Jn 10:36). That consecration (that is, sanctification) is linked to the coming into the world of the Son of God. As the Father sends the Son into the world by the power of the Holy Spirit (the messenger told Joseph: "It is through the Holy Spirit that this child has been conceived in her": Mt 1:20), so he consecrates this Son in his humanity by the working of the Holy Spirit.

The Spirit is the author of the sanctification of all people. He is especially the author of the sanctification of the man conceived and born of Mary, as well as the sanctification of his most pure mother. From the very first moment of the conception of this man who is the Son of God, he received from the Holy Spirit an extraordinary fullness of holiness, in a measure corresponding to the dignity of his divine Person (cf. St. Thomas, *Summa Theol.,* III, q. 7, aa. 1, 9-11).

This sanctification refers to the entire humanity of the Son of God, his soul and his body, as is made clear by John the evangelist, who seems to stress the bodily aspect of the Incarnation: "The Word was made flesh" (Jn 1:14). The power of the Holy Spirit in the Incarnation of the Word overcomes that concupiscence which St. Paul speaks about in the Letter to the Romans (cf. Rom 7:7-25) and which wounds man from within. The "law of the Spirit" (Rom 8:2) liberates a person precisely from that concupiscence, so that the one who lives in the Spirit walks also according to the Spirit (cf. Gal 5:25). The holiness of Christ's full humanity is the result of the action of the Holy Spirit.

The human body of the Son of Mary shares fully in this holiness through a growing dynamism which has its highpoint in the Easter mystery. Thanks to that, the body of Jesus, which the Apostle terms "in the likeness of sinful flesh" (Rom 8:3), achieves the perfect holiness of the body of the risen one (cf. Rom 1:4). Thus a new destiny for the human body is begun— and for every body in the world, created by God and called, even in its materialness, to share in the benefits of the redemption (cf. St. Thomas, *Summa Theol.,* III, q. 8, a. 2).

It must be added at this point that the body, which by the power of the Holy Spirit belongs from the first moment of its conception to the humanity of the Son of God, must eventually become in the Eucharist the spiritual food for men and women. In announcing the institution of this wonderful sacrament, Jesus Christ will stress that in it his flesh (under the species of bread) will be able to become food for people, thanks to the working of the Holy Spirit who gives life.

In this regard, the words he said near Capernaum are very significant: "It is the Spirit that gives life, while the flesh is of no avail" (Jn 6:63). While Christ left us his flesh as spiritual food, he wanted at the same time to teach us about that state of consecration and of holiness which, by the power of the Holy Spirit, was and is a prerogative even of his body in the mystery of the Incarnation and of the Eucharist.

Luke the evangelist, perhaps echoing private conversations with Mary, tells us that, as the Son of Man, "Jesus grew in wisdom, age and favor before God and man (Lk 2:52; cf. Lk 2:40). In an analogous way one can also speak of "growth" in holiness in the sense of an ever more complete manifestation and fulfillment of that fundamental fullness of holiness with which Jesus came into the world. The moment in which the consecration of the Son in the Holy Spirit was made known in a special way, at the level of mission, was at the start of the messianic activity of Jesus of Nazareth: "The Spirit of the Lord is upon me: because he has anointed me; he has sent me" (Lk 4:18).

This activity manifested that holiness which one day Simon Peter will feel obliged to acknowledge with these words: "Lord, depart from me for I am a sinner" (Lk 5:8). And also at another time: "We have come to believe and are convinced that you are the Son of God" (Jn 6:69).

The mystery-reality of the Incarnation, therefore, signals the entrance into the world of a new holiness. It is the holiness of the divine Person of the Son-Word who, in hypostatic union with humanity, permeates and consecrates the entire reality of the Son of Mary: soul and body. By the power of the Holy Spirit, the holiness of the Son of Man constitutes the principal and lasting source of holiness in human and world history.

General audience of June 6, 1990

The Spirit at Work in Mary's Visitation

The truth about the Holy Spirit is clearly given in the Gospel texts which describe moments in the life and mission of Christ. We have already paused to reflect on Jesus' virginal conception and birth from Mary by the power of the Holy Spirit. There are other pages of the infancy Gospel, to which we must direct our attention, because these highlight the working of the Holy Spirit in a special way.

One of these moments is surely the passage in which the evangelist Luke recounts the visit of Mary to the house of Elizabeth. We read that "during those days Mary set out and traveled to the hill country in haste to a town of Judah" (Lk 1:39). It is commonly understood that he is referring to the locality of Ain-Karim, six kilometers west of Jerusalem. Mary went there to be near her relative Elizabeth, who was older than she. Mary went there after the annunciation, to which the visitation was almost a complement. The angel had said to Mary: "Behold, Elizabeth your relative has also conceived a son in her old age, and this is the sixth month of her who was called barren; for nothing is impossible with God" (Lk 1:36-37).

Mary undertook the journey to Elizabeth "in haste," certainly out of a heartfelt need to offer her loving service as a sister during those months of advanced pregnancy. Within her sensitive and gentle spirit a feeling of feminine solidarity was blossoming, as is characteristic of such circumstances. But against that psychological backdrop, there was probably a special communion which was forged between her and Elizabeth during the announcement made by the angel. The son whom Elizabeth was expecting would be the precursor of Jesus and the one who would baptize him in the Jordan.

On the basis of that communion of spirits we understand why the evangelist Luke took so much care in accenting the working of the Holy Spirit during the meeting of the two future mothers: Mary "entered the house of Zechariah and greeted Elizabeth, and when Elizabeth heard Mary's greeting, the infant leaped in her womb, and Elizabeth was filled with the Holy Spirit" (Lk 1:40-41). Elizabeth experienced this work of the Holy Spirit in a particularly profound way as she met Mary. It was related to the mysterious destiny of the son whom she was carrying in her womb. Earlier the baby's father Zechariah was heard to say, as he received the news about the birth of his son during his priestly service in the temple: "He will be filled with the Holy Spirit even from his mother's womb" (Lk 1:15).

At the moment of the visitation when Mary crossed the threshold of Elizabeth's house (and, with her, he who was already the "fruit of her womb" crossed it too), that presence of the Holy Spirit was felt in an experiential way by Elizabeth. She herself bore witness to that in the greeting which she addressed to the young mother who came to visit her.

According to Luke's Gospel, Elizabeth "cried out in a loud voice and said, 'Most blessed are you among women and blessed is the fruit of your womb. And how does this happen to me, that the mother of my Lord should come to me? For at the moment the sound of your greeting reached my ears, the infant in my womb leaped for joy. Blessed are you who believed that what was spoken to you by the Lord would be fulfilled'" (Lk 1:42-45).

In a few lines, the evangelist reveals to us the surprise of Elizabeth, the joyous leaping of the baby in her womb, and her at least somewhat confused understanding of the messianic identity of the baby that Mary was carrying in her womb. The text shows Elizabeth's recognition of Mary's faith in the revelation which was given her by the Lord. Beginning with these passages Luke uses the divine title "Lord" not only to speak of the God who reveals and promises ("the works of the Lord"), but also of the son of Mary, Jesus. In the New Testament the title is attributed to Jesus especially as the risen one (cf. Acts 2:36; Phil 2:11). Here he is yet to be born. But Elizabeth no less than Mary perceived his messianic greatness.

That means that Elizabeth, "filled with the Holy Spirit," was introduced into the depths of the mystery of the coming of the Messiah. Within her the Holy Spirit worked a special enlightenment which found expression in the salutation she addressed to Mary. Elizabeth spoke as if she were participating in and witnessing the annunciation in Nazareth. In her words, she defined the essence of the mystery which was at work at that moment in Mary. By saying "the mother of my Lord comes to me," she called the baby which Mary has been carrying in her womb "my Lord." Then she proclaimed Mary herself "blessed among women," and added: "Blessed is she who has trusted." It was as if she wished to refer to the attitude and behavior of the handmaid of the Lord, who answered the angel with her fiat: "May it be done to me according to your word!" (Lk 1:38).

The text of Luke shows his conviction that the Holy Spirit was acting, enlightening and inspiring both Mary and Elizabeth. Just as the Holy Spirit helped Mary perceive the mystery of her messianic motherhood brought about within her virginity, so the Spirit gave Elizabeth the ability to discover him whom Mary was carrying in her womb. She discovered what Mary was called to be in the economy of salvation: the "mother of the Lord." And the Spirit gave her the inner energy which prompted her to proclaim what she had learned "in a loud voice" (Lk 1:42), with a kind of enthusiasm and joy which are also the result of the Holy Spirit.

The mother of the future preacher and baptizer in the Jordan attributed that joy to the baby whom she had been carrying for sixth months in her womb: "The infant in my womb leaped for joy." Mother and son were united in a kind of spiritual symbiosis, by which the exultation of the baby almost infected her who conceived him. Elizabeth broke out into that shout to express the joy which she profoundly shared with her son, as Luke testifies.

Continuing with the Lucan narrative, the Magnificat, the hymn of joy, welled up from the soul of Mary. In it she too expressed her joy: "My spirit rejoices in God my Savior" (Lk 1:4-7). Raised as she was in the word of God by reading and meditating on the Sacred Scripture, Mary in that moment felt welling up from the depths of her soul the verses of the canticle of Anna, Samuel's mother (cf. 1 Sam 2:1-10) as well as other Old Testament verses. She gave free expression to the feelings of the "daughter of Sion," which found highest fulfillment in her.

That is what the evangelist came to know so well, on the basis of the private conversations which he directly or indirectly shared with Mary. Among what was passed on there must have been news of that joy which the two mothers shared in common during that meeting, as the fruit of the love which beat in their hearts. It was the trinitarian Spirit-Love, who was revealing himself on the threshold of the "fullness of time" (Gal 4:4), inaugurated in the mystery of the Incarnation of the Word. Already in that blessed moment what Paul would later say was being fulfilled: "The fruit of the Holy Spirit...is love, joy, peace" (Gal 5:22).

General audience of June 13, 1990

The Presentation in the Temple

According to the "Gospel of Jesus' childhood" presented by Luke, the Holy Spirit was revealed not only at the annunciation and during Mary's visitation to Elizabeth, as we saw in previous catecheses. He was also revealed during the presentation of the child Jesus in the Temple on the fortieth day after his birth (cf. Lk 2:22-38). That is the first of an entire series of events in the life of Christ in which the truth of the mystery of the Incarnation extends into that of the active presence of the Holy Spirit.

The evangelist writes that "when the days were completed for their purification according to the law of Moses, they took him up to Jerusalem to present him to the Lord" (Lk 2:22). The presentation of the firstborn in the Temple and the offering which accompanied it (cf. Lk 2:24) was a symbolic ransoming of the tiny Israelite, who thus returned to the life of his family and his people. It was prescribed (or at least recommended) by the Mosaic law in force during the old covenant (cf. Ex 13:2, 12-13, 15; Lev 12:6-8; Num 18:15). Pious Israelites practiced that ancient rite.

According to Luke, the rite performed by Jesus' parents in observance of the law was an occasion for a new intervention by the Holy Spirit, who gave the event messianic significance, introducing into it the mystery of Christ the Redeemer. The chosen instrument for this new revelation was a holy old man, of whom Luke writes: "Now there was a man in Jerusalem whose name was Simeon. This man was righteous and devout, awaiting the consolation of Israel, and the Holy Spirit was upon him" (Lk 2:25). Therefore, this took place in the holy city and in the temple toward which the entire history of Israel gravitated and in which the hopes based on the ancient promises and prophecies came together.

That man who awaited the "consolation of Israel," that is, the Messiah, had been especially prepared by the Holy Spirit for the meeting with "the one who is to come." We read that "the Holy Spirit was upon him," that is, acted within him in a habitual fashion, and "had revealed to him that he would not see death before he had seen the Messiah of the Lord" (Lk 2:26).

According to Luke's text, that period of waiting for the Messiah, packed with desire, hope and the inner certainty that it would be granted him to see him with his own eyes, was an indication of the Spirit's activity which is inspiration, enlightenment and movement. The day when Mary and Joseph brought Jesus to the Temple Simeon went there also, "moved by the Spirit," as Luke says (Lk 2:27). The inspiration of the Holy Spirit not only foretold his meeting with the Messiah, and not only suggested to him that he make a visit to the temple, but it moved him and almost drove him. Once he had arrived at the Temple, that inspiration permitted him to recognize the one he was waiting for in the child Jesus, the son of Mary.

Luke writes that "when the parents brought in the child Jesus to perform the custom of the law in regard to him, he took him into his arms and blessed God" (Lk 2:27-28). At that point the evangelist places on Simeon's lips the canticle *Nunc Dimittis* which is known by all. The liturgy has us repeat it daily at compline when the sense of the passing of time is particularly felt. The very touching words of Simeon, who was already close to the moment of "going in peace," create an opening for the ever-new hope for salvation which finds its fulfillment in Christ: "My eyes have seen your salvation, which you have prepared in the sight of all peoples, a light of revelation to the Gentiles and glory for your people Israel" (Lk 2:30-32). It was an advance proclamation of universal evangelization, heralding the salvation which comes from Jerusalem, from Israel, but by the power of the Messiah-Savior who is awaited by his people and by all peoples.

The Holy Spirit working in Simeon was also present and carried out his work in those who, like that holy old man, stayed close to God and believed in his promises at all times. Luke offers us another example of this reality, of this mystery. That example is the prophetess Anna who, having remained a widow since her youth, "never left the Temple, but worshipped night and day with fasting and prayer" (Lk 2:37). Therefore she was a woman consecrated to God and, in the light of God's Spirit, especially capable of grasping God's plan and interpreting God's commands. In this sense she was a "prophetess" (cf. Ex 15:20; Jgs 4:4; 2 Kgs 22:14). Luke does not speak explicitly of the Holy Spirit's action within her. Yet still he associates her with Simeon, both as regards their praise of God and their speaking about Jesus: "And coming forward at that very time, she gave thanks to God and spoke about the child to all who were awaiting the redemption of Jerusalem" (Lk 2:38). Like Simeon she too without a doubt was moved by the Holy Spirit toward her meeting with Jesus.

The prophetic words of Simeon (and of Anna) not only announced the Savior's coming into the world and his presence in Israel's midst, but also his redemptive sacrifice. This second part of the prophecy was directed precisely to Mary: "He is destined for the rise and fall of many in Israel, and to be a sign that will be contradicted (and you yourself a sword will pierce) so that the thoughts of many hearts may be revealed" (Lk 2:34-35).

One cannot fail to see the Spirit as the inspirer of this prophecy of Christ's passion, through which he will bring about salvation. Simeon also spoke of the future sufferings of Christ in directing his thoughts to the heart of Mary, who is associated with her Son in bearing the contradictions of Israel and of the whole world. Simeon did not mention the sacrifice of the cross by name, but transferred the prophecy into the heart of Mary, who will be "pierced with a sword" as co-sharer in the sufferings of her Son.

The inspired words of Simeon take on even more importance if they are considered in the global context of the "Gospel of Jesus' childhood" described by Luke. They fall within that whole period of life which comes under the special action of the Holy Spirit. Thus the evangelist's observation is more understandable when he refers to the astonishment of Mary and Joseph at those events and words: "The child's father and mother were amazed at what was said about him" (Lk 2:33).

The one who mentions those events and words is the same Luke who, as author of the Acts of the Apostles, describes the Pentecost event: the descent of the Holy Spirit on the Apostles and the disciples gathered together in the Cenacle with Mary after the Lord's ascension into heaven, as Jesus himself had promised. The reading of the "Gospel of Jesus' childhood" already shows that the evangelist was especially sensitive to the presence and action of the Holy Spirit in all aspects of the mystery of the Incarnation, from the first to the final moment of Christ's life.

General audience of June 20, 1990

The Spirit and the Child Jesus

Luke concludes "the Gospel of Jesus' infancy" with two texts which include the whole range of Jesus' childhood and youth. Between these two texts is the account of the episode of the losing and finding of Jesus in the Temple during the Holy Family's pilgrimage. Neither of these passages explicitly mentions the Holy Spirit. But anyone who followed the evangelist's narrative of the infancy events and continues to read the next chapter concerning John the Baptist's preaching and the baptism of Jesus in the Jordan, where the unseen protagonist is the Holy Spirit (cf. Lk 3:16, 22), perceives the continuity of Luke's idea and narrative. It includes Jesus' childhood years within the action of the Holy Spirit. Those years were lived in the hidden mystery of Nazareth. The theology of grace and of the gifts of the Holy Spirit helps us to understand the depths of this mystery which will always constitute the most intimate dimension of Jesus' humanity.

After having informed us that, having fulfilled the ritual of the presentation in the Temple, "they returned to Galilee, to their own town of Nazareth," the evangelist adds: "The child grew and became strong, filled with wisdom; and the favor of God was upon him" (Lk 2:40). And again, at the end of the account of the pilgrimage to the Temple and the return to Nazareth, he notes: "And Jesus advanced in wisdom and favor before God and man" (Lk 2:52). From these texts we see that there was a real human development in Jesus, eternal Word of the Father who assumed human nature through his conception and birth of Mary. Infancy, childhood, adolescence and youth are the periods of his physical growth ("in age"), as is true of all those "born of woman," among whom he is rightly numbered, as St. Paul remarks (cf. Gal 4:4).

According to Luke's text, there was also a spiritual growth in Jesus. As a doctor who was attuned to the whole person, Luke took pains to note the total reality of the human facts, including the development of the child, in Jesus' case as well as in that of John the Baptist. Luke wrote about John: "the child grew and became strong in spirit" (Lk 1:80). He more specifically says of Jesus that "the child grew and became strong, filled with wisdom"; "he advanced in wisdom...and favor before God and man"; and again, "the favor of God was upon him" (Lk 2:40, 52).

In the evangelist's terminology, this "being upon" a person chosen by God for a mission is attributed to the Holy Spirit, as in the case of Mary (cf. Lk 1:35) and Simeon (cf. Lk 2:26). This evokes the transcendence, lordship and the intimate action of the one we proclaim as *Dominum et vivificantem* (the Lord and giver of life). The grace which, again according to Luke, was "upon" Jesus and in which he "grew," seems to indicate the mysterious presence and action of the Holy Spirit in which, according to the Baptist's proclamation reported by the four Gospels, Jesus would be baptized (cf. Mt 3:11; Mk 1:8; Lk 3:16; Jn 1:33).

The patristic and theological tradition helps us to interpret and explain Luke's text about Jesus' growth "in wisdom and favor" in relation to the Holy Spirit. St. Thomas, speaking about grace, repeatedly calls it *gratia Spiritus Sancti* (cf.

Summa Theol., I-II, q. 106, a. 1), a free gift which expresses and concretizes God's favor toward the creature eternally loved by the Father (cf. I, q. 37, a. 2; q. 110, a. 1). Speaking of the cause of grace, he expressly says that "the principal cause is the Holy Spirit" (I-II, q. 112, a. 1, ad 1, 2).

It is a question of justifying and sanctifying grace which reinstates the person in God's friendship, in the kingdom of heaven (cf. I-II, q. 111, a. 1). "It is according to this grace that we understand the Holy Spirit's mission and his indwelling in the human person" (I, q. 43, a. 3). The Holy Spirit instilled the fullness of grace in Christ, for the personal union of the human nature with the Word of God, for the extreme nobility of his soul and for his sanctifying and salvific mission for the whole human race. St. Thomas affirms this on the basis of Isaiah's messianic text: "The Spirit of the Lord will rest upon him" (Is 11:2): "The Spirit which is in the person by means of habitual (or sanctifying) grace" (III, q. 7, a. 1, *sed contra*); and on the basis of the other text from John: "And we saw his glory, the glory as of the Father's only Son, full of grace and truth" (Jn 1:14) (III, q. 7, aa. 9-10). However, the fullness of grace in Jesus was in proportion to his age; there was always fullness, but a fullness which increased as he grew in age.

The same can be said of the wisdom which Christ had from the beginning in the fullness proper to the period of childhood. As he advanced in age, this fullness grew in him to a proportionate degree. It was not merely a matter of human knowledge and wisdom about divine things, which God infused into Christ through the communication of the Word subsisting in his humanity. Also, and most of all, we are dealing with wisdom as a gift of the Holy Spirit: the greatest of gifts, which is "the perfection of the faculties of the soul, in order to dispose them to the movement of the Holy Spirit. Now, we know very well from the Gospel that Christ's soul was moved most perfectly by the Holy Spirit. Luke tells us that

'Jesus, filled with the Holy Spirit, returned from the Jordan and was led by the Spirit into the desert' (Lk 4:1). Therefore, the gifts were in Christ in a most exalted manner" (III, q. 7, a. 5). Wisdom had primacy among these gifts.

We would like to continue talking about the marvelous chapters of St. Thomas, as well as of other theologians who studied the sublime spiritual greatness of Jesus' soul, where the Holy Spirit dwelt and worked in a perfect manner from infancy and throughout the entire time of his development. Here we can only indicate the wonderful ideal of holiness which Jesus offers everyone in his own concrete life, even children and young people. They are called to "grow in wisdom and favor before God and man," as Luke writes about the child from Nazareth. The same evangelist will later write in the Acts of the Apostles concerning the primitive Church which "was...built up and walked in the fear of the Lord, and with the consolation of the Holy Spirit" (Acts 9:31). It is a fascinating comparison, not only a linguistic repetition, but a conceptual one as well, of the mystery of grace which Luke saw present both in Christ and in the Church as a continuation of the life and mission of the Incarnate Word in history. The many children whom history and hagiography present to us as especially enlightened and moved by holy gifts are sharers and have leading roles in the Church's growth under the inspiration of the Holy Spirit. In our time also the Church is happy to salute them and present them as particularly shining images of the young Jesus, filled with the Holy Spirit.

General audience of June 27, 1990

The Spirit Helps Mary Understand

An example of the wisdom and grace of the teenage Jesus is found in the episode of Jesus' debate with the doctors in the Temple. Luke inserts this between two texts on Jesus' growth "before God and the people." The Holy Spirit is not mentioned by name in this passage either, but his activity seems to shine through what occurred during the event. The evangelist says that "all who heard him were astounded at his understanding and answers" (Lk 2:47). They were astonished by a form of wisdom which is perceived as coming from on high (cf. Jgs 3, 15, 17; Jn 3:34), that is, from the Holy Spirit.

After having sought him for three days, his parents found Jesus in the Temple in the midst of the doctors. The question they asked him is also significant. Mary complained affectionately to him: "Son, why have you done this to us? Your father and I have been looking for you with great anxiety." Jesus answered with another serene question: "Why were you looking for me? Did you not know that I must be in my Father's house?" (Lk 2:48-49). In that "did you not know" one can perhaps see a reference to what Simeon had foretold to Mary during the presentation of the child Jesus in the Temple. It explains that preview of the future separation, of that first blow of the sword to the mother's heart. It can be said that the words of the holy old man Simeon, inspired by the Holy Spirit, echoed once again at the moment among that group gathered in the Temple, the place where they had been pronounced twelve years earlier.

But Jesus' response also manifested his awareness that he was "the Son of God" (cf. Lk 1:35) and thus his duty to be "in his Father's house," the Temple, to "take care of his Father's business" (according to another possible translation of the Gospel phrase). Thus Jesus publicly declared his Messiahship and his divine identity perhaps for the first time. That happened by strength of the knowledge and wisdom which, under the Holy Spirit's influence, was poured out in his soul, united to the Word of God. At that moment he spoke as one "filled with the Holy Spirit."

Luke calls attention to the fact that Mary and Joseph "did not understand what he said to them" (Lk 2:50). Their astonishment at what they had seen and felt were part of that condition of "being in the dark" in which his parents remained. But we must take into account even more that they, Mary included, were standing before the mystery of the Incarnation and the redemption. Although they were involved in it, that did not mean that they understood it. They too were within the light and the shadow of faith. Mary was the first on faith's pilgrimage (cf. *Redemptoris Mater*, nn. 12-19). She was the most enlightened, but also the one most subject to the test of accepting the mystery. It was her task to remain faithful to the divine plan which she adored and meditated on in the silence of her heart. Luke adds: "His mother kept all these things in her heart" (Lk 2:18-19).

Here we hear the echo of Mary's words uttered in confidence. We can call them her "revelations" to Luke and to the early Church from which we receive the "Gospel of Jesus' infancy and childhood." Mary had kept it in her memory and sought to understand, but above all she believed and meditated on it in her heart. For Mary, sharing in the mystery did not consist only in accepting it and passively holding on to it. She exerted a personal effort: "She meditated," a word which in the original Greek *(symballein)* literally means to put together, to compare. Mary tried to make connections between the events and the words in order to grasp their meaning as well as she could.

These meditations, this interior study, took place under the influence of the Holy Spirit. Mary was the first to benefit from the light which one day her Jesus would promise to the disciples: "The Advocate, the Holy Spirit whom the Father will send in my name will teach you everything and remind you of all I have taught you" (Jn 14:26). The Holy Spirit who makes the Church and believers understand the meaning and the worth of Christ's words was already working in Mary who as mother of the Word Incarnate was the *Sedes Sapientiae,* the Spouse of the Holy Spirit, the bearer and the first mediatrix of the Gospel concerning Jesus' origins.

Even during the successive years in Nazareth, Mary stored in her heart all that regarded the person and destiny of her son and reflected on it silently. Perhaps she could not confide in anyone. Perhaps only at some particular moment was it granted her to grasp the meaning of certain words, of certain glances given by her son. But the Holy Spirit never stopped reminding her in the intimate depths of her soul of the things she saw and experienced. Mary's memory was enlightened by the light which came from above. That light is at the origin of Luke's narrative, which seems to want to help us understand by insisting on the fact that Mary kept these things and meditated on them. Under the influence of the Holy Spirit's action, she was able to discover the higher meaning of the words and the events, through a reflection which she engaged in, in order to "put everything together."

The Spirit Helps Mary Understand

Thus Mary appears to us to be the model of those who like the good seed (cf. Mt 13:23), allow themselves to be led by the Holy Spirit. They accept and keep in their hearts the words of revelation, making every effort to understand them as much as possible in order to penetrate the depths of Christ's mystery.

General audience of July 4, 1990

The Spirit Working at Jesus' Baptism

In the life of Jesus as Messiah, that is, the one who is consecrated by the Holy Spirit's anointing (cf. Lk 4:18), there are key moments when the person of the Holy Spirit is shown to be intimately united to Christ's humanity and mission. We have seen that the first of these moments was the Incarnation. It occurred through the conception and birth of Jesus from the Virgin Mary by the power of the Holy Spirit: "*Conceptus de Spiritu Sancto, natus ex Maria Virgine,*" as the creed professes.

Another moment when the presence and action of the Holy Spirit took on special prominence was at Jesus' baptism in the Jordan. We will look at that in today's catechesis.

All the evangelists have passed on that event to us (Mt 3:13-17; Mk 1:9-11; Lk 3:21-22; Jn 1:29-34). Let us read Mark's text: "It happened in those days that Jesus came from Nazareth of Galilee and was baptized in the Jordan by John. On coming up out of the water, he saw the heavens being torn open and the Spirit, like a dove, descending upon him" (Mk 1:9-10). Jesus had come to the Jordan from Nazareth where he had spent his "hidden" years (we shall return again to that theme in an upcoming catechesis). Before his arrival, he had been heralded by John, who had been exhorting people to a "baptism of repentance." He preached thus: "one mightier than I is coming after me. I am not worthy to stoop and loosen the thongs of his sandals. I have baptized you with water; he will baptize you with the Holy Spirit" (Mk 1:7-8).

Here we are already on the threshold of the messianic era. With John's preaching the long preparatory period ended. It had taken place through the whole of the old covenant, and one could say through the whole of human history, narrated by the Sacred Scriptures. John sensed the greatness of that decisive moment, which he interpreted as the beginning of a new creation. He discovered in it the presence of the Spirit which had hovered over the first creation (cf. Jn 1:32; Gen 1:2). He knew that he was and professed himself to be only the herald, the precursor and minister of him who would come to "baptize with the Holy Spirit."

On his part, Jesus prepared himself by prayer for that moment of great importance in salvation history. In it the Holy Spirit, proceeding from the Father and the Son in the trinitarian mystery, was to manifest himself, though under representational signs, as present in Christ's humanity as the principle of divine life. We read in Luke: "While Jesus was praying, heaven was opened and the Holy Spirit descended upon him in bodily form like a dove" (Lk 3:21-22). That same evangelist will narrate later that one day Jesus, teaching those following him along the byways of Palestine how to pray, said that "the Father in heaven will give the Holy Spirit to those who ask him" (Lk 11:13). He himself asked for this greatest of gifts in order to carry out his own messianic mission. During the baptism in the Jordan he received an especially visible manifestation of it. It marked the messianic "investiture" of Jesus of Nazareth in the presence of John and his hearers. The Baptist bore witness to him "before Israel as the Messiah, that is, the one 'anointed' with the Holy Spirit" *(DViv* 19).

The Father heard the prayer of Jesus, who in his divine Person was the eternal Son of God, yet acting and praying in his human nature. He himself one day had told the Father: "I know that you always hear me" (Jn 11:42). This awareness resonated especially within him at the moment of the baptism, which was the public start of his redemptive mission, as John had understood and proclaimed. He introduced him who had come to "baptize in the Holy Spirit" (Mt 3:11) as the "lamb of God who takes away the sin of the world" (Jn 1:29).

Luke tells us that during Jesus' baptism in the Jordan "heaven opened" (Lk 3:21). Once the prophet Isaiah had invoked God saying: "O that you would rend the heavens and come down!" (Is 63:19). Here at the moment of the baptism, God seemed to have responded to this cry and heard this prayer. That opening of heaven is linked with the descent of the Holy Spirit in the form of a dove upon Christ. It was a visible sign that the prophet's prayer was heard and that his prophecy was fulfilled. That sign was accompanied by a voice from heaven: "And a voice came from the heavens: 'You are my beloved Son; with you I am well pleased'" (Mk 1:11; Lk 3:22). Therefore the sign entered the level of the sight (the dove) and the hearing (the voice) of the privileged beneficiaries of that extraordinary supernatural experience. The manifestation of the Father's eternal pleasure in the Son takes form above all in the human soul of Christ, but also to those present at the Jordan. Thus in the baptism at the Jordan a theophany occurred. Its trinitarian character is highlighted even more than in the narrative of the annunciation. The "opening of heaven" signifies at that moment a particular initiative of communication by the Father and the Holy Spirit with earth through the religious and almost ritualistic inauguration of the messianic mission of the Incarnate Word.

In John's text, what occurred during Jesus' baptism is described by the Baptist himself: "I saw the Spirit come down like a dove from the sky and remain upon him. I did not know him, but the one who sent me to baptize with water told me, 'on whomever you see the Spirit come down and remain, he is the one who will baptize with the Holy Spirit.' Now I have seen and testified that he is the Son of God" (Jn 1:32-34). That means that, according to the evangelist, the Baptist shared that experience of the trinitarian theophany and understood (at least partially, by messianic faith) the significance of those words which the Father had pronounced: "You are my beloved Son; with you I am well pleased." Furthermore, among the other evangelists as well, it is significant that the word "Son" is used instead of the term "servant," found in the first song of Isaiah regarding the Lord's Servant: "Here is my servant whom I uphold, my chosen one with whom I am pleased, upon whom I have put my spirit" (Is 42:1).

In their God-inspired faith, and in that of the early Christian community, the servant was identified with the Son of God (cf. Mt 12:18; 16:16) and the Spirit given him was recognized in his divine personhood as the Holy Spirit. Jesus on the eve of his passion said to the apostles that that very Spirit who descended on him during his baptism would work with him in carrying out the redemption: "He [the Spirit of truth] will glorify me, because he will take from what is mine and declare it to you" (Jn 16:14).

A text of St. Irenaeus of Lyons is interesting in this regard. In commenting on the baptism in the Jordan, he states: "The Holy Spirit had promised through the prophets that in the last days he would be poured out upon his servants and handmaids so that they might prophesy. For that reason he descended upon the Son of God who was made son of man. He became accustomed along with him to dwell among the human race, to 'rest' in the midst of men and women and to reside among those who were created by God, bringing about within them the Father's will and renewing them in a way that transforms them from the 'old man' into the 'newness' of Christ" *(Adv. Haer.*, III, 17, 1). This text confirms that from the earliest centuries the Church has been aware of the association between Christ and the Holy Spirit in bringing about the new creation.

The symbol of the dove which appeared during the baptism at the Jordan was a sign of the Holy Spirit. In baptismal symbolism, the dove is linked to the water. According to certain Fathers of the Church it recalls what happened at the end of the flood, interpreting this too as a type of Christian baptism. We read in Genesis that when Noah "sent the dove out from the ark and the dove returned...there in its bill was a plucked-off olive leaf. So Noah knew that the waters had lessened on the earth" (Gen 8:10-11). The symbol of the dove indicates forgiveness of sins, reconciliation with God and renewal of the covenant. That is what finds its complete fulfillment in the messianic era, with the work of Christ the Redeemer and of the Holy Spirit.

General audience of July 11, 1990

The Spirit Led Jesus into the Desert

Another element belongs to the beginning of the messianic mission of Jesus, a very interesting and evocative one for us. The evangelists relate it and make it depend on the action of the Holy Spirit. That element is the desert experience. We read in Mark's Gospel: "At once (after the baptism) the Spirit drove him out into the desert" (Mk 1:12). In addition Matthew (4:1) and Luke (4:1) say that Jesus "was led by the Spirit into the desert." These texts offer us various indications which lead us to further study of the mystery of the intimate union of Jesus the Messiah with the Holy Spirit, from the beginning of the work of redemption.

First of all, we should make an observation about linguistics. The verbs which the evangelists used ("was led" in Matthew and Luke, "drove" in Mark) express an especially dynamic initiative on the Holy Spirit's part. That initiative is incorporated fully into the logic of Jesus' spiritual life and his psychology. From John he received a "baptism of repentance." Therefore he felt the need for a period of reflection and of austerity, even though he personally had no need for penance since he was "full of grace" and "holy" from the moment of his conception (cf. Lk 1:35; Jn 1:14), in preparation for his messianic mission.

His mission also demanded that he live in the midst of sinful people whom he was sent to evangelize and save (cf. St. Thomas, *Summa Theol.*, III, q. 40, a. 1), in a struggle with demonic powers. Out of this the occasion arises for this pause in the desert "to be tempted by the devil." Therefore Jesus complied with the inner impulse and went where the Spirit willed.

Besides being a place to meet God, the desert is also a place of temptation and spiritual struggle. During their long desert pilgrimage the people of Israel had experienced many temptations and also yielded to them (cf. Ex 32:1-6; Num 14:1-4; 21:4-5; 25:1-3; Ps 78:17; 1 Cor 10:7-10). Jesus went into the desert almost as a way of linking himself with his people's historical experience. But unlike the behavior of Israel, at the beginning of his messianic activity Jesus was above all docile to the action of the Holy Spirit. The Spirit demanded of him a definitive interior preparation for the carrying out of his mission, with the help of God's Word and by prayer.

In the spirit of biblical tradition and in line with Israelite psychology, the number forty could easily be connected with other ancient events, full of meaning for salvation history: the forty days of the flood (cf. Gen 7:4, 17); the forty days that Moses stayed on the mountain (cf. Ex 24:18); and the forty days of Elijah's journey during which he was refreshed by the miraculous bread which gave him new strength (cf. 1 Kgs 19:8). According to the evangelists, by the prompting of the Holy Spirit, Jesus adapted both to this stay in the desert and to the tradition and the almost sacred number (cf. Mt 4:1; Lk 4:1). He did the same thing during the period in which he appeared to the apostles after the resurrection and ascension into heaven (cf. Acts 1:3).

Jesus, therefore, was led into the desert so that he could

face the temptations of Satan and be able to have a freer and more intimate contact with the Father. Here we must also keep in mind that in the Gospels the desert is presented many times as the place where Satan dwells. One need only recall the passage in Luke on the "unclean spirit" which "when it goes out of someone, roams through arid regions searching for rest..." (Lk 11:24); and the other passage about the Gerasene demoniac who was "driven by the demon into deserted places" (Lk 8:29).

In the case of the temptations of Jesus, the impulse to go into the desert came from the Holy Spirit and signified above all the beginning of a manifestation—one can even say of a new awareness—of the struggle which he will have to wage to the bitter end against Satan, sin's craftsman. Overcoming his temptations, he thus showed his saving power over sin and the advent of God's kingdom, as he would one day say: "If I drive out demons by the power of God, then the kingdom of God has come upon you" (Mt 12:28). The Spirit was revealed both in Christ's power over evil and Satan, and in this coming of God's kingdom through Christ's actions.

It is well to observe that in the temptations which Jesus underwent and overcame during the desert experience, one notes Satan's opposition to the coming of God's kingdom into the human world. This opposition is directly or indirectly expressed in the texts of the evangelists. The answers which Jesus gave to the tempter unmask the fundamental intentions of the "father of lies" (Jn 8:44) who tried in perverse fashion to use the words of Scripture to reach his goals. But Jesus refuted him on the basis of the same Word of God, properly applied.

The evangelists' narrative perhaps in some way echoes and establishes a parallel between the analogous temptations of the people of Israel in their forty year pilgrimage in the desert (the search for nourishment: cf. Dt 8:3; Ex 16; the pretext of divine protection for self-satisfaction: cf. Dt 6:13;

Ex 32:1-6) and with various moments in Moses' life. But the episode forms part of the history of Jesus, specifically, one could say, in its biographical and theological logic. Though exempt from sin, Jesus experienced the external seductions of evil (cf. Mt 16:23). It was well that he was tempted in order to become the new Adam, our head, our merciful Redeemer (cf. Mt 26:36-46; Heb 2:10, 17-18; 4:15; 5:2, 7-9).

At the root of all the temptations was the vision of a glorious political messiahship, which was widespread and had penetrated the soul of the people of Israel. The devil sought to lead Jesus to accept this false perspective, because the devil is the adversary of God's plan, of God's law and of God's economy of salvation. He is therefore the enemy of Christ, as is seen in the Gospel and other New Testament writings (cf. Mt 13:39; Jn 8:44; 13:2; Acts 10:38; Eph 6:11; 1 Jn 3:8, etc.). If Christ too were to fall, the empire of Satan who boasts that he is the ruler of the world (cf. Lk 4:5-6) would have the final victory in history. So that moment of struggle in the desert was decisive.

Jesus knew that he was sent by the Father to establish God's kingdom in the world of humanity. On the one hand, for this purpose he accepted being tempted in order to take his proper place among sinners. He had already done this at the Jordan, in order to serve as a model for all (cf. St. Augustine, *De Trinitate* 4:13). But on the other hand, by virtue of the Holy Spirit's anointing, he reached into the very roots of sin and defeated the one who is the "father of lies" (Jn 8:44). Thus he willingly went to face the temptations at the start of his ministry, complying with the Holy Spirit's impulse (cf. St. Augustine, *De Trinitate* 13:13).

One day when his mission was completed he would proclaim: "Now is the time of judgment on this world; now the ruler of this world will be driven out" (Jn 12:31). On the eve of his passion he would repeat once again: "The ruler of the world is coming; but he has no power over me" (Jn 14:30); rather, "the ruler of this world has been condemned" (Jn 16:33). The struggle against the "father of lies" who is the "ruler of this world," begun in the desert, will reach its climax on Golgotha. The victory will come about through the cross of the Redeemer.

Therefore we are called to the full value of the desert as a place for a special experience of God, as it was for Moses (cf. Ex 24:18), and for Elijah (cf. 1 Kgs 19:8), and as it was above all for Jesus. Led by the Holy Spirit, he was willing to go through the same experience. It was one of contact with God the Father (cf. Hos 2:16) in contrast to the powers which oppose God. His experience is exemplary, and can serve as a lesson for us on the need for penance—not for Jesus who was without sin, but for all of us. Jesus himself one day would admonish his disciples about the need for prayer and fasting in order to cast out "unclean spirits" (cf. Mk 9:29). Amidst the tension of his solitary prayer in Gethsemane, he counseled the apostles who were there: "Watch and pray that you may not enter into temptation; the spirit is willing, but the flesh is weak" (Mk 14:38). By conforming ourselves to the victorious Christ of the desert, we will discover that we too have a divine Comforter: the Holy Spirit, the Paraclete. Jesus Christ promised that he would "take from what is mine" and give it to you (cf. Jn 16:14). He will take some of Christ's victory over sin and Satan, sin's first craftsman, to associate with it anyone who is tempted—he who led the Messiah into the desert not only "to be tempted," but also so that he might give the initial proof of his victorious power over the devil and his reign.

General audience of July 21, 1990

The Spirit of Prayer
Fueled the Master's Active Life

After the desert experience, Jesus began his messianic activity among the people. Luke writes that "Numerous crowds came to him to listen to him and be healed" (Lk 5:15). This activity consisted in evangelizing and teaching about the kingdom of God, choosing and training his apostles, healing the sick, and preaching in synagogues while moving from city to city (cf. Lk 4:43-44). It was an intense activity which was accompanied by "signs and wonders" (cf. Acts 2:22). These flowed in their totality out of the anointing in the Holy Spirit which the evangelist speaks of from the beginning of the public life. As the fullness of the gift the presence of the Holy Spirit is constant, although it is mentioned only at some points.

Since he had to evangelize people in order to dispose them for redemption, Jesus was sent to live among them, and not in a desert or other lonely place. His place was in the midst of the people, as Remigius of Auxerre (†908) noted, as quoted by St. Thomas. But the Angelic Doctor himself observes: "Christ's return to normal life after his fasting in the desert did not happen without good reason. That is what suits the life of one who is committed to communicating to others the results of his own contemplation, a commitment which Christ took on: that is, a commitment to devote himself first to prayer and then to go down into the public arena of action by living in the midst of others" *(Summa Theol.,* III, q. 40, a. 2, ad 2).

Though immersed in the crowd, Jesus remained deeply dedicated to prayer. Luke informs us that he "would withdraw to deserted places to pray" (Lk 5:16). He lived by translating the condition of permanent dialogue with the Father in which he lived into eminently religious acts. Luke states that he sometimes spent "the night in communion with God" (cf. Lk 6:12). The evangelists highlight some of these events: the prayer preceding the transfiguration on Tabor (cf. Lk 9:29) and during the agony in Gethsemane where his filial closeness and union to the Father in the Holy Spirit reach a sublime expression in the words: "Abba, Father! All things are possible to you, take this cup from me! But not what I will but what you will" (Mk 14:36).

There is one case in which the evangelist attributes Jesus' prayer explicitly to the Holy Spirit. This reveals the habitual state of contemplation from which that prayer sprang. It happened that during the journey to Jerusalem Jesus spoke with the disciples from whose number he chose seventy-two. After having properly instructed them, he sent them out to evangelize the people in places he was about to visit (cf. Lk 10:1). Upon their return from the mission, the seventy-two told Jesus what they had done, including the casting out of demons in his name (cf. Lk 10:17). After having told them that he had seen "Satan falling like fire from heaven" (Lk 10:18), Jesus exulted in the Holy Spirit and said: "I give you thanks, Father, Lord of heaven and earth, that you have hidden these things from the wise and prudent and have revealed them to the merest children. Yes, Father, such has been your gracious will" (Lk 10:21).

I observed in the Encyclical *Dominum et Vivificantem* that "Jesus rejoices at the fatherhood of God: he rejoices because it has been given him to reveal this fatherhood; he rejoices, finally, as at a particular outpouring of this divine fatherhood on the 'little ones.' And the evangelist describes all this as 'rejoicing in the Holy Spirit....' That which during the theophany at the Jordan came so to speak 'from outside,' from on high, here comes 'from within,' that is to say, from the depths of who Jesus is. It is another revelation of the Father and the Son, united in the Holy Spirit. Jesus speaks only of the fatherhood of God and of his own sonship—he does not speak directly of the Spirit who is Love and thereby the union of the Father and the Son. Nonetheless, what he says of the Father and of himself, the Son, flows from that fullness of the Spirit which is in him, which fills his heart, pervades his own 'I,' inspires and enlivens his action from the depths. Hence that 'rejoicing in the Holy Spirit'" (nn. 20-21).

Added to the text of John which gives the farewell discourse in the upper room (cf. Jn 13:31; 14:31) this Lucan text is especially significant about the revelation of the Holy Spirit in the messianic mission of Christ.

In the synagogue in Nazareth Jesus had applied to himself the Isaian prophecy which began with these words: "The Spirit of the Lord is upon me" (Lk 4:18). That "being upon him" of the spirit extended to all that he "did and taught" (Acts 1:1). As Luke writes, Jesus "returned (from the desert) to Galilee in the power of the Spirit, and news of him spread throughout the whole region. He taught in their synagogues and was praised by all" (Lk 4:14-15); that and wonderment: "All spoke highly of him and were amazed at the gracious words that came from his mouth" (Lk 4:22). The same thing is said of the miracles and of the singular power of attraction of his personality. The entire crowd which "had come out (from all over) to hear him and to be healed of their sicknesses...sought to touch him, because power went out from him which healed all" (Lk 6:17-19). How can we not recognize this also as a manifestation of the power of the Holy Spirit, given in fullness to him as man, to empower his words and actions?

Jesus taught others to ask the Father in prayer for the gift of the Spirit, trusting that what is asked for will be granted: "If you...know how to give good things to your children, how much more will your Father in heaven give the Holy Spirit to those who ask him" (Lk 11:13). When he preached to his disciples about the coming persecution, to be accompanied by imprisonment and interrogations, he added: "Do not worry beforehand about what you are to say. But say whatever will be given you in that hour. For it will not be you who are speaking but the Holy Spirit" (Mk 13:11). "The Holy Spirit will teach you at that moment what you are to say" (Lk 12:12).

The Synoptic Gospels report another statement of Jesus in his instructions to the disciples which is bound to make an impression. It is in regard to "blasphemy against the Holy Spirit." He said: "Everyone who speaks a word against the Son of Man will be forgiven, but the one who blasphemes against the Holy Spirit will not be forgiven" (Lk 12:10; cf. Mt 12:32; Mk 3:29). These words create a vast theological and ethical problem greater than people think after having only superficially read the text. "The 'blasphemy' does not properly consist in offending against the Holy Spirit in words; it consists rather in the refusal to accept the salvation which God offers man through the Holy Spirit, working through the power of the cross.... If Jesus says that blasphemy against the Holy Spirit cannot be forgiven either in this world or in the next, it is because this 'nonforgiveness is linked as to its cause to 'nonrepentance,' in other words, to the radical refusal to be converted.... Blasphemy against the Holy Spirit, then, is the sin committed by the person who claims to have a 'right' to persist in evil—in any sin at all—and who thus rejects redemption. One closes oneself up in sin, thus making impossible one's conversion, and consequently the remission of sins" *(DViv* 46). It is the exact opposite of that state of docility and communion with the Father in which Jesus worked and prayed and which he taught and recommended to people as an inner attitude and as a principle for action.

The totality of Jesus Christ's preaching and action flowed out of his union with the Holy Spirit. It contained an immense richness of heart: "Learn of me, for I am meek and humble of heart and you will find rest for your souls" (Mt 11:29). But at the same time all the power of the truth about the kingdom of God is present, and there also the insistent invitation to open the heart, under the prompting of the Holy Spirit, in order to be admitted to the kingdom and not excluded from it.

All that reveals the power of the Holy Spirit and the Holy Spirit himself with his presence and his action as Paraclete, human comforter, confirmer of divine truths, and uprooter of the "prince of this world."

General audience of July 25, 1990

The Spirit at Work on Calvary

In the Encyclical *Dominum et Vivificantem* I wrote: "The Son of God Jesus Christ, as man, in the ardent prayer of his passion, enabled the Holy Spirit who had already penetrated the inmost depths of his humanity, to transform that humanity into a perfect sacrifice through the act of his death as the victim of love on the cross. He made this offering by himself. As the one priest, 'he offered himself without blemish to God' (Heb 9:14)" (n. 40). The sacrifice of the cross is the culmination of a life in which we have read the truth about the Holy Spirit, according to the Gospel texts, starting with the moment of the Incarnation. It has served as the theme of previous catecheses which centered on moments in the life and mission of Christ when the revelation of the Holy Spirit was particularly clear. Today's topic for catechesis is the event of the cross.

Let us concentrate on the last words pronounced by Jesus during his agony on Calvary. In Luke's text they read thus: "Father, into your hands I commend my spirit" (Lk 23:46). Even though every word except for the word "Father" comes from Psalm 31, they take on another meaning in the Gospel context. The Psalmist prayed to God to save him from death. Instead, using the very words of the Psalmist, Jesus on the cross accepted death, turning over his spirit (that is, "his life") to the Father. The Psalmist turned to God as to a liberator; Jesus offered (that is, handed over) his spirit to the Father with a view to the resurrection. Jesus entrusted the fullness of his own humanity to the Father. However, the divine "I" of the Son united to the Father and to the Holy Spirit subsists in his humanity. Still the presence of the Holy Spirit is not manifested in an explicit way in Luke's text as will happen in the Letter to the Hebrews (cf. 9:14).

Before moving on to this other text, we must consider the slightly different formulation of the dying Christ's words in John's Gospel. There we read: "When Jesus had taken the wine, he said, 'It is finished!' And bowing his head he handed over the spirit" (Jn 19:30). The evangelist does not highlight the "handing over" (or "commending") of the spirit to the Father. The full context of John's Gospel and especially of the pages devoted to Jesus' death on the cross seem rather to indicate that death marks the beginning of the sending of the Holy Spirit, as the gift handed over at Christ's leaving.

Still, here too, no explicit affirmation is made. But we cannot ignore the surprising connection which seems to exist between John's text and the interpretation of Christ's death which is found in the Letter to the Hebrews. Its author speaks of the ritual function of the bloody sacrifices of the old covenant which were used to purify the people of legal guilt. He compares them to the sacrifice of the cross, and ends by exclaiming: "How much more will the blood of Christ, who through the eternal Spirit offered himself up unblemished to God, cleanse our consciences from dead works to worship the living God" (Heb 9:14).

As I wrote in the Encyclical *Dominum et Vivificantem,* "In his humanity (Christ) was worthy to become this sacrifice, for he alone was 'without blemish.' But he offered it 'through the eternal Spirit,' which means that the Holy Spirit acted in a special way in this absolute self-giving of the Son of Man, in order to transform this suffering into redemptive love" (n. 40). The mystery of the association between the Messiah and the Holy Spirit in the messianic activity contained in Luke's account of Mary's annunciation, passes here into the section of the Letter to the Hebrews. It manifests the depths of that activity which enters into human consciences to purify them and renew them by means of divine grace—a far cry from the superficiality of ritual representations.

The Old Testament speaks several times of the "fire from heaven" which burnt the oblations presented by men (cf. Lev 9:24; 1 Kgs 18:38; 2 Chr 7:1). "The fire on the altar is to be kept burning; it must not go out. Every morning the priest shall put firewood on it. On this he shall lay out the holocaust and burn the fat of the peace offerings" (Lev 6:5). Now we know that the ancient holocausts prefigured the sacrifice of the cross, the perfect holocaust. "By analogy one can say that the Holy Spirit is the 'fire from heaven' which works in the depth of the mystery of the cross. Proceeding from the Father, he directs the Son's sacrifice toward the Father, bringing it into the divine reality of the trinitarian communion" *(DViv* 41).

Therefore we add that, reflected in the Trinitarian mystery, one sees the complete fulfillment of the announcement of John the Baptist at the Jordan: "He [the Christ] will baptize with the Holy Spirit and with fire" (Mt 3:11). While in the Old Testament the fire which the Baptist evoked symbolized God's sovereign intervention in an act of purifying consciences through the Holy Spirit (cf. Is 1:25; Zech 13:9; Mal 3:2-3; Sir 2:5), now the reality goes beyond types to the sacrifice of the cross which is the perfect "baptism with which Christ himself had to be baptized" (cf. Mk 10:38). During his life and earthly mission he directed himself with his whole strength toward this baptism, as he himself said: "I have come to light a fire on the earth. How I wish the blaze were ignited! I have a baptism to receive. What anguish I feel till it is over!" (Lk 12:49-50). The Holy Spirit is the saving "fire" which brings about that sacrifice.

In the Letter to the Hebrews we again read that Christ, "Son though he was, learned obedience from what he suffered" (5:8). And on entering the world he said to the Father: "Behold I come to do your will" (Heb 10:9). In the sacrifice of the cross this obedience of his is realized fully: "If sin caused suffering, now the pain of God in Christ crucified acquires through the Holy Spirit its full human expression.... But at the same time, from the depth of this suffering...the Spirit draws a new measure of the gift made to man and to creation from the beginning. In the depth of the mystery of the cross love is at work, that love which brings man back again to share in the life that is in God himself" *(DViv* 41).

Thus in humanity's relationships with God "we have a great high priest who is able to sympathize with our weakness because he has been tested in every way, yet without sin" (Heb 4:15). In this new mystery of Christ's priestly mediation before the Father, there is the decisive intervention of the eternal Spirit who is the fire of infinite love.

"The Holy Spirit descends as love and gift, in a certain sense, into the very heart of the sacrifice which is offered on the cross. Referring to the Biblical tradition we can say: he consumes this sacrifice by the fire of the love which unites the Son to the Father in the Trinitarian communion. And since the sacrifice of the cross is an act proper to Christ, in this sacrifice too he 'receives' the Holy Spirit. He receives the Spirit in such a way that he—and he alone with the Father—can give the Spirit to the apostles, to the Church, to humanity" *(DViv* 41).

Therefore it is proper to see in the sacrifice of the cross the conclusive moment of the Holy Spirit's revelation in

Christ's life. The Pentecost event and the entire effects which will flow from it into the world are rooted in this key moment. The same "eternal Spirit" working in the mystery of the cross will appear in the upper room in the form of "tongues of fire" on the heads of the apostles. This signified that he would gradually penetrate into the arteries of human history through the Church's apostolic service. We too are called to enter into the sphere of activity of this mysterious saving force which started with the cross and the upper room in order, in it and through it, to be drawn into the communion of the Trinity.

General audience of August 1, 1990

The Resurrection of the Body

The First Letter of Peter states: "Christ also suffered for sins once, the righteous for the sake of the unrighteous, that he might lead you to God. Put to death in the flesh, he was brought to life in the spirit" (1 Pet 3:18). The Apostle Paul also states the same truth in his introduction to the Letter to the Romans, where he introduces himself as the herald of the Gospel of God. He writes: "The Gospel is about his Son, descended from David according to the flesh, but established as Son of God in power according to the spirit of holiness through resurrection from the dead, Jesus Christ our Lord" (Rom 1:3-4). In this regard I wrote in the Encyclical *Dominum et Vivificantem*: "It can be said that the messianic 'raising up' of Christ in the Holy Spirit reaches its zenith in the resurrection, in which he reveals himself also as the Son of God, 'full of power'" (n. 24).

Scholars hold that this passage of the Letter to the Romans—as well as the passage from the Letter of Peter (1 Pet 3:18-4:6)—contains an earlier profession of faith which the two apostles took from the living resource of the earliest Christian community. Among the elements in this profession of faith is the statement that the Holy Spirit working in the resurrection is the "Spirit of holiness." Therefore we can say that Christ, who was Son of God from the moment of his conception in Mary's womb by the power of the Holy Spirit, is "constituted" as the source of life and holiness in the resurrection, "full of sanctifying power," by the action of the same Holy Spirit.

Thus the full meaning of the action which Jesus performed on the night of the resurrection, "the first day after the sabbath," is made clear. In appearing to the apostles he showed them his hands and side, breathed on them and said: "Receive the Holy Spirit" (Jn 20:22).

The First Letter of Paul to the Corinthians merits special attention in this regard. We saw earlier in the Christological catecheses that this letter contains the first historical record about the witnesses concerning Christ's resurrection, which in the Apostle's view already belonged to Church tradition: "For I handed on to you as of first importance what I also received: that Christ died for our sins in accordance with the Scriptures; that he was buried; that he was raised on the third day in accordance with the Scriptures; that he appeared to Cephas, then to the Twelve" (15:3-5). Then the Apostle lists various appearances of Christ which followed the resurrection, mentioning finally the one he himself received (cf. 15:4-11).

This is a very important text which documents not only the conviction of the first Christians about the resurrection of Jesus, but also the preaching of the apostles, the developing tradition, and the pneumatological and eschatological content of the faith of the early Church.

In his letter, the Apostle links Christ's resurrection with faith in the universal resurrection of the body and establishes a relationship between Christ and Adam in these terms: "The first man, Adam, became a living being, the last Adam a life-giving spirit" (15:45). Writing about Adam who became a "living spirit," Paul cites the text of Genesis, according to which Adam became a "living being" thanks to the "breath of life" which God "blew into his nostrils" (Gen 2:7). Paul then holds that Jesus Christ, as a risen man, goes beyond Adam. He possesses the fullness of the Holy Spirit, who in a new way must give man life so as to make him a spiritual being. If the new Adam became "a life-giving spirit," that does not mean that he identifies personally with the Holy Spirit who "gives [divine] life." Rather it means that, possessing as man the fullness of this Spirit, he gives the Spirit to the apostles, to the Church and to all humanity. The "Spirit gives life" through Jesus' death and resurrection, or through the sacrifice offered on the cross.

The Apostle's text is part of Paul's instruction on the destiny of the human body whose vital principle is the soul *(psyche* in Greek, *nefesh* in Hebrew: cf. Gen 2:7). It is a natural principle. The body seems to be abandoned by it at the moment of death, an event which poses the question of immortality as an existential problem prior even to being an object of philosophical reflection.

According to the Apostle, the resurrection of Christ responds to this question with the sureness of faith. The body of Christ, filled with the Holy Spirit in the resurrection, is the source of new life for risen bodies: "It is sown a natural body; it is raised a spiritual body" (1 Cor 15:44). The "natural" body (that is, animated by the *psyche)* is destined to disappear to yield place to the "spiritual body," animated by the *pneuma*, the Spirit. He is the principle of new life already present during mortal life (cf. Rom 1:9; 5:5), but which will reach his full effectiveness after death. Then he will be the author of the resurrection of the natural body in the completed reality of the spiritual body through union with the risen Christ (cf. Rom 1:4; 8:11), the heavenly man and the "life-giving Spirit" (1 Cor 15:45-49).

The coming resurrection of our bodies, therefore, is linked to their spiritualization in resemblance to Christ's body, enlivened by the Holy Spirit's power. This is the Apostle's answer to the question he himself asks: "How are the dead raised? With what kind of body will they come back?" (1 Cor 15:35). "You fool!" Paul exclaims. "What you sow is not brought to life unless it dies. What you sow is not the body that is to be, but a bare kernel of wheat, perhaps, or of some other kind; but God gives it a body as he chooses.... So also is the resurrection of the dead...it is sown a natural body; it is raised a spiritual body" (1 Cor 15:36-44).

According to the Apostle, life in Christ is at the same time life in the Holy Spirit: "But you are not in the flesh; on the contrary you are in the spirit, if only the Spirit of God dwells in you. Whoever does not have the Spirit of Christ does not belong [to Christ]" (Rom 8:9). True freedom is found in Christ and his Spirit, "because the law of the spirit of life in Jesus Christ has freed you from the law of sin and death" (Rom 8:2). Sanctification in Christ is at the same time sanctification in the Holy Spirit (cf., for example, 1 Cor 1:2; Rom 15:16). If Christ "intercedes for us" (Rom 8:34), then the Holy Spirit too "intercedes for us with inexpressible groanings.... He intercedes for the holy ones according to God's will" (Rom 8:26-27).

As is clear in these Pauline texts, the Holy Spirit who has acted in Christ's resurrection already infuses new life into the Christian within the eschatological perspective of the future resurrection. There is a continuity between Christ's resurrection, the new life of Christians freed from sin and made sharers in the paschal mystery, and the future reconstitution of the body-soul union in the resurrection of the dead. The author of all growth of new life in Christ is the Holy Spirit.

We can say that Christ's mission truly reaches its zenith in the paschal mystery. In it, the close connection between Christology and pneumatology opens up on the eschatological horizon before the eyes of believers and the research of theologians. But this perspective includes the ecclesiological level also; since "the Church...proclaims the one who gives...life: the life-giving Spirit; she proclaims the Spirit and co-operates with the Spirit in giving life. For, 'although your bodies are dead because of sin, your spirits are alive because of righteousness' (Rom 8:10), the righteousness accomplished by the crucified and risen Christ. And in the name of Christ's resurrection the Church serves the life that comes from God himself, in close union with and in humble service to the Spirit" *(DViv* 58).

At the heart of this service is the Eucharist. In this sacrament, Christ's redemptive gift continues and is renewed incessantly. It contains as well the life-giving power of the Holy Spirit. Therefore, the Eucharist is the sacrament in which the Spirit continues to work and to "reveal himself" as the vital human principle in time and eternity. The Spirit is the source of light for the mind and of strength for conduct, according to the words of Jesus in Capernaum: "It is the Spirit who gives life.... The words which I have spoken to you" (concerning the "bread which comes down from heaven") "are spirit and life" (Jn 6:63).

General audience of August 8, 1990

THE HOLY SPIRIT:
A DIVINE PERSON

The Revelation of the Person of the Spirit

Up to now we have devoted a series of reflections to the action of the Holy Spirit, considering it first of all in the light of the Old Testament and then in different times in Christ's life. Now we turn to examine the mystery of the Person of the Holy Spirit who lives in communion with the Father and the Son in the unity of the divine Trinity. We are in the loftiest phase of that which we have several times referred to as God's self-revelation: the manifestation of his own intimate essence and plan on the part of the God whom Jesus taught us to recognize and invoke as Father. This infinitely true and good God has always kept to a kind of transcendent pedagogy to teach us and draw us to himself. This also happened in the revelation of the Holy Spirit.

St. Gregory Nazianzen recalls this in a beautiful text which explains the main theme of God's progressive action in salvation history in relation to the mystery of the Trinity of the divine Persons in the unity of the divine substance. "In effect," says the great Father of the Church, "the Old Testament expressly told us about the Father, and less clearly, about the Son; the New Testament manifested the Son and suggested the divinity of the Holy Spirit. Now the Spirit dwells in us and manifests himself more clearly. It was not prudent to speak openly about the Son when the divinity of the Father was not yet confessed and to impose upon us even more—here I am speaking quite boldly—the Holy Spirit, before the Son's divinity was recognized" *(Orat. XXXI,* Theol. V, 26: PG 36, 161). Therefore, according to Nazianzen, it was difficult for people to accept the revelation of God as one in nature and three in person because it was greater than human intellectual concepts as they are generally understood. It is difficult, and has always remained so for many people, even those who are sincerely religious, as the history of Judaism and Islam shows us.

In the previous reflections we saw that in many ways and many places, beginning with the opening of the Book of Genesis (cf. Gen 1:2), the Old Testament speaks of the Spirit of God. This pedagogical progress has taken place in divine revelation. However, we always noted that we were dealing with pre-announcements and foretastes, as it were, of the Holy Spirit's activity in human history, and not yet with his Person, at least not directly or explicitly. In the vast range of the Old Testament one can speak of a discovery, a "taste," a progressive understanding of the Spirit's activity. However, it always remains in obscurity about the distinction of persons in the unity of God. Even the most ancient texts show that certain phenomena of the physical, psychological and spiritual world come from the Spirit of God. They speak of "God's breath" which gives life to the universe from the moment of creation, or of a superhuman force given to persons called to special tasks in guiding and defending the People of God, such as Samson's physical strength (cf. Jgs 14:6), Gideon's investiture (cf. Jgs 6:34) and Jephthah's victory in battle against the Ammonites (cf. Jgs 11:29). In other instances we find that the Spirit of God not only "invests" but also "seizes" the person (for example, Elijah: cf. 1 Kgs 18:12), effects prophetic transports and ecstasy, or gives the ability to interpret dreams (Joseph in Egypt: cf. Gen 41:38). In all these cases it is a matter of an action of an immediate and transitory nature—we could say a charismatic one—for the good of the people of God.

On the other hand, the same Old Testament gives us many instances of a constant action by the Spirit of God which, according to Biblical language, "rested upon" a person, as happened to Moses, Joshua, David, Elijah and Elisha. The prophets were especially the bearers of the Spirit of God. The connection between the prophetic word and God's Spirit was already affirmed in the story of Balaam (Num 24:2-3) and was emphasized in an episode from the First Book of Kings (1 Kgs 22:24). After the exile, Ezekiel showed that he was fully aware of the origin of his inspiration: "The Spirit of the Lord came upon me and said to me: 'Speak...'" (Ez 11:5). Zechariah recalls that God had spoken to his people "by his Spirit through the former prophets" (Zech 7:12).

In this period effects of a moral nature were also attributed most of all to the Spirit of God and his action (for example, in Psalms 51 and 143, and in the Book of Wisdom). We have referred to these passages and analyzed them in turn.

However, the most significant and important texts are those which the prophets dedicated to the Spirit of the Lord which would rest upon the Messiah, on the messianic community and its members. The texts of Isaiah's messianic prophecies are especially important. Here is the revelation that the Spirit of the Lord would first be upon the "shoot of Jesse," David's descendant and successor (Is 11:1-2), then upon the "servant of the Lord" (Is 42:1), who will be a "covenant of the people and light for the nations" (Is 42:6), and lastly upon the evangelizer of the nations (Is 61:1; cf. Lk 4:18).

According to the ancient prophecies, the Spirit of the Lord will also renew the spiritual face of the "remnant of Israel," of the messianic community which remains faithful to the divine call. We are told this not only by the passages from Isaiah (cf. 44:3; 59:21), but also in Ezekiel (cf. 36:27; 37:14), Joel (cf. 3:1-2) and Zechariah (cf. 12:10).

In such a way the Old Testament, with its abundant references to the action of the Spirit of God, prepared our understanding for what would be given in the New Testament's revelation concerning the Holy Spirit as a Person in his unity with the Father and the Son. All this developed along the line of the divine pedagogy which led people to the knowledge and recognition of the greatest of mysteries: the Trinity, the Incarnation of the Word, the coming of the Holy Spirit. In the Old Testament everything was concentrated on the truth of monotheism entrusted to Israel. It always had to be defended and consolidated in the face of the temptations to polytheism which came from all directions.

In the new covenant we reach a new phase: greater awareness of the person in regard to man has given us a context in which the revelation of the Holy Spirit as a Person can find fertile ground. The Holy Spirit is he who dwells in the person and living there, sanctifies him or her especially with the power of love which he himself is. In this way the revelation of the Spirit-Person also reveals the interior depth of the human person. And through this more profound exploration of the human spirit, we are more aware that the Holy Spirit becomes the source of communion between humanity and God, as well as of interpersonal communion among people. This is the synthesis of the new revelation of the Person of the Holy Spirit which we shall reflect on in the next catechesis.

General audience of August 22, 1990

The New Testament Fully Reveals the Trinity

After his resurrection, Jesus appeared to the eleven apostles and said to them: "Go, therefore, and make disciples of all nations, baptizing them in the name of the Father and of the Son and of the Holy Spirit" (Mt 28:19). It is the apostle-evangelist Matthew who tells us, at the end of his Gospel, about this order by which Jesus Christ sent his apostles into the whole world that they might be his witnesses and continue his work of salvation. Our Christian tradition, according to which Baptism is administered in the name of the Blessed Trinity, corresponds to these words. However, Matthew's text contains something else which we can consider as the last word of the revelation of the truth about the Trinity, including the revelation of the Holy Spirit as a Person who is equal to the Father and the Son, of one substance with them in the unity of the divinity.

This revelation belongs to the New Testament. In the Old Testament the Spirit of God, in the various ways of acting which were pointed out in our preceding reflections, was the manifestation of God's power, wisdom and holiness. In the New Testament we clearly make the transition to the revelation of the Holy Spirit as a Person.

The Gospel expression in Matthew 28:19 clearly reveals the Holy Spirit as a Person because it names him in the identical way as the other two Persons, without indicating any difference in this regard: "the Father and the Son and the Holy Spirit." Matthew's Gospel clearly shows that the Father and Son are two distinct Persons. "The Father" is the one whom Jesus calls "my heavenly Father" (Mt 15:13; 16:17; 18:35); "the Son" is Jesus himself, designated as such by a voice which came from heaven at the time of his baptism (Mt 3:17) and his transfiguration (Mt 17:5). Simon Peter acknowledged him as "the Christ, the Son of the living God" (Mt 16:16). Now a third Person, the "Holy Spirit," is associated to these two divine Persons in an identical way. This association is made even closer by the fact that the expression speaks of the name of these three, prescribing that they baptize all nations "in the name of the Father and of the Son and of the Holy Spirit." In the Bible the expression "in the name of" is not usually used to refer to anything other than persons. It is also noteworthy that the Gospel's expression uses the term "name" in the singular, even though it mentions several persons. From all of this we have the undeniable result that the Holy Spirit is a third divine Person, closely associated to the Father and the Son in the unit of a single divine "name."

Christian Baptism puts us in close personal relationship with the three divine Persons, thus introducing us into the intimacy of the Godhead. Every time we make the sign of the cross we repeat this Gospel expression in order to renew our relationship with the Father and the Son and the Holy Spirit. Acknowledging the Holy Spirit is an essential condition for the Christian life of faith and charity.

The risen Christ's words about Baptism (Mt 28:19) do not occur without some preparation in Matthew's Gospel. They have a relationship to the baptism of Jesus himself, in which there was a trinitarian theophany. Matthew tells us that when Jesus came up out of the water, "the heavens were opened and they saw the Spirit of God descending like a dove and coming upon him. And a voice came from the heavens, saying, 'This is my beloved Son, with whom I am well pleased'" (Mt 3:16-17). The same scene is described similarly by the other two Synoptics (cf. Mk 1:9-11; Lk 3:21-22). In it we find a revelation of the three divine Persons. The person of Jesus is indicated with the designation of Son; the person of the Father is manifested through the voice which says, "This is my...Son"; and the person of the Spirit of God appears as distinct from the Father and the Son and in relationship to both of them. He is in relationship with the heavenly Father, because the Spirit comes from on high, and with the Son, because the Spirit came upon him. If at first glance this interpretation does not seem convincing, comparing it with the closing phrase of the Gospel (cf. Mt 28:19) assures its foundation.

The light which we are given by Matthew's final phrase allows us to discover the personhood of the Holy Spirit in other texts. The revelation of the Spirit in his relationship with the Father and the Son can also be deduced in the account of the annunciation (Lk 1:26-38).

According to Luke's narrative, the angel Gabriel, sent by God to a virgin named Mary, announced the will of the Eternal Father to her in the following words: "Behold, you will conceive in your womb and bear a Son, and you shall name him Jesus. He will be great and will be called Son of the Most High" (Lk 1:32-32). When Mary asked how this could happen in her virginal condition, the angel replied to her: "The Holy Spirit will come upon you, and the power of the Most High will overshadow you. Therefore, the child to be born will be called holy, the Son of God" (Lk 1:34-35).

Of itself, this text does not tell us that the Holy Spirit is a Person. It merely shows that he is a being in some way distinct from the Most High, that is from God the Father, and from the

Son of the Most High. When it is read, however, as we spontaneously do in the light of faith, "in the name of the Father and of the Son and of the Holy Spirit" (Mt 28:19), it reveals to us the unity of the three divine Persons in the fulfillment of the mystery which is called the Incarnation of the Word. The Person of the Holy Spirit contributes to this fulfillment according to the Father's plan, which is fully accepted by the Son. By the power of the Holy Spirit the Son of God, one in nature with the eternal Father, is conceived as a man and born of the Virgin Mary. In the preceding reflections we have already spoken of this mystery which is both Christological and pneumatological. Here we need only recall that in the annunciation the trinitarian mystery is revealed, especially the Person of the Holy Spirit.

At this point we can also point out a reflection of this mystery on Christian anthropology. There is a connection between the birth of the eternal Son of God in human nature and the "rebirth" of the sons and daughters of humanity by divine adoption through grace. This connection belongs to the economy of salvation. In view of this, Baptism was instituted in the sacramental economy.

Therefore the revelation of the Holy Spirit as a subsistent Person in the trinitarian unity of the Godhead is particularly highlighted both in the mystery of the Incarnation of the eternal Son of God and in the mystery of the divine adoption of the sons and daughters of humanity. In this mystery John's proclamation about Christ at the Jordan is constantly fulfilled: "He will baptize with the Holy Spirit" (Mt 3:11). This supernatural adoption is brought about in the sacramental order precisely through baptism "with water and the Spirit" (Jn 3:5).

General audience of August 29, 1990

The Spirit:
Active Agent in Jesus' Work

In the New Testament the Holy Spirit reveals himself as a Person subsisting with the Father and the Son in the unity of the Trinity, through the actions attributed to him by the inspired authors. One cannot always move from an action to a "property" of a Person in a strict theological sense. But in terms of our catechesis that process is sufficient for discovering what the Holy Spirit is within the divine reality through the deeds which he authors. Besides, this is the path followed by the Fathers and Doctors of the Church (cf. St. Thomas, *Summa Theol.,* I, q. 30, aa. 7-8).

In this catechesis we will limit ourselves to several Synoptic texts. Afterward we will refer also to other books in the New Testament. We have seen that in the annunciation narrative the Holy Spirit manifested himself as the one who is acting: "He will come upon you," the angel said to Mary, "and the power of the Most High will overshadow you" (Lk 1:35). Therefore we can recognize that the Holy Spirit is the principle of action, especially in the Incarnation. Precisely because he is Eternal Love (a property of the third Person), the power of acting—a power of love—is attributed to him.

The first chapters of Luke's Gospel speak several times of the Holy Spirit's action in the people closely connected to the mystery of the Incarnation. Thus it is with Elizabeth, who during Mary's visit was filled with the Holy Spirit. Under divine inspiration she greets her blessed relative (cf. Lk 1:41-45). Thus it is even more so with the elderly holy man Simeon to whom the Holy Spirit manifested himself in a personal way, announcing to him in advance that he would see the "Lord's Messiah" before he died (cf. Lk 2:26). Under the inspiration and movement of the Holy Spirit he took the child in his arms and spoke those prophetic words which encompass in a very full and emotion-laden synthesis the entire redemptive mission of the Son of Mary (cf. Lk 2:27 ff.). More than any other person the Virgin Mary was under the influence of the Holy Spirit (cf. Lk 1:35). The Spirit certainly gave her insight into the mystery and prompted her soul to accept her mission and to sing exultantly as she contemplated the providential plan of salvation (cf. Lk 1:26 ff.).

In these holy people a paradigm is sketched of the action of the Holy Spirit, who is almighty Love and gives light, strength, consolation and active encouragement. But the paradigm is even clearer in the life of Jesus himself. It was lived entirely under the Spirit's impulse and direction, by bringing about within himself Isaiah's prophecy about the Messiah's mission: "The Spirit of the Lord is upon me because he has anointed me to bring glad tidings to the poor. He has sent me to proclaim liberty to captives and recovery of sight to the blind, to let the oppressed go free, and to proclaim a year acceptable to the Lord" (cf. Lk 4:18; cf. Is 61:1). We know that Jesus read these prophetic words aloud in the Nazareth synagogue and stated that from that moment on these words were to be fulfilled in him (cf. Lk 4:21).

The words and deeds of Jesus were the unfolding of his messianic mission in which the Lord's Spirit was at work, according to the prophet's announcement. The Holy Spirit's action was hidden in the unfolding of this whole mission, carried out by Jesus in a visible, public and historical way. Thus it gave witness to and revealed the work and the person of the Holy Spirit as well, according to the statement of Jesus to which the evangelists and other sacred authors refer.

At times the evangelists stress that active presence of the Holy Spirit in Christ in a special way, as when they speak about the fasting and temptation of Christ in the desert: "Jesus was led by the Spirit into the desert to be tempted by the devil" (Mt 4:1; cf. Mk 1:12). The expression used by the evangelist presents the Spirit as a Person who leads another to something. This aspect which the evangelists give to the Holy Spirit's activity in Christ signifies that his messianic mission, carried out to conquer evil, includes from the start a struggle with him who is the "liar and the father of lies" (Jn 8:44): the spirit of rejection of God's kingdom. Christ's victory over Satan at the start of his messianic activity is the prelude and announcement of his final victory in the cross and resurrection.

Jesus himself attributed this victory to the Holy Spirit at every stop in his messianic mission. He stated that "I cast out demons by the Spirit of God" (Mt 12:28). In Christ's struggle and victory the power of the Holy Spirit is manifest. That power is the inner champion and untiring producer of that victory. That is why Jesus is so strong in admonishing his listeners about the sin which he himself calls "the blasphemy against the Holy Spirit" (Mt 12:31-32; cf. Mk 3:29; Lk 12:10). Here too the expressions used by the evangelist present the Spirit as a Person. A parallel is set up between anyone who speaks against the person of the Son of Man and the one who speaks against the person of the Holy Spirit (cf. Mt 12:32; Lk 12:10). The offense to the Holy Spirit is stated to be more serious. "To sin against the Holy Spirit" means to place oneself on the side of the spirit of darkness, with the result that a person closes himself or herself off to the sanctifying action of God's Spirit. This is why Jesus stated that this type of sin cannot be forgiven "either in this world or in the world to come" (Mt 12:32). The inner rejection of the Holy Spirit is the rejection of the very source of life and holiness. Man thus excludes himself freely and by his own initiative from the sphere of God's saving actions.

Jesus' warning about the sin against the Holy Spirit includes at least implicitly an additional revelation of the Person and sanctifying activity of that Person of the Trinity. He is the protagonist in the struggle against the spirit of evil and in the victory of good.

Still according to the synoptics, the Holy Spirit's action is the source of the deepest inner joy. Jesus himself experienced this special "exultation in the Holy Spirit" when he spoke these words: "I give you thanks, Father, Lord of heaven and earth, for although you have hidden these things from the wise and the learned you have revealed them to the childlike. Yes, Father, such has been your gracious will" (Lk 10:21; cf. Mt 11:25-26). In the texts written by Luke and Matthew this is followed by the words of Jesus about the Son's knowledge of the Father and the Father's knowledge of the Son. This knowledge is communicated by the Son himself to these "little ones."

Therefore, it is the Holy Spirit who also gives Jesus' disciples not only the power of victory over evil, over the "evil spirits" (Lk 10:17), but also the supernatural joy of discovering God and life in him through his Son.

The revelation of the Holy Spirit through the force of the action which fills the whole mission of Christ will also accompany the apostles and the disciples in the work which they carry out by divine mandate. Jesus himself tells them that: "You will receive power when the Holy Spirit comes upon you and you will be my witnesses...to the ends of the earth" (Acts 1:8). Even when in the course of this witness they meet with persecution, imprisonment and court interrogations, Jesus assures them: "You will be given at that moment what you are to say. For it will not be you who speak, but the Spirit of your Father speaking through you" (Mt 10:19-20; cf. Mk 13:11). Only persons can speak. Impersonal forces can move, push and destroy, but they cannot speak. But the Spirit speaks. He is the inspirer and the consoler of the apostles and the Church in difficult moments. That is another characteristic of his action, another ray of light shed upon the mystery of his Person.

Therefore we can state that in the synoptics the Holy Spirit manifests himself as a Person who works within the whole mission of Christ. In the lives and history of Christ's followers he frees them from evil, gives them strength in the struggle with the spirit of darkness, and increases the supernatural joy of knowing God and witnessing to him even in trying times. The Spirit is a Person who works with divine strength above all within the messianic mission of Jesus, and afterward in the work of drawing people to Christ and of guiding those who are called to take part in his saving mission.

General audience of September 19, 1990

An Advocate Who Dwells in Us

In his Gospel, John the Apostle highlights more than the Synoptics the personal relationship between the Son and the Father. This can be seen early on in the prologue where the evangelist sets his gaze on the eternal reality of the Father and the Word-Son. He begins by saying: "In the beginning was the Word, and the Word was with God and the Word was God. He was in the beginning with God" (Jn 1:1-2). Then he concludes: "No one has ever seen God. The only Son, God, who is at the Father's side, reveals him" (Jn 1:18). It is a completely new assertion in the history of human reflection on God and within revelation itself. The depth and the wealth of the content it offers to theology will never be exhausted or fully explained. Religious education too must always refer to it, not only on the Christological level but also on the pneumatological level.

The very unity of the Son with the Father, stressed also in other parts of John' Gospel, seems to open up to the apostles the path of revelation of the Holy Spirit as a Person.

Significantly, Christ's words which most directly relate to this topic are found in the farewell discourse in the upper room. Therefore they are made in light of the imminent departure of the Son who returns to the Father by means of the cross and the ascension. At that moment Jesus said: "I will ask the Father and he will give you another Advocate to be with you always, the Spirit of truth which the world cannot accept because it neither sees nor knows him" (Jn 14:16-17). Advocate-Paraclete: this name, given to the Holy Spirit by Jesus, shows that he is a Person, distinct from the Father and the Son. The Greek word *Parákletos* is always applied to a person, since it means advocate, defender, or consoler. Only a person can accomplish those tasks. On the other hand by speaking in terms of "another Advocate," Jesus makes us understand that during his earthly life, he himself was the disciples' first "Advocate." He will assert that even more clearly in his priestly prayer in which he says to his Father: "When I was with them I protected them in your name that you gave me, and I guarded them" (Jn 17:12). After Jesus' departure, the Holy Spirit will take his place in the midst of the disciples still living in the world to defend them in the struggles they must face and to sustain their courage in trial.

In the farewell discourse, the Paraclete is called "the Spirit of truth" several times (cf. Jn 14:17). This title recognizes the mission which is given him regarding the apostles and the Church: "The Advocate—the Holy Spirit whom the Father will send in my name—he will teach you everything and remind you of all that I taught you" (Jn 14:26). "Teach," "remind"; these activities show well that the Spirit is a Person. Only a person can do them. The mission of preaching truth, entrusted to the apostles and the Church by Christ, is and will always remain bound to the personal activity of the Spirit of truth.

The same observation goes for the witness which must be rendered to Christ before the world. "When the Advocate comes whom I will send you from the Father, the Spirit of truth that proceeds from the Father, he will testify to me" (Jn 15:26).

Only a Person can bear witness to another person. The apostles will have to bear witness to Christ. Their testimony as human persons will be supported and confirmed by the testimony of a divine Person, the Holy Spirit.

For that very reason the Holy Spirit is also the invisible master who will continue to impart from one generation to the next the teaching of Christ himself: his Gospel. "But when he comes, the Spirit of truth, he will guide you to all truth. He will not speak on his own, but will speak what he hears, and will declare to you the things that are coming" (Jn 16:13). From this we deduce that the Holy Spirit will not only watch over the Church as regards the solidness and the identification of the truth in Christ. He will also indicate the way to transmit this truth to the coming generations which will continue to appear through various eras, and to peoples and societies in various places, according to their needs and their ability to understand, giving each person the strength to assent interiorly to that truth and conform his or her life to it.

A special aspect of this action, already stressed in the Encyclical *Dominum et Vivificantem* (cf. nn. 27-28), is that which Jesus himself announced with these words: "And when he comes he will convict the world in regard to sin and righteousness and condemnation" (Jn 16:8). This particular power to convict the world, that is, those who are in the world, in regard to sin is an essential aspect of the mission of the Spirit of truth. To convict regarding condemnation means, according to Jesus' owns words, that "the prince of this world has been condemned" (Jn 16:11). He who is to come as Consoler and Advocate, the Holy Spirit, must guide humanity toward victory over evil and over the works of evil in the world.

There is a close connection between the redemptive death of Christ on the cross and what he gave the apostles after his resurrection: "Receive the Holy Spirit; whose sins you forgive are forgiven them" (Jn 20:22-23). This is the route

Lord,

*source of eternal life and truth,
give to your shepherd Benedict
a spirit of courage and right judgement,
a spirit of knowledge and love.*

*By governing with fidelity
those entrusted to his care
may he, as successor to the
apostle Peter and vicar of Christ,
build your Church into a sacrament of unity,
love and peace for all the world.*

*We ask this through our
Lord Jesus Christ, your Son,*

*who lives and reigns with you and the Holy Spirit,
one God for ever and ever*

Amen

through which the road leading to victory over evil passes, the evil which the Spirit of truth must constantly convict the world of.

All of these passages come from Jesus' discourse in the upper room and reveal the Holy Spirit as a Person subsisting in trinitarian unity with the Father and the Son. They show the mission in which he is closely linked to the redemption accomplished by Christ: "For if I do not go," passing from this world to the Father, "the Advocate will not come to you" (Jn 16:7). There are also other passages which are very significant in this regard.

Jesus announced that the Holy Spirit will come to "remain" with us: "And I will ask the Father and he will give you another Advocate to be with you always" (Jn 14:17). These words express the indwelling of the Holy Spirit as inner guest in people's hearts: in the heart of anyone among all the souls belonging to Christ who welcomes the Spirit. The Father and Son too come to "take up residence" in these souls (Jn 14:23). Therefore the whole Trinity is present in them, but, since this is a spiritual presence, that presence refers in a most direct way to the Person of the Holy Spirit.

Through this presence at work in the soul, a person can become that "true worshipper" of God who "is spirit" (Jn 4:24), as Jesus said in the meeting with the Samaritan woman at Jacob's well (cf. Jn 4:23). The hour of those who "adore the Father in spirit and truth" arrived with Christ and becomes a reality in every person who accepts the Holy Spirit and lives according to the Spirit's inspiration and under the Spirit's personal direction. That is the greatest and holiest element in Christian spirituality.

General audience of September 26, 1990

The Spirit in St. Paul's Letters

This is the famous wish with which St. Paul concludes his Second Letter to the Corinthians: "The grace of the Lord Jesus Christ and the love of God and the fellowship of the Holy Spirit be with all of you" (2 Cor 13:13). This is the wish which the liturgy places upon the lips of the priest celebrant at the beginning of the Mass. With this text of obviously trinitarian significance we begin our examination of what the Apostle Paul's letters tell us about the Holy Spirit as a Person in the trinitarian unity of the Father and the Son. The text from the Second Letter to the Corinthians seems to come from the language of the first Christian communities, and perhaps from the liturgy of their assembly. With these words the Apostle expresses the trinitarian unity beginning with Christ. As the one who brought about salvific grace, Christ reveals to humanity the love of God the Father and imparts it to believers in the communion of the Holy Spirit. Thus, according to St. Paul, the Holy Spirit is the Person who brings about the communion of the human being—and of the Church—with God.

The Pauline formula clearly speaks of a one and triune God, even though in different terms than the baptismal formula which Matthew refers to: "In the name of the Father, the Son and the Holy Spirit" (Mt 28:19). It lets us know the Holy Spirit as he was presented in the teaching of the Apostles and received in the life of the Christian communities.

A further text from St. Paul has as its basis for its teaching about the Holy Spirit the wealth of charisms distributed with variety and unified order within the community: "There are different kinds of spiritual gifts but the same Spirit; there are different forms of service but the same Lord; there are different workings but the same God who produces all of them in everyone" (1 Cor 12:4-6). The Apostle attributes to the Holy Spirit the gifts of grace (charisms); to the Son, as Lord of the Church, the ministries *(ministeria);* to God the Father, the creator of everything in everyone, the "working."

The parallel between the Spirit, the Lord Jesus and God the Father is very significant. It indicates that the Spirit is also recognized as a divine Person. It would not be proper to place two Persons, the Father and the Son, in the same phrase with an impersonal force. It is equally significant that the free giving of the charisms and all divine gifts to humanity and the Church is particularly attributed to the Holy Spirit.

All this is further emphasized in the immediate context of the First Letter to the Corinthians: "One and the same Spirit produces all these things, distributing them individually to each person as he wishes" (1 Cor 12:11). Thus the Holy Spirit is manifested as a free and spontaneous donor of the good in the order of charisms and grace; as a divine Person who chooses and bestows diverse gifts upon their recipients. "To one is given through the Spirit the expression of wisdom; to another the expression of knowledge according to the same Spirit" (1 Cor 12:8-9). And again: "The gift of healings...the gift of prophecy...the gift of discernment of spirits...the gift of varieties of tongues and the gift of interpretation of tongues" (1 Cor 12:9-10). And behold: "To each individual the manifestation of the Spirit is given for some benefit" (1 Cor 12:7). Therefore, from the Holy Spirit comes the multiplicity of their gifts, as well as their unity and their co-existence. All this shows the Holy Spirit as a Person who subsists and works within the divine unity, in the communion of the Son with the Father.

Other passages from the Pauline letters also express the same truth about the Holy Spirit as a Person in the trinitarian unity, with the economy of salvation as their departure point. "But we ought to give thanks for you always...because God chose you as the first fruits for salvation through sanctification by the Spirit and belief in truth...to possess the glory of our Lord Jesus Christ." Thus the Apostle writes in his Second Letter to the Thessalonians (2 Thess 2:13-14), to indicate to them the goal of the Gospel preached by him. And to the Corinthians: "But now you have had yourselves washed; you were sanctified; you were justified in the name of the Lord Jesus Christ and in the Spirit of our God" (1 Cor 6:11).

According to the Apostle, the Father is the first principle of sanctification, which is conferred by the Holy Spirit upon the person who believes "in the name" of Christ. The sanctification deep within a person therefore comes from the Holy Spirit, a Person who lives and works in unity with the Father and the Son. In another passage the Apostle expresses the same concept in an evocative manner: "The one who gives us security with you in Christ and who anointed us is God; he has also put his seal upon us and given the Spirit in our hearts as a first installment" (2 Cor 1:21-22). The words "in our hearts" indicate the intimacy of the Holy Spirit's sanctifying activity.

This same truth can be found in the Letter to the Ephesians in a more developed form: "God, the Father of our Lord Jesus Christ...has blessed us in Christ with every spiritual blessing in the heavens, in Christ" (Eph 1:3). Shortly after that the author says to the believers: "You were sealed with the promised Holy Spirit, which is the first installment of our inheritance" (Eph 1:13-14).

Another magnificent expression of St. Paul's thought and intention is that of the Letter to the Romans. In it he writes that the purpose of his Gospel ministry is "so that the offering up of the Gentiles may be acceptable, sanctified by the Holy Spirit" (Rom 15:16). He asks those to whom the letter is addressed to pray to God for this service. He does so through Christ and through "the love of the Spirit" (Rom 15:30). "Love" is a special attribute of the Holy Spirit (cf. Rom 5:5) as well as "communion" (cf. 2 Cor 13:13). From this love comes holiness which makes the offering acceptable. This is also a work of the Holy Spirit.

According to the Letter to the Galatians, the Holy Spirit gives people the gift of adoption as God's children, arousing in them the prayer of the Son himself. "As proof that you are children, God sent the spirit of his Son into our hearts, crying out, 'Abba, Father!'" (Gal 4:6). The Spirit "cries out" and thus reveals himself as a Person who is able to express himself with great intensity. He makes Christian hearts echo with the prayer which Jesus himself addresses to the Father (cf. Mk 14:36) with childlike love. The Holy Spirit is the one who makes us adoptive children and gives us the capacity for childlike prayer.

St. Paul's teaching on this topic is so rich that we will have to take it up again in our next instruction. For now we can conclude that in the Pauline letters the Holy Spirit is seen as a divine Person living in the trinitarian unity with the Father and the Son. The Apostle attributes to him the work of sanctification in a particular manner. He is the direct author of holiness in souls. He is the fount of love and prayer in which the gift of the person's divine "adoption" is expressed. His presence in souls is the pledge and the beginning of eternal life.

General audience of October 3, 1990

The Spirit "Searches Everything"

In our previous instruction we saw that the revelation of the Holy Spirit as a Person in the unity of the Trinity with the Father and Son is expressed in many beautiful and fascinating ways in the Pauline writings. Today we shall continue to touch upon other variations on this one basic theme as found in the letters of St. Paul. It frequently recurs in the Apostle's texts, which are imbued with a lively and life-giving faith in the Holy Spirit's activity and in his Personhood, which is especially made known through his activity.

One of the noblest and most attractive expressions of this faith which under Paul's pen becomes a communication of a revealed truth to the Church, is that of the Holy Spirit's indwelling within the faithful, who are his temple. "Do you know," he admonishes the Corinthians, "that you are the temple of God, and that the Spirit of God dwells in you?" (1 Cor 3:16). Normally persons "dwell." Here it is a question of a divine person's "indwelling" in human beings. This fact is spiritual in nature, a mystery of grace and eternal love which for this very reason is attributed to the Holy Spirit.

This internal indwelling has an effect upon the entire person, on the concrete totality of his or her being, which the

Apostle refers to more than once as a "body." In this same letter, a little bit after the passage we cited, he seems to urge the recipients of his letters with the same question: "Do you not know that your body is a temple of the Holy Spirit within you, whom you have from God, and that you are not your own?" (1 Cor 6:19). In this text the reference to the "body" is all the more meaningful in that it refers to the Pauline concept of the Holy Spirit's activity in the entire person!

Thus we can explain and better understand the other text in the Letter to the Romans about "life according to the Spirit." We read: "But you are not in the flesh; on the contrary, you are in the Spirit, if only the Spirit dwells in you" (Rom 8:9). "If the Spirit of the one who raised Jesus from the dead dwells in you, the one who raised Christ from the dead will give life to your mortal bodies also, through his Spirit that dwells in you" (Rom 8:11).

Therefore, the influence of the divine indwelling in a person is extended to his or her whole being. It extends to his or her whole life, which in all its constitutive elements and operational activities is placed under the action of the Holy Spirit: of the Spirit of the Father and the Son, and therefore also of Christ, the Incarnate Word. This Spirit, alive in the Trinity, by virtue of the redemption won by Christ is present in the entire person who lets himself or herself be "inhabited" by him, and in all of humanity which recognizes and accepts him.

Another characteristic which St. Paul attributes to the Person of the Holy Spirit is that of "searching" everything, as he writes to the Corinthians: "For the Spirit searches everything, even the depths of God" (1 Cor 2:10). "Who knows what pertains to a person except the spirit of the person that is within? Similarly, no one knows what pertains to God except the Spirit of God" (1 Cor 2:11).

This "searching" means the clarity and depth of the knowledge which is proper to the divinity in which the Holy

Spirit lives with the Word-Son in the unity of the Trinity. Therefore he is a Spirit of light, a teacher of truth for humanity, as Jesus Christ had promised (cf. Jn 14:26).

First of all, his teaching concerns divine things, the mystery of God in himself, but also his words and his gifts to humanity. As St. Paul writes: "We have not received the spirit of the world but the Spirit that is from God, so that we may understand the things freely given us by God" (1 Cor 2:12). It is a divine view of the world, of life and history, which the Holy Spirit gives believers. It is a "faith-filled understanding" which enables us to look beyond the human and cosmic dimensions of reality in order to discover in all things the presence of God's saving activity, the working out of his Providence and the reflection of his triune glory.

In the ancient sequence of the Mass of Pentecost, the liturgy has us pray for this: *Veni, Sancte Spiritus, et emitte coelitus lucis tuae radium.* "Come, Holy Spirit, come, and from your celestial home, shed a ray of light divine! Come, Father of the poor! Come, source of all our store! Come, within our bosoms shine!"

This Spirit of light also gives people, especially the apostles and the Church, the ability to teach the things of God as if by an expansion of his own light. We speak about the things freely given us by God, as Paul writes, "not with words taught by human wisdom, but with words taught by the Spirit, describing spiritual realities in spiritual terms" (1 Cor 2:13). The words of the Apostle, the words of the primitive Church and the Church throughout the ages, the words of true theologians and catechists, speak of a wisdom that is not of this world, of "God's hidden mysterious wisdom, which God predetermined before the ages for our glory" (1 Cor 2:6-7).

This wisdom is a gift of the Holy Spirit, which must be implored for all teachers and preachers in every age. It is the gift which St. Paul speaks about in the same Letter to the

Corinthians: "To one is given through the Spirit the expression of wisdom; to another the expression of knowledge according to the same Spirit" (1 Cor 12:8). All this is the gift of the Holy Spirit: wisdom, knowledge, the force of an expression which penetrates minds and hearts, an internal light which, through the proclamation of the divine truth, influences the person who is docile and attentive to the glory of the Trinity.

The Spirit who "searches everything, even the depths of God" and "teaches" divine wisdom is also the one who "leads." In the Letter to the Romans we read: "Those who are led by the Spirit of God are children of God" (Rom 8:14). Here we have an inner guide which touches the very roots of the new creation. The Holy Spirit makes people live as God's children by adoption. In order to live in such a way, the human spirit needs to recognize this divine adoption. "The Spirit himself bears witness with our spirit that we are children of God (Rom 8:16). The personal witness of the Holy Spirit is absolutely necessary so that the person lives out in his or her own life the mystery which God himself has brought about within that person.

In this manner the Holy Spirit comes to the aid of our weakness. According to the Apostle, that happens especially in prayer. Indeed, he writes: "The Spirit comes to the aid of our weakness; for we do not know how to pray as we ought, but the Spirit himself intercedes for us with sighs too deep for words" (Rom 8:26). For Paul, therefore, the Spirit is the internal author of authentic prayer. Through his divine influence, he penetrates human prayer from within and brings it into the depths of God.

A further Pauline expression in some way encompasses and synthesizes all that we have touched upon to this point about this topic. "The love of God has been poured out into our hearts through the Holy Spirit who has been given to us" (Rom 5:5). The Holy Spirit is therefore the one who pours out God's love into human hearts in overflowing measure, and enables us to become sharers in that love.

From all these expressions so frequently and consistently found in the language of the Apostle to the Gentiles, we are able to understand better the Holy Spirit's activity and the Person of the one who acts in a divine way in human beings.

General audience of October 10, 1990

Wind and Fire: Signs of the Spirit

The New Testament contains the revelation about the Holy Spirit as Person, subsistent with the Father and the Son in the unity of the Trinity. But it is not a revelation with well-delineated features, like that regarding the first two Persons. Isaiah's statement, according to which ours is a "hidden God" (Is 45:15), can be seen as a special reference to the Holy Spirit. By becoming man, the Son entered into the realm of the experientially visible for those who were able to see with their own eyes and touch with their hands the Word of Life (cf. 1 Jn 1:1). Their witness offers a concrete reference point for later Christian generations as well. The Father, in his turn, while remaining within invisible and unspeakable transcendence, is manifested in the Son. Jesus said: "He who sees me sees the Father" (Jn 14:9). Furthermore "fatherhood," even on the level of the divine, is well enough understood by analogy with human fatherhood which is a reflection, though imperfect, of that uncreated and eternal fatherhood, as St. Paul said (Eph 3:15).

The Person of the Holy Spirit, on the other hand, is more radically beyond all our means of cognitive awareness. For us the third Person is a hidden and invisible God. This is also because the analogies with the world of human understanding regarding the Spirit are more fragile. The genesis and outpouring of love which is a reflection of uncreated Love within the human soul is not as accessible to the act of understanding, which in a certain way is an act of self-awareness. Out of this comes the mystery of love on the psychological and theological levels, as St. Thomas notes (cf. *Summa Theol.*, I, q. 27, a. 4; q. 36, a. 1; q. 37, a. 1). Thus we can explain that the Holy Spirit, like human love itself, finds expression especially in symbols. These point to his active dynamisms, but also to his Person, present in activity.

Thus it is with the symbol of the wind which is central to the Pentecost experience, a fundamental event in the revelation of the Holy Spirit: "And suddenly there came from the sky a noise like a strong driving wind, and it filled the entire house where they were gathered [with Mary]" (Acts 2:2).

The wind was often presented, in biblical texts and elsewhere, as a person who comes and goes. Jesus spoke of it this way in his conversation with Nicodemus, when he used the example of the wind to speak of the Person of the Holy Spirit: "The wind blows where it will and you can hear the sound it makes, but you do not know where it comes from or where it goes; so it is with everyone who is born of the Spirit" (Jn 3:8). The Holy Spirit's action, through which one is "born of the Spirit" (as happens in the adoptive sonship worked by divine grace) is compared to the wind. This analogy used by Jesus highlights the total spontaneity and generosity of this action, through which people are made participants in God's life. The symbol of the wind seems to bring about in a special way that supernatural dynamism through which God himself draws near to people to transform them from within, to sanctify them and, in a certain sense, as the Fathers say, to divinize them.

We must add that from an etymological and linguistic point of view the symbol of the wind is the one most closely connected with the Spirit. We have already mentioned this in previous catecheses. Here we need only recall the meaning of the word *ruah* (already in Gen 1:2), that is "breath." We know that when after the resurrection Jesus appeared to the Apostles, "he breathed on" them and said "Receive the Holy Spirit" (Jn 20:22-23).

We must also note that the wind symbol, as an explicit reference to the Holy Spirit and the Spirit's action, belongs to the language and doctrine of the New Testament. In the Old Testament the wind, like a "hurricane," is the expression of God's wrath (cf. Ez 13:13), while the "tiny whispering sound" speaks of the intimate nature of his conversations with the prophets (cf. 1 Kgs 19:12).

The same term is used to indicate the breath of life, a symbol of God's power which restores the life of the human skeletons in Ezekiel's prophecy: "From the four winds, come, O Spirit, and breath into these slain that they may come to life" (Ez 37:9). In the New Testament the wind clearly becomes the symbol of the Holy Spirit's action and presence.

Another symbol is the dove which according to the Synoptics and John's Gospel was manifested during the baptism of Jesus in the Jordan. This symbol is more appropriate than that of the wind to indicate the Person of the Holy Spirit, because the dove is a living being, while the wind is only a natural phenomenon. The evangelists speak of the dove in almost identical terms. Matthew writes (3:16): "The heavens opened and he saw the spirit of God descending like a dove and coming upon him" (that is, upon Jesus). Mark (1:10), Luke (3:21-22) and John (1:32) write in a similar manner. Because of the importance of this event in the life of Jesus, who received in a visible way the "messianic investiture," the symbol of the dove is confirmed through artistic imagery, and in imaginative depictions of the mystery of the Holy Spirit, his activity and his Person.

In the Old Testament the dove was the messenger of God's reconciliation with humanity in Noah's time. The dove gave that patriarch the news about the end of the flood covering the face of the earth (cf. Gen 8:9-11).

In the New Testament this reconciliation comes about through Baptism, which Peter speaks about in his first Letter, comparing it to the "persons...saved through water" in Noah's ark (1 Pet 3:20-21). Therefore, we can see this as a foretaste of the pneumatological symbol. The Holy Spirit, who is Love, "pouring out this love in human hearts," as St. Paul says (Rom 5:5), is also the giver of peace, which is God's gift.

Further, the action and Person of the Holy Spirit are also indicated by the symbol of fire. We know that John the Baptist proclaimed at the Jordan: "He [Christ] will baptize you with the Spirit and fire" (Mt 3:11). Fire is the source of warmth and light, but it is also a destructive force. For this reason the Gospels speak of "throwing into the fire" the tree that bears no fruit (Mt 3:10; cf. Jn 15:6); they speak also of "burning the chaff in unquenchable fire" (Mt 3:12). Baptism "in the Spirit and fire" indicates fire's purifying power. It is a mysterious fire that expresses the demand of holiness and purity of which God's Spirit is the bearer.

Jesus himself said: "I have come to set the earth on fire; and how I wish that it were already blazing!" (Lk 12:49). In this example we are dealing with the fire of God's love, of that love which "has been poured out in our hearts by means of the Holy Spirit" (Rom 5:5). When on the day of Pentecost "tongues of fire" appeared upon the heads of the Apostles, they signified that the Spirit brought the gift of participation in the saving love of God. St. Thomas says that the love, the fire which Jesus brought to the earth, is "a kind of participation in the Holy Spirit" *(participatio quaedam Spiritus Sancti; Summa Theol.*, II-II, q. 23, a. 3, ad 3). In this sense fire is a symbol of the Holy Spirit whose Person within the divine Trinity is Love.

General audience of October 17, 1990

Anointing: Biblical Sign of the Spirit

In his discourse at the Nazareth synagogue at the start of his public life, Jesus applied to himself an Isaian text which says: "The Spirit of the Lord is upon me, because he has anointed me" (Is 61:1; cf. Lk 4:18). It is another symbol which passed from the Old to the New Testament with a more precise and new meaning. This also happened with the symbols of wind, the dove and fire; in recent catecheses we saw that these refer to the activity and the Person of the Holy Spirit. Anointing with oil, too, belongs to the Old Testament tradition. Kings above all others received anointing, but so did priests and sometimes prophets. The symbol of anointing with oil was to express the strength needed to exercise authority. The text cited from Isaiah about "consecration through anointing" refers to the spiritual strength needed to carry out the mission God gives to a person he has chosen and sent. Jesus tells us that this chosen one of God is he himself, the Messiah. The fullness of strength conferred on him—the fullness of the Holy Spirit—belongs to him as Messiah (that is, the Lord's Anointed, the Christ).

In the Acts of the Apostles, Peter refers similarly to the

anointing received by Jesus when he recalls "how God anointed Jesus of Nazareth with the Holy Spirit and power; he went about doing good and healing all those oppressed by the devil" (Acts 10:38). Just as oil penetrates wood or other materials, so the Holy Spirit pervades the entire being of the Messiah-Jesus, conferring on him the saving power for caring for bodies and souls. Through this anointing with the Holy Spirit, the Father has carried out the messianic consecration of the Son.

Participation in the anointing in the Holy Spirit of Christ's humanity is transmitted to all those who accept him in faith and love. This happens on the sacramental level in the anointings with oil, a rite which is part of the Church's liturgy, especially in Baptism and Confirmation. As St. John writes in his First Letter, they have "the anointing which comes from the Holy One," and it "remains" in them (1 Jn 2:20, 27). This anointing constitutes the source of knowledge: "You have the anointing which comes from the Holy One and you have all knowledge" (1 Jn 2:20), so that "you do not need anyone to teach you...his anointing teaches you about everything" (1 Jn 2:27). In this way the promise made by Jesus to the Apostles is fulfilled: "You will receive power when the Holy Spirit comes upon you and you will be my witnesses" (Acts 1:8).

The source of knowledge and of understanding is found in the Spirit, as is the strength needed to bear witness to divine truth. The Spirit is also the source of that supernatural "sense of the faith" which, according to the Second Vatican Council *(LG* 12), is the inheritance of the People of God, as St. John says: "All of you have knowledge" (1 Jn 2:20).

The symbol of water also appears often in the Old Testament. Taken in a very general way, water symbolizes the life lavished freely by God upon nature and human beings. We read in Isaiah: "I will open up rivers on the bare heights, and fountains in the broad valleys; I will turn the desert into a marshland and the dry ground into springs of water" (Is 41:18). This is a reference to the life-giving property of water. The prophet applies this symbol to God's Spirit, putting water and God's Spirit in a parallel relationship when he proclaims this oracle: "I will pour out water upon the thirsty ground and streams upon the dry land; I will pour out my Spirit upon your offspring...they shall spring up amid the verdure beside the flowing waters..." (Is 44:3-4). The life-giving property of water symbolizes the life-giving property of the Spirit.

Further, water liberates the land from drought (cf. 1 Kgs 18:41-45). Water also serves to satisfy the thirst of man and of animals (cf. Is 43:20). The thirst for water is likened to the thirst for God, as we read in the Psalms: "As the deer yearns for running streams, so my soul yearns for you, my God. My soul is thirsting for God, the living God; when shall I see him face-to-face?" (Ps 42:2-3; another no less explicit text is Ps 63:2).

Finally, water is a symbol of purification, as we read in Ezekiel: "I will sprinkle clean water on you to cleanse you from all your impurities, and from all your idols I will cleanse you" (Ez 36:25). The same prophet announced the life-giving power of water in a stirring vision: "Then he brought me back to the entrance of the temple and I saw water flowing out from beneath the threshold of the temple toward the east.... He said to me: 'This water flows into the eastern district down upon the Arabah, and empties into the sea, the salt waters, which it makes fresh. Wherever the water flows, every sort of living-creature that can multiply shall live...'" (Ez 47:1, 8-9).

In the New Testament the purifying and life-giving power of water serves for the rite of baptism already practiced by John, who administered a baptism of repentance in the Jordan (cf. Jn 1:33). But it was Jesus who presented water as a symbol of the Holy Spirit, when on a feastday he exclaimed to the crowds: "Let anyone who thirsts come to me and drink.

Whoever believes in me, as Scripture says: 'Rivers of living water will flow from within him.'" And the evangelist gives a commentary: "He said this in reference to the Spirit that those who came to believe in him were to receive; there was, of course, no Spirit yet because Jesus had not yet been glorified" (Jn 7:37-39).

These words also explain all that Jesus said to the Samaritan woman about living water, water which he himself will give. In a person this water becomes "a spring of water welling up to eternal life" (Jn 4:10, 14).

These are all expressions of the truth which Jesus revealed about the Holy Spirit, of whom "living water" is a symbol. In the sacrament of Baptism this is translated into the reality of being born of the Holy Spirit. Here many other Old Testament passages also come together, such as the one about the water which, upon God's orders, Moses made to flow from the rock (cf. Ex 17:5-7; Ps 78:16), and the other about the spring made available to the house of David for washing away sins and impurities (cf. Zech 13:1; 14:8). The crowning text of all is found in the words of the Book of Revelation concerning the crystal clear rivers of living water which will flow forth from the throne of God and the Lamb. In the midst of the city square and on either side of the river there is a tree of life; this tree's leaves serve to heal the nations (cf. Rev 22:1-2). According to the exegetes, the living and life-giving waters symbolize the Spirit, as John himself states several times in his Gospel (cf. Jn 4:10-14; 7:37-38). In this vision from the Book of Revelation one catches a glimpse of the Trinity itself. The reference to the healing of the nations is also significant. This healing comes through the leaves of the tree, which is nourished by the living and salubrious water of the Spirit.

If God's people "drink this spiritual drink," according to St. Paul, it is like Israel in the desert, which drew "from the rock which was Christ" (1 Cor 10:1-4). From his side pierced on the cross "flowed blood and water" (Jn 19:34), as a sign of the redemptive end of his death which he underwent for the salvation of the world. The result of this redemptive death is the gift of the Holy Spirit, which he gave abundantly to his Church.

Truly "springs of living water flowed from within" the paschal mystery of Christ by becoming in people's souls "a spring of water welling up to eternal life" (Jn 4:14) as a gift from the Holy Spirit. This gift comes from a Giver who is quite easily identified in the words of Christ and of his Apostles: the third Person of the Trinity.

General audience of October 24, 1990

The Holy Spirit in the Creed

"I believe in the Holy Spirit, the Lord, the Giver of life, who proceeds from the Father and the Son. With the Father and the Son he is worshipped and glorified; he has spoken through the prophets." With these words the Nicene-Constantinopolitan Creed defines the belief of the Church concerning the Holy Spirit, who is acknowledged as true God, with the Father and the Son, in the trinitarian unity of the Godhead. This is an article of faith, formulated by the First Council of Constantinople (381), perhaps on the basis of a previous text, as a completion of the Nicene Creed (325) (cf. *DS* 150).

This faith of the Church is continually repeated in the liturgy, which is in its way not only a profession but also a witness of faith. This occurs, for example, in the trinitarian doxology, which as a rule concludes liturgical prayers: "Glory to the Father and to the Son and to the Holy Spirit." Thus it is in the intercessory prayers addressed to the Father: "through Christ our Lord, who lives and reigns with you (the Father) in the unity of the Holy Spirit, God for ever and ever."

The hymn "Glory to God in the highest" also possesses a trinitarian structure. It lets us celebrate the glory of God and of the Son, together with the Holy Spirit: "You alone are the Most High, Jesus Christ, with the Holy Spirit, in the glory of God the Father."

This faith of the Church has its origin and basis in divine revelation. God definitively revealed himself as Father in Jesus Christ, the consubstantial Son, who by the working of the Holy Spirit became man and was born of the Virgin Mary. Through the Son the Holy Spirit was revealed. The one God revealed himself as the Trinity: Father, Son and Holy Spirit. The last word of the Son who was sent into the world from the Father was the admonition given to the apostles to "teach all nations, baptizing them in the name of the Father, and of the Son and of the Holy Spirit" (Mt 28:19). We have seen in preceding catecheses examples of revelation concerning the Holy Spirit and the Trinity in the teachings of Jesus Christ.

We have also seen that Jesus Christ revealed the Holy Spirit while he carried out his messianic mission. He declared that he was working "with the power of the Holy Spirit" (for example, in expelling demons: cf. Mt 12:28). But one might say that revelation is concentrated and condensed in the close of his mission with the announcement of his return to the Father. After Jesus' departure, the Holy Spirit will be "a new Advocate." It will be he, "the Spirit of truth," who will guide the apostles and the Church throughout history: "I will ask the Father and he will give you another Advocate to be with you always, the Spirit of truth, whom the world cannot accept, because it neither sees nor knows him" (Jn 14:16-17). He who will come from the Father in Christ's name, "will teach you everything and remind you of all that I taught you" (Jn 14:26). And again: "When he comes, he will convict the world in regard to sin and righteousness and condemnation" (Jn 16:8). This is the promise. This, one can say, is the testament which along with the ones regarding love and the Eucharist, Jesus left to his own during the Last Supper.

After the death, resurrection and ascension of Christ, Pentecost was the fulfillment of his announcement to his apostles and the beginning of his activity among the generations of coming centuries, for the Holy Spirit was to remain with the Church "forever" (Jn 14:16). We have spoken amply about this in preceding catecheses.

That foundational story about the origins of the Church which the Book of Acts records tells us that the apostles were "filled with the Holy Spirit" and "announced God's words with boldness" (Acts 2:4; 4:31). It tells us also that from the times of the apostles "the world" resisted the activity not only of the apostles, but of the invisible worker who was acting through them, as is seen in their accusation of their persecutors: "You always oppose the Holy Spirit" (Acts 7:51). That would also happen in subsequent historical eras. That resistance can reach the point of a special sin, called "blasphemy against the Holy Spirit." Jesus himself adds that this is a sin that will not be forgiven (cf. Mt 12:31; Lk 12:10).

As Jesus predicted and promised, the Holy Spirit has been the giver of all divine gifts in the Church from the beginning and continues to be so in the Church through all ages *(Dator munerum,* as we call him in the Pentecost Sequence). He is the guide both of those gifts destined directly for personal sanctification as well as those granted to some for the good of others (as is the case with certain charisms). "But one and the same Spirit produces all of these, distributing them individually to each person as he wishes" (1 Cor 12:11). Even the "hierarchical gifts," as we can call them along with the Second Vatican Council *(LG* 4), which are indispensable for the guidance of the Church, come from him (cf. Acts 20:28).

On the basis of the revelation made by Jesus and passed on by the apostles, the creed professes faith in the Holy Spirit, of whom it says that he is "Lord," as the Word who took on human flesh is Lord: "You alone are the Lord...with the Holy

Spirit." It adds too that the Holy Spirit gives life. Only God can give life to human beings. The Holy Spirit is God. And, as God, the Spirit is the author of human life. He is author of the new and eternal life brought by Jesus, but also of life in all its forms: human life and the life of all things *(Creator Spiritus)*.

This truth of faith was formulated in the Nicene-Constantinopolitan Creed. It is understood and accepted as revealed by God through Jesus Christ and as belonging to the "deposit of revelation" passed on by the apostles to the first communities, from which it was handed down through the constant teaching of the Church Fathers. Historically one can say that the article was added to the Nicene Creed by the First Council of Constantinople. It had to face certain people who denied the Holy Spirit's divinity, just as other people, especially the Arians, opposed the divinity of the Son-Word Christ. In both cases they almost lost their minds in their pretentious rationalism before the mystery of the Trinity!

The opponents of the Holy Spirit's divinity were called "pneumatomachians" (that means, opponents of the Spirit), or "Macedonians" (from the name of their leader, Macedonius). The great Fathers opposed these erroneous opinions with their authority; among them was Athanasius (†373), who especially in his Letter to Serapion (1, 28-30) affirmed the equality of the Holy Spirit with the other two divine persons in the unity of the Trinity. He did so on the basis of "ancient tradition, the doctrine and faith of the Catholic Church, which we understand as having been given us by the Lord and which the apostles preached and the Fathers safeguarded..." (cf. PG 26, 594-595).

These Fathers who valued the revelation contained in Sacred Scripture in its fullness and with its complete meaning not only defended the true and complete concept of the Trinity. They also noted that by denying the divinity of the Holy Spirit, the raising up of humanity to share in God's life—that is, man's "divinization" by means of grace—would also be annulled. According to the Gospel, that too is the work of the Holy Spirit. Only he who is God can bring about a share in divine life. And it is precisely the Holy Spirit who "gives life," according to Jesus' very own words (cf. Jn 6:63).

We must add that faith in the Holy Spirit as a divine Person, as professed in the Nicene-Constantinopolitan Creed, has been confirmed many times by the solemn magisterium of the Church. The canons of the Roman Synod of 382, for example, are a proof of this. They were published by Pope Damasus I, and in them we read that the Holy Spirit "is of divine substance and is truly God," and that, "as the Son and the Father, so also the Holy Spirit can do all and knows all and is omnipresent" *(DS* 168-169).

The concise formula of the Creed of 381, which says about the divinity of the Holy Spirit that "he is Lord" as the Father and the Son are Lord, logically adds that "with the Father and the Son he is worshipped and glorified." The Holy Spirit is the one who "gives life." That is, with the Father and the Son he possesses creative power, and especially sanctifying and life-giving power in the supernatural order of grace. This power is attributed to his Person. It is right that he be adored and glorified as the first two Persons of the Trinity, from whom he proceeds as the endpoint of their eternal love, in perfect equality and unity of substance.

Still the creed attributes to this third Person of the Trinity in a special way the role of being the divine author of prophecy. He is the one who "has spoken through the prophets." Thus the source of the Old Testament inspiration of the prophets is recognized, beginning with Moses (cf. Dt 34:10) and extending through to Malachi. They left us God's instructions in written form. They were inspired by the Holy Spirit. David, who was also a "prophet" (Acts 2:30), said that about himself (2 Sam 22:2); Ezekiel also said it (Ez 11:5). In his first speech,

Peter expressed the same faith, affirming that the "Holy Spirit had spoken through the mouth of David" (Acts 1:16). The author of the Letter to the Hebrews expresses himself similarly (Heb 3:7; 10:15). With deep gratitude, the Church receives the prophetic Scriptures as a precious gift from the Holy Spirit, who has shown himself to be so near and active from the beginning of salvation history.

General audience of October 31, 1990

The Spirit and the *Filioque* Debate

When we profess our faith "in the Holy Spirit, the Lord, the Giver of Life," we add: "who proceeds from the Father and the Son." As you know, these words were inserted into the Nicene Creed which had read simply: "We believe in the Holy Spirit" (cf. *DS* 125). Already during the Council of Constantinople (381) the explanation that the Holy Spirit "proceeds from the Father" (cf. *DS* 150) was added, and so we refer to the Nicene-Constantinopolitan Creed. The conciliar formula of 381 reads: "We believe in the Holy Spirit, who proceeds from the Father and the Son." The more complete formula: "who proceeds from the Father and the Son" *(qui a Patre Filioque procedit),* was already present in the ancient texts. It was put forth once again by the Synod of Aachen in 809. It was finally introduced in Rome as well in 1014 during the coronation of the Emperor Henry II.

It spread from there throughout the entire West, and was adopted by the Greeks and the Latins at the ecumenical councils of Lyons (II, 1274) and Florence (1439) (cf. *DS* 150 *Nota Introductoria).* It was a clarification that changed nothing in terms of the substance of the ancient faith. The Roman Pontiffs were insistent on adopting it out of respect for the ancient formula which had by then spread to all areas, and was used in St. Peter's Basilica as well. The introduction of the addition, which was accepted without difficulties in the West, gave rise to reservations and debate among our Eastern brethren who said that the West had made a substantial change in a matter of faith. Today we can thank the Lord that even on this point the true meaning of the formula is being clarified in the West and in the East, as well as the relative importance of the question itself. In our present context, however, we must now take a look at the "origin" of the Holy Spirit, taking into consideration as well the matter of the *Filioque*.

In the first place, Sacred Scripture refers to the Holy Spirit's procession from the Father. In Matthew's Gospel, for example, as Jesus sent the Twelve on their first mission, he reassured them in this fashion: "Do not be worried over how you are to speak or what you are to say. For it will not be you who speak but the Spirit of your Father speaking through you" (Mt 10:19-20). In John's Gospel, Jesus states: "When the Advocate comes whom I will send, the Spirit of Truth who comes from the Father, he will testify to me" (Jn 15:26). According to many exegetes, these words of Jesus refer directly to the temporal mission of the Spirit given by the Father. One can legitimately see reflected in them the eternal procession, and therefore the Holy Spirit's origin from the Father.

Clearly since we are referring to God we must free the word "origin" from all reference to created and temporal origin. That is, the communication of existence to someone in an active sense must be excluded, and therefore the prior existence and the superiority of the one over the other, and likewise post-existence and dependence on the other. In God all is eternal, beyond time. The origin of the Holy Spirit is therefore eternal, as is that of the Son within the Trinitarian mystery in which the three divine Persons are consubstantial. It is precisely a procession with spiritual origins, as occurs (to use an analogy which is always very imperfect) in the "production" of thought or of love which remain in the soul united to the mind from which they originated. "It is in this sense," St. Thomas writes, "that the Catholic faith admits processions in God" (*Summa Theol.*, I, q. 27, a. 1; aa. 3-4).

Regarding the procession and the origin of the Holy Spirit from the Son, the New Testament texts, while not openly speaking of them, still stress the very close relationship between the Spirit and the Son. The sending of the Holy Spirit upon the believers is not just the work of the Father, but of the Son too. In the upper room, after Jesus spoke of "the Holy Spirit whom the Father will send in my name" (Jn 14:26), he adds: "If I go, I will send him to you" (16:7).

Other Gospel passages express the relationship between the Spirit and the revelation given by the Son, as in the passage where Jesus says: "He will glorify me because he will take from me what is mine and declare it to you. Everything that the Father has is mine; for this reason I told you that he will take from what is mine and declare it to you" (Jn 16:14-15).

The Gospel clearly says that the Son, not only the Father, "sends" the Holy Spirit. It further states that the Spirit "takes" from the Son what he reveals, since all that the Father has also belongs to the Son (cf. Jn 16:15).

After the resurrection, these words were fulfilled when Jesus, entering through "closed doors" into the place where the apostles were hiding for fear of the Jews, "breathed on" them and said: "Receive the Holy Spirit" (Jn 20:22).

These Gospel passages are the basic ones for our discussion. Along with them there are others in the New Testament which show that the Holy Spirit is not only the Spirit of the Father, but also the Spirit of the Son, Christ's Spirit. Thus we read in the letter to the Galatians that "God has sent the Spirit of the Son into our hearts, crying out: 'Abba, Father!'" (4:6). In other texts the Apostle speaks of "the Spirit of Christ Jesus"

(Phil 1:19) and the "Spirit of Christ" (Rom 8:9). He states that what Christ does through him (the Apostle) he does "by the power of the Holy Spirit" (Rom 15:19). There is no dearth of other texts like this one (cf. Rom 8:2; 2 Cor 3:17 ff.; 1 Pet 1:11).

Truly the question about the "origin" of the Holy Spirit within the trinitarian life of the one God has been the object of long and complex theological reflection based on Scripture. In the West St. Ambrose in his *De Spiritu Sancto* and also St. Augustine in his work *De Trinitate* made a great contribution to the clarification of this problem. The attempt to more deeply penetrate the mystery of the intimate life of God the Trinity, made by these and other Latin and Greek Fathers and Doctors (beginning with St. Hilary, St. Basil, Diogenus, St. John Damascene), certainly prepared the way for the introduction into the creed of that formula referring to the Holy Spirit as one who "proceeds from the Father and the Son." The Eastern brethren, however, held to the pure and simple formula of the Council of Constantinople (381), even more so since the Council of Chalcedon (451) confirmed that council's "ecumenical" character (even though almost all its participants were Oriental bishops). Thus the *Filioque* of the Latin West became in subsequent centuries an occasion for a schism which had already been actuated by Photius (882), but which was consummated and extended to almost all the Christian East in 105. In the creed the Oriental Churches separated from Rome still today profess their faith "in the Holy Spirit who proceeds from the Father," without mentioning the *Filioque*. In the West we expressly say that the Holy Spirit "proceeds from the Father and the Son."

Specific reference to this doctrine is not lacking in the great Fathers and Doctors of the East (Ephraim, Athanasius, Basil, Epiphanius, Cyril of Alexandria, Maximus, John Damascene) and of the West (Tertullian, Hilary, Ambrose, Augustine). Following the Fathers, St. Thomas gave an insightful explanation of the formula on the basis of the principle of the unity and equality of the divine Persons in the trinitarian relationship (cf. *Summa Theol.,* I, q. 36, aa. 2-4).

After the schism various Councils during the second millennium tried to reconstruct the unity between Rome and Constantinople. The issue of the Holy Spirit's procession from the Father and from the Son was the object of clarification especially at the Fourth Lateran Council (1215), the Second Council of Lyons (1274) and finally at the Council of Florence (1439). At this last Council we find a statement which has the value of a historical clarification and at the same time of a doctrinal declaration: "The Latins state that by saying that the Holy Spirit proceeds from the Father and from the Son they do not mean to exclude that the Father is the source and the principle of all divinity, that is, of the Son and the Holy Spirit. Nor do they wish to deny that the Son learned from the Father that the Holy Spirit proceeds from the Son; nor do they hold that there are two principles or two spirations. Rather they assert that one only is the principle and one only the spiration of the Holy Spirit, as they have asserted up to now" (cf. *Conciliorum Oecumenicorum Decreta*, Bologna 1973, p. 526).

That was an echo of the Latin tradition which St. Thomas had well defined theologically (cf. *Summa Theol.,* I, q. 36, a. 3) by referring to a text of St. Augustine, according to which *"Pater et Filius sunt unum principium Spiritus Sancti" (De Trinitate*, V, 14: PL 42, 921).

The problems on the order of terminology seem thus to be resolved and the intentions clarified, to the extent that each party, the Greeks and the Latins, during the sixth session (July 6, 1439) were able to sign this common definition: "In the name of the Holy Trinity, Father, Son and Holy Spirit, with the approval of this sacred and universal Council of Florence, we establish that this truth of faith must be believed and accepted by all Christians: and thus all must profess that the Holy Spirit is eternally of the Father and the Son, that he has his existence and his subsistent being from the Father and the Son together, and that he proceeds eternally from the one and from the other as from a single principle and from a single spiration" *(DS* 1300).

There is an additional clarification to which St. Thomas had devoted an article of the *Summa ("Utrum Spiritus Sanctus procedat a Patre per Filium,"* I, q. 36, a. 3): "We declare," said the Council, "what the holy Doctors and Fathers stated—that is, that the Holy Spirit proceeds from the Father through the Son—tends to make understandable and means that the Son too, like the Father, is the cause, as the Greeks say, and the principle, as the Latins say, of the subsistence of the Holy Spirit. And since all that the Father has he has given to the Son in his generation, with the exception of being Father, this very procession of the Holy Spirit from the Son the Son himself has eternally from the Father, from whom he has been eternally generated" *(DS* 1301).

Today as well this conciliar text is still a useful basis for dialogue and agreement between the Eastern and Western brethren, even more so since the agreed-upon definition ended with the following declaration: "We establish...that the explanation given of the expression *Filioque* has been added to the creed licitly and with reason, in order to render that truth clearer and because of the incumbent needs of those times" *(DS* 1302).

After the Council of Florence the West continued to profess that the Holy Spirit "proceeds from the Father and the Son," while the East continued to hold to the original formula of the Council of Constantinople. But since the time of the Second Vatican Council a fruitful ecumenical dialogue has been developing. It seems to have led to the conclusion that the formula *Filioque* does not constitute an essential obstacle to the dialogue itself and to its development, which all hope for and pray for to the Holy Spirit.

General audience of November 7, 1990

The Spirit as "Love Proceeding"

Today we want to begin the catechesis by repeating a statement previously made on the topic of the One God which the Christian faith teaches us to recognize and to adore as the Trinity. "The reciprocal love of the Father and the Son proceeds in them and from them as a Person: the Father and the Son 'spirate' the Spirit of Love who is of one substance with them." From the start the Church held the conviction that the Holy Spirit proceeds from the Father and from the Son as Love.

The roots of the tradition of the Fathers and Doctors of the Church are found in the New Testament and especially in St. John's words in his first letter: "God is Love" (1 Jn 4:8).

These words refer to the very essence of God, in which the three Persons are one single substance, and all are equally Love, that is, the desire for another's good, an inner drive toward the object which is loved, within and outside of the life of the Trinity.

But the time has come to observe with St. Thomas Aquinas that our language is poor in terminology which can express the act of the will which draws the lover into the beloved. That is due to the interior nature of love. Since it proceeds from the will or the heart, it is not as clear and self-conscious as is an idea which proceeds from the mind. In the sphere of the intellect we have different words which express, on the one hand, the relationship between the knower and the object known (to know, to understand) and on the other hand, the emergence of an idea from the mind in the act of knowing (to speak the word, or *verbum*, to proceed as a word from the mind). The same is not the case in the field of the will and the heart. It is certainly true that, "given the fact that one loves something, an impression is left in that person, in his or her feelings, an impression, so to say, of the object which is loved, by virtue of which the thing loved is within the lover as a thing known is within the person who knows it.

"Thus when a person knows and loves himself, he is in himself, not only because he is identical with himself, but also because he is the object of his own knowledge and of his own love." Yet in human language, "other words have not been coined to express the relationship which exists between the affection, or the impression made by the object which is loved, and the (interior) principle from which it emerges, or vice versa. Therefore, because of the poverty of vocabulary *(propter vocabulorum inopiam)*, these relationships are also expressed by the words *love* and *delight*. It is as though one were applying to the Word the names of conceived knowing or of generated wisdom."

Whence comes the conclusion of the Angelic Doctor: "If in the words love and to love *(diligere)* one wishes to refer only to the relationship between the lover and the thing loved, these words (in the Trinity) refer to God's essence, like the other words knowing and understanding. If instead we use these same words to indicate the relationships which exist between what derives from or proceeds from the act and object of love, and the correlative principle, in a way in which *Love is equal to Love which proceeds,* and *to Love (diligere)* is equivalent *to spirate the proceeding love,* then Love is the name of a person..." and is the name of the Holy Spirit himself *(Summa Theol.,* I, q. 37, a. 1).

The terminological analysis made by St. Thomas is very useful in getting a relatively clear idea of the Holy Spirit as Love-Person, in the heart of the Trinity which in its entirety "is Love." But it must be said that the attribution of love to the Holy Spirit, as the Spirit's proper name, is found in the teachings of the Fathers of the Church which the Angelic Doctor drew on. In their turn the Fathers are the heralds of the revelation of Jesus and of the preaching of the apostles, which we also know through other texts of the New Testament. Thus in his priestly prayer directed to the Father at the Last Supper, Jesus said: "I made known to them your name, and I will make it known, that the love with which you loved me may be in them and I in them" (Jn 17:26). We are dealing here with the love with which the Father has loved the Son "before the creation of the world" (Jn 17:24). According to some modern exegetes the words of Jesus point here, at least in an indirect way, to the Holy Spirit, the Love with which the Father eternally loves the Son, who is eternally loved by him. Earlier St. Thomas had carefully examined a text by St. Augustine concerning this reciprocal love of the Father and the Son in the Holy Spirit (cf. *De Trinitate,* VI, 5; XIV, 7, PL 43, 928, 1065). This was discussed by other scholastics because of the ablative with which it entered into medieval theology: *"Utrum Pater et Filius diligant se Spiritu Sancto"*; he had concluded his literary and doctrinal analysis with this beautiful explanation: "In the same way that we say that the tree blooms with flowers, so we say that the Father says himself and his creatures in the Word, his Son, and that the Father and the Son love each other and us in the Holy Spirit, that is, in Love proceeding" *(Summa Theol.,* I, q. 37, a. 2).

In the same farewell discourse, Jesus also announces that

the Father will send the apostles and the Church the "Comforter...the Spirit of truth" (Jn 14:16-17), and that he, the Son, will also send him (cf. Jn 16:7) "to be with you always" (Jn 14:16-17). The apostles, therefore, will receive the Holy Spirit as the Love which unites the Father and the Son. By the power of this Love the Father and the Son "will make their dwelling with them" (Jn 14:23).

In this same regard, another passage in the priestly prayer when Jesus prays for the unity of his disciples must be considered: "So that they may all be one as you, Father, are in me and I in you, that they also may be one in us, that the world may know that you sent me" (Jn 17:21). If the disciples are to be "one in us," that is, in the Father and the Son, this can happen only by the Holy Spirit's power, whose coming and indwelling in the disciples are announced simultaneously by Christ: he "remains with you and will be in you" (Jn 14:17).

This announcement was accepted and understood by the early Church. Besides the Gospel of John, this is shown in St. Paul's note on the love of God which "has been poured out into our hearts through the Holy Spirit who has been given to us" (Rom 5:5). The words of St. John prove it as well in his first letter: "If we love one another, God remains in us and his love is brought to perfection in us. This is how we know that we remain in him and he in us; that he has given us of his Spirit" (1 Jn 4:12-13).

The tradition about the Holy Spirit as Person-Love has developed from these roots. The trinitarian economy of salvific sanctification allowed the Fathers and Doctors of the Church to "cast a penetrating glance" into the intimate mystery of the God-Trinity.

St. Augustine did this especially in his work *De Trinitate* by contributing in a decisive way to the formulation and the spread of this teaching in the West. His reflections developed the concept of the Holy Spirit as the mutual Love and the bond of unity between the Father and the Son in the communion of the Trinity. He wrote: "As we appropriately call the sole Word of God 'Wisdom,' even though generally speaking the Holy Spirit and the Father himself are Wisdom, the Spirit also is given Love as a proper name, even though the Father and the Son are Love as well in a general sense" *(De Trinitate*, XV, 17, 31; CC 50, 505).

"The Holy Spirit is something in common with the Father and the Son...the same consubstantial and coeternal communion.... They are not more than three: one who loves the one who comes from him; one who loves the one from which he receives his origin; and Love himself" *(De Trinitate,* VI, 5, 7; CC 50, 295, 236).

The same doctrine is found in the East, where the Fathers speak about the Holy Spirit as the one who is the unity of the Father and the Son and the bond of the Trinity. Thus wrote Cyril of Alexandria (†444) and Epiphanius of Salamis (†403) (cf. *Ancoratus,* 7: PG 43, 28 B).

The Eastern theologians of later times kept to the same line. Among them was the monk Gregory Palamas, Archbishop of Thessalonika (14th century) who writes: "The Spirit of the supreme Word is like a certain kind of love which the Father has for the mysteriously generated Word; and it is that same love that the most beloved Word and Son of the Father has for the one who generated him" *(Capita Physica,* 36: PG 150, 1144 D-1145 A). Among more recent authors I am happy to cite Bulgakov: "If God, who is in the most holy Trinity, is love, the Holy Spirit is the Love of the love" *(The Paraclete,* Italian ed., Bologna, 1972, p. 121).

It is the doctrine of the East and West which Pope Leo XIII gathered from the tradition and synthesized in his encyclical on the Holy Spirit, wherein we read that the Holy Spirit "is divine Goodness and the mutual Love of the Father and the Son" (cf. *DS* 3326). But in conclusion, let us turn again to St.

Augustine: "Love is from God and is God: therefore it is appropriately the Holy Spirit through whom God's love spreads in our hearts by making the Trinity dwell in us.... The Holy Spirit is properly called the Gift made in Love" *(De Trinitate*, XV, 18, 32: PL 42, 1082-1083). Because he is Love, the Holy Spirit is Gift. That will be the theme of our next catechesis.

General audience of November 14, 1990

The Spirit as Gift

We are all familiar with the sensitive and inviting words Jesus addressed to the Samaritan woman who came to draw water from Jacob's well: "If only you recognized God's gift" (Jn 4:10). These words lead us into another fundamental aspect of the truth revealed about the Holy Spirit. In that meeting Jesus spoke about the gift of "living water," stating that the one who drinks it "will never be thirsty" (Jn 4:14). On another occasion Jesus spoke in Jerusalem about "rivers of living water" (Jn 7:38). In reporting these words the evangelist adds that Jesus said this "referring to the Spirit which those who came to believe in him were to receive" (Jn 7:39). Afterward the evangelist explains that the Spirit would be given only after Jesus had been "glorified" (Jn 7:39).

Out of a reflection on these and similar texts the conviction emerged that the concept of the Holy Spirit as Gift granted by the Father belongs to Jesus' revelation. Furthermore in Luke's Gospel, in his teaching (which is almost a catechesis) on prayer Jesus tells his disciples that, if people know how to give good things to their children, "how much more will the heavenly Father give the Holy Spirit to those who ask him" (Lk 11:13). The Holy Spirit is a "good" more valuable than any other (cf. Mt 7:11), the "good gift" par excellence!

In his farewell discourse to the apostles, Jesus assured them that he himself will ask the Father to give his disciples this gift above all others: "I will ask the Father and he will give you another Paraclete to be with you always" (Jn 14:16). This is how he spoke on the eve of his passion. After the resurrection he announced that the fulfillment of his prayer was near: "I will send down upon you the promise of My Father...until you are clothed with power from on high" (Lk 24:49). "You will receive power when the Holy Spirit comes down on you; then you are to be my witnesses...to the ends of the earth" (Acts 1:8).

Jesus asks the Father to give the Holy Spirit as a gift to the apostles and to the Church until the end of time. But at the same time he is the one who carries this gift within himself, and possesses even in his humanity the fullness of the Holy Spirit since "the Father loves the Son and has given everything over to him" (Jn 3:35). He is the one whom "God has sent," who speaks the words of God and does not ration his gift of the Spirit" (Jn 3:34).

Even through his humanity the Son of God is the one who sends the Holy Spirit. While the Holy Spirit is fully the Gift of the Father, Christ the man, by accomplishing his redemptive mission through his passion which he embraced and bore in obedience to the Father, an obedience "even to death on the cross" (Phil 2:8), reveals the Holy Spirit as Gift through his redemptive sacrifice as Son and gives the spirit to his disciples. What Jesus in the upper room called his "departure" becomes within the economy of salvation the preordained moment to which the "coming" of the Spirit is connected (cf. Jn 16:7).

Through this climactic moment of self-revelation by the Trinity, we are allowed to enter even more deeply into God's inner life. The Holy Spirit is revealed to us not only as a Gift to humanity, but also as Gift subsistent in the very inner life of God. "God is love," as St. John told us (1 Jn 4:8), essential love which is common to all three Divine persons, according to the clarification by theologians. But that does not exclude that the Holy Spirit, as Spirit of the Father and the Son, is Love in a personal sense, as we explained in prior catecheses. Therefore he "scrutinizes even the deep things of God" (1 Cor 2:10) with the penetrating power that belongs to Love. Therefore he is also the uncreated and eternal Gift shared by the three divine Persons in the inner life of God, one and three. His existence as Love is identified with his existence as Gift. One could even say that "through the Holy Spirit God 'exists' in the mode of gift. It is the Holy Spirit who is the personal expression of this self-giving, of this being-love. He is Person-Love. He is Person-Gift" *(DViv* 10).

St. Augustine writes that, "just as for the Son, to be the being which is born, means that he is from the Father, so for the Holy Spirit, to be the being which is Gift means that he proceeds from the Father and the Son" *(De Trinitate*, IV, 20: PL 42, 908). In the Holy Spirit there is an equality between being Love and being Gift. St. Thomas explains it well: "Love is the reason for a free gift which is given to a person out of love. The first gift, therefore, is love *(amor habet rationem primi doni)*.... Thus, if the Holy Spirit proceeds as Love, he proceeds also as First Gift" *(Summa Theol.*, I, q. 38, a. 2). All the other gifts are distributed among Christ's Body through the Gift which is the Holy Spirit, the Angelic Doctor concludes in harmony with St. Augustine *(De Trinitate*, XV, 19; PL 42, 1084).

The Holy Spirit as Love-Person and uncreated God is at the origin of all other gifts poured out upon creatures, and is a source *(fons vivus)* from which every created thing derives. He is like a fire of love *(ignis caritas),* which showers sparks of reality and goodness upon all things *(dona creata)*. This refers to the giving of existence through the act of creation and the giving of grace to angels and human beings within the economy of salvation. This is why the Apostle Paul wrote: "God's love has been poured out in our hearts through the Holy Spirit who has been given to us" (Rom 5:5).

This Pauline text is also a synthesis of what the apostles taught immediately after Pentecost. "You must reform and be baptized," urged Peter, "each one of you, in the name of Jesus Christ that your sins may be forgiven; then you will receive the gift of the Holy Spirit" (Acts 2:38). Shortly thereafter Peter was sent to baptize the centurion Cornelius. Peter grasped through the experience of a divine revelation "that the gift of the Holy Spirit was to be poured out upon the pagans too" (cf. Acts 10:45). Acts reports also the episode referring to Simon Magus who wanted to buy the gift of the Holy Spirit with money. Simon Peter rebuked him harshly for that, and reasserted that the Holy Spirit is a gift only to be freely received as God's own gift (cf. Acts 8:19-23).

That is what the Fathers of the Church repeat. We read, for example, in Cyril of Alexandria that "our return to God is made through Christ the Savior, and occurs only through the participation and the sanctification of the Holy Spirit. The one who connects us and, so to speak, unites us with God is the Spirit; by receiving the Spirit we are sharers in and consorts of the divine nature; we receive the Spirit through the Son and in the Son we receive the Father" *(Commentary on John's Gospel*, 9, 10: PG 74, 544 D). It is the "return to God" which is brought about continually in individuals and throughout various human generations during the intervening period between the redemptive "departure" of Christ—of the Father's Son—and the always new "coming" in holiness of the Holy Spirit, which will be complete in Jesus' glorious return at the end of history. All things on the sacramental, charismatic, and ecclesiastical-hierarchical levels which serve this "return" by humanity to the Father in the Son are a multi-form and varied outpouring of the one eternal Gift. This gift is the Holy Spirit, under the dimension of created gift, or as a sharing of humanity in infinite Love. It is the "Holy Spirit who gives himself," St. Thomas says *(Summa Theol.*, I, q. 38, a. 1, ad 1). There is a certain continuity between the uncreated Gift and created gifts. That led St. Augustine to write: "The Holy Spirit is eternally Gift, but in time he is [what is] given" *(De Trinitate*, V, 16, 17; CC 50, 224).

Out of this ancient tradition of the Church Fathers and Doctors who are links with Jesus Christ and the apostles comes what was written in *Dominum et Vivificantem:* "The love of God the Father, as a gift, infinite grace, source of life, has been made visible in Christ, and in his humanity that love has become 'part' of the universe, the human family and history. This appearing of grace in human history through Jesus Christ has been accomplished through the power of the Holy Spirit, who is the source of all God's salvific activity in the world. He is the 'hidden God' who as love and gift 'fills the universe'" (n. 54). At the heart of this universal order made up of the gifts of the Holy Spirit is the human being, "a rational creature who, unlike other earthly creatures, can attain the enjoyment of the divine Person and make use of his gifts. The rational creature can arrive at this when he or she becomes a sharer in the divine Word and in Love which proceeds from the Father and the Son so that through free interior openness the human being can truly know God and properly love God...but this happens certainly not through personal merit, but as a gift granted from on high.... In this sense it is up to the Spirit to be given and to be Gift" *(Summa Theol.,* I, q. 38, a. 1).

We will have another opportunity to indicate the importance of this teaching for the spiritual life. For now we will end our catecheses on the Person of the Holy Spirit—Love and Gift of infinite charity—with the beautiful text by the Angelic Doctor.

General audience of November 21, 1990

THE SPIRIT
AND THE CHURCH

The Soul of the Church

Today we begin a new series of catecheses in the cycle on the Holy Spirit in which I have sought to draw the attention of my listeners both near and far to the basic Christian truths about the Holy Spirit. We have seen that the New Testament, led up to by the Old, permits us to come to know the Spirit as a Person of the Blessed Trinity. It is a fascinating truth, because of both its inner meaning and its influence on our lives. We can even say that it is a truth-for-living, just as is all the revelation which is summed up in the creed. In a special way the Holy Spirit has been revealed to us and given to us so that he may be life's light and guide for us, for the whole Church and for all people called to know him.

We are speaking especially about the Spirit as the life-giving principle of the Church. We saw earlier during the Christological catechetical series that from the start of his messianic mission Jesus gathered disciples around himself. From them he chose the Twelve, called apostles. He assigned the prime role as his witness and representative to Peter (cf. Mt 16:18). When on the eve of his sacrifice on the cross he instituted the Eucharist, he commanded and empowered these apostles to celebrate it in his memory (cf. Lk 22:19; 1 Cor 11:24-25). After the resurrection he conferred on them the power to forgive sins (cf. Jn 20:22-23) and gave them the command to evangelize the whole world (cf. Mk 16:15).

We can say that all of that is tied to the announcement and the promise of the Holy Spirit's coming which occurred on the day of Pentecost, as the Acts of the Apostles relates (2:1-4).

The Second Vatican Council gives us several significant texts on the decisive importance of the day of Pentecost, which is often called the birthday of the Church in the world's eyes. We read in the Constitution *Dei Verbum* that "He confirmed with divine testimony what revelation proclaimed, that God is with us to free us from the darkness of sin and death, and to raise us up to life eternal" (n. 4). Therefore there is a close link between Jesus Christ and the Holy Spirit in the work of salvation.

In its turn the Constitution *Lumen Gentium* says: "He is the Spirit of life, a fountain of water springing up to eternal life (Jn 4:47; 7:38-39). To men, dead in sin, the Father gives life through him, until in Christ, he brings to life their mortal bodies" (n. 4). Therefore, through the power and action of the Spirit through whom Christ was raised up, those who are incorporated into Christ will be raised. This is St. Paul's teaching which the Council adopted (cf. Rom 8:10-11).

The Council adds that in descending upon the apostles, the Holy Spirit gave birth to the Church (cf. *LG* 19), which is described in the New Testament and especially in St. Paul as the Body of Christ: "The Son of God...by communicating his Spirit, made his brothers, called together from all nations, mystically the components of his own Body" *(LG 7)*.

Christian Tradition employs the Pauline theme of *Ecclesia Corpus Christi,* whose life-giving principle, according to the Apostle, is the Holy Spirit. It comes to the conclusion in a most beautiful phrase that the Holy Spirit is the

Church's "soul." Here we need only quote St. Augustine who in a speech states that "what our spirit, that is, our soul, is in relation to our other members, so the Holy Spirit is to the members of Christ, that is, the Body of Christ which is the Church" *(Sermon* 269, 2; PL 38, 1232). In speaking of Christ as head of the Body of the Church, St. Thomas Aquinas compares the Holy Spirit to the heart, because "invisibly he gives life to and unifies the Church," just as the heart "carries out its inner influence within the human body" *(Summa Theol.,* III, q. 8, a. 1, ad 3).

The Holy Spirit as "soul of the Church" and "heart of the Church": this is a beautiful aspect of Tradition which we must delve into more deeply.

It is clear that, as theologians explain, the expression: "The Holy Spirit animates the Church" is understood as an analogy. He is not the "substantial form" of the Church as the soul is for the body, together with which it forms the one substance we call the human being. The Holy Spirit is the vital principle of the Church, intimate yet transcendent. He is the Giver of life and unity to the Church, along the lines of the efficient cause, that is, as the author and promoter of divine life in the Body of Christ. The Council calls attention to this and states that "in order that we might be unceasingly renewed in him (cf. Eph 4:23) he has shared with us his Spirit who, existing as one and the same being in the head and in its members, gives life to, unifies and moves the whole body. This he does in such a way that his work could be compared by the Fathers with the function which the principle of life, that is, the soul, fulfills in the human body" *(LG* 7).

Following this analogy one could draw a comparison between the whole process of the formation of the Church, already within the sphere of the messianic activity of Christ on earth, and the creation of the human being according to the Book of Genesis, and especially the breathing in of the "breath of life" by which "man became a living being" (Gen 2:7). The term used in the Hebrew text is *nefesh* (to be animated by a life-giving breath). But in another passage in Genesis the vital breath of the living beings is called *ruah*, that is, "spirit" (Gen 6:17). According to this analogy the Holy Spirit can be considered to be the vital breath of the "new creation" which is realized in the Church.

The Council tells us in another place that "the Holy Spirit was sent on the day of Pentecost in order that he might continually sanctify the Church, and thus, all those who believe would have access through Christ in one Spirit to the Father (cf. Eph 2:18)" *(LG* 4). Holiness is the first and the basic form of life that the Holy Spirit, like the "life-giving soul," infuses into the Church—holiness after the model of Christ "whom the Father consecrated and sent into the world" (Jn 10:36). Holiness constitutes the Church's basic identity as the Body of Christ, given life and sharing in his Spirit. Holiness gives the Body spiritual health. Holiness also determines its spiritual beauty, a beauty which surpasses all natural or artistic beauty; a supernatural beauty in which the beauty of God himself is reflected in a more essential and direct way than in any other created beauty, precisely because it is the Body of Christ. In another catechesis we shall return to the theme of the Church's holiness.

The Holy Spirit is called the "Church's soul" also in the sense that he sheds divine light on all thought within the Church, and "guides to all truth," according to the announcement made by Christ in the upper room: "When the Spirit of truth comes, he will guide you to all truth. He will not speak on his own, but will speak only what he hears...what he will announce to you he will have from me" (Jn 16:13, 15).

Therefore it is by the Holy Spirit's light that the Church comes to the announcement of the revealed truth, and a deepening of faith on all levels of the Body of Christ is at work:

among the apostles, among their successors in the ministry, and regarding the "sense of faith" of all believers, among whom are catechists, theologians and other Christian thinkers. All is and must be enlivened by the Spirit.

The Holy Spirit is also the source of all dynamism in the Church, whether we are referring to the witness she must give to Christ before the world, or to the spread of the Gospel message. In Luke's Gospel when the risen Christ tells the apostles about the coming of the Holy Spirit, he stresses precisely this aspect: "I send down upon you the promise of my Father. Remain here in the city until you are clothed with power from on high" (Lk 24:49). The link between the Holy Spirit and power is still clearer in the parallel account in the Acts of the Apostles where Jesus says: "You will receive power when the Holy Spirit comes down upon you and you will be my witnesses..." (Acts 1:8). In both the Gospel and in the Acts, the Greek word for power or strength is *dynamis* (dynamism). This refers to a supernatural energy which on a person's part requires prayer most of all. This is a further teaching of the Second Vatican Council, according to which the Holy Spirit "dwells in the Church and in the hearts of the faithful, as in a temple. In them he prays on their behalf and bears witness to the fact that they are adopted sons" *(LG* 4). In the same text the Council cites St. Paul (cf. Gal 4:6; Rom 8:15-16, 26). We want to mention especially the passage from the Letter to the Romans: "The Spirit aids us in our weakness for we do not know how to pray as we ought; but the Spirit himself makes intercession for us with groanings that cannot be expressed in speech" (8:26).

To conclude all that we have said so far, let us reread another brief conciliar text which says that the Holy Spirit uninterruptedly renews the Church and "leads it to perfect union with her Spouse. The Spirit and the Bride both say to Jesus, the Lord, 'Come!' (Rev 22:7)" *(LG* 4). This text echoes

St. Irenaeus *(Adv. Haer.* III, 14, 1: PG, 7, 966 B), who communicates to us the certainty of faith of the earliest Fathers. It is the same certainty announced by St. Paul when he said that believers have been freed from slavery to the letter "to serve in the new spirit" (Rom 7:6). The whole Church is under this new spirit and discovers in the Holy Spirit the source of her continued renewal and her unity. This is due to the fact that the power of the Spirit who is life-giving and unifying Love is stronger than all human weakness and sins.

General audience of November 28, 1990

The Spirit of Unity

As we saw in our preceding catechesis, the Holy Spirit is the soul of the Church, according to the Christian Tradition founded on the teaching of Christ and the apostles. But we must immediately add that St. Paul, in drawing his analogy of the Church as a human body, emphasizes for us that "in one Spirit we were all baptized into one body, ...and we were all given to drink of one Spirit" (2 Cor 12:13). If the Church is like a body, the Holy Spirit is like her soul, that is, the principle of her divine life. If, on the other hand, on the day of Pentecost the Spirit established the Church by descending on the primitive community in Jerusalem (cf. Acts 1:13), from that day on and for all other generations that enter the Church, he cannot fail to be the principle and the source of unity, as the soul is for the human body.

Let us say that, according to the texts of the Gospel and St. Paul, this is a matter of a unity in multiplicity. The Apostle expresses this explicitly in his First Letter to the Corinthians: "As a body is one though it has many parts, and all the parts of the body, though many, are one body, so also is Christ" (1 Cor 12:12).

Once this premise of the ontological order on the unity of

the Body of Christ has been posited, the exhortation which we find in the Letter to the Ephesians is explained: "Strive to preserve the unity of the Spirit through the bond of peace" (Eph 4:3). It is apparent that this is not a question of a mechanical unity, nor of a merely organic one (like that of every living being), but rather of a spiritual unity which entails an ethical involvement. According to Paul, peace is the result of reconciliation through the cross of Christ, "for through him we both have access in one Spirit to the Father" (Eph 2:18). In this text "both" refers to converts from Judaism and from paganism. The Apostle asserts and describes at length their reconciliation with God, who makes of everyone one people, one body in one Spirit (cf. Eph 2:11-18). However, this argument holds true for all peoples, nations and cultures from which those who believe in Christ come. With St. Paul we can say about all of them what we find in the next part of the text: "So, then, you are no longer strangers and sojourners, but you are fellow citizens with the holy ones and members of the household of God, built upon the foundation of the apostles and prophets, with Jesus Christ himself as the capstone. Through him the whole structure is held together and grows into a temple sacred in the Lord; in him you [converts from paganism] also [in addition to converts from Judaism] are being built together into a dwelling place of God in the Spirit" (Eph 2:19-22).

"In him [Christ] every construction grows." There is therefore a dynamism in the unity of the Church, which tends toward an ever fuller participation in the trinitarian unity of God himself. The unity of the ecclesial communion is an image of the communion of the Trinity, the summit of infinite height, to which it looks at all times. It is the greeting and wish which is addressed to the faithful at the beginning of the Mass in the renewed liturgy of Vatican II, using the words of Paul himself: "The grace of the Lord Jesus Christ and the love of God and the fellowship of the Holy Spirit be with all of you" (2 Cor 13:13). They contain the truth about the unity in the Holy Spirit as the unity of the Church, which St. Augustine commented upon as follows: "The communion of the Church's unity...is as it were a work of the Holy Spirit himself, with the participation of the Father and the Son, because in a way the Spirit himself is the communion of the Father and the Son.... The Father and the Son have the Spirit in common, because he is the Spirit of both of them" *(Sermon* 71, 28, 33: PL 38, 463-464).

This concept of trinitarian unity in the Holy Spirit as the source of the Church's unity in the form of "communion" is one of the main points of ecclesiology. The Second Vatican Council repeatedly affirms this. We can cite the closing words of the fourth paragraph of the Constitution *Lumen Gentium*, dedicated to the Spirit who sanctifies the Church, which quotes a famous text of St. Cyprian of Carthage *(De Orat. Dominica,* 23: PL, 4, 536): "Thus the Church has been seen as 'a people made one with the unity of the Father, the Son and the Holy Spirit" *(LG* 4; see also *LG* 9; *GS* 24; *UR* 2).

We should also note that, according to Paul's recommendation which we have just heard, ecclesial communion is expressed in the readiness to remain in unity and in constancy, regardless of the multi-faceted plurality and differences among individuals, ethnic groups, nations and cultures. As the source of this unity the Holy Spirit teaches mutual understanding and indulgence (or at least tolerance), showing each person the spiritual wealth of the others. He teaches how to share spiritual gifts with one another in order to unite people and not divide them. As the Apostle says: "One body and one Spirit, as you were also called to the one hope of your call; one Lord, one faith, one baptism" (Eph 4:4-5). On the spiritual and ethical level, yet having profound repercussions on the psychological and social planes, the force which unites is most of all love which is shared and practiced according to Christ's commandment: "Love one another, as I have loved you" (Jn 13:34; 15:12). According to St. Paul, this love is the supreme gift of the Holy Spirit (cf. 1 Cor 13:13).

Unfortunately, this unity of and in the Holy Spirit, which is proper to the Body of Christ, runs up against sin. Thus it came about that during the course of the centuries, Christians have experienced quite a few divisions, some of which were greater and enduring. These divisions are explained—but not justified—by the weakness and limitation which are part of our fallen human nature. These remain and are also expressed in the members of the Church and in her leaders too. However, we must also proclaim our conviction, based on the certainty of faith and the experience of history, that the Holy Spirit is working tirelessly to build up unity and communion, despite our human weakness. This is the conviction which the Second Vatican Council expressed in the Decree *Unitatis Redintegratio* on ecumenism, when it acknowledged that "today, in many parts of the world, under the inspiring grace of the Holy Spirit, many efforts are being made in prayer, word and action to attain that fullness of unity which Jesus Christ desires" *(UR* 4), *Unum corpus, unus Spiritus.* This sincere tending toward unity in the Body of Christ comes from the Holy Spirit, and it is only through his work that the ideal of unity can be fully realized.

Yet in the Church, in addition to the unity of Christians, the Holy Spirit brings about a universal openness to the entire human family, and is the source of universal communion. On the religious plane the Church's missionary activity has emerged from this wonderful and deep source, from the age of the apostles to our own day. The tradition of the Fathers tells us that from the very first centuries the mission was carried out with attention to and understanding of those "seeds of the Word" *(semina Verbi)* contained in various cultures and non-Christian religions, to which the last Council dedicated a document *(Nostra Aetate*: see especially n. 2 in regard to the ancient Fathers, including the *Apologia* by St. Justin, 10. See also *Ad Gentes*, 15; *Gaudium et Spes*, 22). This is because the Spirit who "blows where he wills" (cf. Jn 3:8) is the source of inspiration for all that is true, good and beautiful, according to the magnificent phrase of an unknown author from the time of Pope Damasus (366-384) which states that: "Every truth, no matter who says it, comes from the Holy Spirit" (cf. PL, 191, 1651). St. Thomas repeated this text several times in his writings and commented upon it in this way in his *Summa:* "Every truth, no matter who says it, comes from the Holy Spirit who infuses the natural light [of intelligence] and moves the person to understand and express the truth." Then the Spirit, according to Aquinas, intervenes with the gift of grace added to nature, when it is a question of "knowing and expressing certain truths, and especially the truths of faith, to which the Apostle is referring when he affirms that 'no one can say Jesus is Lord except by the Holy Spirit' (1 Cor 12:3)" (I-II, q. 109, a. 1, ad. 1). Discerning and bringing to light in all their richness the truths and values present in the fabric of cultures is a fundamental task of missionary activity, nourished in the Church by the Spirit of Truth, who as Love leads people to a more perfect knowledge in charity.

The Holy Spirit pours himself out into the Church as Love, the saving force which tends to draw together all people and all of creation. This energy of love ends up overcoming all resistance even though, as we know all too well from experience and history, it must continually struggle against sin and everything there is in the human being which is opposed to love, that is, selfishness, hatred and jealous and destructive rivalry. But the Apostle assures us that "love builds up" (1 Cor 8:1). The building up of the ever new and ever ancient unity will also depend on love.

General audience of December 5, 1990

The Spirit Is
the Source of Holiness

The Second Vatican Council stressed the close relationship which exists in the Church between the gift of the Holy Spirit and the faithful's call and aspiration to holiness: "Christ, the Son of God, who with the Father and the Spirit is praised as 'uniquely holy,' loved the Church as his bride, delivering himself up for her. He did this that he might sanctify her (cf. Eph 5:25-26). He united her to himself as his own body and brought it to perfection by the gift of the Holy Spirit for God's glory. Therefore in the Church everyone...is called to holiness.... This holiness of the Church is unceasingly manifested, and must be manifested, in the fruits of grace which the Spirit produces in the faithful; it is expressed in many ways in individuals, who in their walk of life, tend toward the perfection of charity, thus causing the edification others..." *(LG* 39).

Being the source of holiness is another basic aspect of the work of the Holy Spirit in the Church.

As seen in the conciliar text just cited, the holiness of the Church begins in Jesus Christ, the Son of God, who became man by the work of the Holy Spirit and was born of the most holy Virgin Mary. The holiness of Jesus in his conception and birth by the power of the Holy Spirit is in deep communion

The Spirit Is the Source of Holiness

with the holiness of her whom God chose as his mother. As the Council again notes, "It is no wonder therefore that the usage prevailed among the Fathers whereby they called the Mother of God entirely holy and free from all stain of sin, as though fashioned by the Holy Spirit and formed as a new creature" *(LG* 56). Hers is the first and the highest realization of holiness in the Church, through the power of the Holy Spirit who is the Holy One and the Sanctifier. Mary's holiness is entirely directed toward the supreme holiness of the humanity of Christ, whom the Holy Spirit consecrated and filled with grace from the start of his earthly life until its glorious conclusion when Jesus revealed himself as the "established Son of God in power according to the spirit of holiness through the resurrection of the dead" (Rom 1:4).

On the day of Pentecost this ecclesial holiness shone forth not only in Mary but also in the apostles and in the disciples who with her "were all filled with the Holy Spirit" (Acts 2:4). From that time until the end of time, that holiness, the fullness of which is always Christ from whom we receive all grace (cf. Jn 1:16) is bestowed on all those who open themselves to the power of the Holy Spirit through the apostles' teaching, as the Apostle Peter said in his Pentecost discourse: "Repent and be baptized, every one of you, in the name of Jesus Christ for the forgiveness of your sins; and you will receive the gift of the Holy Spirit" (Acts 2:38).

That day was the beginning of the history of Christian holiness to which both the Israelites and the pagans are called. As St. Paul writes, both can "have access through Christ in one Spirit to the Father" (Eph 2:18). All are called to become, according to the text already referred to in the previous catechesis, "fellow citizens with the holy ones and members of the household of God, built upon the foundation of the apostles and prophets, with Christ Jesus himself as the capstone. Through him the whole structure is held together and grows into a temple sacred in the Lord...to become God's dwelling place in the Spirit" (Eph 2:19-22). This concept of the temple is dear to the Apostle, who asks in another passage: "Are you not aware that you are God's temple and that the Holy Spirit dwells in you?" (1 Cor 3:16). And in another place: "Your bodies are temples of the Holy Spirit" (1 Cor 6:19).

It is clear that in the context of the Letters to the Corinthians and to the Ephesians the temple is not just an architectural space. It is the representative image of holiness which is brought about by the Holy Spirit in people alive in Christ and united to the Church. And the Church is the "place" for this holiness.

The Apostle Peter too in his first letter uses the same vocabulary and gives us the same teaching. Speaking to the "faithful dispersed" (among the pagans), he reminds them that they have been "chosen in the foreknowledge of God the Father, through sanctification by the Spirit, for obedience and sprinkling with the blood of Jesus Christ" (1 Pet 1:1-2). By strength of this sanctification in the Holy Spirit all are "like living stones built into a spiritual house to be a holy priesthood to offer spiritual sacrifices acceptable to God through Jesus Christ" (1 Pet 2:5).

This is a significant special link which the Apostle drew between sanctification and the offering of "spiritual sacrifices," which is really a sharing in the very sacrifice of Christ and in his priesthood. It is one of the basic themes of the Letter to the Hebrews. But also in the Letter to the Romans the Apostle Paul speaks of the "oblation acceptable to God, sanctified by the Holy Spirit"; people (pagans) become that offering through the Gospel (cf. Rom 15:16). And in the Second Letter to the Thessalonians he urges readers to give thanks to God because "he has chosen you as the first fruits for salvation through sanctification by the Spirit and belief in truth" (cf. 2 Thess 2:13). All these are signs of the first Christians' common awareness of the action of the Holy Spirit as the author of holiness within themselves and in the Church. They knew that the Spirit which had been granted to them made them temples of God.

St. Paul insists on this in repeating that the Holy Spirit brings about human sanctification and forms ecclesial communion among believers, as sharers in his very holiness. People who have been "washed, sanctified and justified in the name of the Lord Jesus Christ" become holy "in the Spirit of our God" (1 Cor 6:11). "Whoever is joined to the Lord becomes one spirit with him" (1 Cor 6:17). And this holiness becomes true worship of the living God: "worship in God's Spirit" (Phil 3:3).

This Pauline teaching goes together with the words of Christ referred to in John's Gospel about "true worshippers" who "worship the Father in spirit and in truth.... The Father seeks such people to worship him" (Jn 4:23-24). This "worship in spirit and in truth" has its roots in Christ who carries out the entire program which was brought to life by him in the Holy Spirit, as Jesus himself said at the Last Supper: "He [the Holy Spirit] will glorify me, because he will take from what is mine and reveal it to you" (Jn 16:14). The entire *opus laudis* in the Holy Spirit is the "true worship" paid to the Father by the Son, the Incarnate Word, in which believers share through the Holy Sprit. Therefore it is also the glorification of the Son himself in the Father.

The sharing in the Holy Spirit by believers and by the Church occurs also in all the other aspects of sanctification: purification from sin (cf. 1 Pet 4:8), enlightenment of the mind (cf. Jn 14:26), observance of the commandments (cf. Jn 14:23), perseverance in the journey toward eternal life (cf. Eph 1:13-14; Rom 8:14-16), and listening to what the Spirit himself "has to say to the Churches" (cf. Rev 2:7). In considering this work of sanctification in his catechesis on the Apostles' Creed,

St. Thomas Aquinas finds it easy to pass from the affirmation about the Holy Spirit to the one about the "holy Catholic Church." He writes: "As we see that in a person there is a body and a soul, and still there are various members, so too the Catholic Church is one body made up of various members. The soul which gives life to this body is the Holy Spirit. And therefore, after our profession of faith in the Holy Spirit, we are commanded to believe in the holy Catholic Church, as the creed says. Now 'Church' means assembly; and therefore the Church is the assembly of the faithful, and every Christian is a member of the Church which is holy...through washing in the blood of Christ, through anointing with the grace of the Holy Spirit, through the indwelling of the Trinity and through the invocation of the name of God in the temple of the soul, which must never be violated (cf. 1 Cor 3:17)" *(In Symb. Apost.,* a. 10).

The logic of this explanation is based on the fact that holiness, the source of which is the Holy Spirit, must accompany the Church and her members in the course of their whole pilgrimage toward the eternal dwelling place. Therefore in the creed the articles on the Holy Spirit, the Church and the communion of saints are all connected: "I believe in the Holy Spirit, the holy Catholic Church, the communion of saints." The perfecting of this union—or the communion of saints— will be the eschatological result of holiness which is bestowed by the Holy Spirit on this earth to the Church in her sons and daughters, in every person, in every generation throughout the course of history. Even though during this history the sons and daughters of the Church often "sadden the Holy Spirit" (Eph 4:30), faith tells us that, "marked" by this Spirit "for the day of redemption" (Eph 4:30), they can advance along the paths of holiness, despite their weakness and sins, as far as the journey's end. The ways are many, and great are the various types of saints within the Church. "Star differs from star in brightness" (1 Cor 15:41). But "there is one Spirit" who in his own way and divine fashion brings about holiness in each person. Therefore we can accept with faith and hope the exhortation made by the Apostle Paul: "Therefore, my beloved brothers and sisters, be firm, steadfast, always fully devoted to the work of the Lord, knowing that in the Lord your labor is not in vain" (1 Cor 15:58).

General audience of December 12, 1990

The Spirit: Source of Catholicity

In the creed we affirm that the Church is one, holy, catholic and apostolic. These are the Church's characteristics. The Church's universality is therefore attributed to her with the very same word that is used in speaking of her: the Catholic Church.

This catholicity has its origin in the Holy Spirit, who "fills the universe" (Wis 1:7) and is the universal principle of communication and communion. The "power of the Holy Spirit" tends to spread faith in Christ and the Christian life "to the ends of the earth" (Acts 1:8), extending the benefits of redemption to all peoples.

Before the coming of the Holy Spirit, communion with the true God in divine covenant was not equally accessible to all peoples. The Letter to the Ephesians observes this in addressing Christians who belonged to pagan nations: "You people of Gentile stock, called 'uncircumcised' by those who...call themselves 'circumcised'...remember that in former times you had no part in Christ and were excluded from the community of Israel. You were strangers to the covenant and the promise; you were without hope and without God in the world" (Eph 2:11-12). In order to enter in some way into the divine covenant, they had to accept circumcision and adopt the observances of the Hebrew people, thus cutting themselves off from their own people.

Now, however, communion with God no longer requires these restrictive conditions because it comes about "through the Spirit." There is no longer any discrimination based on race or nation. All human beings can "become a dwelling place for God in the Spirit" (Eph 2:22).

This change of situation was announced by Jesus in his conversation with the Samaritan woman: "An hour is coming and is already here, when authentic worshippers will worship the Father in Spirit and truth. Indeed, it is just such worshippers the Father seeks. God is Spirit, and those who worship him must worship in Spirit and truth" (Jn 4:23-24). That was Jesus' answer to the question about the place for true worship of God. For the Samaritans it was Mount Gerizim, and it was Jerusalem for the Israelites. Christ's answer showed another dimension of true worship of God, the interior dimension ("in spirit and truth"), for which worship was not bound up with a definite place (a national sanctuary), and was therefore a universal worship. The words addressed to the Samaritan woman opened the road to that universality which is a fundamental quality of the Church as the new temple, the new sanctuary built by the Spirit who dwells there. This is the profound root of catholicity.

This root is the origin of the external, visible catholicity, the community and social one, we could say. It is essential to the Church due to the fact that Jesus commanded the apostles and their successors to bring the Gospel "to all nations" (Mt 28:19). The Church's universality under the influence of the Holy Spirit was already manifested at the time of her birth on Pentecost. The Acts of the Apostles testify that at the event in Jerusalem participants included "devout Jews of every nation under heaven" (Acts 2:5) who were staying in the holy city, and with them the proselytes, that is, pagans who had accepted the law of Moses. The Acts of the Apostles lists the names of some of the countries from which the people came, but they also speak more generally of "every nation under heaven." It is a sign of the primitive Church's awareness, interpreted and testified to by Luke, that the "baptism in the Holy Spirit" (Acts 1:5) conferred on that first community of the Church certainly had a universal value and that the Church was born from it with her characteristic of catholicity, that is, universality.

Generated by the action of the Holy Spirit this universality was, from the very day of Pentecost, accompanied by an insistent reference to that which is "particular," in regard to both persons and individual peoples and nations. This results from the fact that, as Luke notes in Acts, the power of the Holy Spirit was manifested through the gift of tongues in which the apostles spoke, so that each of (those present) heard them speaking in his own tongue (cf. Acts 2:4-6). Here we can observe that the Holy Spirit is Love, and to love someone means to respect everything that is a priority for the beloved. This especially goes for language which generally demands sensitivity and respect, but it also holds true for culture, spirituality and customs.

The Pentecost event was attentive to this demand and manifested the Church's unity in the multiplicity of peoples and in cultural pluralism. The Church's catholicity includes respect for the values of all. We could say that the particular is not canceled out by the universal. The one dimension contains and requires the other.

The fact of the multiplicity of languages at Pentecost tells us that in the Church the language of faith—which is universal in that it is an expression of the truth revealed through the Word of God—finds its human expression in various languages; we can say in each and every language. Earliest

The Spirit: Source of Catholicity

Christian history is already proof of this. We know that the language spoken by Jesus was Aramaic, which was used in Israel at that time. When the apostles set off to spread Christ's message, Greek had become the common language of the Greco-Roman world, and thus became the language of evangelization. It is also the language of the Gospel and all the other writings of the New Testament which came about under the inspiration of the Holy Spirit. These writings contain only a few words of Aramaic. This shows that from the beginning, the truth announced by Christ has sought the way to reach all tongues, to speak to all peoples. The Church has always sought, and continues to do so, to follow this principle of methodology and pedagogy of the apostolate according to the opportunities afforded in various eras. Today, we know, the practice of this demand of catholicity is especially felt and facilitated, thanks be to God.

In the Acts of the Apostles we find another example in an event which took place even before the conversion and preaching of Paul, the apostle of catholicity. At Caesarea Peter had accepted into the Church and baptized a Roman centurion Cornelius and his household—therefore, the first pagans. Luke's description of this event, which contains many details, indicates among other things, the fact that, since the Holy Spirit had descended upon all those who were listening to the Apostle's preaching, "the circumcised believers who had accompanied Peter were surprised that the gift of the Holy Spirit should have been poured out on Gentiles also" (Acts 10:44-45). However, Peter himself did not hesitate to confess that he had acted under the influence of the Holy Spirit: "The Spirit instructed me to accompany them without hesitation" (Acts 11:12).

This first "break" toward the universality of the faith immediately received further confirmation in dealing with the apostolic activity of Paul of Tarsus and his companions. The assembly in Jerusalem (which can be considered the first "council") reinforces this direction in the development of evangelization and of the Church. The apostles gathered in that assembly were sure that this direction came from the Spirit of Pentecost. Their words are eloquent, and they will always remain so. They can be considered the very first conciliar declaration: "It is the decision of the Holy Spirit and ours, too" (Acts 15:28). These decisions involved the path of universality which the Church had to take.

There is no doubt that this is the path the Church took then and throughout the centuries. The apostles and missionaries preached the Gospel to all nations, penetrating as much as possible the various societies and milieus. According to the possibilities of the time, the Church has sought to introduce the words of salvation into all cultures (inculturation), at the same time helping them recognize better their own authentic values in the light of the Gospel message.

This is what the Second Vatican Council set as a basic law for the Church when it wrote: "All men are called to belong to the new People of God. Wherefore this people, while remaining one and only one, is to be spread throughout the whole world and must exist in all ages.... It was for this purpose that God sent his Son.... For this too God sent the Spirit of his Son as Lord and Life-giver. He it is who brings together the whole Church and each and every one of those who believe, and who is the wellspring of their unity in the teaching of the apostles and in fellowship, in the breaking of bread and in prayers (cf. Acts 2:42)" *(LG* 13).

In these words the Council proclaimed its own awareness of the fact that the Holy Spirit is the principle and source of the Church's universality.

General audience of January 2, 1991

The Spirit:
Safeguard of the Apostolic Bond

In illustrating the action of the Holy Spirit as the soul of the Body of Christ, we saw in previous catecheses that he is the font and principle of the Church's unity, holiness, and catholicity (universality). Today we can add that he is also the source and principle of the apostolicity which is the Church's fourth property and characteristic: *"unam, sanctam, catholicam et apostolicam Ecclesiam,"* as we profess in the creed. Through the Holy Spirit the Church is apostolic, which means that she is "built upon the foundation of the apostles," with Christ himself as the cornerstone, as St. Paul says (Eph 2:20). This is a very interesting point of ecclesiology viewed in the light of pneumatology (cf. Eph 2:22).

St. Thomas Aquinas highlights this in his catechesis on the Apostles' Creed when he writes: "The Church's main foundation is Christ, as St. Paul affirms in his First Letter to the Corinthians (3:11): 'No one can lay a foundation other than the one that has been laid, namely Jesus Christ.' But there is a secondary foundation, that is, the apostles and their teaching. Therefore we speak of the apostolic Church" *(In Symb. Apost.,* a. 9).

Besides attesting to the ancient concept—of St. Thomas and the medieval era—of the Church's apostolicity, Aquinas' text reminds us that the foundation of the Church is the relationship between Christ and the apostles. Such a relationship comes about in the Holy Spirit. This manifests the theological (and revealed) truth of an apostolicity whose beginning and source is the Holy Spirit. He is the author of the communion in the truth which binds the apostles to Christ and through their teaching, binds Christian generations and the Church in all the centuries of her history to him.

Many times we have repeated Jesus' announcement to the apostles at the Last Supper: "The Paraclete, the Holy Spirit whom the Father will send in my name will instruct you in everything and remind you of all that I told you" (Jn 14:26). These words which Christ spoke before his passion find their complement in Luke's text in which we read that Jesus "having first instructed the apostles...through the Holy Spirit...was assumed into heaven" (Acts 1:2). The Apostle Paul, in turn, writing to Timothy while facing his own death, reminds him: "Guard the rich deposit of faith with the help of the Holy Spirit who dwells within us" (2 Tim 1:14). It is the Spirit of Pentecost, the Spirit who fills the apostles and the apostolic communities, the Spirit who guarantees the handing on of the faith in the Church from generation to generation, helping the apostles' successors to guard the "rich deposit," as Paul says, of the truth revealed by Christ.

In the Acts of the Apostles we read the account of an episode in which we clearly see this truth of the Church's apostolicity in its pneumatological dimension. The Apostle Paul, "compelled by the Spirit," (Acts 20:22), went to Jerusalem feeling and knowing that those he evangelized at Ephesus would never see him again (cf. Acts 20:25). Then he addressed the priests of the church in that city who had gathered around him, saying to them: "Keep watch over yourselves and over the whole flock the Holy Spirit has given you to guard. Shepherd the Church of God, which he has acquired at the price of his own blood" (Acts 20:28). "Bishops" means inspectors and leaders. They are placed to shepherd, therefore, while remaining on the basis of the apostolic truth which, according to Paul's premonition, will undergo distortion and threats from those who spread "false doctrine" (cf. Acts 20:30). Such will seek to cut the disciples off from the Gospel truth preached by the apostles. Paul urged the pastors to watch over their flock, but with the certainty that the Holy Spirit who had placed them there as "bishops" would assist them and sustain them. He himself would guide the successors of the apostles in the *munus* in the power and responsibility of guarding the truth which the apostles received from Christ. There is the certainty that it is the Holy Spirit who safeguards the truth for the People of God and their perseverance in it.

Besides the task of guarding the truth of Christ, the apostles and their successors have the duty of bearing witness to it, and they perform this task with the assistance of the Holy Spirit. As Jesus said to the apostles before his ascension: "You will be my witnesses in Jerusalem, in all of Judea and Samaria and to the very ends of the earth" (Acts 1:8). It is a vocation that binds the apostles to the mission of Christ himself, whom the Book of Revelation refers to as "the faithful witness" (Rev 1:5). In his prayer for the apostles, he said to the Father: "As you have sent me into the world, I have sent them into the world also" (Jn 17:18). In his apparition on Easter evening, before breathing upon them the breath of the Holy Spirit, he said to them: "As the Father has sent me, so I send you" (Jn 20:21). However, the testimony of the apostles, those who continue Christ's mission, is bound up with the Holy Spirit who in turn bears witness to Christ: "The Spirit of truth, who proceeds from the Father, will bear witness to me, and you too will bear witness, because you have been with me from the beginning" (Jn 15:26-27). These words of Jesus from the Last Supper are echoed in his words to the apostles before the ascension. In the light of the eternal plan of Christ's death and resurrection, he said that "in his name penance for the remission of sins is to be preached to all the nations.... You are witnesses of this. I send down upon you the promise of my Father" (Lk 24:48-49). And in a definitive manner he announced: "You will receive power when the Holy Spirit comes down upon you; then you are to be my witnesses" (Acts 1:8). It is the promise of Pentecost, not only in a historical sense, but also in the inner, divine dimension of the witness of the apostles and therefore, we can say, of the Church's apostolicity.

The apostles were aware of this association with the Holy Spirit in "bearing witness" to Christ crucified and risen. We can clearly see this in the response which Peter and his companions gave to the Sanhedrin which sought to silence them and prevent them from speaking about Christ: "The God of our fathers has raised up Jesus whom you put to death, hanging him on a tree. He whom God has exalted at his right hand as ruler and savior is to bring repentance to Israel and forgiveness of sins. We testify to this. So too does the Holy Spirit, whom God has given to those who obey him" (Acts 5:30-32). The Church, too, throughout the development of her history, has had the awareness that the Holy Spirit is with her in bearing witness to Christ. The Church is aware of the limitations and fragility of her people. With dedication in the search and vigilance which Paul recommended to the "bishops" in his farewell at Miletus, the Church knows that the Holy Spirit guards her and defends her from error in bearing witness to her Lord and in the doctrine which she has received from him to announce to the world. As the Second Vatican Council says: "This infallibility with which the divine Redeemer willed his Church to be endowed in defining doctrine of faith and morals, extends as far as the deposit of divine revelation extends, which must be religiously guarded and faithfully expounded" *(LG* 25). The conciliar text clarifies in what way this infallibility extends to the entire college of bishops and particularly to the bishop of Rome, in that they are successors of the apostles and persevere in the truth inherited from them by virtue of the Holy Spirit.

The Holy Spirit is therefore the life-giving principle of this apostolicity. Thanks to him the Church can spread throughout the world, throughout the various epochs of history, becoming implanted in diverse cultures and civilizations, but always preserving her own Gospel identity. As we read in the Decree *Ad Gentes* of the same Council: "Christ sent from the Father his Holy Spirit, who was to carry on inwardly his saving work and prompt the Church to spread out. The Lord Jesus, before freely giving his life for the world, did so arrange the apostles' ministry and promise to send the Holy Spirit that both they and the Spirit might be associated in effecting the work of salvation always and everywhere. Throughout all ages, the Holy Spirit...equips her with various gifts of a hierarchical and charismatic nature, giving life, soul-like, to ecclesiastical institutions and instilling into the hearts of the faithful the same mission spirit which impelled Christ himself..." *(AG* 4). And the Constitution *Lumen Gentium* underlines that "the divine mission, entrusted by Christ to the apostles, will last until the end of the world, (cf. Mt 28:20), since the Gospel they are to teach is for all time the source of all life for the Church" *(LG* 20).

In the next catechesis we shall see that the Holy Spirit intervenes in this Gospel mission, giving the Church a heavenly guarantee.

General audience of January 9, 1991

The Spirit: Guardian of Sacred Tradition

In its deepest meaning, the Church's apostolicity pertains to pastors and faithful together. It pertains to the truth revealed by Christ through the apostles and their successors, with an ever more sufficient knowledge of its content and value for life. It is a truth of divine origin concerning mysteries which surpass the abilities of the vision or powers of the human mind. Only by the power of the Word of God, addressed to humanity through analogy and expressed in human language, can it be understood, preached, believed and faithfully obeyed. And authority of merely human value would not suffice to guarantee the authenticity of the handing on of this truth, nor therefore the deep dimension of the Church's apostolicity. The Second Vatican Council assures us that it is the Holy Spirit who safeguards that authenticity.

According to the Constitution *Dei Verbum,* "by sending the Holy Spirit," Jesus Christ "confirmed with divine testimony what revelation proclaimed, that God is with us to free us from the darkness of sin and death, and to raise us up to life eternal" *(DViv* 4). This passage from the Council's *Constitution on Divine Revelation* finds its justification in the words Christ addressed to the apostles in the upper room as recorded

The Spirit: Guardian of Sacred Tradition

by John the evangelist: "I have much more to tell you, but you cannot bear it now. When he comes, however, being the Spirit of truth, he will guide you to all truth. He will not speak on his own, but will speak only what he hears" (Jn 16:12-13). Therefore it will be the Holy Spirit who gives light to the apostles that they may proclaim "the whole truth" of the Gospel of Christ, "teaching all nations" (cf. Mt 28:19): they and obviously their successors in this mission.

The Constitution *Dei Verbum* continues to say that this order (to preach the Gospel) "was faithfully fulfilled by the apostles who, by their oral preaching by example, and by observances handed on what they had received from the lips of Christ, from living with him, and from what he did, or what they had learned through the prompting of the Holy Spirit. The commission was fulfilled, too, by those apostles and apostolic men who under the inspiration of the same Holy Spirit committed the message of salvation to writing" *(DViv 7)*. As we can see, the Council text refers to the Holy Spirit's assurance of the truth revealed in its oral transmission (the origin of Tradition) and the written version which came about through inspiration and divine assistance in the books of the New Testament.

Again we read that "the Holy Spirit, through whom the living voice of the Gospel resounds in the Church, and through her, in the world, leads unto all truth those who believe and makes the word of Christ dwell abundantly in them (cf. Col 3:16)" *(DViv 8)*. Therefore, "Sacred Scripture is the word of God inasmuch as it is consigned to writing under the inspiration of the divine Spirit, while sacred Tradition takes the word of God entrusted by Christ the Lord and the Holy Spirit to the apostles, and hands it on to their successors in its full purity, so that led by the light of the Spirit of truth, they may in proclaiming it preserve this word of God faithfully, explain it, and make it more widely known" *(DViv 9)*.

Also, "the task of authentically interpreting the word of God...has been entrusted exclusively to the living teaching office of the Church, whose authority is exercised in the name of Jesus Christ. This teaching office is not above the word of God, but serves it, teaching only what has been handed on, listening to it devoutly, guarding it scrupulously and explaining it faithfully in accord with a divine commission and with the help of the Holy Spirit; it draws from this one deposit of faith everything which it presents for belief as divinely revealed" *(DViv* 10).

Therefore, there is a close bond between Sacred Scripture, Tradition, and the Church's magisterium. Through this intimate connection the Holy Spirit guarantees the handing on of divine revelation and consequently the Church's identity of faith.

Particularly in regard to Sacred Scripture, the Council tells us that "holy mother Church, relying on the belief of the apostles, holds that the books of both the Old and New Testaments in their entirety, with all their parts, are sacred and canonical because written under the inspiration of the Holy Spirit, they have God as their author and have been handed on as such to the Church herself.... Everything asserted by the inspired...writers must be held to be asserted by the Holy Spirit..." *(DViv* 11). As a consequence, "Holy Scripture must be read and interpreted in the same Spirit in which it was written..." *(DViv* 12). "For what the apostles preached in fulfillment of the commission of Christ, afterward they themselves and apostolic men, under the inspiration of the divine Spirit, handed on to us in writing: the foundation of faith, namely, the fourfold Gospel, according to Matthew, Mark, Luke and John" *(DViv* 18).

"After the ascension of the Lord the apostles handed on to their hearers what he had said and done. This they did with that clearer understanding which they enjoyed after they had been instructed by the events of Christ's life and taught by the light of the Spirit of Truth" *(DViv* 19).

This close connection between the Holy Spirit, revelation and the handing on of the divine truth is at the basis of the Church's apostolic authority and the decisive argument for our faith in the Word which the Church passes on to us. Besides, as the Council also says, the Holy Spirit intervenes in the inner birth of faith in a person. Indeed, "'the obedience of faith' (Rom 16:26; cf. 1:5; 2 Cor 10:5-6) 'is to be given to God who reveals, an obedience by which man commits his whole self freely to God, offering the full submission of intellect and will to God who reveals,' and freely assenting to the truth revealed by him. To make this act of faith, the grace of God and the interior help of the Holy Spirit must precede and assist, moving the heart and turning it to God, opening the eyes of the mind and giving 'joy and ease to everyone in assenting to the truth and believing it.' To bring about an ever deeper understanding of revelation, the same Holy Spirit constantly brings faith to completion by his gifts" *(DViv* 5).

It is a question of the faith of the Church as a whole and of every believer within the Church. It is also a question of the proper understanding of divine revelation which always flows from faith through the power of the Holy Spirit, and of the development of the faith through "reflection and study by believers." In speaking of the "Tradition which comes from the apostles," the Council says that it "develops in the Church with the help of the Holy Spirit. For there is a growth in the understanding of the realities and the words which have been handed down. This happens through the contemplation and study made by believers, who treasure these things in their hearts (like Mary: cf. Lk 2:19, 51), through a penetrating understanding of spiritual realities which they experience, and through the preaching of those who have received through episcopal succession the sure gift of truth" *(DViv* 8). Concerning Sacred

Scripture it adds that, "inspired by God and committed once and for all to writing, they impart the word of God himself without change, and make the voice of the Holy Spirit resound in the words of the prophets and apostles" *(DViv* 21). Therefore "the Bride of the Incarnate Word, the Church taught by the Holy Spirit, is concerned to move ahead toward a deeper understanding of the Sacred Scriptures..." *(DViv* 23).

The Church, therefore, "has always venerated the Scriptures," and she receives nourishment from them as from the "bread of life" and "has always maintained them, and continues to do so, together with sacred tradition as the supreme rule of faith..." *(DViv* 21). And since, "as the centuries succeed one another, the Church constantly moves forward toward the fullness of divine truth until the words of God reach their complete fulfillment in her" *(DViv* 8), the Church's entire life is animated by the Spirit by which she invokes Christ's glorious coming. As we read in the Book of Revelation: "The Spirit and the Bride say: 'Come!'" (Rev 22:17). In the order of this fullness of truth, the Holy Spirit leads and guarantees the handing on of revelation, preparing the Church and each and every one of us in the Church, for the Lord's final coming.

General audience of January 16, 1991

The Spirit:
Source of Sacramental Life

The Holy Spirit is the source of truth and life-giving principle of the identity of the one, holy, catholic and apostolic Church. The Holy Spirit is also the source and principle of the sacramental life through which the Church draws the strength of Christ, participates in his holiness, is nourished by his grace and grows and advances on her journey toward eternity. The Holy Spirit, who is at the origin of the Incarnation of the Word, is the living source of all the sacraments instituted by Christ and at work in the Church. It is precisely through the sacraments that he gives people "new life," associating the Church to himself as his co-worker in this saving action.

We do not intend to explain the nature, properties and scope of the sacraments to which we shall dedicate, God willing, other future catecheses. But we can always turn to the simple, concise formula of the old catechism according to which "the sacraments are means of grace, instituted by Jesus Christ for our salvation." We can also repeat once again that the Holy Spirit is the author, dispenser and almost the breath of Christ's grace in us. In this catechesis we shall see how, according to the Gospel texts, this connection can be found in the individual sacraments.

This connection is particularly clear in Baptism, which Jesus describes in his conversation with Nicodemus as being "born of water and the Spirit": "What is born of flesh is flesh and what is born of spirit is spirit.... You must be reborn from above" (Jn 3:5-7).

John the Baptist already announced and presented Christ as "the one who baptizes in the Holy Spirit" (Jn 1:33), "in the Holy Spirit and fire" (Mt 3:11). In the Acts of the Apostles and the apostolic writings the same truth is expressed in a different way. On Pentecost those who listened to Peter's message heard an invitation: "Repent and be baptized, every one of you, in the name of Jesus Christ for the forgiveness of your sins; and you will receive the gift of the Holy Spirit" (Acts 2:38). The Pauline letters speak of a "bath of rebirth and renewal by the Holy Spirit" poured out by Jesus Christ our Savior (cf. Titus 3:5-6). The baptized are reminded that "you have had yourselves washed, you were sanctified, you were justified in the name of the Lord Jesus Christ and in the Spirit of our God" (1 Cor 6:11). Again they are told that "in one Spirit [they] were all baptized into one body" (1 Cor 12:13). In Paul's teaching, as in the Gospel, the Holy Spirit and the name of Jesus Christ are linked in the proclamation, conferral and mention of Baptism as the source of sanctification and salvation—of that new life Jesus spoke of to Nicodemus.

Confirmation, the sacrament connected to Baptism, is presented in the Acts of the Apostles in the form of an imposition of hands through which the apostles communicated the gift of the Holy Spirit. Peter and John "laid hands on" the new Christians who had just been baptized "and they received the Holy Spirit" (Acts 8:17). The same was said of the Apostle Paul in regard to the other neophytes: "And when Paul laid [his] hands on them, the Holy Spirit came upon them" (Acts 19:6).

Through faith and the sacraments, therefore, we "were sealed with the promised Holy Spirit, which is the first installment of our inheritance" (Eph 1:13-14). To the Corinthians Paul wrote: "But the one who gives us security with you in Christ and who anointed us is God; he has also put his seal upon us and given the Spirit in our hearts as a first installment" (2 Cor 1:21-22; cf. 1 Jn 2:20, 27; 3:24). The Letter to the Ephesians adds the significant admonition not to grieve the Holy Spirit with which we "were sealed for the day of redemption" (Eph 4:30).

From the Acts of the Apostles we can deduce that the sacrament of Confirmation was administered through the imposition of hands after baptism "in the name of the Lord Jesus" (cf. Acts 8:15-17; 19:5-6).

In the sacrament of Reconciliation (or Penance), the connection with the Holy Spirit is established through the power of the word of Christ after his resurrection. Indeed, John testifies that Jesus breathed on the apostles and said to them: "Receive the Holy Spirit; whose sins you forgive are forgiven them; whose sins you retain are retained" (Jn 20:22-23). These words can also refer to the sacrament of the Anointing of the Sick, concerning which we read in the Letter of James that "the prayer of faith," together with the anointing by the presbyters "in the name of the Lord," "will save the sick person, and the Lord will raise him up. If he has committed any sins, he will be forgiven" (Jas 5:14-15). Christian Tradition has seen in this anointing and prayer an initial form of the sacrament (cf. St. Thomas, *Contra Gentes*, IV, C. 73). This identification was sanctioned by the Council of Trent (cf. *DS* 1695).

As for the Eucharist, in the New Testament its link with the Holy Spirit is marked more or less directly in the text of John's Gospel which recounts Jesus' announcement in the synagogue at Capernaum about the institution of the sacrament of his Body and Blood: "It is the Spirit which gives life, while the flesh is of no avail; the words I have spoken to you are spirit and life" (Jn 6:63). Both the word and the sacrament have life and operative effectiveness from the Holy Spirit.

Christian Tradition is aware of this bond between the Eucharist and the Holy Spirit which was expressed, and still is today, during the Mass when, in the *epiklesis* the Church requests the sanctification of the gifts offered upon the altar: "by the power of your Spirit" (Eucharistic Prayer III); "let your Spirit come upon them" (Eucharistic Prayer II); "bless and approve our offering" (Eucharistic Prayer I). The Church emphasizes the mysterious power of the Holy Spirit for the completion of the Eucharistic consecration, for the sacramental transformation of bread and wine into the Body and Blood of Christ, and for the communication of grace to those who participate in it and to the entire Christian community.

In regard to the sacrament of Orders, St. Paul speaks of the "charism" (or gift of the Holy Spirit) which leads to the imposition of hands (cf. 1 Tim 4:14; 2 Tim 1:6). He emphatically declares that it is the Holy Spirit who "appoints" bishops in the Church (cf. Acts 20:28). Other passages from Paul's letters and the Acts of the Apostles testify to a special rapport between the Holy Spirit and Christ's ministers, that is, the apostles and their collaborators, and later their successors: bishops, priests and deacons. They are heirs not only of their mission, but also of their charisms, as we shall see in our next catechesis.

Finally, I want to recall the sacrament of Matrimony, this "great mystery...in reference to Christ and the Church" (Eph 5:32). In marriage, in Christ's name and through him, a covenant is established between two people, a man and a woman, a life-giving community of love. This sacrament is the human participation in that divine love which has been "poured out into our hearts through the Holy Spirit" (Rom 5:5). According to St. Augustine, the third Person of the Blessed Trinity in God is the "consubstantial communion" *(communion consubstan-*

tialis) of the Father and the Son (cf. *De Trinitate*, VI, 5.7, PL 42, 928). Through the sacrament of Matrimony, the Spirit forms the human "communion of persons" between a man and woman.

In concluding this catechesis in which we at least gave a rough outline of the truth of the presence of the Holy Spirit at work in the Church's sacramental life, as we see from Scripture, Tradition and especially from the sacramental liturgy, we cannot fail to emphasize the necessity of a continual deepening of our knowledge of this wonderful doctrine. Nor can we fail to recommend to everyone a sacramental practice which is ever more consciously docile and faithful to the Holy Spirit who, especially through the "means of salvation instituted by Jesus Christ," brings to fulfillment the mission entrusted to the Church to work for universal redemption.

General audience of January 30, 1991

The Spirit: Source of All Ministry

For the full maturation of the life of faith, for preparation for the sacraments and for continual help to individuals and communities in responding to the grace given through these "salvific means," the Church has a structure of ministries (that is, organs and functions of service, *diakonie*), some of which are of divine institution. These are principally bishops, priests and deacons. Paul's words addressed to the presbyters of the Church of Ephesus, recorded in the Acts of the Apostles, are well known: "Keep watch over yourselves and over the whole flock of which the Holy Spirit has appointed you overseers, in which you tend the Church of God that he acquired with his own blood" (Acts 20:28). This advice from Paul shows the bond which exists between the Holy Spirit and the service of hierarchical ministry which takes place in the Church. The Holy Spirit, operating continually in the Church, helps her persevere in the truth of Christ inherited from the apostles and infuses into her members all the wealth of the sacramental life. He is also the one who "appoints bishops," as we read in the Acts of the Apostles. Appointing them does not simply mean naming them or having them named, but to be from the very beginning the life-giving principle of their ministry of salvation in the Church. Similar to the bishops, this holds true for the subordinate ministries. The Holy Spirit is the Author and Giver of the divine, spiritual, pastoral strength of the entire ministerial structure with which Christ the Lord has endowed the Church which is built upon the apostles. In the Church, as Paul says in the First Letter to the Corinthians, "there are different forms of service, but one Lord" (1 Cor 12:5).

The apostles were quite aware of this truth which first concerned them in their task of evangelization and government. Thus Peter, addressing the faithful spread throughout various regions of the pagan world, reminded them that the preaching of the Gospel was accomplished "through the Holy Spirit sent from heaven" (1 Pet 1:12). Similarly, the Apostle Paul reveals the same awareness several times in his letters. Thus he writes in the Second Letter to the Corinthians: "Our qualification comes from God, who has indeed qualified us as ministers of a new covenant, not of letter but of spirit" (2 Cor 3:5-6). According to the Apostle, the "service of the new covenant" receives life from the Holy Spirit, through whom the proclamation of the Gospel and the entire work of salvation takes place. Paul was called to perform these tasks especially among the nations beyond Israel. He presented himself to the Romans as one who had received the grace of being "a minister of Christ Jesus to the Gentiles in performing the priestly service of the Gospel of God, so that the offering up of the Gentiles may be acceptable, sanctified by the Holy Spirit" (Rom 15:16).

The entire apostolic college knew it was inspired, commanded and moved by the Holy Spirit in the service of the faithful, as can be seen from the concluding declaration of the council held by the apostles and their closest collaborators, the presbyters, at Jerusalem: "It is the decision of the Holy Spirit and of us" (Acts 15:28).

The Apostle Paul repeatedly affirms that, with the ministry which he exercises by virtue of the Holy Spirit, he intends "to show the spirit and his power." In his message there is no "sublimity of word," nor are there "persuasive words of wisdom" (1 Cor 2:1, 4). As an apostle he speaks in a language "not...taught by human wisdom, but with words taught by the Spirit, describing spiritual realities in spiritual terms" (1 Cor 2:13). It is here that he makes that significant distinction between "the natural person" who does not understand "what pertains to the spirit of God" and "the spiritual person" who "can judge everything" (cf. 1 Cor 2:14-15) in the light of the truth revealed by God. The Apostle can say of himself (and of the other preachers of the word of Christ) that "this [the things concerning the divine mysteries] God has revealed to us through the Spirit; for the Spirit scrutinizes everything, even the depths of God" (1 Cor 2:10).

Paul's concept of his apostolate as service corresponds to the awareness of the power of the Holy Spirit present and at work in his ministry. Let us recall that beautiful synthesis of his entire ministry: "We do not preach ourselves but Jesus Christ as Lord, and ourselves as your slaves for the sake of Jesus" (2 Cor 4:5). These words so well express the thought and intention which can be found in Paul's heart. They are decisive for the understanding of every ministry of the Church and in the Church for all time. They are the essential key for understanding it in a Gospel way. They are the basis of the spirituality which must flourish in the successors of the apostles and their collaborators: a humble service of love, although with the awareness that the same Apostle Paul manifests in the First Letter to the Thessalonians where he affirms: "Our Gospel did not come to you in word alone, but also in power and in the Holy Spirit, and with much conviction" (1 Thess 1:5). We could say that they are like two coordinates which allow us to recognize the place of ministry in the

Church: the spirit of service and the awareness of the power of the Holy Spirit who is at work in the Church. Humility of service and strength of soul derive from the personal conviction that the Holy Spirit assists and supports one in ministry, if the person is docile and faithful to his action in the Church.

Paul was convinced that his activity derived from that transcendent source. He did not hesitate to write to the Romans: "In Christ Jesus, then, I have reason to boast in what pertains to God. For I will not dare to speak of anything except what Christ has accomplished through me to lead the Gentiles to obedience by word and deed, by the power of signs and wonders, by the power of the Spirit..." (Rom 15:17-19).

Paul told the Thessalonians that "our Gospel did not come to you in word alone, but also in power and in the Holy Spirit and with much conviction. You know what sort of people we were among you for your sake." Paul then felt that he was able to offer them this beautiful testimony: "You became imitators of us and of the Lord, receiving the word in great affliction, with joy from the Holy Spirit, so that you became a model for all the believers in Macedonia and in Achaia..." (1 Thess 1:6-7). This is the most splendid perspective, and it must be the most important task for all those who are called to fulfill ministries in the Church: to be, like Paul, not only preachers, but also witnesses of faith and models of life. They should also tend to act so that the faithful also all become so within the Church herself and among the various particular churches.

This true glory of the ministry, according to Jesus' command to the apostles, must serve for preaching "conversion and forgiveness" (Lk 24:47). Yes, it is a ministry of humility, but one of glory, too. All those who are called to exercise it in the Church can make their own two expressions of Paul's sentiments. First of all: "All this is from God, who has reconciled us to himself through Christ and given us the ministry of reconciliation; namely, God was reconciling the world to himself in Christ.... So we are the ambassadors for Christ, as if God were appealing through us. We implore you on behalf of Christ, be reconciled to God" (2 Cor 5:18-20). The other text is the one in which Paul, considering the "ministry of the new covenant" as a "ministry of the Spirit" (2 Cor 3:6) and comparing it to the ministry of Moses on Sinai as mediator of the old law (cf. Ex 24:12), observes: if he "was so glorious that the Israelites could not look intently at the face of Moses because of its glory that was going to fade, how much more will the ministry of the Spirit be glorious?" This reflects the glory of the new covenant which is not surpassed in glory (2 Cor 3:7-10).

It is the glory of the reconciliation which has taken place in Christ. It is the glory of service given to one's brothers and sisters through the preaching of the message of salvation. It is the glory of having preached "not ourselves, but Christ Jesus the Lord" (2 Cor 4:5). Let us repeat it once and for all: it is the glory of the cross!

The Church has inherited from the apostles the awareness of the presence and assistance of the Holy Spirit. This is attested to by the Second Vatican Council when it writes in the Constitution *Lumen Gentium:* "The Spirit dwells in the Church and in the hearts of the faithful, as in a temple (cf. 1 Cor 3:16; 6:19). In them he prays on their behalf and bears witness to the fact that they are adopted sons (cf. Gal 4:6; Rom 8:15-16, 26). The Church, which the Spirit guides in the way of all truth (cf. Jn 16:13) and which he unified in communion and in works of ministry, he both equips and directs with hierarchical and charismatic gifts and adorns with his fruits (cf. Eph 4:11-12; 1 Cor 12:4; Gal 5:22)" *(LG* 4).

From this intimate awareness derives the sense of peace which the shepherds of Christ's flock maintain even at times when the world and the Church are in turmoil. They know that beyond their limitations and inadequacies, they can count on the Holy Spirit who is the soul of the Church and the guide of history.

General audience of February 6, 1991

The Spirit:
Source of Spiritual Gifts

We concluded the preceding catechesis with a text of the Second Vatican Council which we must take as our starting point for the present catechesis. In the Constitution *Lumen Gentium* we read: "The Spirit dwells in the Church and in the hearts of the faithful, as in a temple (cf. 1 Cor 3:16; 6:19). In them he prays on their behalf and bears witness to the fact that they are adopted sons (cf. Gal 4:6; Rom 8:15-16, 26). The Church, which the Spirit guides in the way of all truth (cf. Jn 16:13) and which he unified in communion and in works of ministry, he both equips and directs with hierarchical and charismatic gifts and adorns with his fruits (cf. Eph 4:11-12; 1 Cor 12:4; Gal 5:22)" *(LG* 4).

After having spoken in the preceding catechesis about the Church's ministerial structure which is inspired and sustained by the Holy Spirit, we are now going to discuss, following the Council's line of thought, the spiritual gifts and charisms given to the Church by the *dator munerum*, the giver of gifts, as the Spirit is called in the Pentecost sequence.

Here also we can draw upon the letters of St. Paul for the doctrine to explain it synthetically as is required by catechesis. In the First Letter to the Corinthians we read: "There are different gifts but the same Spirit; there are different ministries but the same Lord; there are different works but the same God who accomplishes all of them in everyone" (1 Cor 12:4-6). In these verses the diversity of charisms is placed together with the diversity of ministries and works. This suggests to us that the Holy Spirit is the one who gives a multiform wealth of gifts which accompanies the ministries and the life of faith, charity, community and fraternal collaboration of the faithful, as was already seen in the story of the apostles and the first Christian communities.

St. Paul pauses to emphasize the multiplicity of gifts: "To one the Spirit gives wisdom in discourse, to another the power to express knowledge. Through the Spirit one receives faith; by the same Spirit another is given the gift of healing, and still another miraculous powers. Prophecy is given to one.... One receives the gift of tongues" (1 Cor 12:8-10). Here we must note that the Apostle's list is not meant to be exhaustive. Paul is indicating the gifts which were particularly significant for the Church at that time. These gifts were still manifested in later eras, but without limiting, neither at the beginning nor later, all of the room available for the ever new charisms which the Holy Spirit can give in response to new needs. Therefore, "to each person the manifestation of the Spirit is given for the common good" (1 Cor 12:7). When new demands and new problems arise for the community, the history of the Church reveals the presence of new gifts.

In any case, whatever type of gift it may be, even when it seems primarily to serve the person who receives it (for example in glossolalia, which the Apostle speaks about (cf. 1 Cor 14:5-18), they all merge together in some way for the common good. They serve to build up "a Body": "It was in one Spirit that all of us...were baptized into one body. All of us have been given to drink of the one Spirit" (1 Cor 12:13). Hence Paul's recommendation to the Corinthians: "Since you have set your hearts on spiritual gifts, try to be rich in those that build up the Church" (1 Cor 14:12). In the same context we find the exhortation to "seek...the gift of prophecy" (1 Cor 14:1), which is more "useful" to the community than that of tongues. "Whoever speaks in a tongue is talking not to people but to God. No one understands him because he utters mysteries in the Spirit. The prophet on the other hand, speaks to people for their upbuilding, their encouragement, their consolation. He...builds up the Church" (1 Cor 14:2-3).

Evidently Paul prefers the "edifying" charisms, we could say those of the apostolate. However, above all the gifts he recommends that which is even more useful for the common good: "Seek eagerly after love" (1 Cor 14:1). Fraternal charity, rooted in the love of God, is the "more perfect way" which Paul insists on and exalts in a hymn of great lyrical power and sublime spirituality (cf. 1 Cor 13:1-3).

In the *Constitution on the Church* the Second Vatican Council takes up Paul's teaching on the spiritual gifts, and especially on the charisms, in order to specify them: "These charisms, whether they be the more outstanding or the more simple and widely diffused, are to be received with thanksgiving and consolation for they are perfectly suited to and useful for the needs of the Church. Extraordinary gifts are not to be sought after, nor are the fruits of apostolic labor to be presumptuously expected from their use; but judgment as to their genuinity and proper use belongs to those who are appointed leaders in the Church, to whose special competence it belongs, not indeed to extinguish the Spirit, but to test all things and hold fast to that which is good (cf. 1 Thess 5:12; 19:21)" *(LG* 12). This text is filled with pastoral wisdom. It is entirely in line with the recommendations and norms which, as we have seen, St. Paul gave the Corinthians in order to help them to a proper understanding of charisms and the necessary discernment of the true gifts of the Spirit.

The Spirit: Source of Spiritual Gifts

According to the Council, among the charisms special importance is given to those that serve the fullness of the spiritual life, especially those which are expressed in the various forms of consecrated life according to the evangelical counsels, which the Holy Spirit has always raised up among the faithful. In the Constitution *Lumen Gentium* we read: "The evangelical counsels of chastity dedicated to God, poverty and obedience are based upon the words and examples of the Lord. They were further commended by the apostles and the Fathers of the Church, as well as by the doctors and pastors of souls. The counsels are a divine gift, which the Church received from its Lord and which it always safeguards with the help of his grace. Church authority has the duty, under the inspiration of the Holy Spirit, of interpreting these evangelical counsels, of regulating their practice and finally to build on them stable forms of living.... The religious state...clearly shows all men both the unsurpassed breadth of the strength of Christ the King and the infinite power of the Holy Spirit marvelously working in the Church. Thus, the state which is constituted by the profession of the evangelical counsels, though it does not belong to the hierarchical structure of the Church, nevertheless, undeniably belongs to its life and holiness.... The hierarchy, following with docility the prompting of the Holy Spirit, accepts the rules presented by outstanding men and women and authentically approves these rules" *(LG* 43-45).

This concept of the religious state as a work of the Holy Spirit is especially important. Through it the third Person of the Trinity almost makes visible the activity which he performs in the entire Church in order to lead the faithful to the perfection of charity.

It is also legitimate to recognize the presence of the Holy Spirit at work in the efforts of all those—bishops, priests, deacons and lay men and women of all types—who try to live the Gospel in their own state of life. It is a matter of "various orders," as the Council put it *(LG* 13), which all manifest the "multiform grace of God." What counts for everyone is that "as each one has received a gift, use it to serve one another" (1 Pet 4:10). The communion of the Church is a result of the abundance and variety of gifts; she is one and universal in the variety of peoples, traditions, vocations and spiritual experiences.

The Spirit's action is manifested and at work in the multiplicity and richness of the charisms which accompany ministries in various forms and degrees as required by the needs of time and place. For example, we see this in helping the poor, the sick, the unfortunate, the handicapped or those suffering from various types of disability; or on a still higher level, in counsel, spiritual direction, making peace between opposing factions, conversion of sinners, drawing people to the word of God, the efficacy of preaching and writing, teaching the faith, encouraging people to do good, etc. There is an enormous range of charisms through which the Holy Spirit shares his charity and holiness with the Church, similar to the general economy of creation in which, as St. Thomas observes, the one divine Being gives things a share in his infinite perfection (cf. *Summa Theol.*, II-II q. 183, a. 2).

These charisms are not in contrast with the hierarchical nature of the ministries and, in general, with the "offices" which were also established for the unity, proper functioning and beauty of the Church. The hierarchical order and the entire ministerial structure of the Church are also under the action of the charisms, as Paul pointed out in his letter to Timothy: "Do not neglect the gift you received when, as a result of prophecy, the presbyters laid their hands on you" (1 Tim 4:14); "I remind you to stir into flame the gift of God bestowed when my hands were laid on you" (2 Tim 1:6).

There is, therefore, the charism of Peter; there are the charisms proper to bishops, priests and deacons; there is a charism granted to those called to assume an ecclesiastical office, a ministry. It is a question of discovering and recognizing these charisms and of supporting them, but without presumption. Therefore the Apostle writes to the Corinthians: "I do not want to leave you in ignorance about spiritual gifts" (1 Cor 12:1). And then Paul begins his instruction on the charisms in order to give some instructions about behavior to the converts of Corinth who, when they were still pagans, let themselves be "led astray to mute idols, as impulse" drove them (improper behavior which they now had to avoid). "That is why I tell you...that no one can say 'Jesus is Lord' except in the Holy Spirit" (1 Cor 12:3). This is a truth which, together with that of the Trinity, is fundamental for the Christian faith. The profession of faith in this truth is a gift of the Holy Spirit. Therefore it is an act far greater than an act of purely human knowledge. In this act of faith, which is and must be on the lips and in the hearts of all true believers, the Holy Spirit "is manifest" (cf. 1 Cor 12:7). This is the first and the most basic fulfillment of what Jesus said at the Last Supper: "He [the Holy Spirit] will give glory to me, because he will have received from me what he will announce to you" (Jn 16:14).

General audience of February 27, 1991

The Spirit: Another Comforter

In his farewell discourse to the apostles during the Last Supper on the night before he died, Jesus promised: "I will ask the Father, and he will give you another Comforter to be with you always" (Jn 14:16). The word "Comforter" here translates the Greek word *Parákletos*, the name which Jesus gave the Holy Spirit. "Comforter" is one possible meaning of Paraclete. In his discourse in the upper room Jesus suggested this meaning because he promised his disciples the continuing presence of the Spirit as a remedy against the sadness caused by his departure (cf. Jn 16:6-8).

The Holy Spirit, sent by the Father, will be "another Comforter" sent in the name of Christ, whose messianic mission must come to a close with his departure from this world to return to the Father. This departure, which took place through his death and resurrection, was necessary so that "another Comforter" could come. Jesus clearly affirmed this when he said: "If I do not go, the Comforter will not come to you" (Jn 16:7). The Second Vatican Council's Constitution *Dei Verbum* presents this sending of the "Spirit of truth" as the concluding moment of the revelatory and redemptive process responding to God's eternal plan (cf. n. 4). And all of us, in the sequence of Pentecost, invoke him: "Come, of comforters the best."

In Jesus' words about the Comforter we hear an echo of the books of the Old Testament, especially the "Book of Israel's Consolation" contained in the writings gathered under the name of the prophet Isaiah: "Comfort, give comfort to my people, says your God.... Speak tenderly to Jerusalem and proclaim to her that her servitude is at an end, her guilt is expiated" (Is 40:1-2). And later, "Sing out, O heavens and rejoice, O earth; break forth into song, you mountains, for the Lord comforts his people" (Is 49:13). For Israel the Lord is like a woman who cannot forget her child. In Isaiah the Lord says: "Even should [a mother] forget, I will never forget you" (Is 49:15).

In the objective finality of Isaiah's prophecy, besides the proclamation of Israel's return to Jerusalem following the exile, the promised "consolation" has a messianic content which the pious Israelites, faithful to the heritage of their ancestors, kept present up to the threshold of the New Testament. Thus we can explain what we read in Luke's Gospel about the aged Simeon who was "awaiting the consolation of Israel; the Holy Spirit was upon him. It had been revealed to him that he should not see death before he had seen the Messiah of the Lord" (Lk 2:25-26).

According to Luke, who is speaking of things that took place and narrates them in the context of the mystery of the Incarnation, it is the Holy Spirit who fulfills the prophetic promise connected with the coming of the first Comforter, Christ. It is he, in fact, who brings about in Mary the conception of Jesus, the incarnate Word (cf. Lk 1:35); it is he who enlightens Simeon and leads him to the Temple at the exact time of Jesus' presentation (cf. Lk 2:27); it is in him that Christ, at the beginning of his messianic ministry, in a reference to the prophet Isaiah, declares: "The Spirit of the Lord is upon me because he has anointed me to bring glad tidings to the poor. He has sent me to proclaim liberty to captives and recovery of sight to the blind, to let the oppressed go free" (Lk 4:18; cf. Is 61:1 f.).

The Comforter whom Isaiah spoke of, seen from the perspective of prophecy, is the one who brings the Good News from God, confirming it with "signs," that is, with works containing the salutary good of truth, justice, love and liberation—the "consolation of Israel." And when Jesus Christ, after having accomplished his work, left this world to return to the Father, he announced "another Comforter," that is the Holy Spirit, whom the Father will send in his Son's name (cf. Jn 14:26).

The Comforter, the Holy Spirit, will be with the apostles; when Christ is no longer on the earth there will be long periods of affliction, lasting for centuries (cf. Jn 16:17 ff.). He will be with the Church and in the Church, especially during times of strife and persecution, as Jesus himself promised the apostles in the words contained in the Synoptic Gospels: "When they take you before synagogues and rulers and authorities, do not worry about how or what your defense will be or about what you are to say. For the Holy Spirit will teach you at that moment what you should say" (Lk 12:11-13; cf. Mk 13:11). In fact, "It will not be you who speak but the Spirit of your Father speaking through you" (Mt 10:20). These words refer to the tribulations suffered by the apostles and the Christians of the communities which they founded and presided over. But they also refer to all those who, throughout the world and in all centuries, have to suffer for Christ. In reality many people throughout the centuries, and recently too, have experienced this help of the Holy Spirit. They know and can testify to the joy of the spiritual victory which the Holy Spirit granted them. The whole Church of today knows it and testifies to it.

From her beginning in Jerusalem, the Church has never lacked opposition and persecution. However, in the Acts of the

Apostles we read: "The Church throughout all Judea, Galilee and Samaria was at peace. It was being built up and walked in the fear of the Lord, and with the consolation of the Holy Spirit it grew in numbers" (Acts 9:31). It was the Spirit-Comforter promised by Jesus who sustained the apostles and the other disciples of Christ in the first trials and sufferings, and continued to grant the Church his comfort during periods of peace and calm as well. This peace depended on him, as did the growth of individuals and communities in the Gospel truth. That is how it has always been throughout the centuries.

The conversion and baptism of Cornelius, a Roman centurion, was a great "consolation" for the primitive Church (cf. Acts 10:44-48). He was the first "pagan" to enter the Church, together with his family, baptized by Peter. From that moment the number of those who converted from paganism began to multiply, especially through the apostolic activity of Paul of Tarsus and his companions; their number reinforced the multitude of Christians. In his discourse to the assembly of the apostles and the "elders" gathered in Jerusalem, Peter recognized in that fact the working of the Spirit-Comforter: "Brothers, you are well aware that from early days God made his choice among you that through my mouth the Gentiles would hear the word of the Gospel and believe. And God, who knows the heart, bore witness by granting them the Holy Spirit just as he did us" (Acts 15:7-9). For the apostolic Church the "consolation" was that, in giving the Holy Spirit, as Peter says, God "made no distinction between them and us, for by faith he purified their hearts" (Acts 15:9). Another "consolation" was also the unity expressed in this regard by that meeting in Jerusalem: "It is the decision of the Holy Spirit and of us" (Acts 15:28). When the letter regarding the liberating decision made at Jerusalem was read to the community of Antioch, everyone was "delighted with the consolation *(paraklesei)* it contained" (Acts 15:31).

Another "consolation" of the Holy Spirit for the Church was the spread of the Gospel as the text of the new covenant. If the books of the Old Testament, inspired by the Holy Spirit, were already a source of consolation and comfort for the Church, as St. Paul says to the Romans (Rom 15:4), how much more so were the books which related "all that Jesus did and taught from the beginning" (Acts 1:1). Of these we can even more truly say that they were written "for our instruction, that by endurance and by the consolation of the scriptures we might have hope" (Rom 15:4).

Another consolation to be attributed to the Holy Spirit (cf. 1 Pet 1:12) is the fulfillment of Jesus' preaching, that is, that "the Gospel of the kingdom will be preached throughout the world as a witness to all nations" (Mt 24:14). Among these nations, covering every era, there are also the people of the contemporary world, who seem so distracted and even led astray by success and the attraction of a too one-sided, material progress. To these people too, and to all of us, the work of the Spirit-Paraclete extends, who does not cease giving consolation and comfort with the Good News of salvation.

General audience of March 13, 1991

The Spirit:
Dwelling in Individuals

In a preceding catechesis I announced that we would return to the topic of the Holy Spirit's presence and action in the soul. Based on theology and rich in spirituality, these themes exert a certain attraction and, one could say, a supernatural fascination for those who desire an interior life. They attract those who are docile and attentive to the voice of the one who dwells in them as in a temple and who enlightens them from within and sustains them on paths consistent with the Gospel. It was these people whom my predecessor Leo XIII had in mind when he wrote the Encyclical *Divinum Illud* on the Holy Spirit (May 9, 1897) and later the letter *Ad Fovendum* on the devotion of the Christian people to the Spirit's divine Person (April 18, 1902), establishing the celebration of a specific novena in his honor, especially aimed at obtaining the good of Christian unity *(ad maturandum Christianae unitatis bonum).* The Pope of *Rerum Novarum* was also the Pope of devotion to the Holy Spirit. He knew from what source it was necessary to draw the energy to bring about true good on the social level also. I wanted to call the attention of the Christians of our day to that same source with the Encyclical *Dominum et Vivificantem* (May 18, 1986), and I shall now dedicate the concluding part of our pneumatological catechesis to it.

We can say that, on the basis of a Christian life characterized by interiority, prayer and union with God, there is a truth which—like all theology and pneumatological catechesis—derives from the texts of Sacred Scripture and especially from the words of Christ and the apostles: that of the indwelling of the Holy Spirit as a divine guest in the souls of the just.

The Apostle Paul asks in his First Letter to the Corinthians (3:16): "Do you not know that...the Spirit of God dwells in you?" Of course, the Holy Spirit is present and at work in the whole Church, as we have seen in preceding catecheses. But the concrete fulfillment of his presence and action comes about in relationship with the human person, with the soul of the just person in whom he establishes his dwelling and pours out the gift which Christ obtained through the redemption. The action of the Holy Spirit penetrates the depths of the person, the hearts of the faithful, and pours out upon them the light and grace which gives life. This is what we ask in the sequence of the Mass of Pentecost: "O most blessed light divine, shine within these hearts."

The Apostle Peter, in turn, in his discourse on Pentecost, after having urged his listeners to convert and be baptized, added the promise: "You will receive the gift of the Holy Spirit" (Acts 2:38). From this context we see that the promise personally concerns every person who converts and is baptized. Peter expressly addressed "each one" of those present (cf. 2:38). Later, when Simon the magician asked the apostles to give him the sacramental power, he said: "Give me this power, too, so that anyone upon whom I lay my hands may receive the Holy Spirit" (8:19). The gift of the Holy Spirit is understood as a gift given to individual persons. This same affirmation can be verified in the episode of the conversion of

Cornelius and his household. While Peter was explaining the mystery of Christ to them, "the Holy Spirit fell upon all who were listening" (10:44). The Apostle therefore recognized that "God gave them the same gift he gave to us" (11:17). According to Peter, the descent of the Holy Spirit signifies his presence in those to whom he communicates himself.

In regard to this presence of the Holy Spirit in the person, we must recall the successive ways in which we find the divine presence in salvation history. In the old covenant, God is present and manifests his presence first in the "tent" in the desert, then later in the "Holy of Holies" in the Temple in Jerusalem. In the new covenant, his presence is fulfilled in and identified with the Incarnation of the Word. God is present among people in his eternal Son through the human nature he assumed in unity of person with his divine nature. By this visible presence in Christ, God prepares a new presence through him, an invisible one that is fulfilled in the coming of the Holy Spirit. Indeed, Christ's presence "in the midst" of people opens up the path for the presence of the Holy Spirit, which is an inner presence, a presence in human hearts. Thus Ezekiel's prophecy is fulfilled (36:26-27): "I will give you a new heart and place a new spirit within you.... I will put my spirit within you."

On the night before his departure from this world to return to the Father through his cross and ascension into heaven, Jesus himself announced the coming of the Holy Spirit to the apostles: "I will ask the Father, and he will give you another advocate to be with you always, the Spirit of truth.... He will be in you" (Jn 14:16-17). But Christ himself said that this presence of the Holy Spirit, his indwelling in human hearts which also infers the indwelling of the Father and Son, has a condition, that of love: "Whoever loves me will keep my word, and my Father will love him, and we will come to him and make our dwelling with him" (Jn 14:23).

The reference to the Father and the Son contained in Jesus' discourse includes the Holy Spirit. St. Paul and patristic and theological tradition attributes the trinitarian indwelling to the Spirit because he is the Person-Love, and besides, this inner presence is necessarily spiritual. The presence of the Father and Son comes about through love, and therefore in the Holy Spirit. It is in the Holy Spirit that God, in his trinitarian unity, communicates himself to the spirit of each person.

St. Thomas Aquinas says that it is only in the spirit of the human person (and of an angel) that this manner of divine presence is possible (through indwelling) because only a rational creature is capable of being raised to knowledge, conscious love and enjoyment of God as an inner guest. This takes place through the Holy Spirit, who, therefore, is the first and most basic gift *(Summa Theol.,* I, q. 38, a. 1).

Through this indwelling, however, people become "temples of God" (of the triune God) because it is "the Spirit of God [who] dwells in" them, as the Apostle reminds the Corinthians (1 Cor 3:16). God is holy and makes holy. Paul points out shortly after this: "Do you not know that your body is a temple of the Holy Spirit within you, whom you have from God?" (1 Cor 6:19). Therefore the indwelling of the Holy Spirit implies a particular consecration of the whole human person (whose bodily dimension Paul emphasizes) similar to a temple. This consecration is sanctifying. It is the very essence of the saving grace through which the person is able to participate in God's trinitarian life. Thus an internal source of holiness opens up within the person, from which comes life "according to the Spirit," as Paul says in the Letter to the Romans (8:9): "You are not in the flesh; on the contrary, you are in the Spirit, if only the Spirit of God dwells in you." Here is the basis for the hope of bodily resurrection because "if the Spirit of the one who raised Jesus from the dead dwells in you, the one who raised Christ from the dead will give life to your mortal bodies also, through his Spirit that dwells in you" (Rom 8:11).

We must take note that the indwelling of the Holy Spirit, who sanctifies the entire person, body and soul, bestows a greater dignity on the human person. It gives new value to interpersonal relations, bodily ones too, as St. Paul notes in the text we quoted from the First Letter to the Corinthians (6:19).

Therefore, through the indwelling of the Holy Spirit the Christian is placed in a particular relationship with God, which also extends to all interpersonal relationships, in the family and in society too. When the Apostle says "not to grieve the Holy Spirit" (Eph 4:30), he is speaking on the basis of this revealed truth: the personal presence of an interior guest who can be "grieved" by sin—by every sin—because sin is always contrary to love. He himself, as the Person-Love dwelling in the human being, creates in the soul an inner demand to live in love. St. Paul suggests this when he writes to the Romans that "the love of God" (that is, the powerful stream of love which comes from God) "has been poured into your hearts by the power of the Holy Spirit who has been given to us" (Rom 5:5).

General audience of March 20, 1991

The Spirit: Source of New Life

The Holy Spirit, the soul's guest, is the inner source of the new life which Christ shares with those who believe in him. It is a life according to the "law of the Spirit," which in the power of the resurrection already prevails over the power of sin and death at work in man since the original fall. St. Paul himself identifies with this dramatic conflict between the inner feeling for what is good and the attractiveness of evil, between the tendency of the "mind" to serve the law of God and the tyranny of the "flesh" which subjects one to sin (cf. Rom 7:14-23). He exclaims: "Miserable one that I am! Who will deliver me from this mortal body?" (Rom 7:24).

But here is the new interior experience which corresponds to the revealed truth about the redemptive action of grace: "Hence, now there is no condemnation for those who are in Christ Jesus. For the law of the Spirit of life in Christ Jesus has freed you from the law of sin and death" (Rom 8:1-2). It is a new state of life begun in our hearts "through the Holy Spirit that has been given to us" (Rom 5:5).

The whole Christian life is lived in faith and charity, and in the practice of all of the virtues, according to the interior action of this renewing Spirit, who imparts the grace which justifies, vivifies and sanctifies. With this grace comes all the new virtues which constitute the fabric of the supernatural life. This life is developed not only by the natural faculties of man—the intellect, will, and senses—but also by the new capacities that are added on along with grace, as St. Thomas Aquinas explains *(Summa Theol.,* I-II, q. 62, aa. 1, 3). They give to the intellect the ability to adhere to God-Truth in faith; to the heart the ability to love in charity, which in man is like "a participation in the divine Love itself, the Holy Spirit" (II-II, q. 23, a. 3, ad 3). They also give to all the powers of the soul and in some way to the body, too, a participation in the new life with acts worthy of men elevated to participating in the nature and life of God in grace: *consortes divinae naturae,* as St. Peter says (2 Pet 1:4).

This state is like a new interior organism, in which the law of grace is made manifest: a law written in hearts rather than on stone tablets or manuscripts. St. Paul calls this law, as we have seen, "the law of the Spirit of life in Christ Jesus" (Rom 8:2; cf. St. Augustine, *De spiritu et littera,* c. 24: PL 44:225; St. Thomas, *Summa Theol.,* I-II, q. 106, a. 1).

In the preceding catechetical talks dedicated to the Holy Spirit's influence on the life of the Church, we have emphasized the variety of gifts which he gives for the development of the whole community. This same variety is evident in the personal life of the Christian: every person receives the gifts of the Holy Spirit in the concrete, existential situation in which he or she lives, according to the measure of God's love from which each one's vocation, journey and spiritual history take their origin.

We read in the account of Pentecost that the Holy Spirit fills the entire community, but also each person present. While the wind, symbolizing the Spirit, is said to have "filled the entire house in which they were" (Acts 2:2), it is said precisely that the tongues of fire, another symbol of the Spirit, "came to rest on each one of them" (2:3); then, "they were all filled with the Holy Spirit" (2:4). The fullness is given to each one; this fullness implies a variety of gifts for all the aspects of one's personal life.

Among these gifts we wish to recall and briefly highlight those which the catechism and theological tradition particularly call gifts of the Holy Spirit. It is true that everything is a gift, both in the order of grace and that of nature, and more generally, in all of creation. In the language of theology and of the catechism however, the name gifts of the Holy Spirit is reserved for those exquisitely divine energies which the Holy Spirit pours into the soul to perfect the supernatural virtues in order to give the human spirit the capacity to act *in modo divino* (cf. *Summa Theol.*, I-II, q. 68, aa. 1, 6).

It must be said that the first description and list of the gifts is found in the Old Testament, more exactly, in the book of Isaiah, where the prophet attributes to the messianic king "a spirit of wisdom and of understanding, a spirit of counsel and of strength, a spirit of knowledge and of fear of the Lord." Then he names the sixth gift a second time, saying that the king's "delight shall be the fear of the Lord" (Is 11:2-3).

In the Greek Septuagint translation and in the Latin Vulgate of St. Jerome, the repetition is avoided. "Piety" is listed as the sixth gift instead of "fear of the Lord," so that the prophecy finishes with these words: "a spirit of knowledge and of piety, and he will be full of the spirit of the fear of the Lord" (vv. 2-3). But one can say that this duplication of fear and piety does not depart from the biblical tradition regarding the virtues of the great figures of the Old Testament. In the Christian theological, liturgical and catechetical tradition it becomes a fuller rereading of the prophecy in its application to the Messiah and an enrichment of its literal sense. In the synagogue of Nazareth, Jesus himself applies another messianic text of Isaiah (cf. 61:1) to himself: "The Spirit of the Lord is upon me..." (Lk 4:8). This citation corresponds to the beginning of the prophecy just quoted and goes like this: "The Spirit of the Lord shall rest upon him" (Is 11:2). According to the tradition taken up by St. Thomas, the gifts of the Holy Spirit "are named by Scripture as they exist in Christ, according to the text of Isaiah," but they are met again, derived from Christ, in the Christian soul (cf. *Summa Theol.,* I-II, q. 68, a. 1).

The biblical references just cited have been compared to the fundamental dispositions of the human soul, considered in light of its supernatural elevation and the infused virtues themselves. The medieval theology of the seven gifts was thus developed, which, although not having an absolutely dogmatic character and so not claiming to limit the number of gifts or the specific categories in which they can be distributed, has been and remains very useful both in understanding the variety of the gifts in Christ and the saints, and in giving a good structure to the spiritual life.

St. Thomas (cf. I-II, q. 68, aa. 4, 7) and other theologians and catechists have found in this same text of Isaiah a guide for arranging the gifts in their relationship to the spiritual life in an explanation which can only be synthesized here:

1) First of all there is the gift of wisdom, by means of which the Holy Spirit enlightens the intellect. He enables it to know the "highest reasons" of revelation and the spiritual life, and form sound and right judgments concerning the faith and Christian living; as a "spiritual" man *(pneumatikòs)* or even "carnal" man (cf. 1 Cor 2:14-15; Rom 7:14).

2) Then there is the gift of understanding, which is a particular keenness, given by the Spirit, producing intuitive knowledge of the Word of God in its height and depth.

3) The gift of knowledge is the supernatural capacity to see and to determine with precision the content of revelation and to distinguish the things of God in one's knowledge of the universe.

4) With the gift of counsel the Holy Spirit gives a supernatural ability to regulate one's personal life in regard to the difficult actions to be accomplished and the hard choices to be made, as well as in the governance and direction given to others.

5) With the gift of fortitude the Holy Spirit supports the will and makes it prompt, active, and persevering in facing difficulties and even extreme suffering. This happens especially in martyrdom; in martyrdom of blood, but also in that of the heart and in the martyrdom of illness, weakness and infirmity.

6) Through the gift of piety the Holy Spirit directs the heart of man toward God with feelings, affections, thoughts and prayers which express our filiation with the Father revealed by Christ. It causes us to penetrate and assimilate the mystery of "God with us," especially in union with Christ, the incarnate Word, in filial relations with the Blessed Virgin Mary, in company with the angels and saints in heaven, in communion with the Church.

7) With the gift of the fear of the Lord the Holy Spirit puts in the Christian soul a profound respect for the law of God and its imperatives for Christian living. This gift frees the soul from the temptations of "servile fear," enriching it instead with a "filial fear" steeped in love.

This doctrine of the gifts of the Holy Spirit continues to be a very useful teaching of the spiritual life. It helps us to give direction to ourselves and to train others, for whom we have a responsibility of formation, in an unceasing dialogue with the Holy Spirit and in a loving and trusting abandonment to his guidance. This doctrine is connected with and always refers back to the messianic text of Isaiah. When applied to Jesus, it tells of the greatness of his perfection. When applied to the Christian soul, it teaches us the fundamental moments in the dynamism of the interior life: to understand (wisdom, knowledge, and understanding); to decide (counsel and fortitude); to remain and grow in a personal relationship with God, in the life of prayer and in an upright life according to the Gospel (piety and fear of the Lord).

Thus there is a fundamental importance to being in tune with the eternal Spirit-Gift who must be known from revelation in the Old and New Testament. He is a unique, infinite Love given to us with a multiplicity and variety of manifestations and gifts, in harmony with the general plan of creation.

General audience of April 3, 1991

The Spirit: Source of Interior Life

In the preceding catechesis St. Paul spoke to us about "the law of the spirit of life in Christ Jesus" (Rom 8:2). We must live according to this law if we wish "to follow the Spirit" (Gal 5:25), accomplishing the works of the Spirit and not those of the "flesh."

The Apostle highlights the opposition between "flesh" and "Spirit," and between the two types of works, thoughts and life which result from them: "For those who live according to the flesh are concerned with the things of the flesh, but those who live according to the Spirit with the things of the Spirit. The concern of the flesh is death, but the concern of the Spirit is life and peace" (Rom 8:5-6).

It is distressing to see the "works of the flesh" and the conditions of spiritual and cultural decadence the *homo animalis* reaches. But this should not make us forget the very different reality of life "according to the Spirit," which is also present in the world and opposed to the spread of the forces of evil. St. Paul speaks of this in the Letter to the Galatians where, in opposition to the "works of the flesh" which exclude one from the "kingdom of God," he highlights the "fruit of the

Spirit" which is "love, joy, peace, patience, kindness, generosity, faithfulness, gentleness and self-control" (cf. 5:19-22). According to St. Paul, these things are suggested to the believer from within, from the "law of the Spirit" (Rom 8:2), which is in him and which guides him in the interior life (cf. Gal 5:18, 25).

At issue is a principle of the spiritual life and of Christian conduct which is interior and at the same time transcendent, as can be deduced already from the words of Jesus to the disciples: "The Spirit of truth, which the world cannot accept, because it neither sees nor knows it...will be in you" (Jn 14:17). The Holy Spirit comes from on high, but penetrates and resides in us to animate our interior life. Jesus did not only say: "He remains with you," which might suggest the idea of a presence which is merely close, but added that it is a presence within us (Jn 14:17). St. Paul in turn wishes for the Ephesians that the Father grant them "to be strengthened with power through his Spirit in the inner self" (Eph 3:16). For the human person what counts is not the external life, often superficial, but the intention of living in the "depths of God," scrutinized by the Holy Spirit (1 Cor 2:10).

St. Paul's distinction between the "psychic" man and the "spiritual" man (cf. 1 Cor 2:13-14) helps us to understand the difference and the distance between the natural maturing of the human soul's capacities and the properly Christian maturing which entails the development of the life of the Spirit, a maturing in faith, hope, and love. Knowledge of this divine Source of the spiritual life, which spreads from within the soul into all areas of life, even those exterior and social, is a fundamental and sublime aspect of Christian anthropology. The basis of this knowledge is the truth of faith by which I believe that the Holy Spirit dwells in me (cf. 1 Cor 3:16), prays in me (cf. Rom 8:26; Gal 4:6), guides me (cf. Rom 8:14), and has Christ live in me (cf. Gal 2:20).

Even the simile Jesus used in his conversation with the Samaritan woman at Jacob's well about the living water which he would give to those who believe, water which "will become in him a spring of water welling up to eternal life" (Jn 4:14), means the interior spring of the spiritual life. Jesus himself clarified this on the occasion of the "feast of Tabernacles" (cf. Jn 7:2), when he "stood up and exclaimed, 'Let anyone who thirsts come to me and drink. Whoever believes in me, as Scripture says [cf. Is 55:1]; rivers of living water will flow from within him.'" John the evangelist comments, "He said this in reference to the Spirit that those who came to believe in him were to receive" (Jn 7:37-39).

In the believer, the Holy Spirit develops the entire dynamism of the grace which gives new life and of the virtues which translate this vitality into fruits of goodness. From "within" the believer the Holy Spirit is also at work like a fire, according to another simile, used by John the Baptist regarding baptism: "He will baptize you with the Holy Spirit and fire" (Mt 3:11). Jesus himself also used it regarding his messianic mission: "I have come to set the earth on fire" (Lk 12:49). The Spirit, therefore, stirs up a life with that fervor which St. Paul recommends in his letter to the Romans: "Be fervent in the Spirit" (12:11). This is the "living flame of love" which purifies, enlightens, burns and consumes, as St. John of the Cross has explained so well.

Under the action of the Holy Spirit in the believer an original sanctity is so developed that it assumes, elevates and brings the personality of each one to perfection without destroying it. Thus, every saint has his own physiognomy. As St. Paul can say: "Star differs from star in brightness" (1 Cor 15:41), not only in the "future resurrection" to which Paul refers but also in the present condition of the person who is no longer merely psychic (endowed with natural life), but spiritual (enlivened by the Holy Spirit) (cf. 1 Cor 15:44 ff.).

Holiness consists in the perfection of love. Nevertheless, it varies according to the different aspects which love assumes in the various conditions of personal life. Under the action of the Holy Spirit, each person conquers the instinct of egoism with love, and develops the best forces in his own original way of self-giving. When the expressive and expansive force of his originality is particularly strong, the Holy Spirit causes groups of disciples and followers to form around these people (even if they sometimes remain hidden). In this way, currents of spiritual life, schools of spirituality and religious institutes are born, whose variety is thus the effect of that divine intervention. It is the Holy Spirit who puts to use the capacities of all in persons and groups, in communities and institutions, among priests and lay people.

The new value of liberty which characterizes the Christian life derives from this interior source. As St. Paul says: "Where the Spirit of the Lord is, there is freedom" (2 Cor 3:17). The Apostle is referring directly to the freedom acquired by the followers of Christ in regard to the Jewish law, in harmony with the teaching and attitude of Jesus himself. But the principle which he states has a general value. He often talks about freedom as the vocation of the Christian: "You were called for freedom, brothers" (Gal 5:13). And he gives a good explanation of what he means. According to the Apostle, whoever "lives by the Spirit" (Gal 5:16) lives in freedom, because he is no longer under the oppressive yoke of the flesh: "Live by the Spirit and you will certainly not gratify the desire of the flesh" (Gal 5:16). "The concern of the flesh is death, but the concern of the Spirit is life and peace" (Rom 8:6).

The "works of the flesh" from which the Christian who is faithful to the Spirit has been freed are those of egoism and the passions, which prevent entrance into the kingdom of God. The works of the Spirit are those of love: "Against such there is no law" (Gal 5:23).

According to the Apostle, the result of this is that "if you are guided by the Spirit, you are under the law" (Gal 5:18). Writing to Timothy, he does not hesitate to say: "The law is not meant for a righteous person" (1 Tim 1:9). And St. Thomas explains: "The law does not have coercive power over the just, as it does for the wicked" *(Summa Theol.,* I-II, q. 96, a. 5, and 1), because the just do nothing contrary to the law. Rather, guided by the Holy Spirit, they freely do everything which the law enjoins (cf. Rom 8:4; Gal 5:13-16).

This is the wondrous harmonization of freedom and law which is the fruit of the Holy Spirit's work in the just. Jeremiah and Ezekiel foretold this, announcing the interiorization of the law of the new covenant (cf. Jer 31:31-34; Ez 36:26-27).

"I will put my Spirit within you" (Ez 36:27). This prophecy was realized and continues to be active among the faithful and in the community of the Church. It is the Spirit who makes it possible to be not a mere observer of the law, but one who freely, fervently and faithfully accomplishes God's plan. They do all that the Apostle says: "Those who are led by the Spirit of God are children of God. For you did not receive a spirit of slavery to fall back into fear, but you received a spirit of adoption, through which we cry, "Abba, Father!"" (Rom 8:14-15). It is the freedom of children which Jesus proclaimed as the true freedom (cf. Jn 8:36). It is a fundamental, interior freedom, but one which is always oriented toward the love which makes access to the Father in the one Spirit possible and almost spontaneous (cf. Eph 2:18). It is the guided freedom which shines in the lives of the saints.

General audience of April 10, 1991

The Spirit:
Source of Prayer Life

The first and most excellent form of the interior life is prayer. The teachers and masters of the spiritual life are so convinced of this that they often present the interior life as a life of prayer. The principal author of this life is the Holy Spirit, as he was already in Christ. Indeed, we read in the Gospel of Luke: "At that very moment Jesus rejoiced in the Holy Spirit and said, 'I give you praise, Father, Lord of heaven and earth'" (Lk 10:21). This is a prayer of praise and thanksgiving which, according to the evangelist, wells up from Jesus' exultation "in the Holy Spirit."

We know that during his messianic activity Jesus often retired in solitude to pray, and that he spent entire nights in prayer (cf. Lk 6:12). For this prayer he preferred those deserted places which prepare one for conversation with God, who is so responsive to the need and inclination of every spirit sensitive to the mystery of divine transcendence (cf. Mk 1:35; Lk 5:16). Moses and Elijah acted in a similar way, as the Old Testament tells us (cf. Ex 34:28; 1 Kgs 19:8). The book of the prophet Hosea enables us to see that deserted places have a particular inspiration to prayer. God "will lead [us] into the desert and speak to [our] heart" (cf. Hos 2:16).

In our lives, as in the life of Jesus, the Holy Spirit is revealed as the Spirit of prayer. The Apostle Paul tells us this eloquently in a passage from the letter to the Galatians which we have cited before: "As proof that you are children, God sent the Spirit of his Son into our hearts, crying out, 'Abba, Father!'" (Gal 4:6). In some way, then, the Holy Spirit transfers into our hearts the prayer of the Son, who raises that cry to the Father. So too our prayer expresses our "adoption as children," which has been granted to us in Christ and through Christ (cf. Rom 8:15). Prayer professes our faith to be conscious of the truth that "we are children" and "heirs of God," "coheirs with Christ." Prayer allows us to live this supernatural reality because of the action of the Holy Spirit who "bears witness with our spirit" (cf. Rom 8:16-17).

Since the beginning of the Church the followers of Christ have lived in this same faith, which has also been expressed at the hour of death. We are familiar with the prayer of Stephen, the first martyr, a man "filled with the Holy Spirit." During his stoning, he gave proof of his particular union with Christ by exclaiming, as did his crucified Teacher, in reference to his executioners, "Lord, do not hold this sin against them!" And then, still at prayer, he looked intently at the glory of Christ standing "at the right hand of God" and cried out: "Lord Jesus, receive my spirit" (cf. Acts 7:55-60). This prayer was a fruit of the Holy Spirit's action in the martyr's heart.

One also finds the same interior inspiration of prayer in the acts of martyrdom of others who have confessed Christ. These pages express a Christian consciousness formed in the school of the Gospel and the letters of the apostles that has become the consciousness of the Church herself.

In reality, above all in the teaching of St. Paul, the Holy Spirit appears as the author of Christian prayer, first of all because he urges us to pray. He it is who begets in us especially at the time of temptation, the needs and the desire to obey that "watch and pray" recommended by Christ, because "the spirit is willing, but the flesh is weak" (Mt 26:41). An echo of this encouragement seems to resound in the exhortation of the Letter to the Ephesians: "With all prayer and supplication, pray at every opportunity in the Spirit. To that end, be watchful with all perseverance...that speech may be given to me to open my mouth, to make known with boldness the mystery of the Gospel" (Eph 6:18-19). Paul realizes that he is in the condition of those who need prayer to resist temptation and not to fall victim to their human weakness, and to face up to the mission to which they have been called. He always remembers and is sometimes dramatically aware of the charge given to him: to be a witness of Christ and the Gospel in the world, especially in the midst of pagans. And he knows that what he has been called to do and to say is also and primarily the work of the Spirit of truth, of whom Jesus has said: "He will take from what is mine and declare it to you" (Jn 16:14). The Holy Spirit uses "the things of Christ" to "glorify him" through the missionary message. So it is only by entering into the sphere of Christ's relationship with his Spirit, in the mystery of unity with the Father, that one can accomplish a similar mission. The way to enter such a communion is prayer, stirred up in us by the Spirit.

With particularly penetrating words, the Apostle shows in the Letter to the Romans how "the Spirit comes to the aid of our weakness; for we do not know how to pray as we ought, but the Spirit itself intercedes with inexpressible groanings" (Rom 8:26). Paul hears similar groanings arising from the very depths of creation, which "awaiting with eager expectation the revelation of the children of God" in the hope of being "set free from slavery to corruption, is groaning in labor pains even until now" (Rom 8:19, 21-22). Against this historical and spiritual backdrop, the Holy Spirit is at work: "The one who searches hearts [God] knows what is the intention of the Spirit, because he intercedes for the holy ones according to God's will" (Rom 8:27). We are at the most intimate and profound source of prayer. Paul explains to us and enables us to understand that the Holy Spirit not only urges us to pray, but he himself prays in us!

The Holy Spirit is at the origin of the prayer which most perfectly reflects the relationship existing between the divine Persons of the Trinity: the prayer of glorification and thanksgiving, by which the Father is honored, and with him the Son and the Holy Spirit. This prayer was on the lips of the apostles on the day of Pentecost, when they announced "the mighty acts of God" (Acts 2:11). The same things happened in the case of the centurion Cornelius, when during Peter's discourse, those present received "the gift of the Holy Spirit" and "glorified God" (cf. Acts 10:45-47).

In the Letter to the Colossians, St. Paul interprets this first Christian experience that became the common patrimony of the early Church. After expressing the desire that "the word of Christ dwell in you richly" (Col 3:16), he exhorts the Christians to remain in prayer, "singing with gratitude in your hearts to God," teaching and admonishing one another with "psalms, hymns and spiritual songs." And he asks them to transmit this prayerful style of life to whatever they do in word or in deed. "Do everything in the name of the Lord Jesus, giving thanks to God the Father through him" (Col 3:17). A similar recommendation is given in the Letter to the Ephesians: "Be filled with the spirit, addressing one another in psalms and hymns...singing and playing to the Lord in your hearts, giving thanks always and for everything in the name of our Lord Jesus Christ to God the Father" (Eph 5:18-20).

This brings us back to the trinitarian dimension of Christian prayer according to the teaching and exhortation of the Apostle. One also sees how, according to the Apostle, it is the Holy Spirit who urges this sort of prayer and forms it in the human heart. The "prayer life" of the saints, the mystics, the schools and currents of spirituality which developed in the Christian centuries is in line with the experience of the primitive communities. The Church's liturgy is maintained along the same line, as appears, for example in the *Gloria* when we say: "We give you thanks for your great glory"; similarly in the *Te Deum*, we praise God and proclaim him Lord. In the prefaces, there is the invariable invitation: "Let us give thanks to the Lord our God," and the faithful are invited to give their response of assent and participation: "It is truly right and just." How beautiful it is to repeat with the praying Church, at the end of each psalm and on so many other occasions, the short, dense and splendid doxology of the *Gloria Patri*: "Glory be to the Father, and to the Son, and to the Holy Spirit...."

The glorification of the Triune God, under the action of the Holy Spirit who prays in us and for us, occurs principally in the heart. But it is also translated into vocal praises from a need for personal expression and community association in celebrating the marvels of God. The soul which loves God expresses itself in words and easily in song, too, as has always happened in the Church, since the first Christian communities. St. Augustine informs us that "St. Ambrose introduced song into the Church of Milan" (cf. *Confessions*, 9, c. 7: PL 32,770). He remembers that he wept, hearing "the hymns and sweetly echoing songs of your Church, and was touched with profound emotion" (cf. *Confessions*, 9, c. 6: PL 32, 769). Even sound can be of help in praising God, when instruments serve to "transport human feelings upward" (St. Thomas Aquinas, *Expositio in Psalmos*, 32, 2). This explains the value of songs and music in the Church's liturgy, inasmuch as "they serve to stir up feelings for God...with various melodies" *(Summa Theol.,* II-II, q. 92, a. 2; cf. St. Augustine, *Confessions*, 10, c. 22: PL 32, 800). If liturgical norms are observed, one can also experience today what St. Augustine recalled in another passage of his *Confessions* (9, c. 4, n. 8): "What songs I raised to you, O my God, in reading the psalms of David, canticles of faith, the music of piety.... What songs I would raise to you in reading those psalms! How I was inflamed with love for you and with desire to recite them over the face of the whole world, if I could have...." All this happens when either individual souls or communities follow the intimate activity of the Holy Spirit.

General audience of April 17, 1991

The Holy Spirit: Light of the Soul

The spiritual life needs enlightenment and guidance. For this reason, in establishing the Church and sending the apostles into the world, Jesus entrusted to them the task of teaching all nations, as we read in the Gospel according to Matthew (cf. 28:19-20), and also of "proclaiming the Gospel to every creature," as the canonical text of Mark's Gospel says (16:15). St. Paul, too, speaks of the apostolate as an "enlightenment of all" (Eph 3:9).

But the Church's work of evangelizing and teaching belongs to the ministry of the apostles and their successors, and in a different way, to all the members of the Church. It is to continue for all time the work of Christ, the "one Teacher" (Mt 23:8), who has brought to humanity the fullness of God's revelation. There is still the need for an interior teacher who penetrates the human heart and spirit with Jesus' teaching. This is the Holy Spirit, whom Jesus himself calls the "Spirit of truth," and whom he promises as the one who will guide them to all truth (cf. Jn 14:17; 16:13). If Jesus has said to himself: "I am the truth" (Jn 14:6), the Holy Spirit makes this truth of Christ known and spreads it: "He will not speak on his own, but he will speak what he hears...he will take from what is mine and declare it to you" (Jn 16:13-14). The Spirit is the light of the soul: *Lumen cordium*, as we call him in the sequence of Pentecost.

The Holy Spirit was a light and interior teacher for the apostles, who had to know Christ in depth to be able to fulfill their task as his evangelizers. He was and is the same for the Church, and in the Church, for believers of every generation, and in a particular way, for theologians and spiritual directors, for catechists and those responsible for Christian communities. He was and is the same for all inside or outside the visible boundaries of the Church who want to follow the ways of God with a sincere heart and, without fault of their own, do not find someone to help them solve the riddle of life and discover revealed truth. May the Lord grant all our brothers and sisters—millions and even billions of human beings—the grace of acceptance and docility to the Holy Spirit in what can be the decisive moments of their life.

For us Christians, the interior teaching of the Holy Spirit is a joyous certitude. It is founded on the word of Christ about the coming of "another Advocate," whom he said "the Father will send in my name—he will teach you everything and remind you of all that I told you" (Jn 14:26). "He will guide you to all truth" (Jn 16:13).

One can conclude from this text that Jesus did not entrust his word only to the memory of his listeners. This memory would be assisted by the Holy Spirit, who would continually revive in the apostles a recollection of the events and the meaning of the Gospel mysteries.

The Holy Spirit has guided the apostles in handing on the word and life of Jesus. The Spirit inspired both their oral preaching and their writings, as well as the editing of the Gospels, as we have seen in the catechesis on the Holy Spirit and revelation.

He also helps the readers of Scripture to understand the divine meaning within the text, of which he is the inspiration and the principal author. He alone enables one to know "the depths of God" (1 Cor 2:10) which are contained in the sacred text. It was he who was sent to instruct the disciples in the teachings of their Master (cf. Jn 16:13).

The apostles themselves, the first to hand on the word of Christ, speak of this interior teaching of the Holy Spirit. St. John writes: "But you have the anointing that comes from the Holy One [Christ], and you all have knowledge. I write to you not because you do not know the truth but because you do, and because every lie is alien to the truth" (1 Jn 2:20-21). According to the Fathers of the Church and the majority of contemporary exegetes, this "anointing" *(chrisma)* signifies the Holy Spirit. St. John even states that those who live according to the Spirit do not need other teachers: "As for you, the anointing that you received from him remains in you, so that you do not need anyone to teach you. But his anointing teaches you about everything and is true and not false; just as it taught you, remain in him" (1 Jn 2:27).

Even the Apostle Paul speaks of an understanding according to the Spirit which is not the fruit of human wisdom, but of divine enlightenment: "Now the natural person *(psychikòs),* however, can judge everything but is not subject to judgment by anyone" (1 Cor 2:14-15).

Christians, therefore, having received the Holy Spirit, the anointing of Christ, possess in themselves a source of knowledge of the truth, and the Holy Spirit is the sovereign teacher who enlightens and guides them.

If they are docile and faithful to his divine teaching, the Holy Spirit preserves them from error by giving them victory in the continual struggle between the "spirit of truth" and the "spirit of deceit" (cf. 1 Jn 4:6). The spirit of deceit which does not acknowledge Christ (cf. 1 Jn 4:3) is spread by the "false prophets" who are always present in the world, even among Christian people, with an activity that is sometimes open and even sensational, or sometimes underhanded and sly. Like Satan, they too sometimes masquerade as "angels of light" (cf. 2 Cor 11:14) and present themselves with apparent charisms of prophetic and apocalyptic inspiration. This already occurred in apostolic times. For this reason, St. John warns: "Do not trust every spirit but test the spirits to see whether they belong to God, because many false prophets have gone out into the world" (1 Jn 4:1). The Holy Spirit, as Vatican II recalls (cf. *LG* 12), protects the Christian from error by enabling him to discern what is genuine from what is false. The Christian will always need good criteria to discern the things he hears or reads in matters of religion, Sacred Scripture, manifestations of the supernatural, etc. These criteria are conformity to the Gospel, harmony with the teaching of the Church established and set by Christ to preach his truth, the moral conduct of the person speaking or writing and the fruits of holiness which result from what is presented or proposed.

The Holy Spirit teaches the Christian the truth as a principle of life. He shows the concrete application of Jesus' words in each one's life. He enables one to discover the contemporary value of the Gospel for all human situations. He adapts the understanding of the truth to every circumstance, so that this truth does not remain merely abstract and speculative, but frees the Christian from the dangers of duplicity and hypocrisy.

To this end, the Holy Spirit enlightens each one personally, to guide him in his conduct, by showing him the way to go and by giving him just a glimpse of the Father's plan for his life. St. Paul seeks this great grace of light for the Colossians: "the spiritual understanding" which can enable them to understand the divine will. In fact, he assures them: "We do not cease praying for you and asking that you may be filled with

The Holy Spirit: Light of the Soul 399

the knowledge of his [God's] will through all wisdom and spiritual understanding, to live in a manner worthy of the Lord, so as to be fully pleasing, in every good work bearing fruit..." (Col 1:9-10). For all of us this grace of light is necessary to have a good knowledge of God's will for us and to be able to live our personal vocation fully.

Problems are never lacking and they sometimes seem insoluble. But the Holy Spirit helps us in our difficulties and gives us light. He can reveal the divine solution, as he did at the time of the annunciation in regard to the problem of reconciling motherhood with the desire for preserving one's virginity. Even when it is a question of a unique mystery such as the role of Mary in the Incarnation of the Word, the Holy Spirit can be said to possess an infinite creativity, proper to the divine mind, which knows how to loosen the knots of human affairs, even the most complex and inscrutable.

All of this is given and accomplished in the soul by the Holy Spirit through his gifts, the graces which one can carefully discern, not according to the criteria of human wisdom, which is foolishness in God's sight, but with that divine wisdom which can seem foolishness in the eyes of men (cf. 1 Cor 1:18-25). Only the Holy Spirit "scrutinizes everything, even the depths of God" (1 Cor 2:10-11). And if there is opposition between the spirit of the world and the Spirit of God, Paul reminds Christians: "We have not received the spirit of the world but the Spirit that is from God, so that we may understand the things freely given us by God" (1 Cor 2:12). Unlike the "natural person," the "spiritual person" *(pneumatikòs)* is sincerely open to the Holy Spirit, docile and faithful to his inspirations (cf. 1 Cor 2:14-16). Thus, he habitually possesses the ability to make right judgments under the guidance of divine wisdom.

A sign that our discernment is in real contact with the Holy Spirit is and will always be adherence to revealed truth as it is proposed by the Church's Magisterium. The interior teacher does not inspire dissent, disobedience or even merely an unjustified resistance to the pastors and teachers established by him in the Church (cf. Acts 20:29). It belongs to the Church's authority, as the Council said in the Constitution *Lumen Gentium* (n. 12), to "not quench the Spirit, but to test everything and retain what is good" (cf. 1 Thess 5:12; 19-21). This is the direction of ecclesial and pastoral wisdom which also comes from the Holy Spirit.

General audience of April 24, 1991

The Holy Spirit Is the Vital Principle of Faith

Faith is the fundamental gift given by the Holy Spirit for the supernatural life. The author of the Letter to the Hebrews puts much emphasis on this gift as he writes to Christians suffering persecution: "Faith is the realization of what is hoped for and evidence [or conviction] of things not seen" (Heb 11:1). One knows that this text from the Letter to the Hebrews can be read as a sort of theological definition of faith. As St. Thomas explains in citing the passage, faith does not have for its object realities grasped by the intellect or experienced with the senses, but the transcendent truth of God *(Veritas Prima),* proposed to us in revelation (cf. *Summa Theol.,* II-II, q. 1, a. 4; and a. 1).

To encourage Christians, the author of the Letter offers the example of Old Testament believers, summarizing the hagiography of the book of Sirach (cf. ch. 44-50), when he says that they all were moved toward the Invisible One because they were supported by faith. There are seventeen examples cited in the letter: "By faith Abel...by faith Noah...by faith Abraham...by faith Moses...." And we can add: by faith Mary...by faith Joseph...by faith Simeon and Anna...by faith the apostles, the martyrs, the confessors, the virgins and the bishops, priests, religious and lay people of all the Christian centuries.... By faith the Church has journeyed through the centuries and journeys today toward the Invisible One, under the breath and guidance of the Holy Spirit.

The supernatural virtue of faith can assume a charismatic form, as an extraordinary gift reserved only for certain individuals (cf. 1 Cor 12:9). But in itself it is a virtue which the Spirit offers everyone. As such, therefore, it is not a charism, one of the special gifts which the Spirit "distributes to each person as he wishes" (1 Cor 12:11; cf. Rom 12:6). It is one of the spiritual gifts necessary for all Christians, among which the greatest is charity: "So faith, hope, love remain, these three; but the greatest of these is love" (1 Cor 13:13).

It is certain that faith, according to the teaching of St. Paul, although a virtue, is first of all a gift: "For to you has been granted...to believe in Christ" (Phil 1:29). It is inspired in the soul by the Holy Spirit (cf. 1 Cor 12:3). It is a virtue inasmuch as it is a "spiritual" gift, a gift of the Holy Spirit, which enables a person to believe. It is a gift from its very beginning, as the Council of Orange (529) defined: "Even the beginning of faith, in fact, the very disposition to believe...is present in us as the result of a gift of grace, i.e., from the inspiration of the Holy Spirit, who brings our will from disbelief to faith" (can. 5: *DS* 375). This gift has a definitive value, as St. Paul says, "it remains." And it is intended to influence a person's entire life, until the time of death, when faith finds its fulfillment as it gives way to the beatific vision.

The attribution of faith to the Holy Spirit is stated by St. Paul in the letter he wrote to the Corinthians. He reminded them that their introduction to the Gospel took place through preaching in which the Spirit was at work: "My message and my proclamation were not with persuasive words of wisdom, but with a demonstration of the Spirit and power" (1 Cor 2:4). The Apostle is not only referring to the miracles which accompanied his preaching (cf. 2 Cor 12:12), but also to the other outpourings and demonstrations of the Holy Spirit which Jesus promised before the ascension (cf. Acts 1:8). The Holy Spirit granted St. Paul, particularly in his preaching, to know nothing while he was with the Corinthians "except Jesus Christ, and him crucified" (1 Cor 2:2). The Holy Spirit compelled St. Paul to present Christ as the essential object of faith, according to the principle enunciated by Jesus as he spoke in the upper room: "He will glorify me" (Jn 16:14). The Holy Spirit is thus the one who inspired the apostolic preaching. St. Peter says this clearly in his letter: the apostles "preached the Good News to you through the Holy Spirit sent from heaven" (1 Pet 1:12).

The Holy Spirit is also the one who confirmed this preaching, as the Acts of the Apostles states concerning Peter's preaching to Cornelius and his companions: "The Holy Spirit fell upon all who were listening to the word" (Acts 10:44). And Peter appealed to this confirmation for approval of his act of admitting non-Israelites into the Church. The Spirit himself inspired these pagans to accept Peter's preaching and introduced them to the faith of the Christian community. And again it is the Spirit—as in Paul, so in Peter—who makes Jesus Christ the center of preaching. Peter declared in summary fashion: "God anointed Jesus of Nazareth with the Holy Spirit and power...we are witnesses of all that he did..." (Acts 10:38-39). Jesus Christ is presented as the one who, consecrated in the Spirit, demands faith.

The Holy Spirit gives life to the profession of faith in Christ. According to St. Paul, the act of faith stands before and above all particular "charisms." About this act he says: "No one can say, 'Jesus is Lord,' except by the Holy Spirit" (1 Cor 12:3). Recognizing Christ, following him and witnessing on his behalf are the work of the Holy Spirit. This doctrine is found in the Council of Orange, cited above, and Vatican Council I (1869-1870), according to which no one can hold to the apostolic preaching "without the enlightenment and inspiration of the Holy Spirit who gives everyone docility in assenting to and believing in the truth" *(Const. Dei Filius*, c. 3: *DS* 3010).

Citing the Council of Orange, St. Thomas explains that from its very beginning faith is a gift of God (cf. Eph 2:8-9). This is because "man, in assenting to the truth of faith, is raised above the level of his nature...and that can only occur through a supernatural principle which acts from within, i.e., God. Therefore, faith comes from God who works interiorly by means of his grace" *(Summa Theol.,* II-II, q. 6, a. 1).

After the beginning of faith, all of its succeeding development occurs under the action of the Holy Spirit. The ongoing deepening of faith which brings one to a greater knowledge of the truths believed is especially the work of the Holy Spirit, who gives the soul an ever new keenness in penetrating the mystery (cf. *Summa Theol.,* II-II, q. 8, aa. 1, 5). St. Paul writes about the "wisdom which does not belong to this world," which is granted to those who journey in a way conformed to the demands of the Gospel. Citing some texts of the Old Testament (cf. Is 64:3; Jer 3:16; Sir 1:8), he demonstrates that the revelation accepted by him and by the Corinthians surpasses even the highest human aspirations: "What eye has not seen, and ear has not heard, and what has not entered the human heart, what God has prepared for those who love him, this God has revealed to us through the Spirit. For the Spirit scrutinizes everything, even the depths of God" (1 Cor 2:9-10). "We have not received the spirit of the world but the Spirit that is from God, so that we may understand the things freely given us by God" (1 Cor 2:12). Therefore, as ones who are mature in the faith, "we speak a wisdom" (1 Cor 2:6) under the action of the Holy Spirit which brings an ever new discovery of the truths contained in the mystery of God.

Faith demands a life in conformity with the truth which is recognized and professed. According to St. Paul, "faith works through love" (Gal 5:6). Referring to this Pauline text, St. Thomas explains that "charity is the form of faith" (II-II, q. 4, a. 3): that is, the vital principle which gives it life and energy. The result of this is that faith is a virtue (II-II, q. 4, a. 5) and that it continues in an increasing attachment to God and has implications for conduct and human relations, under the guidance of the Holy Spirit.

Vatican Council II reminds us of this when it says: "That discernment in matters of faith is aroused and sustained by the Spirit of truth. It is exercised under the guidance of the sacred teaching authority.... Through it, the People of God adheres unwaveringly to the faith given once and for all to the saints, penetrates it more deeply with right thinking, and applies it more fully in its life" *(LG* 12). One thus understands the exhortation of St. Paul: "Live by the Spirit" (Gal 5:16). One understands the necessity of prayer to the Holy Spirit so that he will give us the grace of knowledge, but also that of conforming our life to the truth that is known. And so we ask him in the hymn *Veni, Creator Spiritus*:

"Through you may we the Father know,
through you the eternal Son...";
but we also pray as well:
"O guide our minds with your blest light,
With love our hearts inflame;
And with your strength which ne'er decays
Confirm our mortal frame.
Far from us drive our deadly foe;
True peace unto us bring;
And from all perils lead us safe
Beneath your sacred wing."

And in the sequence of Pentecost we profess:

"Where you are not, man has naught,
Nothing good in deed or thought."
Then we ask him: "Heal our wounds, our strength renew;
On our dryness pour your dew;
Wash the stains of guilt away.
Bend the stubborn heart and will;
Melt the frozen, warm the chill;
Guide the steps that go astray."

In faith we put our whole life under the active power of the Holy Spirit.

General audience of May 8, 1991

The Spirit: Life-Giving Source of New Love

In the Christian's soul there is a new love by which he shares in God's own love: "The love of God," says St. Paul, "has been poured out into our hearts through the Holy Spirit who has been given to us" (Rom 5:5). This love is divine in nature, and so it is higher than the connatural abilities of the human soul. In theological terminology it is called charity. This supernatural love plays a fundamental role in Christian life, as St. Thomas shows when he clearly emphasizes that charity is not only "the noblest of all the virtues" *(excellentissima omnium virtutum),* but is also "the form of all the virtues, because through charity their acts are ordered to their right and ultimate end" (*Summa Theol.,* II-II, q. 23, aa. 6 and 8).

Therefore, charity is the central value of the new person, "created in God's way in righteousness and holiness of truth" (Eph 4:24; cf. Gal 3:27; Rom 13:14). If the Christian life is compared to a building under construction, it is easy to see that faith is the foundation of all the virtues that comprise it. The Council of Trent teaches that "faith is the beginning of human salvation, the foundation and source of all justification" (cf. *DS* 2532). But union with God through faith has as its goal union with him in the love of charity, a divine love in which the human soul shares as an active and unifying force.

In communicating this vital energy to the soul, the Holy Spirit makes it capable in virtue of supernatural charity, of observing the twofold commandment of love, given by Jesus Christ: love for God and for one's neighbor.

"You shall love the lord your God with all your heart..." (Mk 12:30; cf. Dt 6:4-5). The Holy Spirit enables the soul to share in Jesus' filial love for the Father, so that, as St. Paul says: "Those who are led by the Spirit of God are children of God" (Rom 8:14). He enables the Father to be loved as the Son has loved him, i.e., with the filial love which is shown in the cry of "Abba" (cf. Gal 4:6; Rom 8:15), but it pervades the entire activity of those who, in the Spirit, are children of God. Under the Spirit's influence their whole life becomes an offering to the Father, filled with reverence and filial love.

The capacity to observe the other commandment, love of neighbor, comes from the Holy Spirit, too. "Love one another as I have loved you," Jesus commands his apostles and all his followers. With these words, "as I have loved you," the new value of supernatural love is present, which is a sharing in Christ's love for human beings, and therefore, is a sharing in the eternal charity which is the very beginning of the virtue of charity. As St. Thomas writes: "The divine essence in itself is love, as it is wisdom and goodness. Therefore, just as one can say that we are good because of the goodness which is God, and wise because of the wisdom which is God, because the goodness which makes us formally good is the goodness of God, and the wisdom which makes us formally wise is a participation in the divine wisdom; so the charity by which we formally love our neighbor is a participation in divine charity" *(Summa Theol.,* II-II, q. 23, a. 2, ad 1). This participation is activated by the Holy Spirit who thus makes us able to love not only God, but also our neighbor, as Jesus Christ loved him.

Yes, we can love even our neighbor because, given that the love of God has been poured into our hearts, with that love we can love other persons and even in some way, irrational creatures (cf. *Summa Theol.*, II-II, q. 25, a. 3) as God loves them.

Historical experience tells us how difficult the concrete practice of this precept is. Nevertheless, it is at the center of Christian ethics, as a gift which comes from the Spirit and for which we must ask him. St. Paul confirms this in the Letter to the Galatians in which he exhorts them to live in the freedom they have received by the new law of love: "But do not use this freedom as an opportunity for the flesh; rather, serve one another through love" (Gal 5:13). "For the whole law is fulfilled in one statement, namely, 'You shall love your neighbor as yourself'" (Gal 5:14). After he recommends: "I say, then: live by the Spirit and you will certainly not gratify the desire of the flesh" (Gal 5:16), he identifies the love of charity *(agápe)* as the first "fruit of the Holy Spirit" (Gal 5:22). Thus, it is the Holy Spirit who enables us to walk in love and to overcome all obstacles to charity.

In the First Letter to the Corinthians St. Paul purposely seems to linger over the list and description of the characteristics of charity for one's neighbor. Indeed, after recommending that one aspire to the "greatest spiritual gifts" (1 Cor 12:31), he praises charity as a good higher than all the extraordinary gifts which the Holy Spirit can give and as something more basic to the Christian life. The hymn to charity springs from his speech and his soul and can be considered a hymn to the influence of the Holy Spirit on human behavior. In this context charity assumes an ethical dimension with practical application: "Love is patient, love is kind. It is does not envy or boast, it is not conceited, it is not rude, it is not self-seeking, it is not quick-tempered, it does not brood over injury, it does not rejoice over wrongdoing but rejoices with the truth. It bears all things, believes all things, hopes all things, endures all things" (1 Cor 13:4-7).

In listing the "fruits of the Spirit" (Gal 5:22), it could be said that St. Paul, in a parallel with the hymn, wishes to indicate some essential attitudes belonging to charity. Among these are:

1) Patience, first of all: "Love is patient" (1 Cor 13:4). One could remark that the Spirit himself gives the example of patience toward sinners and their wrongful conduct, as we read in the Gospels about Jesus, who was called "a friend of tax collectors and sinners" (Mt 11:19; cf. Lk 7:34). It is a reflection of the very love of God, St. Thomas observes, "who shows mercy with love, because he loves us as something belonging to himself" *(Summa Theol.,* II-II, q. 30, a. 2, ad 1).

2) Kindness is a fruit of the Spirit: "Love is kind" (1 Cor 13:4). It is also a reflection of the divine kindness toward others, regarded and treated with sympathy and understanding.

3) There is also goodness: "It does not seek its own interests" (1 Cor 13:5). This love is ready to give generously, as the love of the Holy Spirit increases his gifts and shares the Father's love with believers.

4) Finally, there is gentleness: "It is not quick-tempered" (1 Cor 13:5). The Holy Spirit helps Christians to reproduce in themselves Christ's "meek and humble heart" and to practice the beatitude of meekness which he preached (cf. Mt 5:5).

In enumerating the "works of the flesh" (cf. Gal 5:19-21), St. Paul clarifies the demands of charity, from which flow concrete duties, in opposition to the tendencies of the *homo animalis,* i.e., the victim of his passions. In particular, this means to avoid jealousies and rivalries, to want one's neighbor's good, to avoid enmities, dissension, division, quarrels, and to promote everything which brings unity. There is an allusion to this in the verse of the Pauline hymn which says that charity "does not brood over injuries" (1 Cor 13:5). The Holy Spirit inspires generous forgiveness for injuries received and losses suffered and, as Spirit of light and love, enables the

The Spirit: Life-Giving Source of New Love

faithful to do this as he reveals to them the unlimited demands of charity.

History confirms the truth of what we have just explained. Charity shines in the lives of the saints and the Church, from the day of Pentecost to today. All the saints and every age of the Church's history bear the marks of charity and the Holy Spirit. It could be said that in some historical periods, under the inspiration and guidance of the Spirit, charity assumed forms especially characterized by activity which organized help and support for those suffering hunger, illness and epidemics both ancient and new. Thus, there were many "saints of charity," as they were especially called in the 1800's and in our own century. They are bishops, priests, men and women religious and lay Christians. All of them are "servants" of charity. Many have been glorified by the Church, and others by biographers and historians who are able to see with their eyes or discover in documents the true greatness of those followers of Christ and servants of God. Nevertheless, the majority remain anonymous in that charity which continuously and effectively fills the world with good. Glory be to these unknown soldiers, to these silent witnesses of charity! God knows them; God truly glorifies them! We must be grateful to them because they are the historical proof of the "love of God poured out into human hearts" by the Holy Spirit, the first craftsman and vital principle of Christian love.

General audience of May 22, 1991

The Spirit: Principle of Peace

Peace is the great desire of contemporary humanity. It comes in two principal forms: the elimination of war as a way to solve disputes between nations or states, and the resolution of social conflicts by achieving justice. Can anyone deny that the spread of these sentiments represents a progress in social psychology, in political mentality and in the very organization of national and international co-existence? Especially in regard to the dramatic experiences of late, the Church, whose task it is to preach and pray for peace, cannot fail to rejoice when she observes the new achievements in law, social and political institutions, and, more fundamentally, in the human awareness itself of peace.

Profound conflicts, however, remain even in the world today and are the origin of many ethnic and cultural disputes, in addition to economic and political ones. To be realistic and sincere, one cannot fail to recognize the difficulty, even the impossibility, of preserving peace without a higher principle which operates with divine power deep within the human mind.

According to revealed doctrine this principle is the Holy Spirit, who gives spiritual peace to individuals, an inner peace which becomes the basis of peace in society.

Jesus himself, speaking to his disciples in the upper room, announced his peace: "My peace I give to you" (Jn 14:27). This peace is shared with the disciples by the gift of the Holy Spirit who gives this peace to human hearts. In John's text, the promise of peace follows the promise of the Paraclete's coming (cf. Jn 14:26). Christ's work of peacemaking is achieved through the Holy Spirit who was sent to fulfill the Savior's mission.

It should be noted that Christ's peace is announced and offered along with forgiveness of sins, as can be seen in the words of the risen Jesus to his disciples: "Peace be with you.... Receive the Holy Spirit. Whose sins you forgive they are forgiven them" (Jn 20:21-23). This peace is the result of the redemptive sacrifice, accomplished on the cross, which reaches its fulfillment in the glorification of Christ.

This is the first type of peace which human beings need: the peace obtained by overcoming the obstacle of sin. It is a peace which can only come from God, by the forgiveness of sins through Christ's sacrifice. The Holy Spirit, who accomplishes this forgiveness in individuals, is for human beings the operative principle of that fundamental peace which consists in reconciliation with God.

According to St. Paul peace is a "fruit of the Holy Spirit" connected with charity: "The fruit of the Spirit is love, joy, peace..." (Gal 5:22). It is opposed to the works of the flesh, among which (according to the Apostle) are "hostilities, arguing, jealousy, outbursts of rage, selfish rivalries, dissensions, factions, envy..." (Gal 5:20). This is a list of primarily interior obstacles which impede peace of soul and social peace. Precisely because he transforms interior dispositions, the Holy Spirit inspires a basic attitude of peace in the world, too. Paul says of Christ that "he is our peace" (Eph 2:14), and explains that Christ has made peace by reconciling all people with God through his sacrifice, from which one new man is born upon the ashes of human dissension and hostility. But the Apostle himself adds that this peace is accomplished in the Holy Spirit: "Through Christ we have access in one Spirit to the Father" (Eph 2:18). It is always the one, true peace of Christ, but is poured into hearts and experienced under the impulse of the Holy Spirit.

In the Letter to the Philippians the Apostle speaks of peace as a gift given to those who, even in the difficulties of life, turn to God "in every form of prayer and in petitions full of gratitude...." He assures them: "God's own peace, which is beyond all understanding, will stand guard over your hearts and minds, in Christ Jesus" (Phil 4:6-7).

The lives of the saints are a testimony and a proof of the divine origin of peace. They appear to us with an inner serenity in the midst of the most painful trials and storms which seem to sweep them away. Something—indeed Someone—is present and at work in them to protect them not only from the shifting tides of external events, but from their own weakness and fear. It is the Holy Spirit who is the author of that peace which is the fruit of the love which he pours out into human hearts (cf. *Summa Theol.*, II-II, q. 29, aa. 3-4).

According to St. Paul, "the kingdom of God...is justice, peace and joy in the Holy Spirit" (Rom 14:17). The Apostle formulates this principle when he admonishes Christians not to judge the weakest among them harshly when the latter do not succeed in freeing themselves from certain ascetical practices which are based on a false idea of purity, such as the prohibition against eating meat and drinking wine which was practiced by some pagans (e.g., the Pythagoreans) and some Jews (e.g., the Essenes). Paul invited them to follow the rule of an enlightened and certain conscience (cf. Rom 14:5-6, 23), but especially to be inspired by charity, which should direct the conduct of the strong: "Nothing is unclean in itself.... If your brother is being hurt by what you eat, your conduct is no longer in accord with love. Do not because of your food destroy him for whom Christ died!" (Rom 14:14-15).

Paul's recommendation, then, is not to create trouble in the community, not to stir up conflict and not to scandalize others. He exhorts: "Let us then pursue what leads to peace and to building up one another" (Rom 14:19). Everyone should be concerned with preserving harmony by not using the Christian's freedom in a way which offends or harms one's neighbor. The principle formulated by the Apostle is that charity should direct and regulate freedom. In dealing with a particular problem, Paul enunciates a general principle: "The kingdom of God is peace in the Holy Spirit."

The Christian should be committed to complying with the Holy Spirit's activity by fostering in his soul "the tendency of the Spirit toward life and peace" (Rom 8:6). This is the reason for the Apostle's repeated exhortations to the faithful to "preserve the unity which has the Spirit as its origin and peace as its binding force" (Eph 4:3); to act "with perfect humility, meekness and patience, bearing with one another lovingly" (Eph 4:2); and to continue to turn away from "the tendency of the flesh, which is at enmity with God" and conflicts with the tendency of the Spirit which "is toward life and peace" (Rom 8:6-7). Only if they are united in the "binding force of peace" do Christians appear "united in the Spirit" and as true followers of him who came into the world to bring peace.

The Apostle's wish is that they receive from God that great gift which is an essential element of life in the Spirit: "May the God of hope fill you with all joy and peace in believing...by the power of the Holy Spirit" (Rom 15:13).

To conclude this catechesis, I too wish peace in the Holy Spirit to all Christians and to everyone. And I wish to recall again that, according to the teaching of Paul and the witness of saintly souls, the Holy Spirit makes his inspirations recognized by the inner peace which they bring to the heart. The promptings of the Holy Spirit go in the direction of peace, not in the direction of anxiety, discord, dissent and hostility about the good. There can be a legitimate difference of opinion on particular points and on the ways of reaching a common goal, but the impulse of charity, which is a sharing in the Holy Spirit, is toward profound concord and unity in the good willed by the Lord. St. Paul is categorical: "God is not the God of disorder but of peace" (1 Cor 14:33).

This is obviously true for peace of mind and heart within Christian communities. But when the Holy Spirit reigns in hearts, he stirs up the desire to use every effort to establish peace in relationships with others on every level: family, civic, social, political ethnic, national and international (cf. Rom 12:18; Heb 12:14). In particular, he motivates Christians to engage in prudent mediation to reconcile people in conflict and to use dialogue as the means to be employed against temptations and the threat of war.

Let us pray that Christians, the Church and all persons of good will may be ever more committed to obeying faithfully the Spirit of peace.

General audience of May 29, 1991

Only the Holy Spirit Gives True Joy

We have already heard many times from St. Paul that "joy is a fruit of the Holy Spirit" (Gal 5:22), as are love and peace, which we have discussed in earlier catecheses. It is clear that the Apostle is speaking of the true joy which fills the human heart, and certainly not of a superficial, transitory joy, which worldly joy frequently is.

It is not difficult for an observer who operates solely on the level of psychology and experience to discover that degradation in the area of pleasure and love is in proportion to the voice left in man from the false and deceptive joys sought in those things which St. Paul called the "works of the flesh": "immorality, impurity, licentiousness...drinking bouts, orgies and the like" (Gal 5:19, 21). One can add to these false joys—and there are many connected with them—those sought in the possession and immoderate use of wealth, in luxury, in ambition for power, in short, in that passion for an almost frantic search for earthly goods which can easily produce a darkened mind, as St. Paul mentions (cf. Eph 4:18-19), and Jesus laments (cf. Mk 4:19).

Paul refers to the pagan world to exhort his converts to guard against wickedness: "That is not how you learned Christ, assuming that you have heard of him and were taught in him, as truth is in Jesus, that you should put away the old self of your former way of life, corrupted through deceitful desires, and be renewed in the spirit of your minds, and put on the new self, created in God's way in righteousness and holiness of truth" (Eph 4:20-24). It is the "new creation" (cf. 2 Cor 5:17), which is the work of the Holy Spirit, present in the soul and in the Church. Therefore, the Apostle concludes his exhortation to good behavior and peace in this way: "Do not grieve the Holy Spirit of God, with which you were sealed for the day of redemption" (Eph 4:30).

If a Christian "grieves" the Holy Spirit who lives in his soul, he certainly cannot hope to possess the true joy which comes from him: "The fruit of the Spirit is love, joy, peace..." (Gal 5:22). Only the Holy Spirit gives a profound, full and lasting joy, which every human heart desires. The human person is being made for joy, not for sadness. Paul VI reminded Christians and all our contemporaries of this in the Apostolic Exhortation *Gaudete in Domino*. True joy is a gift of the Holy Spirit.

In the Letter to the Galatians Paul has told us that joy is connected with love (cf. Gal 5:22). Therefore, it cannot be an egotistical experience, the result of a disordered love. True joy includes justice in the kingdom of God, which St. Paul says "is righteousness, peace and joy in the Holy Spirit" (Rom 14:17).

It is a matter of Gospel justice, which consists in conformity to the will of God, obedience to his laws and personal friendship with him. Apart from this friendship there is no true joy. Rather, as St. Thomas explains: "Sadness, as an evil or vice, is caused by a disordered love for oneself, which...is the general root of all vices" *(Summa Theol.,* II-II, q. 28, a. 4, ad 1; cf. I-II, q. 72, a. 4). Sin is particularly a source of sadness, because it is a deviation or almost a distortion of the soul away from the just order of God, which gives consistency to one's life. The Holy Spirit, who accomplishes in man the new righteousness in love, removes sadness and gives joy, the joy which we see blossoming in the Gospel.

The Gospel is an invitation to joy and an experience of true and profound joy. At the annunciation, Mary was invited: "Rejoice, full of grace" (Lk 1:28). This is the summation of a whole series of invitations formulated by the prophets of the Old Testament (cf. Zech 9:9; Zep 3:14-17, Joel 2:21-27, Is 54:1). Mary's joy is realized with the coming of the Holy Spirit, who was announced to Mary as the reason for rejoicing.

At the visitation, Elizabeth was filled with the Holy Spirit and with joy, participating naturally and supernaturally in the rejoicing of her son who was still in her womb: "The infant in my womb leaped for joy" (Lk 1:44). Elizabeth perceived her son's joy and showed it, but according to the evangelist, it is the Holy Spirit who filled both of them with this joy. Mary, in turn, exactly at that moment felt rising in her heart that song of rejoicing which expresses the humble, clear and profound joy which filled her, almost as a realization of the angel's "rejoice": "My spirit rejoices in God my savior" (Lk 1:47). In these words, too, Mary echoed the prophets' sound of joy, such as in the Book of Habakkuk: "Yet will I rejoice in the Lord and exult in my saving God" (Hab 3:18).

A continuation of this rejoicing took place during the presentation of the infant Jesus in the Temple, when Simeon met him and rejoiced under the impulse of the Holy Spirit, who had made him desire to see the Messiah and compelled him to go to the Temple (cf. Lk 2:26-32). Then, the prophetess Anna, as she was called by the evangelist, who therefore presents her as a woman consecrated to God and an interpreter of his thoughts and commands according to the tradition of Israel (cf. Ex 15:20; Jgs 4:9; 2 Kgs 22:14), by praising God expresses the interior joy which in her, too, takes it origin from the Holy Spirit (cf. Lk 2:36-38).

In the Gospel texts which concern the public life of Jesus, we read that at a certain moment he himself "rejoiced in the Holy Spirit" (Lk 10:21). Jesus expressed joy and gratitude in a prayer which celebrates the Father's loving kindness: "I give you praise, Father, Lord of heaven and earth, for although you have hidden these things from the wise and the learned you have revealed them to the childlike. Yes, Father, such has been your gracious will" (Lk 10:21). In Jesus, joy assumes all its force in enthusiasm for the Father. The same is true for the joys inspired and sustained by the Holy Spirit in human life. Their hidden, vital energy directs individuals toward a love which is full of gratitude to the Father. Every true joy has the Father as its final goal.

Jesus invited his disciples to rejoice, to overcome the temptation to sadness at the Master's departure, because this departure was the condition planned by God for the coming of the Holy Spirit: "It is better for you that I go. For if I do not go, the Advocate will not come to you. But if I go, I will send him to you" (Jn 16:7). It will be the Spirit's gift to provide the disciples with a great joy, even the fullness of joy, according to Jesus' intention. The Savior, after inviting the disciples to remain in his love, said: "I have told you this so that my joy might be in you and your joy might be complete" (Jn 15:11; cf. 17:13). It is the task of the Holy Spirit to put into the disciples' hearts the same joy that Jesus had, the joy of faithfulness to the love which comes from the Father.

St. Luke attests that the disciples, who had received the promise of the gift of the Holy Spirit at the time of the ascension, "returned to Jerusalem with great joy, and they were continually in the Temple praising God" (Lk 24:52-53). In the Acts of the Apostles, it turns out that after Pentecost a climate of profound joy came to pass in the apostles. This was shared with the community in the form of exultation and enthusiasm in embracing the faith, in receiving Baptism and in community life, as can be seen in the passage: "They ate their meals with exultation and sincerity of heart, praising God and enjoying favor with all the people" (Acts 2:46-47). The Acts notes: "The disciples were filled with joy and the Holy Spirit" (Acts 13:52).

The sufferings and persecutions which Jesus predicted in announcing the coming of the Paraclete-Consoler (cf. Jn 16:1 ff.) would come soon enough. But according to Acts, joy lasts even during trials. One reads that the apostles, brought before the Sanhedrin, were flogged, warned and sent home. They returned "rejoicing that they had been found worthy to suffer dishonor for the sake of the name. And all day long, both at the temple and in their homes, they did not stop teaching and proclaiming the Messiah, Jesus" (Acts 5:41-42).

Moreover, this is the condition and the lot of Christians, as St. Paul reminds the Thessalonians: "And you became imitators of us and of the Lord, receiving the word in great affliction, with joy from the Holy Spirit" (1 Thess 1:6). According to Paul, Christians reproduce in themselves the paschal mystery of Christ, whose foundation is the cross. But its crowning glory is "joy in the Holy Spirit" for those who persevere in the time of trial. It is the joy of the beatitudes, particularly the beatitude of the mourning and the persecuted (cf. Mt 5:4, 10-12). Did not Paul the Apostle say: "I rejoice in my sufferings for your sake..." (Col 1:24)? And Peter, in his turn, urged: "But rejoice to the extent that you share in the sufferings of Christ, so that when his glory is revealed you may also rejoice exultantly" (1 Pet 4:13).

Let us pray to the Holy Spirit that he may always enkindle in us a desire for the good things of heaven and enable us one day to enjoy their fullness: "Grant us virtue and its reward, grant us a holy death, give us eternal joy." Amen.

General audience of June 19, 1991

The Spirit Gives Strength to Christians

The people of today, who are particularly exposed to assault, temptation and the seduction of the world, need the gift of fortitude. This gift gives courage and constancy in the struggle against the spirit of evil which lays siege to those who live upon this earth. This evil tries to turn people away from the road to heaven. Many people risk wavering and giving in, especially during times of temptation of suffering. For Christians too there is always the risk of falling from the heights of their vocation, of deviating from the logic of the baptismal grace which was granted to them as a seed of eternal life. For this very reason Jesus revealed and promised to us the Holy Spirit as our Comforter and Defender (cf. Jn 16:5-15). From him we are given the gift of supernatural fortitude, which gives us a share of the power and strength of the divine Being (cf. *Summa Theol.*, I-II, q. 61, a. 5; q. 68, a. 4).

In the Old Testament we already find many proofs of the action of the divine Spirit who sustained not only individuals, but also the whole people in the difficulties they encountered throughout their history. However, it is especially in the New Testament that the power of the Holy Spirit is revealed and believers receive the promise of his presence and activity in every struggle, until the final victory. We spoke of this several times in preceding catecheses. Here I will limit myself to mentioning that in the annunciation the Holy Spirit was revealed and granted to Mary as "the power of the Most High," who shows that "nothing will be impossible for God" (cf. Lk 1:35-37).

On Pentecost, the Holy Spirit, who manifests his power through the symbolic sign of a driving wind (cf. Acts 2:2), gave the apostles and all those gathered with them "all in one place" (Acts 2:1), the new strength promised by Jesus in his farewell discourse (cf. Jn 16:8-11) and shortly before the ascension: "But you will receive power when the Holy Spirit descends upon you" (Acts 1:8; Lk 24:49).

It is a question of an inner strength which is rooted in love (cf. Eph 3:17), which St. Paul writes about to the faithful of Ephesus: may the Father "grant you in accord with the riches of his glory to be strengthened with power through his Spirit in the inner self" (Eph 3:16). Paul prays to the Father to give this higher power to those to whom he is writing. Christian tradition lists this power among the "gifts of the Holy Spirit," deriving them from the text of Isaiah which lists them as the characteristics of the Messiah (cf. Is 11:2 ff.). Among the gifts with which Christ's most holy soul is filled, the Holy Spirit also gives to Christ's followers the fortitude which he was champion of in his life and death. One can say that the Christian who is involved in the "spiritual combat" has a share in the strength of the cross!

The Spirit intervenes with a deep, continuing action at every moment and under all aspects of Christian life in order to guide human desires in the right direction, which is the direction of generous love of God and neighbor, following the example of Jesus. For this purpose the Holy Spirit strengthens the will, making the person capable of resisting temptations and of gaining victory in internal and external struggles. The Spirit enables the Christian to overcome the power of evil and especially Satan, like Jesus who was led by the Spirit into the desert (cf. Lk 4:1), and of fulfilling the demands of a life according to the Gospel.

The Holy Spirit gives the Christian the strength of fidelity, patience and perseverance on the path of good and in the struggle against evil. In the Old Testament the prophet Ezekiel told people of God's promise: "I will put my spirit within you." The purpose was to obtain the fidelity of the people of the new covenant (cf. Ez 36:27). In his Letter to the Galatians, among the "fruits of the Holy Spirit," St. Paul lists "patience," "fidelity" and "self-control" (cf. Gal 5:22). These virtues are necessary for a consistent Christian life. Among them "patience" is singled out; it is a property of charity (cf. 1 Cor 13:4) and is infused into the soul by the Holy Spirit with charity itself (cf. Rom 5:5), as part of the fortitude to be practiced in confronting evil and the tribulations of life and death. This is accompanied by "perseverance" which is continuity in the exercise of good works with the victory over difficulties represented by the length of the road to be traveled. It is similar to "constancy" which makes people continue to do good despite all external obstacles. Both of these are fruits of the grace which he gives the person in order to reach life's goal on the way of good (cf. St. Augustine *De Perseverantia*, c. 1: PL 45:993; *De corr. et gratia*, c. 12: PL 44:937).

This courageous practice of the virtues is required of every Christian who, even in the state of grace, is still weak in his or her freedom. St. Augustine emphasized this in his controversy with the followers of Pelagius (cf. *De corr. et gratia*, c. 12 cit.). However, it is the Holy Spirit who gives the supernatural strength to fulfill the divine will and conform our life to Christ's precepts. St. Paul writes: "For the law of the spirit of life in Christ Jesus has freed you from the law of sin and death." Thus Christians have the possibility of "walking in the Spirit" and of fulfilling "the justice of the law," that is, of fulfilling the divine will (cf. Rom 8:2-4).

The Holy Spirit also gives people the strength to fulfill the apostolic mission which was entrusted to those designated to proclaim the Gospel and, in some measure, to all Christians. Therefore, at the moment when he sent his disciples on mission, Jesus asked them to wait until Pentecost, so that they might receive the power of the Holy Spirit: "But you will receive power when the Holy Spirit comes upon you" (Acts 1:8). Only with this power can they be witnesses to the Gospel to the ends of the earth, following Jesus' command.

At all times, even to this very day, it is the Holy Spirit who gives the commitment to use all one's faculties and resources, to use all one's talents, to spend and if necessary, to offer one's life in the mission that has been received. It is the Holy Spirit who does wonders in the apostolic activity of men and women of God and the Church, who are chosen and motivated by him. It is the Holy Spirit who most of all assures the efficacy of such an action, regardless of the human capacity of those who have been called. St. Paul said so in his First Letter to the Corinthians, speaking of his own preaching as a "demonstration of spirit and power" (1 Cor 2:4). It was an apostolate, therefore, that was carried out "by word and deed, by the power of signs and wonders, by the power of the Spirit" (Rom 15:18-19). Paul attributes the value of his work of evangelization to this power of the Spirit.

Even amid the sometimes enormous difficulties which are encountered in the apostolate, the Holy Spirit gives the strength to persevere, renewing courage and helping those who are tempted to renounce the fulfillment of their mission. It is the experience of the very first Christian community, where the brothers and sisters who were persecuted by the enemies of the faith prayed: "And now, Lord, take note of their threats, and enable your servants to speak your word with all boldness" (Acts 4:29). And behold, "As they prayed, the place where they were gathered shook, and they were all filled with the Holy Spirit and continued to speak the word of God with boldness" (Acts 4:31).

The Holy Spirit sustains those who are persecuted, to whom Jesus himself promised: "For it will not be you who speak but the Spirit of your Father speaking through you" (Mt 10:20). Martyrdom especially, which the Second Vatican Council calls "the highest gift and supreme test of love" *(LG* 42), is a heroic act of fortitude inspired by the Holy Spirit. This is shown by the holy martyrs of all ages, who faced death because abundant charity burned in their hearts. When St. Thomas examined a good number of cases of ancient martyrdom including those of very young children and the patristic texts concerning them, he concluded that martyrdom is "the most perfect human act," because it is the result of the love of charity, and is proof of its greatest perfection (cf. *Summa Theol.,* II-II, q. 124, a. 3). This is what Jesus himself affirms in the Gospel: "No one has greater love than this, to lay down one's life for one's friends" (Jn 15:13).

In closing, we must refer to Confirmation, the sacrament in which the Holy Spirit is conferred for strength. Its finality is to communicate the fortitude which will be needed in the Christian life and apostolate of witness and action to which all Christians are called. It is quite significant that the rite of the blessing of the chrism alludes to the anointing which the Spirit gives to martyrs. Martyrdom is the highest form of witness. The Church knows this and entrusts the Spirit with the task of sustaining, if necessary, the witness of the faithful to a heroic degree.

General audience of June 26, 1991

The Spirit: Pledge of Eschatological Hope

Hope is among the greatest gifts which last, as St. Paul tells the Corinthians (cf. 1 Cor 12:31). It has a basic role in Christian life, as do faith and charity, although "the greatest of these is love" (1 Cor 13:13). It is clear that hope is not to be understood in its limited meaning as a particular, extraordinary gift granted to some people for the good of the community, but rather as a gift of the Holy Spirit offered to each person who is open to Christ in faith. Special attention should be given to this gift, especially in our day. Today many people, including quite a few Christians, are floundering in the illusion and myth of an unlimited capacity for self-redemption and self-fulfillment, and the temptation to pessimism from the experience of frequent disappointment and defeat.

Although it includes the psychological motivation of the soul which strives toward the more difficult good, Christian hope is found on the supernatural level of the virtues. It derives from grace (cf. *Summa Theol.,* III, q. 7, a. 2), as a gift which God makes to believers in the order of eternal life. It is a virtue which is typical of *homo viator,* of the person on pilgrimage who, although he knows God and his eternal vocation through faith, has not yet arrived at the vision of God. In a certain sense, hope makes him reach "into the interior, beyond the veil," as the Letter to the Hebrews says (cf. Heb 6:19).

The eschatological dimension, however, is essential to this virtue. On Pentecost the Holy Spirit came to fulfill the promises included in the proclamation of salvation, as we read in the Acts of the Apostles: "Exalted at the right hand of God, [Jesus] received the promise of the Holy Spirit from the Father and poured it forth" (Acts 2:33). However, this fulfillment of the promise is projected upon the whole of history, even to the last days. For those who possess faith in the word of God which resounds in Christ and was preached by the apostles, eschatology has begun to be fulfilled, or we could say rather that it is already fulfilled in its fundamental aspect: the presence of the Holy Spirit in human history, which from the Pentecost event takes its meaning and vital impulse on the plane of the divine goal of every person and all humanity. The hope of the Old Testament has as its foundation the promise of God's lasting presence and providence, which would be manifested in the Messiah. In the New Testament, hope already gives us an anticipation of future glory through the grace of the Holy Spirit which is its origin.

In this perspective St. Paul affirms that the gift of the Holy Spirit is like a pledge of future happiness. To the Ephesians he writes: "You were sealed with the promised Holy Spirit, who is the first installment of our inheritance toward redemption as God's possession, to the praise of his glory" (Eph 1:13-14; cf. 4:30; 2 Cor 1:22).

We could say that in Christian life on earth, it is like an initiation into full participation in the glory of God. The Holy Spirit constitutes the guarantee for achieving the fullness of eternal life when, by means of the effects of the redemption, all the other effects of sin will also be overcome, such as suffering and death. Thus Christian hope is not only a guarantee, but also an anticipation of the future reality.

The hope which the Holy Spirit enkindles in the Christian also has a dimension which could be called cosmic, including heaven and earth, that which can be experienced, and that which is beyond our reach, the known and the unknown. "Creation itself," St. Paul writes, "awaits with eager expectation the revelation of the children of God. Creation was made subject to futility, not of its own choice but because of the one who subjected it, in hope that creation itself would be set free from slavery to corruption and share in the glorious freedom of God's children. We know that all creation groans and is in labor even until now; and not only that, but we ourselves, who have the first fruits of the Spirit, we also groan within ourselves as we wait for adoption, the redemption of our bodies" (Rom 8:19-23). Conscious of man's vocation and the destiny of the universe, the Christian understands the meaning of this universal gestation and learns that it is a question of divine adoption for all people, who are called to participate in the glory of God which is reflected in all creation. The Christian knows that he already possesses the first fruits of this adoption in the Holy Spirit, and therefore looks with confident hope to the destiny of the world, even amid the tribulations of time.

Enlightened by faith, he understands the meaning and almost experiences the truth of the subsequent passage from the Letter to the Romans where the Apostle assures us that "the Spirit comes to help us in our weakness; for we do not know how to pray as we ought, but the Spirit himself intercedes with inexpressible groanings. He who searches hearts knows the intention of the Spirit, because he intercedes for the holy ones according to God's will" (Rom 8:26-28).

As you see, it is in the depths of the soul that the Holy Spirit lives, prays and works. He makes us enter more and more fully into the perspective of the ultimate end, God, conforming our whole lives to his saving plan. Therefore he himself helps us pray, praying in us, with the sentiments and words of God's children (cf. Rom 8:15, 26-27; Gal 4:6; Eph 6:18), in intimate spiritual and eschatological relationship with Christ who sits at the right hand of God, where he intercedes for us (cf. Rom 8:34; Heb 7:25; 1 Jn 2:1). Thus he saves us from illusion and from false paths of salvation. While moving hearts toward the authentic purpose of life, he frees us from pessimism and nihilism. These temptations are especially insidious for those who do not begin with the premise of faith, or at least with the sincere desire to search for God.

We must add that the body is also involved in this dimension of hope which the Holy Spirit gives to the human being. St. Paul also tells us so: "If the Spirit of him who raised Jesus from the dead dwells in you, he who raised Christ from the dead will give life to your mortal bodies also, through his Spirit dwelling in you" (Rom 8:11; cf. 2 Cor 5:5). Let us be content for now with having considered this aspect of hope in its personal anthropological dimension as well as in its cosmic and eschatological plane. We shall return to it in the catecheses which, God willing, we shall dedicate to these fascinating, basic articles of the Christian creed: the resurrection of the body and the eternal life of the whole person, body and soul.

One further point should be made: life's earthly journey has an end which, if a person reaches it in friendship with God, coincides with the first moment of eternal bliss. Even, if in that passage to heaven, the soul must undergo the purification of its last impurities through purgatory, it is already filled with light, certitude and joy, because the person knows that he or she belongs forever to God. At this culminating moment the soul is led by the Holy Spirit, the author and giver not only of the justifying "first grace" and of sanctifying grace throughout one's earthly life, but also of the glorifying grace in the hour of death. It is the grace of final perseverance, according to the teaching of the Council of Orange (cf. *DS* 183, 199) and the

Council of Trent (cf. *DS* 806, 809, 832). This is founded upon the teaching of the Apostle, according to which it is up to God "to desire and to work" good (Phil 2:13), and the person must pray in order to obtain the grace to do good until the end (cf. Rom 14:4; 1 Cor 10:12; Mt 10:22; 24:13).

The words of the Apostle Paul teach us to see in the gift of the third divine Person the guarantee of the fulfillment of our hope of salvation: "Hope does not disappoint, because the love of God has been poured out into our hearts through the Holy Spirit who has been given to us" (Rom 5:5). And therefore, "What will separate us from the love of Christ?" The response is a decisive one: nothing "will be able to separate us from the love of God in Christ Jesus our Lord" (Rom 8:35, 39). Therefore Paul's wish is that we may have an abundance of "hope by the power of the Holy Spirit" (Rom 15:13). This is the source of Christian optimism, an optimism about the world's destiny, the possibility of salvation at all times, even in the hardest, most difficult moments in the development of history toward the perfect glorification of Christ ("He will glorify me": Jn 16:14) and the believer's full participation in the glory of the children of God.

In this perspective the Christian can hold his head high and join in the invocation which, according to the Book of Revelation, is the deepest cry which the Holy Spirit raises up throughout history: "The Spirit and the Bride say, Come!" (Rev 22:17). Now listen to the final invitation of the Book of Revelation and of the whole New Testament: "Let the hearer say, Come! Let the one who thirsts come forward, and the one who wants it receive the gift of life-giving water.... Come, Lord Jesus!" (Rev 22:17, 20).

General audience of July 3, 1991

Index

A
Abraham
  covenant by God with, 68
Acts of the Apostles, 130, 147–48. *See also* Holy Spirit, and primitive Church; Holy Spirit, and mission to the Gentiles; Pentecost, fruitfulness of; Peter, Saint, first discourse by; preaching, apostolic
  and anointing of Jesus Christ, 287–88
  and Church
    apostolicity of, 342–43
      missionary activity of, 95–96
      primitive, 225, 370–71
      universality of, 101–102, 337–38
    and Confirmation, 352, 353
    and conversion of first pagan, 132–35, 339, 371, 374–75
    and evangelization, 107, 138, 403
    and fulfillment of history of salvation, 132
    and gift of tongues, 97–98, 338
    and Holy Spirit, 294, 313, 320, 428
      arrival of, 22, 32, 105, 221. *See also* Pentecost
        description of, 54, 63
        preparation for, 37
      and hierarchical ministry, 356
      power of, 323

    and invocation of Jesus Christ's name, 121
    and Jesus' ascension, 16
    and joy, 420–21
    and Mary, 42
    and mission to the Gentiles, 138
    and new People of God, 78
    and Orders (Holy), 354
    and prayer of apostles, 37–39
    and presence of God, 173
    and proclamation by the apostles, 98–99
    and Saint Stephen, 29
    and transformation of apostles, 58

Ad Gentes
    and Holy Spirit in the Church, 345
    and missionary activity of the Church, 95

Ambrose, Saint
    and Mary, 43
    and origin of Holy Spirit, 301
    and prayer, 393, 393–94

Anna
    and presentation of Jesus Christ, 220, 419

anointing, 162–65
    of kings, 163
    as symbol, 287–91
    of the sick, 353
    by Holy Spirit, 80

Antioch, Church of, 138–39, 139, 140–41, 371

Apostles' Creed
    and foundation of the Church, 341
    and Holy Spirit, 15
        sanctification by, 333–34

Arians, 295

Athanasius, Saint
    and equality of Holy Spirit, 295

Augustine, Saint
    and Holy Spirit, 34, 301, 308–309, 327
        as Gift, 312
        as Love, 306, 307–308

and Matrimony, 354–55
and practice of virtues, 424

B

baptism. *See also* John the Baptist, Saint, and baptism
   and divine adoption, 264
   of first pagans, 135, 143, 146, 313, 339, 371
      criticism of, 137. *See also* coucil of Jerusalem
   and Holy Spirit, 80, 84–89, 117, 118, 290, 352
   and Jesus Christ
      invocation of name of, 121–22
   and oil, 288
   and reconciliation with God, 286
   and Trinity, 261, 262, 293
   and water symbol, 289

Barnabas, Saint
   and Church of Antioch, 138–9

Bible. *See* Scripture

Bulgakov
   and Holy Spirit, 308

C

catechesis of Jerusalem, 107, 134–35. *See also* Peter, first discourse by

charisms. *See* Holy Spirit, gifts of

Chronicles
   first book of
      and spirit of God and the word, 182
   second book of
      and spirit of God and the word, 182–83

Church. *See also* Scripture, as source of consolation; Tradition, guarded by the Holy Spirit; Vatican Council, Second
   apostolicity of, 346
      Holy Spirit as source of, 341–45
   beginning of, 80–83, 84, 91, 95–99, 225, 320
      Holy Spirit in, 126–30
      basic forms of organization, 128
      increase in believers, 144–45
   as Body of Christ, 320–21
   divisions in, 328

and Eucharist, 90–1, 94
and evangelization, 395
and Holy Spirit
   as Comforter of, 368–72
   guidance of, 104, 269
   as soul of, 319–24, 341
   as source of spiritual gifts, 362–67
   as source of ministry, 356–61
   unity in, 101
and multiplicity of languages, 338–39
as new People of God, 79. *See also* Pentecost,
as gift of divine adoption
and peace, 412
and Pentecost, 64
and pneumatological utopianism, 123–24
prayer for unity of, 38–39
and preparation through prayer, 38
sacramentality of, 84
   Holy Spirit as source of, 351–55
unity in multiplicity of, 325–29, 328, 338
universality of, 98, 336–40
   and diversity, 100–104
   Holy Spirit as source of, 336–40
and wisdom of God, 280
communion of saints, 334
Confirmation, 288, 352–53
Constitution on Divine Revelation
and Holy Spirit, 57, 346–47
Constitution on the Church
and Mary, 43
and gifts of the Holy Spirit, 364
Council of Chalcedon
and Eastern Catholics, 301
Council of Constantinople, first (381)
and changes to creed, 292, 295, 298
and Eastern Christians, 301, 303
Council of Florence
and procession of Holy Spirit, 302–303, 303
council of Jerusalem, 102

Index

and question of pagan admittance, 141, 340
Council of Orange
and work of the Holy Spirit, 403–404
and faith, 404
Council of Trent
and Reconciliation, 353
and faith, 407
covenant
bond between old and new, 36
fulfillment of promises made in old, 33, 67–71
new, 80
law of, 73–5
prophecy of, 33–34, 72–73
old, 80, 375
history of, 69
nature of, 76–77
of Sinai, 68, 68–71

creed, changes to, 299, 301. *See also* Nicene-Constantinopolitan Creed; Nicene Creed
disagreements between East and West on

Cyprian of Carthage, Saint
and Church, 327

Cyril of Alexandria, Saint
and Holy Spirit, 308, 313

D

Damasus I, Pope
and Holy Spirit, 296
truth of, 329
Daniel, Book of
and spirit of God and wisdom, 183
De Spiritu Sancto
and origin of Holy Spirit, 301
De Trinitate
and Holy Spirit
as Love, 307–308
origin of, 301
Decalogue, 72

Dei Verbum
  and Jesus Christ, 320
  and Holy Spirit, 346, 368–69
  and order to preach the Gospel, 347

demon. *See* Satan

Deuteronomy, Book of
  and People of God, 77
  impartiality of God, 136

devil. *See* Satan

Dominum et Vivificantem
  and beginning of the Church, 81–82
  and Eucharist, 92
  and Holy Spirit, 61–62, 87, 91
    action of, 24–25
    fullness of, 50, 208
    as Gift, 314
    mission of, 125
    victory over sin, 118, 272
  and Jesus Christ, 241–42
    conception and birth of, 206
    death of, 245, 246–47
    resurrection of, 250
  and judgement of Satan, 30
  and Peter
    as witness to Jesus Christ, 110
    first discourse by, 113
  and repentance, 116
  and salvific plan of God, 19

dove (as symbol), 234, 285–86

E

East-West schism, 301, 302

Eastern Church. *See also* East-West schism
  doctrine on Holy Spirit, 301, 303, 308–309
    disagreements with Western Church on, 298–99, 302
    theologians of, 301, 308

Elizabeth. *See* Mary (mother of Jesus Christ), and Holy Spirit, and visit to Elizabeth

Eucharist. *See also* Church, and Eucharist

and Holy Spirit, 90–94, 254, 353–54
and Jesus Christ, 91, 92, 212
    instituted by, 319–20

evangelization. *See* Acts of the Apostles, and evangelization; Church, and evangelization; Jesus Christ, and evangelization; Peter, Saint, and evangelization; redemption, and evangelization; Vatican Council, Second, and evangelization

Exodus, Book of
  and covenant of Sinai, 68
  and God, 150, 151
    People of, 77

Ezekiel
  and analogy to birth of the Church, 82–83
  and God
    gift of spirit by, 156, 174, 424
    inspiration from, 259
    presence of, 54–55
  and *Miserere*, 177–78
  prophecies of
    resurrection, 157–58
    new covenant, 71, 72
    Holy Spirit, 33, 34, 50, 59, 67, 70–71, 259–60
  and prophets, 169
  and sign of divine pardon, 180
  and water symbol, 289
  and wind symbol, 285

F

Father. *See* God

feast of the Pasch, 47

Feast of the Tabernacles, 47

Filioque doctrine
  as basis of East-West schism, 301
  and debate about Holy Spirit, 298–303
  scholars of, 301

fire (as symbol), 54
  of Holy Spirit, 55, 56, 85, 86, 86–87, 87–88, 286, 379
  manifestation of God, 96–97, 247

G

Genesis, Book of
    and analogies to the Church, 82, 321–22
    and multiplicity of languages, 98–99
    and spirit of God, 54, 61, 155, 157, 258

glossolalia, 97, 107, 111, 363

God. *See also* Holy Spirit; Jesus Christ; Trinity
    and covenant of Sinai, 68–71
    gift of self, 203, 205
    kingdom of, 35–36, 237, 388. See also Jesus Christ, kingdom of
    universality of, 132
    and Mary, 200, 202
    presence of, 201–202
    reconciliation with, 286, 359–60
    relationship with man, 204–205
    return to, 313–14
    salvific plan of, 16, 19, 30, 112, 191, 238, 429
    self-communication by, 64, 131, 257
    spirit of, 151–54, 155–56
        attributes of, 185, 187
        guiding action of, 160–65, 166
        presence of, 54–55, 173–74
        prophetic action of, 166–71
        purification by, 177–81
        and wisdom, 182–87, 280–81
    symbols of presence, 54–55, 55

Gospels, 348. *See also* New Testament; *and individual authors*
    and dove symbol, 285
    and Holy Spirit, 39, 12, 146, 214, 245
        blasphemy against, 243
        coming of, 26, 35
        proclamation through, 357, 358, 359
        relationship of Jesus Christ with, 300
        sanctifying grace of, 176
    and iconography, 208
    and Jesus Christ, 194, 250
        birth of, 196–97
        desert experience of, 235, 236, 237–38
    law of, 74

purpose of, 22, 276, 277
and sacraments, 351–55
and style of Jesus Christ's teaching, 108–109
and the desert, 237–38
truth presented in, 23
and unity in multiplicity, 325

Gregory Nazianzen, Saint
and salvation history, 257–58

H

Haggai
and prophetic action, 169–70

Holy Spirit. *See also* God; Jesus Christ; Trinity
as advocate, 26–31, 270–73, 396
activity of, 278–82
guiding, 99, 142, 146, 265–69, 329, 396
anointing by, 287–91
belief in, 15–19
blasphemy against, 243–44, 267–68, 294
as Creator Spirit, 36, 82
descent of, 16, 72
elements of, 54
linked with feast of harvest, 47–48
universality of, 64
as distinct Person, 17–19
revelation of, 257–60, 261–64, 283
divine adoption through, 65–66, 264, 277, 429
dwelling in individuals, 278–79, 373–77
effect on human spirit, 66, 73
and enlightenment, 395–400
and establishing justice, 164–65
and faith, 401–406
fruits of, 384–85, 410, 413, 417, 418, 424
of apostolic ministry, 144
as fulfillment of covenant with God, 76, 149
as guardian of Tradition, 346–50
as Gift, 19, 34–35, 309, 310–15
gifts of, 97, 280–81, 362–67, 399
diversity of, 103–104, 275–76, 294, 380
and revelation, 349

as giver of life, 63–64, 74, 88, 90, 208, 295
as hidden God, 46–47, 52, 143, 283, 283–84, 314
and hope, 427–31
and the Incarnation, 206, 207, 209, 210, 230, 265
   hidden at, 52
   and redemption, 17
   as source of sacraments, 351
law of, 72–75, 378, 388, 424–25
as Love, 304–309, 312–13, 314, 329
   doctrine of Eastern Church on, 308–309
and martyrdom, 129–30, 143
in mission to the Gentiles, 137–42
new anthropology from, 206–209
and new People of God, 78–79, 80
opponents to divinity of, 295–96
and peace, 412–16
and prayer, 37–39, 127, 280, 389–94, 425–26, 430
preparation for coming of, 37–40
procession from Father and Son
   as object of clarification, 302
   councils on, 298, 301, 302, 303
revelation by, 22–23, 349, 358
as sanctifier, 172–76, 211, 276–77, 331
   aspects of sanctification, 332, 333
as soul of the Church, 319–24, 341
as source of
   apostolicity of the Church, 341–45
   charity, 407–11
   holiness, 330–35, 341
   interior life, 384–88
   ministry, 356–61
   new life, 61, 351, 378–83
   sacramentality of the Church, 351–55
   universality of the Church, 336–40, 341
as Spirit of truth, 19, 20–25, 82, 271, 272, 395–96, 397–98
   and multiplicity of languages, 98–9
   work of, 391
as strength to Christians, 145, 422–26
symbols of, 283–86, 290
and true joy, 417–21

and unity in multiplicity, 325–29, 341
as word and wisdom, 182–87, 280–81

Hosea
and prophets, 169
and restoration of Israel, 83

humanity. *See* man

I

Incarnation. *See* Holy Spirit, and the Incarnation; Jesus Christ, virginal conception of

Irenaeus of Lyons, Saint
and baptism of Jesus Christ, 233–34
and Church, 324

Isaiah
and Comforter, 369, 370
and establishing justice, 164
and God, 232
promise of, 156
and prophecies
of Holy Spirit, 61, 242
gifts of, 380
messianic, 86, 224, 259, 266
and *Miserere,* 177–78
and prophecy of new covenant, 70
and restoration of Israel, 83
and salvation, 180
and sign of divine pardon, 180
and spirit of God, 164, 175, 179
holy, 172
renewal by, 259–260

J

Jeremiah
and prophecies of
Holy Spirit, 33–34, 34
new covenant, 69–70, 72
and sign of divine pardon, 180

Jerusalem
as place of fulfillment, 36

Jesus Christ. *See also* Eucharist, and Jesus Christ; Peter, Saint, first discourse by; Torah,

Jesus Christ as new; Trinity
  and activities of apostles, 122–23, 359
  baptism of, 38
    desert experience after, 235–39
    Holy Spirit in, 230–34
    passion and death as, 86, 247–48
  bearing witness to, 29, 35, 343–44
  childhood of, 226–27
    Holy Spirit in, 222–25
  and Church, 80–81, 320, 326
  conception of, 195–200, 201, 206, 207–208, 214, 251. *See also* Mary, and Holy Spirit
  death of
    Holy Spirit in, 245–49, 272–73
  and establishing justice, 165
  and evangelization, 395
  as first Paraclete, 27–31
  and God
    fulfillment of law of, 74
    man's return to, 313–14
    presence of, 174
    self-revelation of, 46
    unity with, 270
    universal worship of, 337
  and his identity, 20–21
  holiness of, 210–13, 330–31
  as Holy Spirit's greatest wonder, 191–94
  kingdom of
    presence in human history, 120–25
  messianic activity of, 319
    Holy Spirit in, 265–69
    and joy, 420
  and parable of the prodigal son, 179-80
  and prayer, 38, 39, 240–44, 343, 389
  presentation in the Temple, 218–21
  reconciliation in, 360
  resurrection of, 250–254
  revelation by, 22, 47, 294–95, 310

of Holy Spirit, 17–19, 52, 192, 293, 300, 306–307
    true worship of, 333
    through sacrifice, 311
  sanctification of by the Holy Spirit, 211–12
  second phase of redemptive work, 148. *See also* Pentecost
  teaching, 108–109, 146
  and water symbol, 289–90
Joachim of Fiore
  and third kingdom, 124
Joel
  and prophecy of Holy Spirit, 33, 51, 96, 111, 259–60
  and prophetic inspiration, 170–1
  and God's promise, 156
John, Saint
  and divine adoption, 64–65, 65
  and dove symbol, 285
  and Eucharist, 353
  and God
    as love, 304, 312
    salvific action of, 19
    spirit of, 54
    true worship of, 333
  and Holy Spirit, 307, 347, 386, 397
    anointing by, 288
    fullness of, 50
    harvest of, 48
    as source of knowledge, 288
    as Spirit of truth, 21, 30, 299
  and Jesus Christ, 224
    as advocate, 27
    baptism of, 232–33
    birth of, 197
    death of, 16, 246
    gift of the Holy Spirit by, 16, 32, 242
    relationship with God, 270–73
  and the Incarnation, 211
  and water symbol, 290, 310
John the Baptist, Saint
  and baptism

by Jesus Christ, 84–85, 90, 231, 247, 264, 386
   of Jesus Christ, 85–86, 230, 232–33, 235
   and water symbol, 289
  childhood of, 223
Joseph
  and spirit of God, 161
Judges, Book of
  and spirit of God, 162–63

K

kerygma, 48, 107, 111–12, 118
kingdom of God. *See God*, kingdom of

L

Leo XIII, Pope
  and Holy Spirit, 308, 373–74
Luke, Saint. *See also* Acts of the Apostles
  and dove symbol, 285
  and Holy Spirit, 263, 266, 310–11, 323
    description of coming of, 49, 54
    and Jesus Christ, 268
    as Comforter, 369
  and Jesus Christ
    baptism of, 231, 232
      desert experience after, 235
    birth of, 195, 196, 201, 202–203, 204
      and Holy Spirit, 208
    childhood of, 212–13, 218–21, 222–23, 225
      and parents' understanding, 227–28
    death of, 245–46
    fulfillment of promises, 32
    messianic activity of, 240, 242–43, 247
    prayer by, 241
    woman followers of, 40
  and links to Old Testament, 192
  and Mary, 41–42, 44, 192, 198, 201, 228
    visit to Elizabeth by, 214–17, 419
  and Peter, 119
  and prayers of apostles, 127

and primitive Church
   disciples' relationship with God, 145
   Holy Spirit in, 128, 225
   increase in believers, 144–45
   institution of seven deacons in, 145

Lumen Gentium
   and connection between Paschal mystery and Pentecost, 81
   and Holy Spirit
      in the Church, 100, 104, 360, 362
      and Jesus Christ, 320
      evangelical counsels, 365
      and Church authority, 400
   and Mary, 44–5
   and mission of the Church, 345
   and new People of God, 79
   and unity in the Church, 101, 327

M

Maccabees
   and establishing justice, 164

Macedonians, 295

Mark, Saint
   and dove symbol, 285
   and Jesus Christ
      desert experience of, 235
      and evangelization, 395
   Mary (mother of Jesus Christ)
   and God, 202
   holiness of, 331
   and Holy Spirit, 42–43, 201–205, 266
      preparation for coming of, 40, 41–45
      and understanding, 226–29
      and visit to Elizabeth, 214–17, 419
   and joy, 419
   role in Incarnation, 197-200, 203–204
   virginity of, 196, 197–200, 203–204, 207, 208, 216

Matrimony, 354–55

Matthew, Saint
   and dove symbol, 285

and Holy Spirit, 299
and Jesus Christ, 268
    baptism of, 262–63
    birth of, 195–196, 201, 207
    desert experience of, 235
    and evangelization, 395
and links to Old Testament, 192
and Trinity, 261, 262, 274

Miserere (Psalm 51), 177–81

Moses
    and theophany of the burning bush, 55
    and guidance of God, 161, 162, 167

Mulieris Dignitatem
    and equality of women in kingdom of God, 40

multiplication of languages, symbolism of, 56–57, 98–99

N

New Testament. *See also* Church, and Scripture; Gospels; *and individual authors*
    and anointing, 287
    and Eucharist, 353–54
    and Holy Spirit
        meaning of, 149, 152
        as Love, 265, 304, 306
        as Person, 191, 283, 319
        as Spirit of Jesus Christ, 300–301
        as strength, 423
    and hope, 428
    and Incarnation, 201
    and Jesus Christ, 216
        Church as Body of, 320
    and Mary, 42
    and miraculous births, 203
    and old covenant, 192
    and pneumatology, 15
    and reconciliation with God, 286
    revelation in, 191, 283, 383
    and Trinity, 93, 261–64, 265, 319
    and water symbol, 289–90

and wind symbol, 285
Nicene Creed
  additions to, 292, 295, 298
Nicene-Constantinopolitan Creed
  and Holy Spirit, 15, 292–97, 295, 296, 298
  spread of, 298–99
Noah
  covenant by God with, 8

O

Old Testament. *See also* Church, and Scripture
  analogies
    with the Holy Spirit in, 87
    with conception of Jesus Christ, 207
  and anointing, 287. *See also* anointing
  and Comforter, 369
  and coming of Holy Spirit, 32–36
  and dove symbol, 285–86
  and establishing justice, 164–65
  and holiness, 173, 176
  and Holy Spirit, 257, 319
    gifts of, 380
  and hope, 428
  and meaning of Pentecost, 47
  Messiah tradition of, 131, 197, 202
  messianic psalm, 112–13
  and miraculous births, 198, 203
  and new covenant, 73, 78
    prophecy of, 67, 72
  and pneumatology, 15
  and prayer, 389
  promises in, 32–36
  and purification, 85
  revelation in, 191–92, 383
  and sacrificial offerings, 247
  and God
    manifestations of, 55, 58, 96
    spirit of, 160, 177, 181, 191, 258–60, 261. *See also* anointing
      guiding action of, 160–61

        as inspiration of prophets, 296
        meaning of, 149–54
        and the word, 182, 259
        strength given by, 422, 424
    and joy, 419
    and water symbol, 288–89, 290
    and wind symbol, 285
Orders (Holy), 354

P

Palamas, Gregory
    and Holy Spirit, 308
Paraclete. *See also Holy* Spirit
    meaning of, 27
Parákletos, meaning of, 27
Paul, Saint
    and Antioch, 141
    and apostolicity of the Church, 342–43, 344
    and baptism, 89, 352
        of disciples, 141–42
    and Christ-Church reality, 50
    and Confirmation, 352
    conversion of, 140
    and divine adoption, 65, 66
    and faith, 401–403, 405
    and guarding against wickedness, 417–18
    and God
        fatherhood of, 283
        new People of, 76, 78
        spirit of, 152, 158, 175, 175–76
    and Holy Spirit, 59, 129, 274–77, 430
        activity of, 19, 23, 278–82
        aid from, 18, 323, 374
        and children of God, 408
        and *Ecclesia Corpus Christi,* 320–21
        and freedom, 387, 409
        fruits of, 384–85, 410, 413, 417, 418, 424
        gifts of, 103–104, 328, 362–64, 366, 367, 386, 427
            greatest of, 409–11
        and hierarchical ministry, 356, 357

inspiration of, 194
and enlightenment, 397, 398–99
as inspiration of prophets, 297
law of, 73–74, 75, 212, 378, 384, 388, 424–25
and love of God, 307, 313, 329, 377, 407
ministry through, 357, 358–59
sealed by, 352–53
sanctification by, 332–33
strength from, 423, 425
as Spirit of Jesus Christ, 300–301
as spiritual drink, 290, 325
and hope, 427, 428, 429, 430, 431
and invocation of Jesus Christ's name, 121–22
and Jesus Christ, 61, 64, 223
   Church as Body of, 320
   death of, 246
   parallelism with Adam, 88, 90, 125, 159, 185, 251–52
   resurrection of, 251–53
   working for, 335
and joy, 417, 418, 421
and Orders (Holy), 354
and peace, 413–15, 416
and prayer, 390, 390–93
profession of faith in writing of, 250–51
and salvation, 121–22
and spiritual life, 385
and temple metaphor, 331–32, 376
and Trinity, 93, 326–27
and unity in multiplicity, 325, 326, 327
and universality of faith, 339–40
and victory over socio-religious particularism, 138
and works of flesh, 417

Penance. *See* Reconciliation

Pentecost. *See also* Peter, Saint, Pentecost
  and baptism, 84–85, 352
  and holiness, 331
  and law of Holy Spirit, 72–75
  and People of God, 76–79
  as beginning of the Church, 81–82, 83, 84, 91, 95–99, 320, 325, 337–38

beginning of new morality, 75, 294
fruitfulness of, 143–48
as fulfillment of new covenant, 67–71
of Gentiles, 131–36, 139, 141, 142
as gift of divine adoption, 63–66, 119
as harvest festival, 46–51, 67
and Jesus Christ, 116, 249
in Jewish religious tradition, 47
manifestation of God, 52–57
   elements of, 54, 58
   symbolism of multiplication of languages, 56–57
new meaning of, 50–51, 67–68
other names for, 47
as outpouring of divine life, 58–62, 379–80
of pagans. *See* Pentecost, of Gentiles
theophany of, 53–54, 61

Peter, Saint. *See also* Acts of the Apostles, and conversion of first pagan; Pentecost, of Gentiles
and Confirmation, 352
and evangelization, 357, 403
first discourse by, 33, 48, 96, 105–109, 110–14
   effect of, 115–19
and God
   new People of, 76, 79
   reconciliation with, 286
and Holy Spirit, 297, 342
   received through baptism, 313, 331, 352, 374
   and bearing witness to Jesus Christ, 344
   and Gentiles, 371
and Jesus Christ
   anointing of, 287–88
   holiness of, 213, 262
   suffering of, 250
and prophetic inspiration, 171
and Simon Magus, 147, 313, 374
and spiritual life, 379
and temple metaphor, 332
and trance at Joppa, 133, 144
profession of faith by, 107–108
   in writings of, 250–51

Philip, Saint, 146–47

pneuatomachians, 295

pneumatological utopianism, 123–24

pneumatology, 193
   based on Scripture, 15, 46
   and account of Last Supper, 20, 26
   and Christology, 253–54

prayer
   in preparation for the Holy Spirit, 37–40, 41, 44
      unity of, 38–39
      perseverance of, 39
      women and, 39–40
   with Mary, 44
   and apostles, 127

preaching, apostolic, 134, 306, 357, 403–404. *See also* Acts of the Apostles, and evangelization; Vatican Council, Second, and evangelization
   initial, 110–14, 115

prophets
   false, 168–69
   prompted by God, 166–67, 168

Psalms
   and death, 245–46
   and God
      the Creator, 157
      spirit of, 259
   messianic, 112–13
   and spirit of holiness, 172, 177
   used in prayers of apostles, 127
   and water symbol, 289

Q

Qumran
   and purification by Holy Spirit, 176

R

Reconciliation, 353

redemption, 23, 429. *See also* God, salvific plan of; salvation
   and evangelization, 240
   and Holy Spirit, 117, 334, 428

and resurrection of Jesus Christ, 117, 135, 311
universality of, 17, 64, 132
and sacraments, 355

Redemptoris Mater
and Mary, 42

Remigius of Auxerre
and messianic activity of Jesus Christ, 240

resurrection of the human body, 252–53

Revelation, Book of
and Jesus Christ, 343
and kingdom of heaven, 91
and new People of God, 76
and water symbol, 290
and Tradition, 350
and salvation, 431

revelation. *See also* Holy spirit, revelation by; Jesus Christ, revelation by; New Testament, revelation in; salvation; Scripture, and revelation
of Holy Spirit, 47, 150, 152, 153, 154, 155
as distinct person, 257–60, 261–64
as gift for everyone, 313
and Jesus Christ, 22, 26, 242, 245
and law of Gospel, 74
of God, 33, 270
in Nicene-Constantinopolitan Creed, 295
of the Incarnation, 206
of Trinity, 191, 242, 261–64, 293, 311
pneumatological truth in, 33
process of, 150
through Jesus Christ, 116–17, 192, 193
and Tradition, 349, 350

Roman Synod of 382
and Holy Spirit, 296

ruah
breath of God, 54, 61, 155, 156, 162, 164, 285, 322
communication aspect, 152–53
dynamic aspect, 151–52, 154
multiplicity of meanings of, 153–54

S

sacraments. *See* anointing, of the sick; baptism; Church, sacramentality of; Confirmation; Eucharist; Matrimony; Orders (Holy); Reconciliation

salvation. *See also* God, salvific plan of; redemption; Scripture, as source of consolation
- comprehending plan of, 107, 220
- and divine adoption, 264
- and faith, 407
- and gift of God's self, 64
- and God, 157, 180
- and Holy Spirit, 19, 30–31, 149, 191, 297, 357, 375, 430
  - against, 243, 268
  - and sanctification, 117–18
- and hope, 431
- and Jesus Christ
  - as advocate, 27–8, 30
  - invocation of name of, 121–22
  - mission of, 46, 355
  - relationship with Holy Spirit, 28, 121, 311, 320
- and Mary, 217
- and new heart, 179
- and Pentecost, 61, 428
- and the Incarnation, 210
- fulfillment of history of, 131–32
- Trinity, 19, 59, 276
- universality of, 30, 340

Samuel
- and Saul, 163
- second book of
  - and presence of God, 54

Satan, 30, 241
- temptation of Jesus Christ by, 237, 238, 267

Saul. *See Paul*, Saint, conversion of

Scripture. *See also* Church, and Scripture; Gospels; New Testament; Old Testament
- and anointing, 287–91
- and fire symbol, 55
- and Holy Spirit, 295 299, 300, 397
- from Holy Spirit, 182, 297, 347
  - and authentic interpretation of, 348

and multiplication of languages, 56
and revelation, 295–96
as source of consolation, 372
and spirit of God, 156–57, 172
and term "name," 262
and theophany, 54, 55
and Trinity, 295
and Tradition, 348

Simeon
and presentation of Jesus Christ, 219–21, 266, 369, 419

simony, 147

sin, 33, 418–19. *See also* redemption; salvation
and Holy Spirit, 27–28, 30, 31, 118, 272, 293. *See also* Holy Spirit, blasphemy against
forgiveness of, 36, 82, 116, 117, 413
freedom from, 253
repentance of, 116–17, 344. *See also* baptism, and Holy Spirit
and suffering of Jesus Christ, 250
versus unity, 328
victory over, 31, 61, 118, 119, 239. *See also* Holy Spirit, and work of salvation

Solomon
and wisdom, 185

Son. *See* Jesus Christ

spiritus. See ruah

Stephen, Saint, 29, 123, 129, 390
and presence of God, 173

Summa Theologica
and Holy Spirit
procession of, 303
truth of, 329

Synod of Aachen (809)
and changes to creed, 298

T

Talmud
and fire in Jewish tradition, 96

theophany
at baptism of Jesus Christ, 232, 233, 242, 262–63
of Pentecost, 53–54, 61, 64

sign of, 54–55
of Sinai, 72

Thomas Aquinas, Saint
and basis of supernatural gifts, 35
and charity, 408
and creation, 366
and faith, 404
and foundation of the Church, 341–42
and grace, 206, 223–24
and Holy Spirit, 34, 284, 286
as Gift, 312, 314, 376
gifts of, 381–82
in Jesus Christ, 225
sanctification work of, 333–34
as soul of Church, 321
terminological analysis, 304–306
truth of, 329
and martyrdom, 426
and messianic activity of Jesus Christ, 240–41
pneumatological utopianism, 123–24
and sadness, 418
and spiritual life, 379, 407
and Trinity, 93, 300, 301–302, 302
and love, 305
and procession of Holy Spirit, 303

Torah
Jesus Christ as new, 96

Tradition
guarded by the Holy Spirit, 346–50
explanation of, 347
and Scripture, 348
and sacraments, 353, 354

Trinity, 93, 283, 290, 293. *See also* salvation, and Trinity
and baptism, 121–22
and Church, 326, 393
and Holy Spirit, 18, 19, 65, 268, 291, 296, 309
as Love, 286, 307, 308
and Jesus Christ, 46, 232, 274
relationship of with Holy Spirit in, 28, 124–25, 195, 300, 391

in liturgical prayers, 292–93
as Love, 304, 305
and Mary, 202
and new covenant, 71
opponents to members of, 295
processions in, 299
revelation of, 257–58, 261–64, 311–12
   and Islam, 258
   and Judaism, 258
scholars of mystery of, 301
self-communication of, 206, 217
and the Incarnation, 210
theophany, 232, 232, 262–63
unity in, 87, 247, 248, 249, 265, 274, 276

Triune God. *See* Trinity

U

Unitatis Redintegratio
  and ecumenism, 328

V

Vatican Council, First
  and work of Holy Spirit, 403–404

Vatican Council, Second. *See also Ad Gentes; Constitution on the Church; Constitution on Divine Revelation; Dei Verbum; Lumen Gentium; Unitatis Redintegratio*
  and Church
    and Holy Spirit, 321, 322, 368–69. *See also* Holy Spirit, as guardian of Tradition
      gifts from, 99, 294, 360, 362
     sacramentality of, 84
     unity of, 326–27, 328
     universality of, 340
  and dialogue with the Eastern Churches, 303
  and evangelization, 106–107
  and faith, 405
  and holiness of Church, 330
  and Holy Spirit, 57, 100, 106, 323
    gifts of, 364–65
    and infallibility, 344–45

Index

and Jesus Christ, 320
and martyrdom, 426
and Mary, 42, 43
and preparation through prayer, 38

W

water (as symbol), 234, 288–91
    of Holy Spirit , 86, 100, 156, 310
    of spiritual life, 386
wind (as symbol). *See also ruah*
    and Holy Spirit, 60 , 284–85
    and spirit of God, 54, 151–52, 153, 154, 155, 156, 160 , 379
Wisdom, Book of
    and spirit of God, 152, 259
        holy, 172
    and wisdom, 184–87
women
    and motherhood, 199
    names of followers of Jesus Christ, 40
    and preparation for coming of Holy Spirit, 39–40, 41
    role in Incarnation, 197-98

Z

Zechariah, Book of
    and destruction of spirit of uncleanliness, 174
    and prophetic action, 169–70, 259
    and spirit of God, 259–60

Pauline BOOKS & MEDIA

ALASKA
 750 West 5th Ave., Anchorage, AK 99501; 907-272-8183

CALIFORNIA
 3908 Sepulveda Blvd., Culver City, CA 90230; 310-397-8676
 5945 Balboa Ave., San Diego, CA 92111; 619-565-9181
 46 Geary Street, San Francisco, CA 94108; 415-781-5180

FLORIDA
 145 S.W. 107th Ave., Miami, FL 33174; 305-559-6715

HAWAII
 1143 Bishop Street, Honolulu, HI 96813; 808-521-2731

ILLINOIS
 172 North Michigan Ave., Chicago, IL 60601; 312-346-4228

LOUISIANA
 4403 Veterans Memorial Blvd., Metairie, LA 70006; 504-887-7631

MASSACHUSETTS
 50 St. Paul's Ave., Jamaica Plain, Boston, MA 02130; 617-522-8911
 Rte. 1, 885 Providence Hwy., Dedham, MA 02026; 617-326-5385

MISSOURI
 9804 Watson Rd., St. Louis, MO 63126; 314-965-3512

NEW JERSEY
 561 U.S. Route 1, Wick Plaza, Edison, NJ 08817; 908-572-1200

NEW YORK
 150 East 52nd Street, New York, NY 10022; 212-754-1110
 78 Fort Place, Staten Island, NY 10301; 718-447-5071

OHIO
 2105 Ontario Street, Cleveland, OH 44115; 216-621-9427

PENNSYLVANIA
 Northeast Shopping Center, 9171-A Roosevelt Blvd., Philadelphia, PA 19114; 215-676-9494

SOUTH CAROLINA
 243 King Street, Charleston, SC 29401; 803-577-0175

TENNESSEE
 4811 Poplar Ave., Memphis, TN 38117; 901-761-2987

TEXAS
 114 Main Plaza, San Antonio, TX 78205; 210-224-8101

VIRGINIA
 1025 King Street, Alexandria, VA 22314; 703-549-3806

CANADA
 3022 Dufferin Street, Toronto, Ontario, Canada M6B 3T5; 416-781-9131